CW01214122

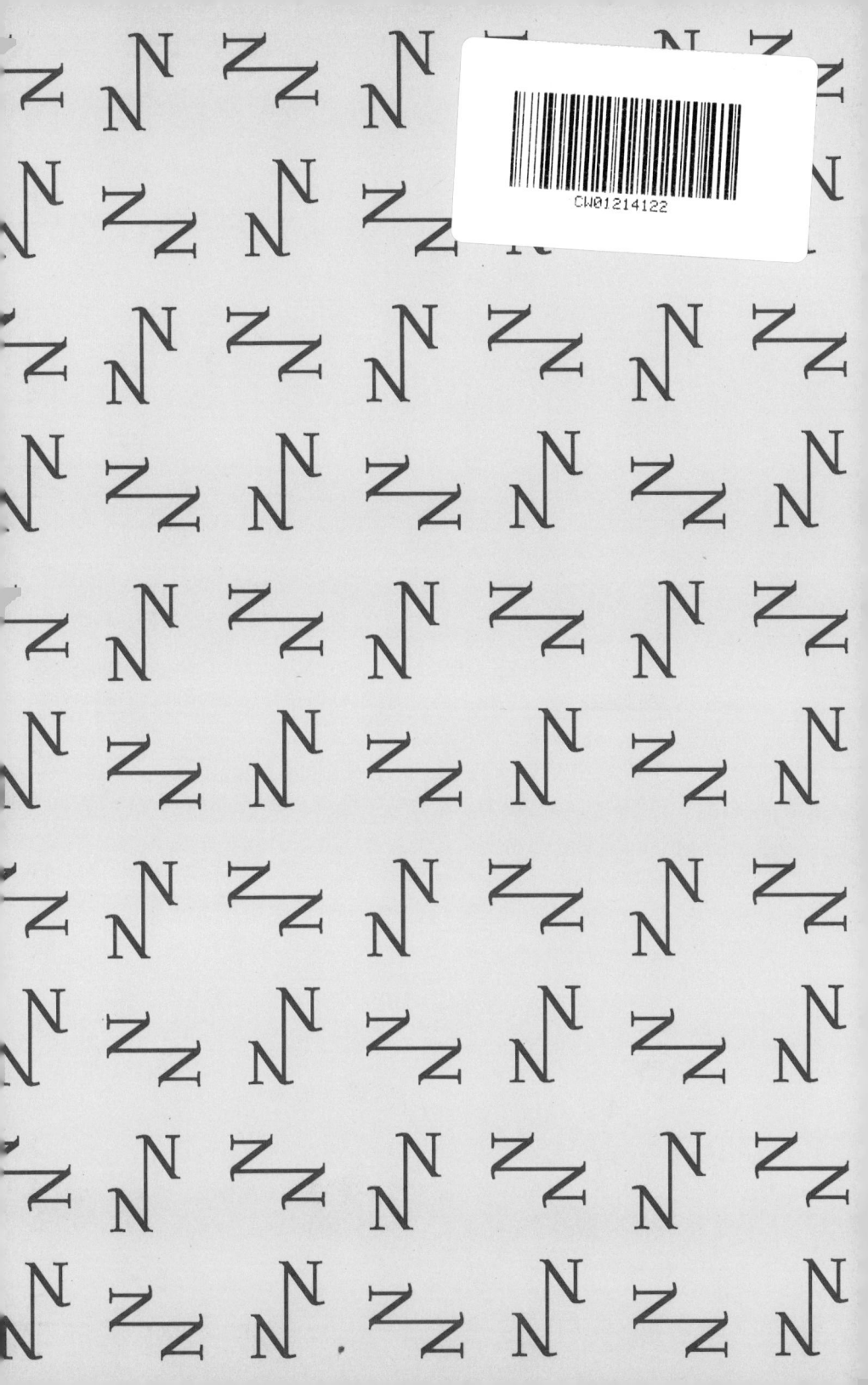

THE NEW NATURALIST LIBRARY

A SURVEY OF BRITISH NATURAL HISTORY

DARTMOOR

EDITORS
SARAH A. CORBET, ScD
Prof. RICHARD WEST, ScD, FRS, FGS
DAVID STREETER, MBE, FIBiol
JIM FLEGG, OBE, FIHort
Prof. JONATHAN SILVERTOWN

*

The aim of this series is to interest the general reader in the wildlife of Britain by recapturing the enquiring spirit of the old naturalists. The editors believe that the natural pride of the British public in the native flora and fauna, to which must be added concern for their conservation, is best fostered by maintaining a high standard of accuracy combined with clarity of exposition in presenting the results of modern scientific research.

THE NEW NATURALIST LIBRARY

DARTMOOR

A Statement of its Time

IAN MERCER

Collins

For Pam – for her reading and her patience

This edition published in 2009 by Collins,
An imprint of HarperCollins Publishers

HarperCollins Publishers
77–85 Fulham Palace Road
London W6 8JB
www.collins.co.uk

First published 2009

© Ian Mercer, 2009

All rights reserved.
No part of this publication may be
reproduced, stored in a retrieval system or
transmitted in any form or by any means,
electronic, mechanical, photocopying,
recording or otherwise, without the
prior written permission of
the copyright owner.

A CIP catalogue record for this book is available
from the British Library.

Edited, set in FF Nexus and designed by
Tom Cabot/ketchup

Printed in Hong Kong by Printing Express
Reprographics by Saxon Photolitho, Norwich

Hardback
ISBN 978-0-00-718499-6

Paperback
ISBN 978-0-00-718500-9

All reasonable efforts have been made by the author to trace the copyright owners of the material quoted in this book and of any images reproduced in this book. In the event that the author or publishers are notified of any mistakes or omissions by copyright owners after publication of this book, the author and the publisher will endeavour to rectify the position accordingly for any subsequent printing.

Contents

Editors' Preface   vii
Author's Foreword and Acknowledgements   ix

1   A Layman's Topography, Brief History and Political Guide   1

2   The Physical Anatomy of Dartmoor   30

3   Plants and People Return: Into the Prehistoric   79

4   Dartmoor Vegetation in the Last Millennium   104

5   The Dartmoor Fauna in the Twenty-First Century   165

6   Weather and Living Water   217

7   Working the Landscape: Dartmoor Men and Their Masters Through Historic Time   245

8   Farming Dartmoor and Sustaining Moorland: The Last Hundred Years   299

9   The Contemporary Conservation Scene: Its History and Its Future   321

10   Dartmoor From Now On   357

References and Further Reading   385
Select Bibliography   388
Index   392

Dartmoor National Park in its immediate setting.

Editors' Preface

The British landscape has been a central theme of the New Naturalists library since its inception and was given early expression by volumes devoted to individual national parks. The tradition was initiated by *Snowdonia* sub-titled *The National Park of North Wales*, and published in 1949, the same year as the Act of Parliament that established the parks came into being. Dartmoor was created a national park in 1951 and two years later we published Professor L. A. Harvey's and D. St. Leger-Gordon's *Dartmoor* as number 27 in the series. Over the next 25 years this ran to three editions and several reprints.

At the time our predecessors wrote that, 'the competing claims of national defence, water-supply, mineral working, afforestation, hill sheep-farming, public recreation and nature conservation which affect so many of the remoter parts of Britain are here all concentrated in one compact area in the heart of a single county.' Today, more than 30 years later, these are still burning issues and all feature prominently in the present volume. However, it is also the case that much has changed and the fruits of new research and a changing political and social environment pointed to the need for a fresh and updated approach to the area.

Professor Mercer is uniquely qualified for this task. As he writes in his Foreword, he has had a long association with the moor since first being introduced to it as an undergraduate in the early 1950s. In 1973, he became the first chief officer of the new Dartmoor National Park Authority, a post that he held for the next 17 years, and he is now chairman of the Dartmoor Commoners' Council. Not only that, but he is one of the country's foremost authorities on national parks and countryside conservation. For five years he was chief executive of the newly formed Countryside Council for Wales and on returning home to Dartmoor was appointed secretary-general of the Association of National Park Authorities.

If all of this sounds like the CV of a typical high-flying bureaucrat, the truth, as the reader will soon discover, is different. Ian Mercer is a geographer and naturalist at heart, never happier than when revealing the secrets of a landscape to a party of entranced and riveted students from the pulpit of a convenient Dartmoor tor or educating the nation on radio from the vantage of a hot air balloon. This is an intensely personal account, written with passion, authority and understanding and in a style that anyone familiar with the author will instantly recognise.

In the preface to the third edition of the original *Dartmoor*, the authors acknowledge assistance from, among others, a Mr Ian Mercer. With this book another of Ian Mercer's Dartmoor circles has been neatly closed.

Author's Foreword and Acknowledgements

THIS BOOK IS ABOUT my perception of a landscape and what knowledge is needed as a foundation to that perception. The landscape in question is that of a compact, discrete, upland national park in Southwest England called Dartmoor and this is my interpretation of its anatomy and at least part of the spectrum of its inhabitants in the twenty-first century – fully acknowledging that there are many who know both better than me. This interpretation recognises that all things alive, natural and human (for we have for a long time drawn an artificial distinction between them) may contribute to that perception – but I do not dwell upon those things that have, or have had, little impact in the landscape itself. That we now know that moorland is for the most part a human imposition upon the upland, and has been maintained by graziers for some 5,000 years, means that the book necessarily involves itself with the contemporary state of that maintenance, its workforce, their difficulties and their would-be overseers.

I have written for the lay reader, mostly of the secular kind, and have used the language and terminology of whatever stage in the development of scientific thinking I have found most comfortable over my fifty-year intermittent observation of this singular hill. Scientific information and its language, shared for the most part between academic peers, seems to become increasingly abstruse. It is not always amenable to instant translation for the rest of us, and space for long and detailed explanation in a book like this is in short supply. None of this denies the need to delve into the far distant past, or helpful theory of any age, on the many occasions when a better understanding of things seen now is the purpose. Equally where good readable descriptions and explanations already exist I have seen no need to repeat the detail – they should be listed near the back of the book.

That said, there is a vast Dartmoor literature with a landscape reference and all that goes with it. It begins with the Domesday Book, but is then patchy for seven hundred years or so. It mushrooms as the nineteenth century progresses and gathers momentum through the twentieth. In the latter part of that century there is an interesting dichotomy. Scientific work on natural and archaeological detail on the one hand increases, and its publication matches its volume, however difficult it is to track down. On the other hand popular writing keeps pace volumetrically, partly because of its huge range: from serious amateur exploration of much moorland detail, through new editions of earlier classics such as the Crossing essays, to a multitude of later guides for walkers, riders and 'letterbox' hunters. (For the stranger: 'letterboxes', except the nineteenth century original at Cranmere Pool, lie hidden in thousands of locations and contain a rubber stamp whose imprint is the evidence for the success of the hunt.)

Between these two large literary branches runs a slim central procession of general Dartmoor 'statements of their time', for lack of a better definition. After the unique Domesday essay there is that long gap, but Samuel Rowe, in the Preface to his *A Perambulation of the Forest of Dartmoor and its Venville Precincts* in 1848, encapsulates the idea and thus really sets off my procession. He says: 'within its [Dartmoor's] limits there is enough to repay, not only the historian and antiquary but the scientific investigator for the task of exploring the mountain wastes of the Devonshire wilderness'. He goes on to point to tors 'for the geologist', Wistman's Wood 'for the botanist' and the 'aboriginal circumvallation of Grimspound' for the antiquary. He does not neglect the economic activity evident on the Dartmoor of his day, but in the thrusting and somewhat innocent Victorian manner concentrates on cultivation and reclamation opportunity and regards common rights as an inhibition to logical ambition in the agricultural developer.

The modern sequence starts, I think, with Worth's *Dartmoor* edited by Malcolm Spooner and the first New Naturalist *Dartmoor* by Harvey and St Leger Gordon, both published in 1953. Then the Devonshire Association published a volume of (scientific) *Dartmoor Essays* in 1964 edited by Ian Simmons. In 1970, *Dartmoor a New Study*, another set of essays, was edited by Crispin Gill. Harvey revised his New Naturalist volume in 1974 by adding two chapters; Eric Hemery's *High Dartmoor* of 1983 deserves a place in this list despite its implied outer boundary and the 1992 *Dartmoor Bibliography* by Peter Hamilton-Leggett does too, though for very different reasons. It has 7,000 entries and thus saves me much space here! It must be apparent that I hope this book can take its place in that procession, though only the objective reader on the one hand and the Dartmoor generalist on the other can determine its fitness for such a place.

I am a Black Country boy, but I was introduced to Dartmoor in 1952, by my tutor at university, where I read geography. He, Gilbert Butland, was born in Dartmouth but his grandparents, who lived at Play Cross on the outskirts of Holne village above the gorge of the Double Dart, were commoners with grazing rights on Holne Moor. They, his great-grandparents and their immediate predecessors are all listed among the Homage in the book of presentments of the Court Baron. By strange chance and nearly 25 years later I became Steward of the Manor of Holne and wrote more presentments in that same 200-year-old book. Gilbert examined the book in my office when on leave from Australia in 1980. He was mightily pleased and wrote to say so when he got home. (He had left his Devon books with me when he emigrated in 1959.) For me a first Dartmoor circle was nicely closed.

Within that quarter century I taught geographers and ecologists on Dartmoor almost weekly from a field centre at Slapton in Start Bay, of which I was the first warden for a decade from 1959. From 1971, as the County Conservation Officer of Devon I had responsibility for the Warden and the Information Services of the Dartmoor National Park Committee and then in 1973 I became the first chief officer of the new National Park Authority (NPA). It was because the NPA bought Holne Moor and unintentionally became Lord of the Manor of Holne that I became its Steward. That involvement with the commoners on their patch was a huge benefit when the NPA was asked to help the Dartmoor Commoners' Association seek an Act of Parliament to provide a better frame for the management of the commons of Dartmoor and legal public access to them. The Dartmoor Commons Act of 1985 was the climax of that process and established a precedent for upland commons management some 20 years before government got round to arranging it for all common land in the Commons act of 2006. From teaching about Dartmoor's landscape to being charged with managing its public benefits and being allowed to work closely with the real managers of its plant cover and habitats was a whole procession of privilege.

The privilege didn't end there. After an essay into Wales to set up and lead a new landscape and nature conservation agency – its Countryside Council – for five years, we returned to Dartmoor in what is euphemistically called retirement. From home in Moretonhampstead I led the Association of National Park Authorities as its Secretary General for another five years, which allowed comparisons with other national parks and with other hills to be more easily made. In 2001, the fifth year of that term, a national outbreak of foot and mouth disease reached Devon – and within that county, Dartmoor (as it did a number of other national parks). I was asked to chair a public inquiry into that outbreak, its handling and its aftermath in Devon, which brought me close to Dartmoor farmers once again. Three years later the Dartmoor Commoners' Council, created by that Act of 1985 and thus then 19 years old, lost its long-serving chairman. To my complete surprise, members of the Council asked whether I would take that chair if they co-opted me. Was ever such an honour offered to someone who felt he already owed the landscape, which the Council oversees, so much? I readily accepted the chair, and so far, they claim, I have been useful to its members. A second Dartmoor circle neatly closed.

Despite spending three-quarters of my working life as a rural public servant, and it doubtless shows, I have always been a geographer. The attraction of true local geography is that it depends upon the wielding of a broad brush much of the time, but allows the display of intricate detail to illuminate corners of the canvas whenever necessary. I thus make no apology for the breadth of canvas I have tried to cover, but for the errors and omissions that Dartmoor experts will identify, I have to take full responsibility. That the landscape lives must not be forgotten as shapes and surfaces, flats and slopes, rocks and pebbles appear to dominate. The denizens of all corners of this National Park in all its ecological variety in their turn react to all those physical components of it whether they are springtails on the right slope in woodland leaf litter or farmers seeing cattle while evading bog pools on the high tops. The wholeness of this contemporary ecosystem is what this book is meant to be about, though it is merely a snapshot in the 280 million years on the record.

Its reader, especially the stranger to the Moor or even the casual visitor, will find it invaluable to have a map at their elbow, for identifying every location mentioned in the text on a map within the book would take up many pages at an adequate scale. I have tried to ensure that the reader knows where to look from the descriptions, but I am well aware that this may not be a foolproof formula. The Ordnance Survey's *Explorer* OL 28 at 1:25,000 covers the greater part of the National Park, in two halves, on either side of the same sheet (the well off might have two copies and avoid continual turning over and refolding as part of the reference exercise). Even then adjacent sheets are needed to cover the extreme eastern and western edges of the Park. The British Geological Survey's three 1:50,000 sheets named *Ivybridge* 349, *Dartmoor Forest* 338 and *Okehampton* 324, also cover the bulk of the Park but *Exeter and Newton Abbot* are needed to complete the eastern edge, and Brentor and the north end of Roborough Down slip off the western margin of the Forest sheet.

Many people have helped me over the last five years especially, while the writing has continued, though disrupted by many a meeting and latterly photographic weather too good to miss. I hope I will miss no one out of the next few lines.

All the maps and diagrams are the ultimate work of an exceptional cartographer, Hanno Koch, who has translated my sketches, aerial photographs, the original Vision map by Fiona Waldon and the other two more elderly vegetation maps (Fig. 79) into what you see here. Professor Charles Tyler, almost a denizen of Holne Moor himself, has provided most of the animal images and a number of 'landscapes' – Dart Valley and Wistman's Wood interior for instance. Tracey Elliot-Reep and Chris Chapman, two of Dartmoor's better-known image makers have both provided 'farmers at work' pictures. The skills of these three show among the bulk of the rest, which are my own.

My successor chief officers of the NPA, Nick Atkinson and Kevin Bishop, have allowed me continuous access to the library, the maps and the aerial photographs at Parke. There, Norman Baldock and Debbie Griffith have provided photographs and advice, Kerenza Townsend and David Partridge have shared their IT technical skills with me and others on the book's behalf.

Tess Walker, archivist extraordinary by any other name, has never failed to come up with the necessary reference. Gordon Clark and Tina Ainsley of the Environment Agency helped me to understand better the Dartmoor freshwater regimes and its rainfall, as did Gary Cox on my home patch.

Conversations with Professor Ian Simmons of Durham, Dan Charman and Ralph Fyfe of Plymouth, and especially their writings, brought my palaeo-ecology more up to date, and reminded me of discussions with Andrew Fleming, the king of Bronze Age Reaves, as he excavated on Holne Moore in the late 1970s and early 1980s. Photographs I took at the time are in Chapter 3. I have stuck with Ian's generalised pollen diagram of 1964 for our purposes in the same chapter, and apologise to the others for not illustrating their detailed and very recent work. Lack of appropriate space is the excuse. Richard Scrivener, then of the British Geological Survey's Exeter office, talked to me about the latest geological thinking around the granite, and the explosive ruthlessness of earlier experts preparing faces for imminent inspection by conference attendees. David Streeter has been my ecological mentor throughout, and as editor has helped enormously with the central chapters. To all these friendly scientists I am very grateful, for forbearance as well as for information.

There are some who have worked around the Moor at the fringe of farming who have unknowingly helped me as we have talked: Karen Aylward, Simon Bates and Eamon Crowe, all now of Natural England, John Loch of DE and John Waldon, once of the RSPB and prime arranger of the Dartmoor Vision for 2030. They all have tricky jobs. Colin Sturmer and Chris Gregory of the Duchy of Cornwall have given more help than they may realise. James Paxman of the Dartmoor Preservation Association and Tom Greeves of the Dartmoor Society have both helped me and both will know why I should list Lady Sayer here, for when calm, relaxed and not in Joan of Arc mode she was happy to share an immense knowledge of her father's Grand Old Moor with conservation striplings like me.

It remains to thank all those who actually manage the Dartmoor landscape, for sometimes just the odd word, or the clarification of things inadequately observed. Among them are those I must name, some to acknowledge time readily given for longer and focused conversation. Colin Abel and his father Cyril, Layland Branfield, Anton Coaker, Phillip and Christine Coaker, Arnold Cole who also took me to Blacklane Brook where Ian Simmons worked, John Hodge who showed me detail on Okehampton Hamlets and Belstone Common in the 1980s, John Jordan from Gidleigh, Brian Lavis of Sourton Common, Michael and Rosemary Mudge (whom we have just lost), Martin Perryman, David Powell, Foreman of the Homage of Holne, Maurice Retallick, John Shears. They have all given me wise counsel, and will know why I must also register here the Dartmoor debt I owe to the late Herbert Whitley.

For the mistakes, errors and misinterpretations only I am to blame, but read on and ignore them if they don't interrupt the story.

CHAPTER 1

A Layman's Topography, Brief History and Political Guide

I have looked long on this land
Trying to understand
My place in it

                  R. S. Thomas

THE MOOR WHERE THE River Dart rises has always been a special place, a high place. Bronze Age settlers divided it meticulously between them; Britons circled it with hill forts; Anglo-Saxons peopled all its valleys, though the Dark Ages were as dark here as anywhere. King John retained its heart as royal Forest or hunting ground in 1204; his son Henry (III), gave it away as a 'chase' but Edward I got it back and invented the Duchy of Cornwall to hold it in 1337. It still does. All Devonians, bar those in Totnes and Barnstaple, had rights of common grazing on it for at least 1,000 years. Its minerals and stone have been exploited for longer than that; and for 5,000 years someone somewhere has been tinkering with its soil and vegetation, moving its boulders into walls, splitting some for gateposts, manipulating its water or, having to cross it regularly, has marked the way (Fig. 1).

It is now, has been for more than 50 years, a National Park. That modern special status recognises all those historic processes that have contributed to it and its landscape through time. The national park purpose points up the need to keep some of these processes going, to care for the evidence of the others and of course to conserve the contemporary natural Dartmoor that veils but does not obscure them. It also demands that enjoyment and understanding of all its special qualities are facilitated and promoted.

FIG 1. Sennett's Cross, in the col where the B3212 crosses the Two Moors Way. Crosses marked routes, and often boundaries too.

THE NATURAL SHAPE OF THINGS

'The Moor', as everyone in South Devon refers to it, is a compact upland lying between the rivers Tamar and Exe or, if you prefer it, between the A30 and the A38 just after they have diverged at the end of the M5. The National Park boundary contains 953 square km (368 square miles). It is just over 38.6 km from Sticklepath in the north to Bittaford under Western Beacon at the southern extremity, and 37.8 km from westward Brentor to the River Teign below east-facing Hennock. Its highest hill – High Willhays – reaches 621 m above sea level or Ordnance Datum (OD) and the River Dart leaves the Park at it's lowest point just below Buckfast, 30 m OD. The great bulk of Dartmoor is a granite mass with a narrow border palisade of hard, baked and twisted country rock, its aureole (see Fig. 16), and the whole now stands well proud of the rest of the South Devon landscape (Fig. 2). That landscape is effectively a set of descending level surfaces dissected by radiating narrow valleys and fashioned from the older rocks that once wholly contained the granite.

The molten granite – rather like a blister on an extensive deep-seated igneous body stretching from Dartmoor westwards beneath the southwest peninsula and beyond – was intruded into these folded and finely divided rocks some 280 million years ago (Ma). Between then and now the granite has been exposed to the air and

FIG 2. Dartmoor rising above the South Hams landscape, the profile from Western Beacon through Ryder's Hill on to Holne Moor.

we know had been blocked out and the main river pattern set (perhaps only 3 million years ago), the whole of Dartmoor was isolated as an island by a short-lived marine invasion reaching up to what we now measure at about 210 m OD and thus creating, however briefly, a 'Dartmoor' island. It was pauses in the sea's retreat from that island's shores that produced the wave-cut surfaces that provide those step-like summit 'flats' of the South Hams. Not long after that retreat began – perhaps it had reached halfway, the present 120 m OD mark, and only 1.6 million years ago in time – the northern hemisphere's 'Great Ice Age' intervened. It lasted more than 1.5 million years and involved some 50 or more glacial advances southwards with related interglacials, many of which were sub-tropical.

Throughout the glaciations Dartmoor always sat just south of the extended polar ice cap and its surface was never subject to moving ice, but sculpted and moulded by all those forces evident in the sub-arctic zone today. The North West Territories of Canada, Alaska, Novaya Zemlya or, nearer at hand, Spitsbergen will demonstrate to the visitor now what was going on in Dartmoor as recently as 15,000 years ago (BP or 'before the present'). Compare 15,000 with 280 million and you will perceive the span of the Dartmoor's earthen landscape history. The 'grand old Moor' of Robert Burnard, joint founder of the Dartmoor Preservation Association, owes its singularity and its gross anatomy to the beginning of that span and the detail of the physical features that *we* see, to the end of it. The contemporary living clothing of the whole, in all its great variety of plants, began on a 'clean' surface only 14,000 BP. But, while we humans have lived here longer than that, we have actually only worked with and around the surface rocks, that vegetation and its dependent animals for just a little more than half that time.

In all the postglacial period Dartmoor stands up from the rest of the South Devon landscape whose roughly east–west geological grain is interrupted only by the parents of our contemporary rivers carving their way across it to either of the Devon coasts and thus to the Western Approaches. Throughout, Dartmoor's altitude has secured a far greater annual rainfall than any other part of Devon, and thus most of those rivers have had their birth in one of its two plateaux as Figure 38 shows.

All of the River Dart's headstreams, but one, flow out of the substantial northern plateau. The exception is the Swincombe, which feeds and then issues from Foxtor Mire just south of Princetown and joins the West Dart downstream of Sherberton. The West Dart has by then already collected the Blackbrook, the Cowsic and the Cherry Brook. The East Dart is joined by the Walla Brook (one of three with the same name within the Park) before Dartmeet and then the so-called Double Dart is strengthened by the West and East Webburns which come together about a mile before they join it on its left bank a third of the way round the great Holne Chase meander between New Bridge and Holne Bridge (Fig. 3). The Double Dart picks up some short minor streams from the northern flank of the southern plateau, the O Brook and Venford Brook among them, and then it collects the longer and eastward flowing Holy Brook at Buckfast, the Mardle at Buckfastleigh where it also collects the Ashburn (or Yeo) from the north. Much nearer the sea, within its tidal reach and well out of the National Park, it is joined by the Harbourne which rises on the southeastern edge of that same plateau. The whole upper catchment of this extensive river system occupies some 25 per cent of the National Park, and the nomenclature suggests that early historic settlers

FIG 3. Medieval New Bridge (above left) and Holne Bridge (above right) which mark the limits of the Double Dart gorge's deeply incised meander round Holne Chase.

approached the moor up the main arterial valley whose river may have been named already. Physical features on the whole have older names than settlements and other artefacts, so even the Anglo-Saxon pioneers who arrived in South Devon by sea ahead of the military invasion of Wessex may have inherited 'Dart', whose root is a British word meaning oak. The sides of the Dart valley from Totnes to Dartmouth are clothed in oakwoods now, as are those of the Double Dart within the Moor (Fig. 4).

The land not in the Dart catchment in the northern plateau is drained in a radiating clockwise order from the southwest corner by the Walkham which joins the Tavy, the Lyd, West and East Okements, Taw and the Teign. This last is joined by the Blackaton Brook; the Bovey, which has already collected the Wray; the Sig and the Lemon, which rise and join within the Park, but are confluent with the Teign at Newton Abbot. Like the Dart the Teign has two main headstreams: the North and the South Teign, whose confluence is upstream of Chagford. From 4 km above that small town the river flows generally eastward and below it enters a deep gorge, seen in Figure 57, some 12 km long across the northeast of the national park and then turns south forming its eastern boundary for another eight, collecting many small right-bank tributaries on the way. The southern plateau in its turn is largely drained (from west to east) by the Meavy which joins the Plym, and the Yealm, Erme and Avon which traverse the South Hams fairly directly to lengthy estuaries flooded twice daily by the waters of the English Channel.

FIG 4. The Double Dart's wooded gorge from Bench Tor. (C. Tyler)

FIG 5. Dartmoor's northern edge from north of Cosdon, the dome on the left, and stretching to the Yes Tor–High Willhays ridge on the far right.

The summits of the landscape surrounding Dartmoor oscillate around 150 m OD, sometimes reaching 200 m closer in, but even at its lowest end the Moor's southern extremity, Western Beacon, is 334 m OD which is gained in less than 400 m, as the crow flies, from the slate country below. On the northern flank Cosdon (Cawsand Beacon to some) and Yes Tor rise spectacularly steeply from the in-country in 1.5 and 3 km respectively (Fig. 5). On all but the northeastern boundary, then, where the National Park would run into the Haldon Hills were it not for the Teign valley, Dartmoor rises abruptly out of its landscape setting.

Approached from the northern arc of the compass – eastwards or westwards on the A30, or across country from Bideford, South Molton or Tiverton, northern Dartmoor is a blue-grey escarpment above the green foreground. As Figure 2 showed, the same colour contrast occurs in the south, though perhaps the foreground is often more chequered here than in the north – more bare red soil in winter, more barley, maize and oil seed rape later on. Travelling northward on some lanes and on some days through the South Hams, Western Beacon presents a narrow blue dome – for all the world like the bow of a large submarine on the surface cleaving through a greenish sea.

The maritime analogy can be more helpful than you might think, particularly in north–south section. If Western Beacon is the prow then Yes Tor to Cosdon is the transom of a taller poop. Recall the long axis of Henry VIII's *Mary Rose*, and even the waist between has its reference in the central basin of the upper Dart separating the northern plateau from the southern as after-castle and forecastle, of different size and height. For that is the north–south profile of the Dartmoor mass. Highest at the extreme northern edge and its summits all the way to the southernmost hill steadily lessening on a remarkably steady gradient of 7.6 m to the kilometre when it was first perceived. That slope is broken only by the width of the central basin, perhaps 6.5 km from Beardown to Ter Hill, 9 km from Hameldown Beacon to Holne Ridge. The basin, of course, has a western rim linking the two plateaux through the Hessary Tors near Princetown and Nun's Cross – as though the Tudor ship was listing heavily to port.

You can actually see the north–south slope – from the right viewpoint at the right distance away. Looking westwards from Lawrence Tower on the northern tip of Great Haldon just west of Exeter, or eastward from Caradon Hill on Bodmin's edge, the southerly slope of the Dartmoor's summit profile is clear. Indeed from Caradon Hill the western rim of the central basin makes that slope seem continuous.

But Dartmoor as a discrete upland appears on the skyline from much further away. It springs into view just before the A35 drops off the East Devon plateau to Honiton. From Exmoor the whole northern escarpment looms above the wide vale of the Culm and red-Devon country in between. From Start Point (that south-southeastern extremity of South Devon) across the corrugated South Hams the other Dartmoor scarp from Lee Moor to Hay Tor is a splendid 27-km two-dimensional backdrop. From a boat at the Eddystone it dominates the landfall, indeed it is visible from anywhere on the arc from Portland Bill to the Dodman on a clear day. On a very good day you can see it from as far away as the Lizard. It is after all the highest, widest – biggest in all senses – of the granite hills and, counting Exmoor in, of all the southwestern piles.

THE CURTAIN WALL

From any distance it is the mass that is impressive – closer to, specific features mean more. Distinctive silhouettes like the dome of Cosdon are easily memorised, and in an anti-clockwise direction, so are the Yes Tor–High Willhays ridge, the jagged profile of Sourton Tors and Great Links Tor's double peak (Fig. 6). Down the west side the chain of Arms Tor, Brat Tor, Hare Tor and Ger Tor mark the outer edge of the plateau and then Blackdown leads the eye out to

FIG 6. Great Links Tor dominating the northwestern skyline.

Brentor with its summit church (Fig. 7). The heap of Cox Tor almost hides Great Staple's twin columns seen in Figure 52. Pew Tor and Vixen Tor are a 100 m lower but still unmistakable. Sharpitor and Sheepstor, shaped as named (Fig. 8), regain height but then there's a gap where china clay waste tips take the eye until the southern extremity that Western Beacon declares. Ugborough Beacon and Brent Hill (Fig. 9) in the aureole are close up the southeast edge, then there's a glimpse of Rippon Tor just before the double asymmetry of Hay Tor looms. All are major landmarks from 'off' the Moor.

Unmistakable Hay Tor is visible from an arc that runs from beyond Moretonhampstead in the northeast round to well west of Salcombe in the South Hams. It was almost certainly a terrestrial navigational marker for prehistoric metal traders and eventually Anglo-Saxon settlers, even if their undulating

FIGS 7 & 8. (above left) Brentor, the western extremity, with its crowning church seen from the south across Whitchurch Down; (above right) Sheepstor crouching above Burrator.

progress on the watershed route-ways from the coast through the in-country demanded other intervening 'signposts'. The 'Hay' was 'Hey' or 'high' before the nineteenth-century map makers wrote down what they thought they heard locals say – simply because of its universal and singular visibility as the observer straightened his back and looked upward from his plodding journey or his cultivating toil (Fig. 10).

FIGS 9 & 10. (above left) Brent Hill. a southeastern dolerite tor on the Devonian/Carboniferous boundary; (above right) The well-known double peak of Hay Tor looming over the middle east, looking south from Langstone Cross .

FIG 11. Inside the plateaux: (top) from above Dinger Tor towards Cranmere Pool and (above) from above Plym Head eastward to Ryder's Hill.

The origin of those tors, rocky piles with necklaces of boulders called clitter, will be examined not so long hence. For a huge number of visitors – from 'up country' (beyond Exeter), from other countries in increasing numbers and from Devon's own in-country – tors define Dartmoor. They are crowded at its edges and thus easily seen from the approaches, they crown many hills and they are never far from roads in popular eastern Dartmoor. They loom over riverside footpaths. They are remarked because they are very rare in visitors' home landscapes. Surprisingly, although odd ones exist there, they are equally uncommon in both soft-rock metropolitan England and in the harsher, harder 'Highland Britain' beyond the Bristol Channel, where moving ice smoothed so much and melting ice dumped 'drift' on so much more.

They are rare too, at home as it were, in the interior of the two Dartmoor plateaux. Away from the 'edges', whether of the whole Moor, of the central basin or of some narrower, deeper valleys the Dartmoor surface and thus its skyline, seen from within a plateau, is smooth as Figure 11 shows. Long low interfluves separate wider shallower troughs, sometimes long themselves – sometimes short depressions. In both, peat accumulates because water from surrounding slopes gathers there, oxygen is excluded and plant remains cannot rot completely. This water is surplus to the below-ground capacity, but the rainfall has been so high for most of the vegetated last 9,000 years that there has been a prehistoric and historic inhibition on rotting even on the wider ridge crests and the low summits from which many of them radiate. The result there is blanket peat – a wonderfully appropriate name – commonly half-a-metre thick on the southern plateau, but 2 m over the northern and reaching 4 to 5 m around the heads of the East Dart and the Taw and at Cranmere Pool (Fig. 11 – top). In the moorland valley bottoms and in even more 'civilised' hollows, 'mires' and 'raised bogs' occur: they are the specialist labels for the other peat-based features which are not necessarily confined to the uplands. Mires in Dartmoor have near-horizontal peat surfaces riddled with pools and small water channels as in Foxtor Mire south of Princetown or Muddilake east of it, Taw Marsh in the north, in Halsanger Common in the east and along the Walla Brook and West Webburn among the fields. In raised bogs – a small one lies in the valley west of Crockern Tor, a larger one above Statts Bridge, both close to the B3212 – the peat swells upwards in the centre creating a low cambered surface, making for easier cutting for early fuel seekers. Both of these bogs can vary considerably in area and the smallest patches of peat, which occur in isolation and often perched on valley sides where springs break out, are known as 'eyes' to commoners and their stockmen, whose sheep and cattle may blunder into them in poor visibility.

Blundering is not confined to lame or sickly stock. Peat surfaces in all their forms do affect people's progress on foot and on horseback and the traveller needs to be able to see the route ahead. A nineteenth-century huntsman called Philpotts caused 'passes' to be cut through the peat on some of the regular routes his pack took, one is in Figure 12, and some are shown on the modern 1:25,000 map. Given that the plateaux at almost any time can protrude into the cloud base, visibility can change with disturbing rapidity. This combination bedevils Dartmoor myth

FIG 12. Peat pass in the upper east Dart valley – an upright stone marks each end of the cutting. (DNPA)

and legend but it is as well to take it seriously and adequate precautions in any case before and during an excursion into the moorland heart. Whatever else, make sure someone knows where you intend to go and how long you intend to take.

Immediately around the two peat blankets on the plateau tops the surface still bears peaty damp soils in a great, slightly fragmented, figure-of-eight zone enveloping them both (Fig. 94). They carry coarse grasses and heather and extend off the open moorland commons into elderly and extensive enclosures – the 'newtakes', 'taken' from the commons or the Forest over at least the 700 years into the late nineteenth century. There are many 'islands' of these poor soils separated from that main zone, most are small but the largest, east of Widecombe, is big enough to hold that same, roughly concentric, pattern of common and enclosure even at its smaller scale. The newtakes still largely bear moorland vegetation. However, because they are in single occupation (as opposed to being grazed in common by a number of stockmen) they have been treated variably over the centuries, depending on altitude and the proportion of bare rock at the surface: that treatment ranging from simple liming to wholesale ploughing and re-seeding in rare cases.

A LAYMAN'S TOPOGRAPHY, BRIEF HISTORY AND POLITICAL GUIDE · 13

MIDDLE EAST AND FAR EAST DARTMOOR

(The appellations used in Figure 13, below, are my own, but the National Park does fall naturally into five topographic divisions for which the main roads, all original turnpikes, provide a convenient guide – though only that. They are not boundaries. This sketch map offers a reference for the rest of this book.)

At slightly lower levels just outside that figure-of-eight of damp peaty soils, narrowly along the western edge, but much more extensively to the east of the high plateaux with their Yes Tor to Western Beacon north–south axis – and, significantly, right within their rain shadow – the granite bears much more amenable soils from the cultivable point of view. 'Brown earths' in the pedologists' language (and named by them here the Moretonhampstead and the Moorgate Series), they are the basis of the early enclosure and historic mixed farming of most of this lower and largely eastern Dartmoor landscape. (The low

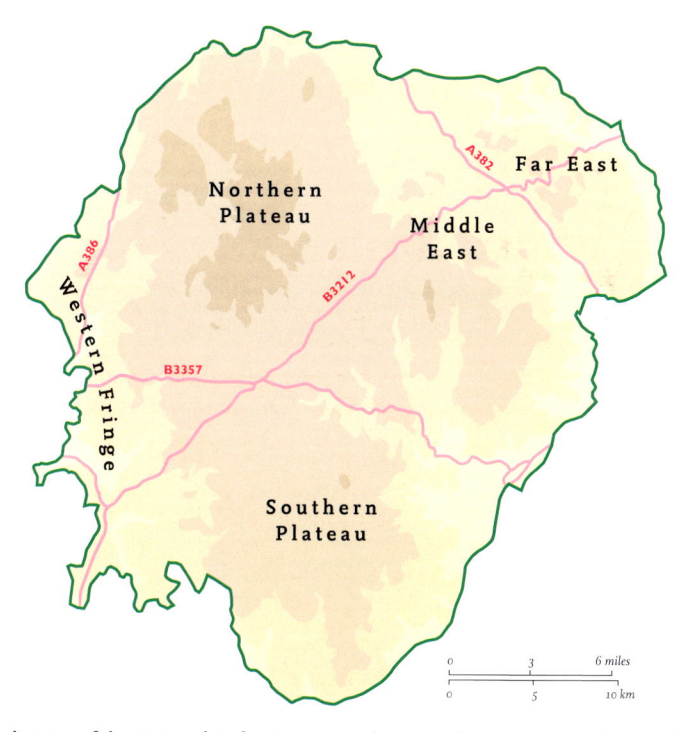

FIG 13. A division of the National Park into topographic areas for our purposes. The roads are simply markers, not boundaries.

western fringe of the National Park also bears a narrow strip of such soils though here its prevailing rainfall is only mitigated by altitude.) On the brown earths lie *all* the villages that are within the granite boundary except Princetown (a specialised nineteenth-century imposition) and Lee Moor (the original but historically recent labour dormitory for working china clay). Almost all the rest are recorded in the Domesday Book so are certainly more than 1,000 years old. Here, also, there are a multitude of living and working farmsteads still: some now the lone representatives of whole eighteenth-century hamlets like Babeny, others still grouped physically and by name like the Drewstons near Chagford, where one farm is active. There are the remains of many others nearly at ground level and now 'waste' in the proper historic sense. The Houndtor medieval village is a classic of the genre, however it is but one of many as Fig. 218 demonstrates. Challacombe and Blackaton Down bear such sites.

A good, and wider, demonstration of that particular historic land-use change is on Holne Moor, nowadays the major part of a broad common rising from the right bank of the Double Dart to Ryders Hill the highest point of the southern plateau (Fig. 14). Archaeological survey has revealed its total enclosure between 300 and 350 m OD at more than one phase of farming history from the Bronze Age on and with at least three mediaeval farmsteads at its centre. Below the once-enclosed belt the land falls steeply another 100 m to the river and is clothed in ancient and coppiced

FIG 14. Looking north across Holne Moor from Ryder's Hill. Combestone Tor is in the sunshine, Dartmeet is beyond it and the north plateau forms the skyline.

FIG 15. Contemplating the landscape north of Widecombe from below Saddle Tor. (DNPA)

oakwood on granite clitter; above it, moorland with no vestige of modern enclosure rises to the summit at 550 m. While there is no evidence of a continuous physical boundary between the wood and the contemporary open common, there seems to have been a pretty precise and straight line at the upper edge of the old enclosures – itself a Bronze Age construction. Above that line peaty soils dominate, whereas they are only in isolated patches below it.

The largest 'island' of poorer soils, east of Widecombe, with other outliers west and southwest of the village, also bear evidence of prehistoric and historic enclosure. Like Holne Moor they carry a mosaic of brown earths and peatier soils, and on the open land bracken, a choosy plant, will often tell you where the brown earths are. Here, with the exception of blanket bog, is a microcosm of the whole Dartmoor soil pattern, even twenty-first-century land use reflects it. Perhaps because of its smaller scale and the juxtaposition of less extensive wild patches between field-patterned valleys, it is enormously popular with both regular visitor and newcomer. Stand on bare rock and stare at a wild skyline or struggle through heather and gorse and shoulder-high bracken briefly, but turn round and there, just below, are the reassuring fields, a village, even men at work, to make 'holiday' feel real (Fig. 15).

This eastern 'half' of gentler Dartmoor itself has two parts – separated by a trough from Chagford through Moretonhampstead to Bovey Tracey whose origins will be explained. The 'far' east is a small plateau-like quadrilateral perhaps 16 km

FIG 16. Halsanger Mire from the southwest. The single file of sheep give something of a scale.

by 6.5 km, with the Teign valley as its eastern boundary. The 'middle east', although extended north to Whiddon Down, is centred historically and geographically on Widecombe, on which converge many of the roads and paths that cross and recross the patch. Widecombe's fame in fable and primary school singing means that those routes carry as heavy a load of visitor traffic by vehicle and on foot as any in the National Park. A large proportion of the total number of annual visitors, then, are treated here to a sample of all the components of the Dartmoor natural scene except those of the high and remote wild country where peat creates the long view and provides the feel of the land underfoot. Even here, quite close to the road and certainly in cotton-grass flowering time visible from it, are all sizes of those valley mires: at Blackslade due east of Widecombe, in Bagtor Newtake or Halshanger Common (seen in Figure 16) either side of Rippon Tor and downstream of Challacombe. Here too are famous tors like Haytor and Hound Tor and lesser-known ones like Yar Tor and Sharp Tor, Bench Tor and Beltor, Chinkwell and Honeybags, Top Tor and Pil Tor, Saddle Tor and Bonehill Rocks.

The Webburn and its East and West headwaters that drain the 'middle east' are crossed by roads many times, famously at Ponsworthy Splash and Buckland Bridge, but also at Cockingford, Shallowford, Cator and Widecombe itself. Water is magnetic to visitors – it is to paddle in, even sit in on a hot day (Fig. 17). Tors

FIG 17. Enjoying the Cherry Brook on Dunnabridge Common.

are to clamber on, see from or just marvel at. A bright mix of ling, bell heather and western furze flowering together and the odd bilberry to find in late August, russet bracken dying at half-term in October, short-cropped grass near the cattle-grid or car park all the year round to run across, kick a ball or just sit on – all creates the human habitat contrast with their own at home that visitors appear to crave. The 'middle east' encompasses all the characteristics of 'lower' Dartmoor, that which surrounds the old high and wild heartland, which in contrast, beckons the intrepid, the energetic and the forever challenged. It is too, remember, in the rain shadow of that heartland.

A fairly dense pattern of streams in lower Dartmoor was still not enough for the eventual density of the need for water. Leats – or water channels of the lowest possible gradient – were engineered ('to lead' is from the same root) to run from streams along near-contours to water fields and drive mills, and on their way to pass through villages as pot-leats and town gutters (Fig. 18). Sometimes they branched to pass even through scullery sinks to yard troughs and the lagoon beyond the midden. They accidentally but valuably add a slower dimension to the scope for freshwater living by plant and animal. Here, as Chapters 4, 5 and 6 will show, is a rich flora and fauna unused to swift currents. Their leaks and overflows create tiny mires where the plants otherwise content in valley mires can also

FIG 18. Holne Moor leat from the west. It is fed by the O Brook and snakes along the contour right across the common towards the parish fields.

flourish. They need constant attention by their users if their original function, or even part of it, is to persist. They are not confined to eastern Dartmoor, nor yet are they all domestic. The slopes of the high moor are themselves contoured by leats whose names as often as not tell their termini – 'Grimstone and Sortridge', 'Prison' and, largest of all, 'Devonport', begun by Francis Drake to water the ships and provide the power in his new dockyard. The early watermen organised the use of Dartmoor's hydrological bounty by hand with a sophistication to make modern engineers and their equipment look innocent. There is not a stream in the whole National Park that has not contributed to this early lending of its water for temporary human use. Their own gradients and those of their valleys' steep sides have always aided the leat makers.

It is on those valley sides too that Dartmoor woodland has persisted through postglacial time. The intensity of Bronze Age enclosure following Neolithic and possibly even Mesolithic settlement proclaims a clearance of prehistoric woodland that surrounded the blanket bog from all the manageable surface slopes. Wood – accidentally or deliberately – was maintained as the most useful crop on rock-strewn and precipitous valley sides. After all, it was already there – the natural climax of the Holocene vegetation succession. Having made room for food

FIG 19. The oakwood-covered sides of the West Webburn just before it joins its East counterpart at Lizwell Meet.

production and hunting space by removing trees, some better be kept for fuel at least and for domestic construction. Weather and soil poverty since might only support scrubby oak, ash, rowan and birch, but firewood, charcoal and tanning bark do not rely on shape or bulk. The relative density of zig-zagging but still steep packhorse paths and charcoal burner's hearths in Dartmoor's valley woodlands more than matches, in-like-for-like space, that of leat and pond out in the open.

Mid-twentieth-century forestry with financial incentive and hydraulic power achieved conversion of some such sloping woods to conifer plantation, notably along 6.5 km of the south side of the Teign valley between Whiddon Park and Clifford Bridge, but oak and ashwood still dominate the sides of the Double Dart, the lower Webburns (seen in Figure 19), the middle Teign, the Bovey and the Wray – all in the east – and the Walkham and lower Tavy in the west. The National Park thus has its share of classic British upland oakwoods, with mossy boulders and fern-with-bilberry floors and the characteristic bird assemblage that flits from here, at the southernmost end of its range, through the Marches to the northern Pennines.

Conifer planting was not confined to the valley sides in the headier days of early national forestry. Indeed, in the mid-nineteenth century the Duchy of

Cornwall's resident land steward had planted conifers in Brimpts Newtake alongside the Ashburton–Two Bridges road above Huccaby in a rather late reaction to the timber shortages of the Napoleonic Wars. The Duchy was for the time being then without a Duke – who only exists when the monarch has a son. He who will become Prince of Wales when he reaches his 21st birthday, but is Duke of Cornwall from his birth. The present Duke of Cornwall's great uncle decided that he should do his bit for the timber reserve which the First World War had exposed again as inadequate, and replanted Brimpts which had been felled during that war and began plantations at Fernworthy and Beardown. The new Forestry Commission had advised him and in 1930 he leased Brimpts Plantation to it and threw in more newtakes, at Bellever, Laughter Hole and at Soussons, for planting too (Figs 20 & 21). Together with that Teign 'valley side' conifer plot of the 1920s and early 1930s and Plymouth city's plantation around the head of the Burrator Reservoir in the Meavy catchment, Dartmoor suddenly, in relative terms, bore more than 2,000 ha of plantation, nearly matching the broad-leaved cover in area. That planting is now, at the beginning of the twenty-first century, well into its first harvest. The hitherto extensive dark blocks of seemingly even-aged and dense conifers are broken up, light is round every corner, and replacement planting is more sophisticated, informed as it is by landscape architects and a need to meet public aspiration.

FIG 20. Bellever Forest from Yar Tor, a hint of Brimpts conifers is in the left middle ground.

FIG 21. The hard edges of Soussons Plantation before recent harvesting.

PUBLIC OPINION AND THE DARTMOOR STAKEHOLDERS

That aspiration is itself a complex consideration in Dartmoor, incorporating as it does the desire of some walkers to use well-drained forest rides if only to get to high moorland more quickly and still dry-shod; that of others to walk the dog where chaseable sheep are technically absent; and those of the birdwatcher who knows there should be species here that occur in no other habitat in the Park. None of them may be adversely exercised about the high plantations placed here at all. But there are those who, viewing from a distance, see the hard cliff-like boundary of a dark cover and alien colours in a moorland landscape, and wonder why.

There is also of course the sizeable army of Dartmoor devotees and defenders for whom anything intruding on moorland, since their original predecessors defeated the enclosers in the nineteenth century, should be confronted. I do not mean to disparage them. Most belong to or look up to the Dartmoor Preservation Association – the oldest 'amenity' society in the country. Founded in 1883, to fight the enclosure of common land, by the serious if amateur moorland 'students' of the day, it persists as the focus of careful examination of proposed developments of all kinds. Its vigorous protest campaigns against any organisations or individuals who appear to it to be wandering from the straight and narrow, dominated the Dartmoor political scene for most of the second half of the twentieth century. For a large part of that time it was led and its representations marshalled by the granddaughter of its best-known founder Robert Burnard, one Lady Sayer. She was the scourge of farmers, foresters, quarrymen, civil – especially water and road – engineers, of generals and even of the National Park Authority (NPA) when its professed pragmatism appeared to her, in the sort of words she would use, to be 'snivelling cowardice'. She fought for national park status, and sat on the Park's first committee. No modern history of Dartmoor would be valid without reference to her, but quite naturally reactions to her actions and statements divided the world of Dartmoor stakeholders for 50 years.

A rival in the 'Dartmoor leadership' stakes through the second half of the twentieth century was Herbert Whitley of Welstor, above Ashburton, who founded the Dartmoor Commoners' Association (a federation of local associations) in 1954 to give evidence to the Royal Commission on Common Land which sat from 1955 to 1958. In 1974, there still being no sign of promised national legislation to give effect to its evidence, he persuaded the new NPA to share with his Association the effort to bring order to the use of common land on Dartmoor by seeking 'private' legislation. An 11-year-long campaign finally delivered the Dartmoor Commons Act in 1985. It created a Commoners' Council to protect and manage the use of the commons and gave a right of access on foot and horseback to the public in perpetuity. (Until then all the wanderers on most of the commons were trespassers in law, the commons did not constitute a statutory 'open space' and therefore things like the Litter Act did not apply.) The partnership that achieved the 1985 Act was recognised within it. Elected commoners were to regulate commoners and be responsible for their activities, protect their rights and the commons; the NPA was to take responsibility for the behaviour of the public, now at large on the commons legally. Nether would act formally without consulting the other. The detail is in Chapter 9.

Common is still the legal status of much the greater part of Dartmoor's moorland and half of the whole national park. Its core is an ellipse with a north–south axis from Cullever Steps to just south of Redlake and only 7.2 km across at its widest point. That core is still called the 'Forest of Dartmoor'. It technically became a 'chase' in 1225 when the monarch gave it to his brother the Earl of Cornwall. (If it wasn't the King's, it couldn't be a Forest.) The earldom eventually became the Dukedom under Edward III, and he passed it to his son (the Black Prince) and the eldest son of the monarch still retains it. In 1967 the Duchy decided not to object to the registration of the 'Forest' as common under the Commons registration Act of 1965 and so it is, oddly, the youngest of the

Dartmoor Commons. It has some outliers such as Dunnabridge and Riddon Ridge and the two main blocks are separated by Princetown, the Prison Farm and a belt of nineteenth-century newtakes. The commons that abut the Forest are called the Commons of Devon, and most Devonians had the right to graze them until the last century. Now only those who have undisputed registrations under the 1965 Act have that right. There is then an outer scattered ring of manorial commons, some detached from the main mass. To complete the moorland picture, almost all of that which is not common is enclosed, sometimes in very large parcels, the later 'newtakes' already named. Most of the area involved was enclosed under Duchy authority and other landowners used the Enclosure Acts in the eighteenth and nineteenth centuries. The process had its origins however in Forest law, and smaller enclosures had been (legally) newly 'taken' from the Forest probably from Saxon times but certainly by Duchy tenants from the fourteenth century on, as a right at the change of a tenancy generation, for instance. The niceties of the common and newtake relationship will be expanded later.

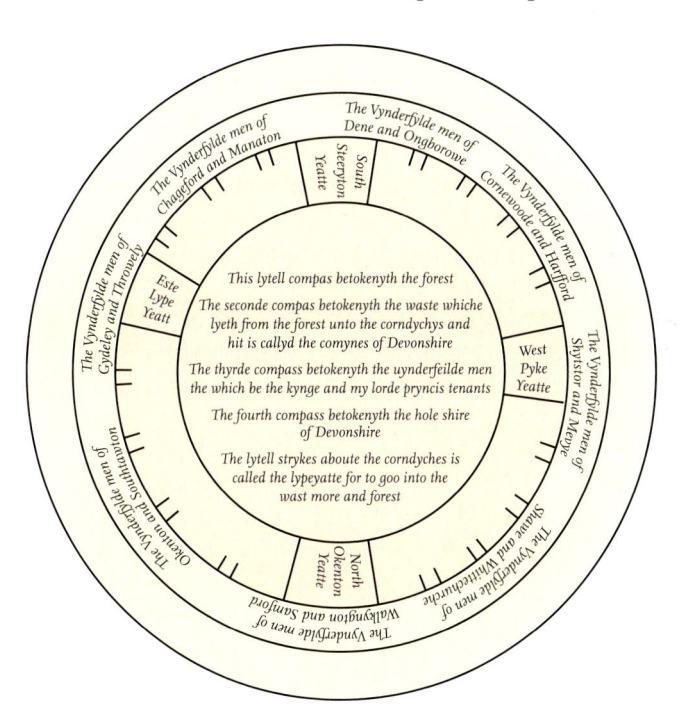

FIG 22A. The distribution of common land: a cartogram dated 1541, made for a commission inquiring into Buckfast Abbey land and rights after its dissolution (DoC).

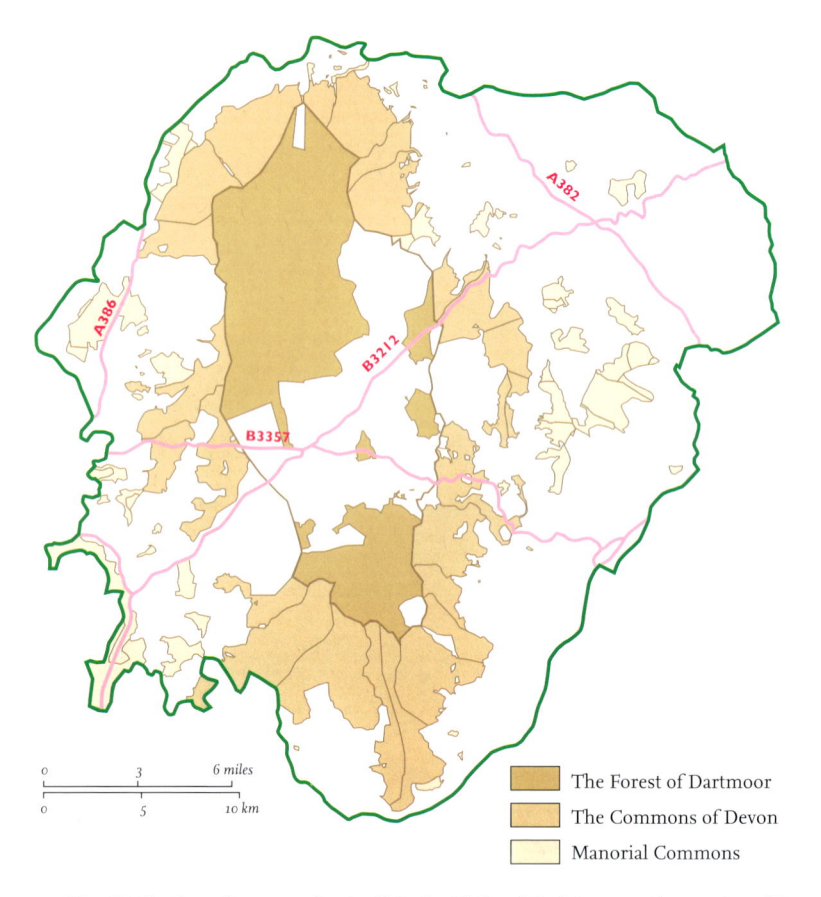

FIG 22B. The distribution of common land within the National Park in 2009: the angular white belt across the Forest includes the Ancient Tenements and all the newtakes.

To return to the Dartmoor 'stakeholder' story, there are of course many other such contemporary groups, though neither commoners with a 5,000-year background, burghers of the stannary towns of Ashburton, Chagford and Tavistock with a 1,000-year one regulating the marketing of tin, or even environmental campaigners with only a 150-year one would regard them all as particularly worthy aspirants to that status.

Military men in all their guises have been here nearly 200 years, off and on for the first 100 but now occupying some 9,193 ha as live firing ranges – though, since 1996, only firing small arms and mortars rather than the artillery which was their original motive in the nineteenth century. They also use another 3,850 ha or so for

FIG 23. Artillery men arriving at Okehampton Camp before the First World War

'dry training'. Water engineers have created eight reservoirs and one pumping extraction from a large mire, Taw Marsh, and, while they had remarkable antecedents as we have seen, only began their 'modern' operations at the end of the nineteenth century, perhaps 90 years after the soldiers. Domestic and industrial water from high rainfall areas seems logical enough and the early leat builders showed how old the logic is, but interestingly they drew or 'led' it off, they didn't try to store it up there. The lower down a river system water can be stored the easier it is to keep the storage topped up – and the River Dart, which has only one small Edwardian reservoir in its catchment, is now tapped at Totnes through its floodplain gravel just above its tidal high-water mark.

The foresters have been spoken for already, and the china clay extractors have been now confined to the biggest of the three outcrops of kaolinite on the southern moor. Since the 1990s they are outside the National Park after a boundary review, of which more anon. There have been many other mineral extractors from prehistoric times onwards and their details will also be revealed, granite and its associated metalliferous ores were their prime targets and none is worked now. A brave few toyed with the commercial extraction of peat and oils from it, and even braver souls, the agricultural improvers, thought they might plough after blasting rocks out of the way. Only the Prison Farm (now divided up among other farmers) is testimony to what improvement might be possible, and that with free labour. In the nineteenth century Duchy leaseholders, ignoring climatic truths, contemplated growing large acreages of flax, rye and other crops alongside the turnpikes. The two main turnpikes are the so-called 'scissor' roads that cross Dartmoor from Moretonhampstead to Yelverton and Ashburton to Tavistock and thus each other at Two Bridges, already portrayed in Figure 13. They were almost certainly the creatures of those improvers. While in plan they might have looked as though they would shorten some journeys, their investors' motivation was exploitation of the open land.

So, the Moor over 5,000 years has seen many 'stakeholders' come and many go. There are clearly honourable exceptions to the going, and the hill-farming commoners and Forest tenants take pride of place in that, for the longevity of their stay and their own tenacity. The Duchy of Cornwall can also stand up to be counted as it's been there, if originally as an earldom, for some 750 years, and still takes its responsibilities very seriously. If one wanted an example of environmental benevolent despotism at its best then the Duchy on Dartmoor is it.

But since the mid-nineteenth century the new 'stakeholders' in Dartmoor, now the numerically vast majority, are 'the visitors'. Many different groups in society make the millions of visits that populate each year, and they will also be analysed. In many ways they have been represented on the spot by the NPA since 1951. It exists to promote their understanding and enjoyment of all the special qualities of this wonderful place and of course to conserve and enhance those qualities for the nation. These two purposes, written in reverse order in the statute, exist because those who wanted a stake in the most beautiful areas of England and Wales mounted a sufficiently effective campaign in the 1930s and 1940s to persuade society and its government that those areas and access to them should be protected from potentially damaging development. The history of that protection and its evolution through the last 50-odd years is a story in itself to be told in Chapter 9, but its firm establishment is now clear for all to see.

The oldest stakeholders – the commoners – now have a partnership with the youngest – the NPA. Their shared purposes, as we have seen, are enshrined in the Dartmoor Commons Act of 1985. They effectively take joint and several responsibility for the management of the moorland and of its visitation. The Commoners' Council manages the agricultural use of the commons and protects them and their commoners against most if not all ills. The NPA manages visitors' activities whether they are from just over the boundary every weekend, or once a year from all over the globe.

Even at this stage in this book it would be wrong to leave things just like that. National Park Authorities have had to have due regard for agriculture since 1949; the Commoners' Council is enjoined by law to take natural beauty into account

FIG 24. A true commoner's daily business – 'looking at' stock. Highland cattle and their owner on the south slope of Cosdon. The inevitable Hay Tor on the far skyline, one of the 'long views' for which Dartmoor is renowned. (T. Eliot-Reep)

when making its own agricultural decisions. Since 1995 NPAs have had a duty to foster the social and economic well being of all the resident communities in their parks and Dartmoor NPA is no exception. Its working relationship with the commoners is clear. There are many farmers within the Park who are not commoners, but various incentives exist to tie their management into the national park purposes and many in that way participate in the pursuit of them. The County Council and the Districts (soon perhaps to be combined as a Unitary Authority) and parishes that overlap the park or lie entirely within it have representative seats on the NPA. By this means – and those seats add up to a majority – the communities within the park have a considerable say in its governance and management. The Secretary of State for Environment, Food and Rural Affairs appoints folk to the remaining 12 seats to represent the national interest and strives in doing that to strike a balance between those who might defend the landscape, those who represent those seeking access to it and those who own and work it. Most of them will be locally based and thus wear more than one hat. The NPA is the planning authority and thus regulates land use change and the appearance of structures in the landscape. It is empowered to aid and abet communities and individuals in their own endeavours when a wider interest and public benefit can be identified within them. Such benefits can range from the perception of upland vegetation in good condition to the visitor facilities in a well-kept village. Ideally local resident, visitor and land manager should all benefit from a benevolent NPA that acts as catalyst for mutual betterment and regulator of individual selfish excess. In its duty towards wildlife the NPA is itself aided and abetted by Natural England, offspring of an uneasy marriage between the Countryside Agency and English Nature. It is technically *in loco parentis* to an NPA and has staff in the region with responsibilities for nature reserves, other protective designations, *and* the administration of agri-environmental schemes to reward farmers for conservation work. Likewise English Heritage and the Environment Agency do their thing in Dartmoor that supports the NPA in its work and helps it towards the fulfilment of the statutory National Park Management Plan.

So, many hands are employed in one way or another in maintaining the surface appearance of this southwestern hill in the twenty-first century. It is in the nature of these things that motives vary and mutual understanding is thought at times to be unlikely, even impossible. That ramblers and hill-farmers may share a real objective – in having vegetation below knee height – may not be acknowledged for decades for quasi-political reasons. But things change. Just as King John agreed to give up hunting throughout lower Devon in 1204, and by chance drew the boundary of Dartmoor's heartland, so the commoners conceded a right of public access to the commons in perpetuity in 1985 and agreed to trust the NPA to manage public recreation on them. The NPA recognised formally, at the same time and in the same instrument, that the commoners could be trusted to manage the commons, now including the Forest, by going about their own well-understood business.

Since then there have been massive changes in the relationship between farming, landscape and its enjoyment – largely through European consensus. The payments for production and protection of 'public goods' are now a potential part of every farmer's balance sheet – not least in national parks, though not as good a part as they were a decade ago. In 2005, the farmers of Dartmoor's moorland persuaded the NPA to get all the other agencies for particular 'public goods' together with them and agree, and sign up to, a shared 'Vision' for that moorland in 2030. The sharing was the crucial need. The map of that vision, essentially a broad-brush portrayal of vegetation communities with 'premier archaeological landscape' insets, bears the signatures and logos of English Nature and the Countryside Agency (now together as Natural England),

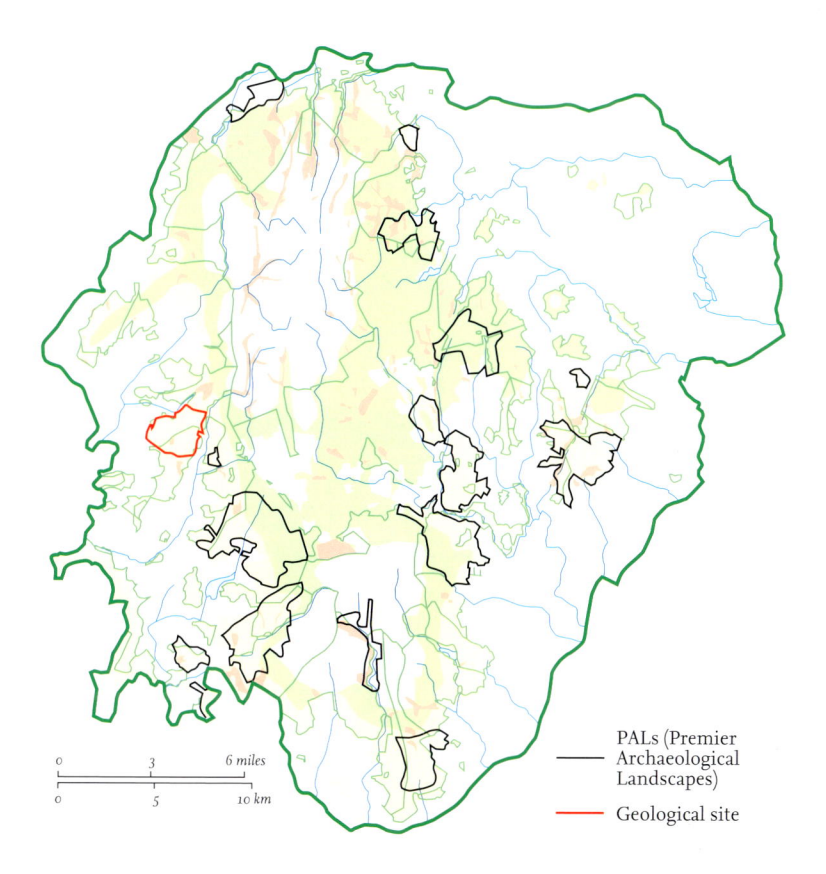

A LAYMAN'S TOPOGRAPHY, BRIEF HISTORY AND POLITICAL GUIDE · 29

FIG 25. The Dartmoor Vision for the farmed landscape of 2030 AD. See Figure 79 to show only the vegetation in other colours. Here the black outlines are premier archeological landscapes (PALs), the red one is a geological site. (DNPA)

English Heritage, the Environment Agency, DEFRA, Defence Estates, the NPA and the Commoners' Council. Here is as powerful an alliance to assure the future welfare of the moorland as has ever existed. As always that future, and the security of the moorland farmers, without whose work nothing will be done, demands a proper investment by society in the joint achievement.

The Dartmoor Vision and the process by which its underlying consensus has been achieved are already regarded as a model for other national parks – if not all upland blocks. It will be referred to again more than once as this latest general update on the state of Dartmoor proceeds.

CHAPTER 2

The Physical Anatomy of Dartmoor

A landscape is the function of structure, process and time.
                                        W. M. Davis, 1884

THIS CHAPTER ANALYSES DARTMOOR'S whole terrain – the stage on which all things ecological, cultural and economic have been acted out over the last 10,000 years – according to Davis's all-time truth. Only it survives of Davis's great body of theoretical work, which dominated geomorphology for more than 50 years, but that troika – structure, process and time – is as critical to the appreciative understanding of any landscape now as it always was. Rocks, once emplaced on or within the earth's crust, may be modified by geologic process and temperature change. When eventually exposed to the air they are attacked by all that the weather can throw at them, both directly, and through the water regimes it sustains, at the surface. All of those processes have varied in type and intensity through time. In Dartmoor's case it has taken a lot of time, so long that rocks intruded into others have been exposed, buried again and re-exhumed. It is then that some evidence of their earlier exposure becomes part of the contemporary scene. As in any landscape, the nearer in time a particular process has been at work the fresher is its visible effect and at the same time the chance that it has removed or masked the effect of earlier processes is higher.

THE SOLID GEOLOGY

The granite

So Bill Dearman could write on the first page of a volume of *Dartmoor Essays* published in 1964: 'The granite has itself determined naturally and almost exclusively the character of the [National] Park ... even when it is not present at the surface its influence is obvious.' Essays that follow his in that volume deal in the work of processes culminating (as far as the physical surface is concerned) in those of the Pleistocene 'Ice Ages' which produced the dramatic detail that takes the immediate attention of most casual observers of Dartmoor. That visible detail is on all steep slopes and mostly round the edges of Dartmoor's two plateaux; but the intervening essayists also apply their reasoning to the wide landscape of long, low profiles and hidden hollows of the hinterlands leading to the plateaux' summits, and the 'flats' of the upper Dart basin which lies between them. In both these cases the product of much older processes dominates the surface.

It better be said now that apart from the acts of faith which laymen must inevitably indulge in dealing with geological time, and despite much improved radio-chemical means of measuring the age of rocks and their derivatives, imagination and controversy about the origin of particular surface forms, even by field scientists, increase in proportion to the distance back in time of the events under discussion.

However, even since Dearman wrote, we have established a new and more precise age for the emplacement of the Dartmoor granite. Its first intrusion came to rest, still superheated and plastic, 280 Ma, nearer the surface of the earth's crust than my school textbook had me believe. It turns out that Dartmoor is the youngest of the six upward intrusions from the single pluton that lies under the southwest peninsula and westward, from Dartmoor to beyond the Scillies.

In the Dartmoor case, three main phases of intrusion of molten magma were originally recognised. The first was thought to have produced the 'giant' granite characterised now by scattered large whitish crystals (megacrysts) of orthoclase feldspar up to 170 mm in length (but most of 'side of matchbox' size) embedded in the ground-mass of quartz, feldspar and mica (mainly dark biotite) typical of most granites. Though these latter crystals average 2–3 mm in diameter they are still at the coarse end of a granite spectrum. The megacrysts may comprise anything up to 30 per cent of the volume of the giant granite as Figure 26 shows. It is the main granite of most of the tors, though percentages of megacrysts by volume are low in an area of the northern plateau bounded by High Willhays, Cosdon, Cut Hill and Brat Tor, and again around Trowlesworthy, Shaugh and Lee Moor in the south, with odd small patches elsewhere. The whole intrusion should be visualised as a thick domed sheet spreading outwards, but mainly northwards, from a 'feeder' column centred under Ryders Hill (the highest point of the southern plateau). It was followed sooner rather than later by a second sheet of what was to become the 'blue' granite, of more

FIG 26. A weathered face of giant granite. Felspar phenocrysts, the size of the side of a matchbox, dominate the matrix of quartz, mica and small felspars. A felspathic vein runs diagonally across the face.

evenly distributed crystals of similar size of the three common granite minerals. It is now thought that the giant and blue granites are so closely related that they may be simply phases of the same intrusive event, and together make up 90 per cent of the area of the exposed granite. Both appeared to early fieldworkers to have suffered further intrusion by a finer-grained granite in dyke- and sill-like form (crudely: dykes appear to cut across existing structure, sills to follow it). However the origin of these finer granites has since been described as 'enigmatic' and include sheet-like bodies of aplite (rich in tourmaline and lacking biotite). Evidence suggests that they may predate the growth of the feldspar megacrysts, for some straddle the exposed boundary between fine and coarse granites. It is even suggested that they may have originally been sandstones that were caught up and melted in the molten magma as it arrived. Mineral veins are locally clustered throughout the whole pluton especially those bearing cassiterite or tin. For our immediate purposes the most important thing is that the considerable and easily recognisable variations in the whole mass of granite exist at Dartmoor's surface and can make different contributions to the landscape detail (Fig. 27).

All this emplacement activity may have been topped off by further intrusion into the original roof over the main mass and even of extrusion in volcanic form at the aerial surface soon after that. There are detectable chemical affinities in the family of rocks from one magmatic source wherever they come to rest vertically in the 'column' from pluton to volcano. Volcanic fragments and crystal particles in surface deposits in the Permian beds of the Crediton trough just north of Dartmoor closely following the 280 Ma date suggest such a state of affairs, even demonstrating the order of denudation of the volcanic rocks, roof and granite in an inversion of the resulting deposits, i.e. volcanic fragments first,

FIG 27. The west side of Haytor. Rounded, chemically-weathered giant granite overlies the finer 'blue granite', or elvan, which – more densely jointed – has retreated faster under mechanical attack.

overlain by roof material and then by granite. So, though the granite was shallow to geologists but deep to you and me, very soon after emplacement (in geological time) it had already been unroofed and landscape-forming processes were at work on it. All this was a very long time ago.

(If you are still having difficulty with geological time, to reduce it to a relative matter compare the 600 million years of fossiliferous earth history (give or take some earlier algae) with a calendar year. Fish appear in early May in the Devonian, big reptiles in September (dinosaurs climax in October), grasses grow first at the end of November, and the main glaciations of the Pleistocene occur at about 1800 on 31 December. The Dartmoor granite was thus emplaced in early July and being eroded in the air before St Swithin's, or even Bastille, Day.)

The country rock

Igneous rocks must obviously be younger than the rocks into which they have been intruded. The geological sketch map that is Figure 28 shows that our granites are in contact with the Devonian (Middle and Upper) shales, slates and grits and with the shales, slates, cherts and sandstones of the Culm Measures of

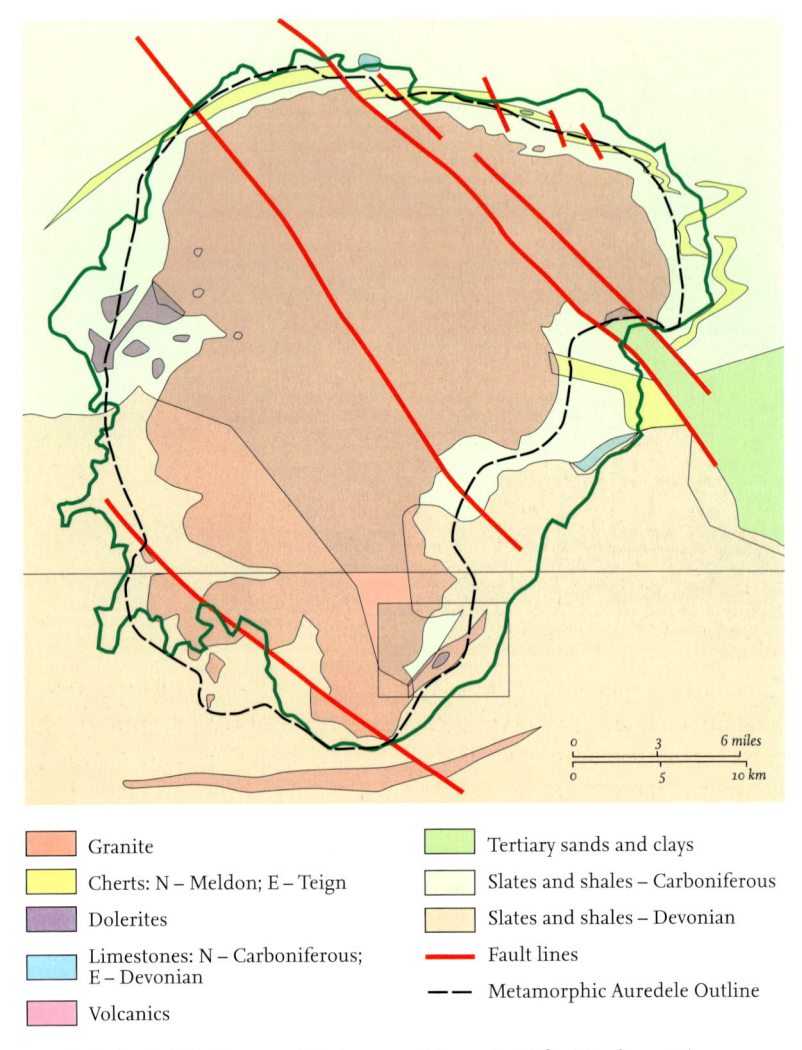

FIG 28. Geological sketch map of Dartmoor and its context (after Dineley, 1986).

Legend:
- Granite
- Cherts: N – Meldon; E – Teign
- Dolerites
- Limestones: N – Carboniferous; E – Devonian
- Volcanics
- Tertiary sands and clays
- Slates and shales – Carboniferous
- Slates and shales – Devonian
- Fault lines
- Metamorphic Auredele Outline

FIG 29. Bulley Cleave Quarry, Buckfastleigh, in 1964 when the Devonian Limestone was still being worked.

the Carboniferous system. Outside the contact zone itself some of these rocks play a significant if local part in the National Park landscape. The Devonian limestones of the Ashburton/Buckfastleigh axis are perhaps the most intriguing, for they contain the whole span of the solid geological time scale of the National Park (Fig. 29). They are among the oldest solid rocks inside its boundary and like most limestones they contain underground passages and caves. Within the caves are the youngest mineral formations we have. They are interglacial in age, perhaps only 120,000 years old, dated by the fossil remains of many mammals in cones of talus or scree under solution holes in the original surface that clearly formed 'elephant traps'. Their detail will be sorted out below. There are tiny patches of limestone in the Culm too, notably exposed in quarries just north of South Tawton and at Drewsteignton.

All of the country rocks, together with the Lower Devonian of the South Hams, Cornwall and Exmoor, were already intensely folded and physically metamorphosed. (Hence the slates, for instance, where compression has turned the flat mica crystals, abundant in the original clay, all on to the same axis and thus created a grain that makes for easy splitting.) For the late Carboniferous had seen the extensive mountain-building crustal movements most widely known as the Variscan, but also as Armorican and Hercynian. Armorica was Brittany, and the east–west trend (strike) of the folding in Devon and Cornwall is sub-parallel with the long axis of that peninsula. Geologists know the resultant mountains as Cornubian and the Dartmoor granite's emplacement into the roots of the Cornubian Mountains might be regarded as the penultimate surge in this whole Variscan crustal disturbance. (The rich mineralisation which made southwest Britain a tin, copper and iron miners' paradise was the ultimate phase.) Nevertheless, by the time these intrusions were taking place the mountain range was already being rapidly eroded and, as we have just seen, the granites themselves were soon exposed and attacked.

The basal beds of the New Red rocks, the Permian, which follow immediately in the geological sequence the uppermost rocks of the Carboniferous, are breccias and the evidence for that attack. They are coarse, iron-rich (thus bright red) sands containing a host of broken angular, many-sized fragments of other older rocks, including Dartmoor granite and its chemical derivatives. Their colour and angularity proclaim erosion and deposition on the edge of a desert basin, typical of the sludged deposits of desert-mountain gullies where, after 364 dry hot days but very cold nights – such temperature change continually cracking off angular fragments – on the 365th day the heavens open and all is sluiced down-valley. This was the start of a long period of arid conditions that begins the Mesozoic Era.

There are tiny outliers of this material at Slapton and Thurlestone in the South Hams, and at Kingsand in southeastern Cornwall but the main outcrop of the Permian breccias lies just east of Dartmoor in a long north–south band from west Somerset to Torbay. During its deposition there was also more volcanic activity, some within that band and best expressed around Exeter, whose Roman remains and mediaeval fortifications are largely built of purplish red lava and related clastic rocks (breccias of volcanic origin). There is a long tapering tongue of Permian rocks extending westward from the main outcrop north of Dartmoor. It is clear that these rocks occupy a valley bottom of great age, at least contemporary with the Dartmoor granite's first exposure, and its west–east trend is an indicator of an erosional and depositional direction that was to dominate southwestern landscape history for millions of years on. It is also, as it now lies

FIG 30. Meldon Chert in Meldon Quarry near Okehampton.

along the modern Vale of Creedy-with-Yeo, a nice demonstration of an ancient contribution to contemporary landscape via exhumation and re-working of a fossil surface feature.

But we must return to the granites and consider the effect of their intrusion on their 'host' rocks that have already been listed. They are often referred to collectively for convenience as the 'country rock' in circumstances such as these. The mechanical intrusive action pushes country rock aside, heaves it upwards and outwards, and prises its beds and the axes of its folds apart. The superheated fluidity of the intruder consumes and in many cases digests great chunks of country rock whose chemistry alone may remain as evidence within the granite of such activity.

On the grand scale, a long thin but distinctive band comprising outcrops of Lower Carboniferous shale, chert and limestone all intruded by dolerite lying just north of Dartmoor today displays in plan a shallow arc sub-parallel with the northern boundary of the granite. The pressure of the mobile granitic magma moving northwards from its feeder appears to have bent the east–west strike of the country rock northwards. A slight bend southwards in the band of Middle Devonian volcanic rocks which runs from Plymouth to Totnes immediately south of Western Beacon (Dartmoor's southernmost point) suggests the same story at the opposite end of the pluton. Figure 28 displays both phenomena. In small-scale terms the faults and tiny but tight folds exposed in quarry faces in

Meldon's three pits near Okehampton (Fig. 30) and others just north of South Tawton have been interpreted by Dearman as evidence of the influence of the emplacement of the northern granite 'toe' on its closest contacts.

The metamorphic aureole

At close contact it is of course the heat of the magma that has greatest effect and in a zone all round the intrusion – the 'metamorphic aureole' – the host rocks have all been altered. Most have been baked, and thus hardened. Slates have become chemically 'spotted' and the spots get bigger towards the granite contact where the most intense conversion is into hornfels, a dark tough compact, flinty-looking rock. Sandstones' quartz grains have recrystallised, and tourmalinisation is common in some places, notably at Leigh Tor above the Dart at Newbridge (Fig. 31) and in boulders on Mardon Down near Moretonhampstead.

At the present surface the aureole, which is shown in Figure 28, appears to average just over 1.5 km in width, though it reaches nearly 6.5 km briefly near Mary Tavy, and shrinks to 400 m near Wotter in the southeast and and a similar width near South Zeal in the north, though later faulting here may have affected such things. Where the actual surface slope of the granite contact can be observed or calculated, a more precise idea of the thickness of the aureole can be obtained.

FIG 31. Leigh Tor. Part of a reef of quartz schorl running across the Dart valley through Holne Chase, middle distance, to Ausewell Rocks on the skyline.

The slope of that contact near Mary Tavy is in fact very shallow at 10 degrees or so, and the true thickness of the aureole (at right angles to the granite surface) thus turns out to be only some 400–500 m there. Figure 28 shows three tiny outcrops of Culm rock sitting on the granite, remnants of its erstwhile roof, just in from Mary Tavy, in passing confirming the shallow angle of the contact just here.

The significance of the aureole in landscape terms is that it extends resistance to erosion and weathering beyond the boundary of the granite since both were exposed. Economically it has provided tougher, harder rocks that break up into more angular fragments than either the unaltered parent, or the granite next door. Granite, as we shall see, is physically strong but chemically weak – so the provision of hard angular, less soluble rocks as by-products of its emplacement has a nice utilitarian irony. Where the granite has succumbed to chemical disintegration totally the aureole rocks stand like the sponge fingers around a charlotte russe fencing in protectively the otherwise easily eroded kaolinite-mica-quartz sand mixture.

Kaolinisation and faulting

The chemical history of the granite is complex and still the subject of argument among those who delve into the mysteries of crustal chemistry, temperatures and pressures. Whether, for instance, the largest feldspar phenocrysts of the giant granite are an original feature, or the result of chemical change after emplacement, has not yet been determined.

I was taught that the slower the cooling the bigger the crystals (which helped separate plutonic (deep-seated) igneous rocks from extruded ones (volcanic glass has the finest grain of all). Equally, the lighter the colour the more acid is the rock. Silica and its derivatives provide the lightness, quartz and feldspars (aluminium silicates) dominate granite – and hence the physical hardness that quartz particularly provides. The feldspars, however, also lead to a chemical weakness because they are readily convertible under attack from the right liquids and gases into mixtures dominated by clay minerals. Kaolinisation is the process and it can occur at depth (through hydro-thermal activity and pneumatolysis) perhaps before, or as the magma cooled. It can also occur as chemical weathering at the surface, more effective in hot, damp tropical conditions, but wherever acid rainwater enhanced by acids in the soil and peat has free access to the crystalline surface. It is happening now, but has been even more effective when this granite has suffered tropical climates – as it has more than once during its long erosional history.

Both forms of kaolinisation have affected the Dartmoor granite, and two deposits in the southwest of the present outcrop (at Lee Moor and Redlake) appear to have been converted at depth, if only because there is still some

FIG 32. China clay being worked with a high-pressure water jet in Lee Moor pit on the edge of southwest Dartmoor.

250 m measured thickness of kaolinised granite (now china clay and micaceous sand) under Lee Moor, hardly a likely weathering depth (Fig. 32). There is much evidence of kaolinisation by weathering in the subsequent geological history of Dartmoor. Three substantial deposits of 'ball' clay (so-called because it was originally worked by hand and cut into spade blade sized cubes or 'balls') lie either side of the granite, one to the southeast and two to the northwest, on the same line which separates the middle east from the far east of Dartmoor.

FIG 33. Oligocene ball clay interbedded with lignite being worked with pneumatic spades in the Bovey basin in the 1960s.

The former lies between Bovey Tracey and Newton Abbot (Fig. 33) and the latter two at Petrockstowe in North Devon and in the Stanley Bank basin in the seabed just east of Lundy Island. They are related to each other and to the granite by the southeast–northwest line of the Sticklepath Fault – a major wrench fault with a horizontal throw of some 1.5 km – which runs from Torbay through the places already listed, out to sea west of Bideford and on between the Pembrokeshire islands and the Welsh mainland. Where the fault crosses the northern and southern boundaries of the granite (at Sticklepath and near Lustleigh) they are displaced as Figure 28 shows, and to the northwest both the narrow Lower Carboniferous chert outcrop and the tongue of New Red rocks in the Vale of Creedy already noted are dislocated by the same distance.

All the evidence points to the fact that this is not a simple single fault, but a zone of faulting, and there seems to have been sufficient vertical movement as well as the horizontal sliding to have created rift-like valleys (Fig. 34). Both the Bovey Basin and the Petrockstowe deposits (of sands, ball clay and lignite) have faulted boundaries and those dislocations north of the granite, because of the contrasted rocks involved, make it possible to map a myriad faults in close proximity. Within the granite such mapping is very difficult, but the fact that the pattern of parallel

FIG 34. The wide trough northwest of Moretonhampstead. Part of the Sticklepath Fault zone which runs from Torbay northwestward to beyond the Bristol Channel.

valleys, notably the Bovey, the Wray and those flooded by the Torquay reservoirs at Tottiford, conforms closely with the main fault direction amounts to circumstantial evidence for the zone rather than for a single fault. Between Sandy Park (near Chagford) and Whiddon Down, there are at least three deposits of pale clay and sand. With one there are quartz tourmaline and quartz grit blocks, the latter very similar to beds at the north end of the Bovey basin. These tiny outliers point to fluvial movement of Dartmoor-weathered material along the rifts.

The ball clay and its accompaniments are of Oligocene (or early mid-Tertiary) age, when a tropical climate held sway over what is now Britain. The lignite interleaved with the clay, as seen in Figure 33, is composed of up to 60 per cent fossil sequoia fragments, broken and battered, and few roots – although scattered rootlet beds occur at the margins of the Bovey basin. The picture then is of tropical forest timber and weathered granite products carried tumultuously but rhythmically into a rift-valley lake. The floor of the rift appears to have continued to sink as the deposits accumulated, making room for more deposition and suggesting a contemporaneous date for faulting, climate and deposition.

The faulting is the first crustal disturbance of any moment since the Variscan phase that ended with the granite's emplacement. Some 240 million years had elapsed during which relatively stable conditions dominated this part of the earth's surface and the deserts of New Red (Permo-Triassic) times had gently given way to invasive Jurassic and Cretaceous seas of varying depth (and to which we must return). But, the Alpine orogeny of the Oligocene changed all that. Southeast England was flexed into the broad folds of the Weald and the Hampshire and London basins, it gave us the Sticklepath Fault, sub-parallel ones to its northeast and from Prewley southeastwards across to Buckland (parts of the West Okement and the upper East Dart are close to the line). A significant fault also runs from Callisham Down to Harford in the extreme southwest (see Fig. 28). In addition Southwest England was almost certainly tilted to the south during the Alpine.

Within all that time Dartmoor granite was exposed to the air, drowned, covered with chalk, and its summits emerged again, for the last time, as far as we are concerned. Evidence of that first exposure we have already seen, in the upper parts of the New Red basement (Permian) whose outcrop has already been described. Characteristic grains and crystals from granite sources are also found in Lower Cretaceous rocks in what is now southeast Devon, which sit unconformably on the New Red, with no Jurassic remains in between. The earliest (New Red) phase was under desert conditions. The later transfer of Dartmoor detritus must have been by rivers flowing eastwards towards westward-advancing seas whose waves would have played their erosive role before the sea submerged the old Cornubian Mountain roots entirely.

Then began the warm-water deposition of the Chalk sheet that probably covered the whole of the southern half of what are now the British Islands and upon which *inter alia* elements of our present drainage pattern developed. In (younger) flint gravels on the Haldon Hills just east of Dartmoor and at Orleigh Court in North Devon there is fossil evidence from the Upper Chalk, and abundant chalk and flint deposits off the South Devon coast and in the Western Approaches add to the evidence for the westward extension of the Chalk 'sea' and thus beyond Dartmoor. But the uppermost beds of the European Cretaceous are missing from the British sequence, suggesting that that sea retreated more rapidly than it originally advanced and left us with a surface sloping gently eastwards (chalk easily trimmed by the waves of the withdrawing sea) upon which the landscaping of the Tertiary Era could begin. The Cretaceous alone had lasted 70 million years, within half that time again the Alpine orogeny would be in full swing, and that Sticklepath Fault would disrupt the developing Dartmoor landscape.

During the Eocene (the first 18 million years of the Tertiary Era) those flint gravels with their Cretaceous components were deposited throughout east Devon and beyond and now lie on the summits of that landscape, capping hills carved out of New Red and younger rocks. They also contain, on the Haldon, pieces of all manner of earlier rocks including fragments from the Dartmoor aureole and, most importantly for the Dartmoor story, granitic sand and whitish kaolinitic clay, a major symptom of granite decomposition. Some beds in these gravels contain abraded flint pebbles with rounded surfaces covered with 'chatter marks' (semi-circular fine cracks caused by flint pebbles continually hitting each other, as in a river or on a beach). It is argued that these must be fluvial in origin from the west because if they were deposited on a beach there would be other exotic material from the east, and there is none. Significantly kaolinitic components in these Tertiary gravels extend as far eastwards as the Hampshire basin (Dorset ball clays are worked near Wareham). There is, however, geological dispute about their origin and about the final modification of river courses that until then, having crossed proto-Dartmoor, extended eastward enough to have carried Dartmoor-derived material so far.

To that question and its context we will return when we consider the evolution of the surfaces we now see on Dartmoor, but before we complete this account of their geological basement and the processes and time involved in its history we have to consider the macro-structure of the granite itself.

Joints

When a Dartmoor granite face is observed from some yards away, the thing that hits the observer first is the network of cracks and fissures in it (Fig. 35). They are 'joints' to a geologist and in most giant granite exposures have a most remarkably rectilinear pattern dividing the rock mass into large blocks. (Joints because they are where blocks join.) In most faces there will be two sets, those near the horizontal and those near the vertical, but there are many other joint directions and their origins explain some.

The pre-eminent cause of jointing in all igneous rocks is related to the cooling process. In all intrusive cases it begins at the contact with the country rock. Its first effect is to cause separations sub-parallel with the outer surface of the igneous body as cooling in layers proceeds, and thus over wide areas in a broad pluton the beginning of the near-horizontal joints. But remember that it is likely to be an irregular surface related to the way the country rock and the magma in our case have accommodated each other and the joints should be sub-parallel with that. Cooling close to that surface is fastest and slows as depth from it increases. Quarrymen go deeper to find bigger blocks and slabs because at depth the joints are further apart and that distance increases at least as far as the centre of the granite body. (Calculations point to a 9.5 km thickness for the Dartmoor granite.) Shrinkage goes with cooling too, so the layers formed by the

FIG 35. The classic joint pattern of the giant granite seen in Sharp Tor above the Dart.

FIG 36. The north end of Bench Tor. Joints sub-parallel with the valley side. Sharp Tor cuts the skyline on the far side of the Dart valley.

horizontal joints break up into blocks of a locally fairly consistent size by vertical jointing. Tensions and the fractures involved are themselves complex and patterns will also be geared to variations in the composition of the rock. Some extrusive rocks and those less deeply intruded than granite often exhibit very formal patterns in which the repeated block becomes a more striking feature than the joints. The Giants Causeway's basalt and the Whin Sill's dolerite are impressive examples where the tall vertical polygonal columns are what takes the eye.

The other main cause of jointing in granite is usually referred to as unloading. Granite was emplaced deep in the earth's crust, that it is now exposed at the surface means that a great volume, and a great weight, of rock that lay on top of it and bore down upon it, has been removed. As that pressure is modified and eventually released so the granite springs apart to its own relief, and cracks develop parallel with the surface from which the weight has been lifted. That last is important because the phenomenon appears to work locally too, where a deep narrow valley or gorge has been cut rapidly in geological terms down through granite and pressure is thus released 'sideways' the granite springs outwards. Joints are then seen in valley side exposures sub-parallel with the surface slope (Fig. 36).

Since their own origin, joints have offered access to the granite interior to anything mobile enough to take advantage of them. Subsequent intrusions of later granites, the vapours and gases which brought about kaolinisation and tourmalinisation, and the mineral rich fluids, which Dearman described as arriving 'in one great and prolonged exhalative' spasm, all took advantage of the joints in the cooling or cold 'giant granite'. So eventually would the acid water from rainfall, which passed down through soil and peat, once the granite was exposed to the air. Both the underground vapours and surface waters by chemical attack widen joints, round off the corners of blocks and leave the subsequent spaces full of 'rotten' granite. Surface waters also break down the surface itself entirely, into what is known locally, and now geologically, as growan. In growan *in situ* the constituent crystals of the parent rock have been separated but still lie in the original relationship with each other.

Kaolinisation has been dealt with, but tourmalinisation is also very common on Dartmoor, in it tourmaline (typically black and in the form of microscopic bundles of needle-like crystals) replaces micas and makes feldspars cloudy. Joints are often seen to be 'armour-plated' with tourmaline and separated boulders to be coated in a black layer 2 or 3 mm thick on one or more sides. Sometimes a quartz (white) and tourmaline (black) combination called schorl is produced and can form veins and reefs along joint spaces. It is very resistant and can form landscape features such as at Leigh Tor shown in Figure 30.

That the density of joint distribution throughout the granite varies in all three main dimensions must be emphasised. Their origins clearly presume that those sub-parallel with the surface will be closer together the nearer they are to the original roof over the intrusion. The Mary Tavy contact slope measurement and outliers of Carboniferous rocks on Standon Hill and near Hare Tor already mentioned suggest that the summits we see today are not far from where the roof once was. So in exposures on such summits joints can be very close together. Variation in the density of near-vertical joints is substantial and its explanation unclear. However, it is demonstrable that there are large-scale patterns of these joints best compared to the patterns which can be created by expanding and narrowing a wooden trellis. It is these that are reflected in the landscape of northeast Dartmoor at the gross scale, producing in their turn a surface pattern extending for many square kilometres which Ronald Waters analysed in a study of the differential weathering of 'oldlands' in the 1950s and which are detailed a little later.

The next chapter will deal with all weathering effects in detail but it is as well to emphasise here that it is as conductors of potentially corroding liquids that granite joints should be most carefully regarded by the student of the Dartmoor landscape. Their distribution, as we have just seen, can affect the large-scale form of the countryside in question, and with the blocks they individually circumscribe they can provide the constituents of the dramatic detail which may dominate the immediate view and punctuate the distant prospect.

GEOMORPHOLOGY – A HISTORY OF THE DARTMOOR SURFACE AND ITS SETTING

Between the North and the South Hams (for that is the ancient name) lieth a chain of hills consisting of a blackish earth, both rocky and heathy, called, by a borrowed name of its barrenness, Dartmoor ... from these hills or rather mountains the mother of many rivers, the land declineth either way; witness there [sic] divers courses, some of which disburthen themselves into the British Ocean, others by long wandering seek the Severn Sea.

Tristram Risdon, A Survey of Devon, 1630

Risdon, whose 'survey' is largely about the landowners and their estates, for they sponsored his work, provided this remarkably economic but accurate summary description of the gross landscape of Dartmoor within Devon nearly 400 years ago. Needless to say the detail has been filled in, and scientifically analysed largely in the last 50 of those years. Just as with the solid geology, evidence about the evolution of the present surface of Dartmoor a) gets better – or at least is less contaminated or masked – the nearer relevant time approaches the present, and b) is subject to more imagination and theoretical controversy the further back we go. Davis's theories referred to at the beginning of this chapter were still being applied to Dartmoor in the 1960s. What is observable on the ground now will be described and more recent theoretical explanations for it will be registered. As always there is probably a grain of truth in most ideas, and their combination is the most fruitful exercise for the newcomer attempting to understand a landscape.

The granite-with-aureole massif is nearly 37 km north to south and 33 km east to west, but those two longest axes cut each other only a third of the way in from the north and the west respectively. Dartmoor, especially its granite core, is essentially a great asymmetric, inverted right-angle triangle, with rounded angles and long sides tapering irregularly to the south. The metamorphic aureole smooths out those sides somewhat, and the National Park boundary extends the smoothing, at least of the whole 'cultural' unit. The greater granite bulk in plan forms an 18 x 18 km northern plateau, separated from a smaller, 13.5 x 9.6 km, southern version by the broad basin of the upper River Dart and its headwaters. To the east of the northern plateau, the 'far east' of the topography, is a slightly lower block, 16 x 6.5 km, separated from the middle east by the valleys following the Sticklepath Fault line.

The highest point of the whole, as we have seen, is that short Yes Tor–High Willhays ridge reaching 621 m OD and the southern extremity of the southern plateau, Western Beacon above Ivybridge, is 334 m OD. The summits between

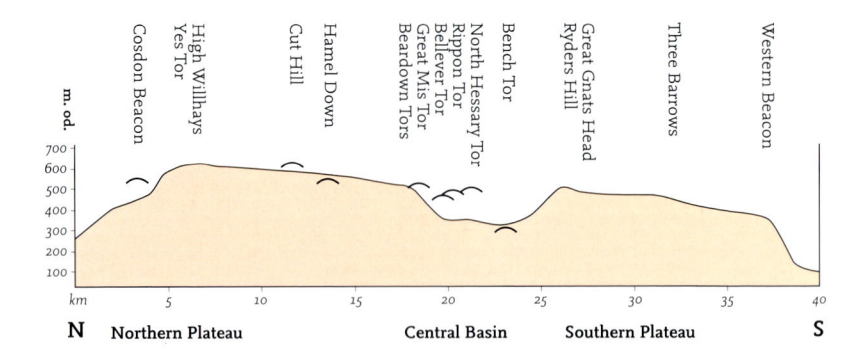

FIG 37. Consolidated north–south profile of the surface of the Dartmoor mass. Significant summits are shown in their latitudinal position, but some are off the line of the virtual profile. Vertical scale exaggerated.

these two accord in the main with a remarkably consistent slope southwards of 1 in 132, or 40 feet to the mile when it was first worked out! It is portrayed in generalised form in Figure 37. The significance of the consistency of that slope must be examined, but to complete the altitudinal data set a reminder that the River Dart leaves the National Park at 30 m OD and that this is the lowest of the river exits, is apposite. So, the total relief within the National Park is 587 m in a relatively small, 953 square km, landscape unit.

Development of the drainage pattern

The contemporary drainage pattern within the park is of a dominantly southerly orientation as Figure 38 indicates. Its rivers have been listed already but arranged for these geomorphological purposes: from the southern plateau the Plym, Yealm, Erme, Avon and Harbourne radiate round from west to east. The Plym has collected the Meavy before it leaves. Further up the west side but out of the northern plateau the Tavy flows south from the moment it enters Tavy Cleave collecting the similarly southward flowing and long Walkham on its way to join the Tamar. The Lyd has substantial southerly reaches within the granite and through its own spectacular gorge before turning west to join the Tamar in due course. The West and East Okements and the Taw are the only substantial rivers (in Devon terms) rising on Dartmoor that flow, significantly quite briefly, northwards and off the northern edge. The Dart basin's main river however is the major exception to the southerly trend, meandering across the central basin, as the West Dart, on a course just south of east from near Princetown (adding in the Black-a-Brook) and as the Double Dart as far as Buckfast. Even then it has

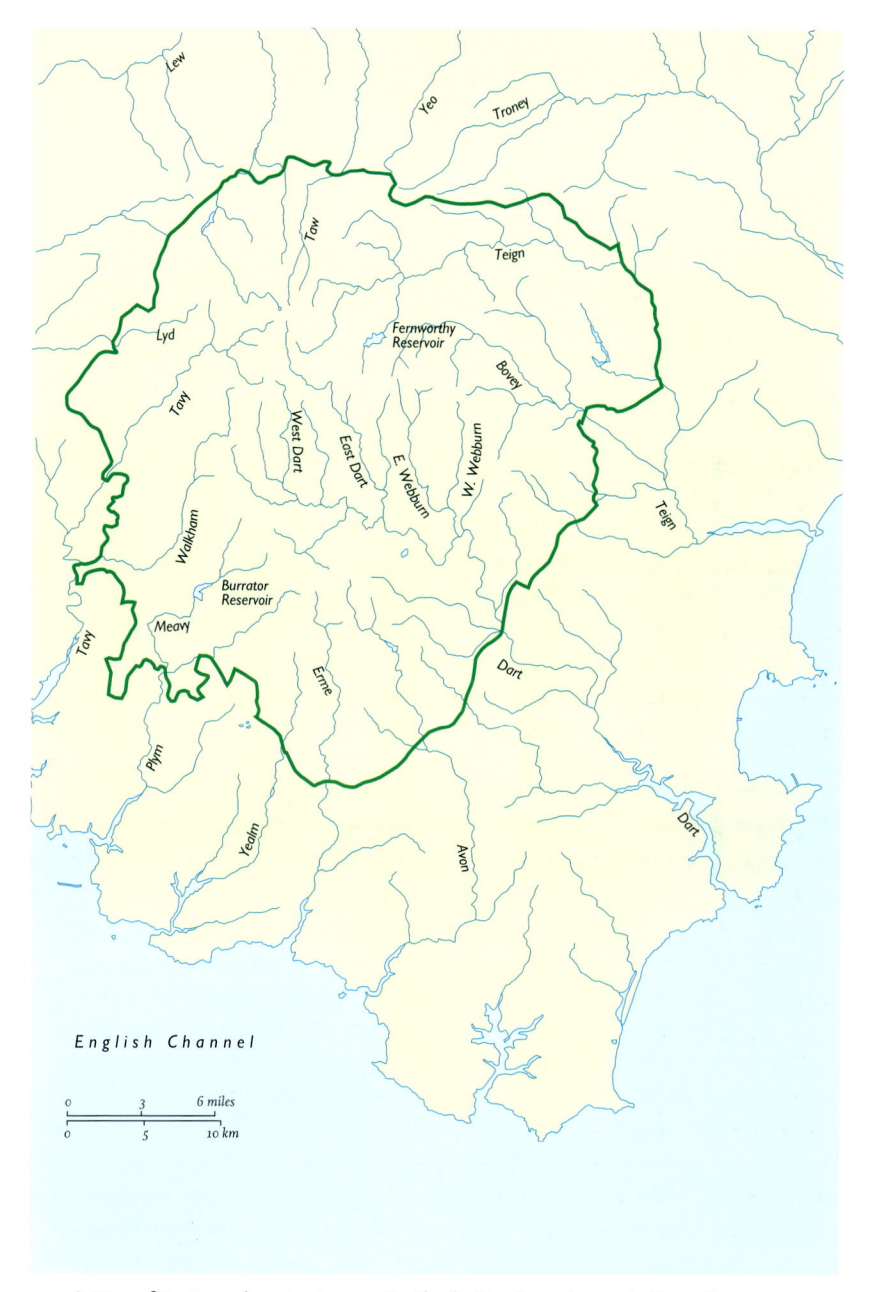

FIG 38. Map of Dartmoor's main streams. Southerly directions dominate the pattern.

collected all its main headstreams on its left bank; the Blackbrook, Cowsic, upper West and East Dart, Cherry Brook, Walla Brook, West and East Webburn all flowing southwards out of the northern plateau to join it and the Ashburn repeats the direction if not the source. This eastward direction of the West and Double Dart in the central basin has a historic significance of its own, as will be seen. But up the east side of the northern Moor the Sig, the Lemon, the Bovey and the Wray flow just east of south and join the Teign. Another Wallabrook, the North Teign and the main Teign *in tandem* flow for some 20 km slightly north of east (sub-parallel with the main Dart) before the latter turns sharply southward just east of Dunsford and runs for 8 km more down the eastern boundary of the National Park, and for a further 8 km beyond that.

Putting together this dominantly southerly directed drainage on Dartmoor and that mean southward slope of the summits is the equation which led to the theory about a crustal southerly tilt during the Alpine orogeny which was referred to earlier. Off Dartmoor but close at hand on either side, the Exe and the Tamar both rise quite close to the northern coast of the Southwest Peninsula (7 km and 4 km respectively) and flow all the way across it to the English Channel. The Fal and the Fowey in Cornwall flow south from source to mouth and the Camel and the Torridge both have extraordinary courses with long southerly reaches before they turn on their heels and flow out from the north coast into the Atlantic. All this adds to the circumstantial tilting evidence.

But, we must recall quickly that fluvial deposits in the Eocene (before the Alpine earth movements) had been brought eastwards from across the granite and, in the same direction but long before that, into the proto Vale of Yeo-and-Creedy just north of Dartmoor from the Cornubian mountains. So, to most authorities, a dominantly eastward drainage pattern is, geologically, of long standing. It had developed during or soon after the granite's origin, was submerged under a Cretaceous sea, buried under the resulting chalk and exhumed as rivers which also flowed eastward on the chalk slowly removed that cover. Eocene gravels with granite-derived minerals lie close to Dartmoor's eastern boundary on the Haldon Hills, and on eastwards as far as the Hampshire basin – though some think the kaolinite there may not necessarily have its entire origin in Dartmoor. Nevertheless all this strongly supports largish rivers flowing eastwards in the early Tertiary Era. We have just recorded that on Dartmoor, now, 20 km of the Teign's head-streams are in eastward-directed valleys, and 8 km of the West Dart and its tributaries flow east in a wide, shallow vale – that upper Dart basin already mentioned, and the Double Dart continues this line for the same length again, though now in a deep, narrow gorge of incised meanders.

FIG 39. Looking east down the valley occupied now by the West Dart. The wide floor and extensive 'flats' above it proclaim the elderly, even fossil, nature of the Moor's central basin. The distant flat is c. 350 m OD around Prince Hall.

Of these easterly directed drainage landscape units it is the basin containing reaches of the West Dart and two of its feeders, the Black-a-Brook and Swincombe, which has been most carefully examined by geomorphologists. Within its confines there is a series of well-developed 'flats' ranging from 280 to 420 m OD (Brunsden, 1963) and their appearance as 'steps' related to each other on substantial spurs suggests strongly that they are remnants of former valley floors (Fig. 39). While, in modern thinking, the whole business of relating such features to distinctive former river base levels is now a dubious art, in practical terms and especially under conditions of diminishing discharge, fragments of one-time valley floors of bigger rivers are bound to be left on the later valley sides of their smaller successors. These examples lie in a wide shallow basin with a long axis roughly aligned with the equally wide vale in which the Teign estuary now sits (strangely at right angles to its main supply river). In between is a broad-bottomed trough between Ashburton and Bickington now carrying the A38 (Fig. 40), and then a segment of the River Lemon valley north of Newton Abbot. All this adds up to a corridor in the landscape of some age clearly not related to any present-day through stream. Moreover, the valley floor remnants up on Dartmoor are still higher than the flat-topped hills with Eocene fluvial deposits

FIG 40. The wide dry trough carrying the A38 between Bickington and Ashburton on a line running through central Dartmoor and the Teign estuary.

further east. The breadth of the valley floors that they define must also imply a catchment extending 'upstream' well west of the present Dartmoor limits. It was developed in weaker rocks long since reduced below the levels preserved now only in the tough granite-with-aureole mass.

Just to the north, head-streams of the Teign are sub-parallel with the direction of the proto-Dart, and to the south is a fainter line through a col near Erme Head and Redlake, seen partly in Figure 205, to the upper Avon at Huntington Cross on the southern flank of Dean Moor (a route nicely taken by the mediaeval Abbot's Way from Buckfast to Tavistock).

These lines, on a moment's lateral reflection in Dartmoor's British context, are themselves sub-parallel with the Thames, the middle Trent, the Calder/Aire/Humber, the Tees, the Tyne, the Forth and the Tay. All are probably the successors of Eocene rivers initiated on that chalk sheet and flowing east to join a proto-Rhine, itself flowing north up a basin whose position is now occupied by the North Sea. This strategic lay-out is impressive enough, but the tactical scene supports its message. Why should the Double Dart, now deeply entrenched, follow meanders with an amplitude of more than 2 km between Sharp Tor and Holne Park which cut across the structural trend of tough rocks so dramatically? The reef of quartz-schorl from Aish Tor through Leigh Tor to Ausewell Rocks, for instance, runs straight across the Holne Chase meander as though it had had no influence at all upon the processes at work (Fig. 30). The answer must lie in the elementary landscape textbook, those meanders were superimposed on the present rock outcrops from some other substrate which overlaid them then and on which the meandering pattern was initiated … in this case, an elderly stage of the landscape developed on the chalk cover already described.

A gentle southerly tilt applied to such a pattern would disturb least those river courses running across it at right angles to the tilt. A bias in favour of left-bank tributaries would be likely, and captures by south-flowing streams with new incentives a distinct possibility. The upper Dart exhibits the former state and the strangely rectilinear pattern of the modern Teign from Castle Drogo to its mouth the latter. The disruption of the original pattern by a northwest/southeast fault zone, complex enough to throw rift valleys across west–east paths and divert stream loads into them, is almost certainly part of the mechanism for the major change in the proto-Dart at least.

Before pursuing that change – and those which followed – we should register one more thing about the uppermost – and thus the oldest – surfaces of Dartmoor now. That still-visible segment of the broad valley of the proto-Dart – which flowed from somewhere west and through the Princetown 'gap' – sat between chunks of landscape that also still exist. It had its own context then and some of that persists today. Correct the Alpine southerly tilt back to near the horizontal and the present flats of high northern Dartmoor that lie between 580 m and 520 m OD accord roughly with the present 493–463 m surfaces of the southern plateau in a north–south cross section. The levels, of which they are but remnants, are variously interpreted as the legacy of very mature landscapes related to base levels associated with long-term crustal stability under warm, humid climates, and with contemporary African analogies of the inselberg-and-pediplain type.

Long-past climatic weathering influences

Such warm and humid climatic conditions certainly pertained from the late Mesozoic into the Eocene and beyond. It is worth remembering that grass (or better, grasses) appeared for the first time in the fossil pollen record in the Eocene. It is a reasonable assumption that the sub-aerial denudation of a landscape by running water, downslope sludging and even wind were very different, more rapid and more efficient processes, before grasses existed and thus before turf could become a cover. Leaps of faith previously exhorted, in this case about the earliest erosion of the surfaces *we* still see, may be more easily made given that information.

Throughout the first part of the Tertiary Era, and in fact later in that era and parts of the next, it was undoubtedly much warmer and wetter than now. It was to all intents and purposes tropical and under such conditions granite, mechanically strong though much divided, but chemically weak because of its unstable felspars, suffers deep weathering. The effect of that attack is still evident, though not to say a controlling factor, in the medium-level detail of the land surface we still move over. The intensity of the weathering breakdown of the granite and thus its depth varied according to the distribution of the partings – vertical joints and faults – both in density and direction. In the northeast of the northern plateau Waters showed that two trends: NNE–SSW and NNW–SSE can be ascertained in both positive (ridge) and negative (valley) elements. Moreover cols in the ridges and widenings to basin-like form in the valleys are evident where perceived lines of weakness cross stronger ones. Where strong lines cross, summits with tors are the marker and they can be plotted on those two direction lines (say, Little Hound Tor–Hound Tor–Wild Tor, and Oke Tor–Steeperton Tor–Wild Tor–Watern Tor and see Figure 58). In the southern plateau, where Waters also worked, the Plym's long profile shows an alternation of narrow and broader cross sections coinciding with steep and gentler gradients. The pattern of the Plym's headwaters is also instructive. Five of its 11 km-long tributaries join its left bank on sub-parallel courses from the southeast, and the other two join the right bank having flowed parallel with the mainstream for most of their route. All this suggests a substantial degree of structural control involving first the pattern of partings in the granite and then the 'etching' of the granite on the basis of the density of the partings in that pattern. The significance of tropical phases in the history of the surface we now enjoy cannot be underestimated, even if as we shall see, cooler times have had a more recent and, some would say, more dramatic effect.

The story so far is thus of a landscape of low relief drained to the east and developed under the conditions just described over maybe 50 million years. It is suddenly, in geological terms, tilted south, dislocated from its original base levels, and 10 million years of turmoil ensues. Faulting probably continues and *inter alia* separates the Dartmoor mass from the rest of Cornubia at the same time. The differential strengths of granite-with-aureole and the country rocks begin to tell, now that the various 'covers' have been stripped away, and that differential is enhanced as the late Tertiary Era progresses. Dartmoor begins to stand proud; and its drainage begins to conform to something approaching a radial pattern albeit with that pronounced southerly bias.

The Dartmoor Island

Then, suddenly, the southwest of Britain along with the Mediterranean and the bulk of the North Atlantic basin sees a substantial end-of-Tertiary rise in sea level. All is engulfed to a height of about 210 m OD as we measure it now. Figure 41 reconstructs the scene. There is a widespread set of 'flats' at this height backed by a decayed low cliff in many cases, in both southwest (they surround Dartmoor) and southeast England. In the latter case there are marine

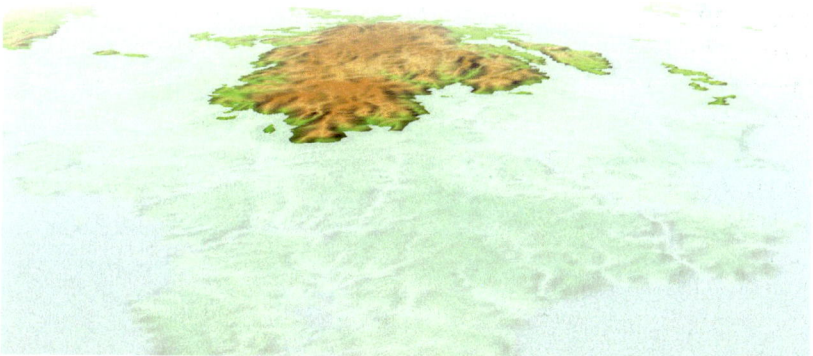

FIG 41. The virtual Dartmoor island, when sea level appears to have stood briefly at what is currently the c. 200 m OD contour given the disposition of flats in the surface right round the upland block.

FIG 42. Southern Hanger Down, a 'flat' at 200 m.

deposits on some flats whose fossils give them a Lower Pleistocene age, i.e. early in the Quaternary. The classic sites in the Mediterranean give this hemispherical sea level its name – the Calabrian. True geomorphologists standing on Headley Heath in Surrey, Plasterdown near Tavistock, Hanger Down or on a bench in Whiddon Park near Chagford can hear the waves of the Calabrian sea breaking!

At the end of the Tertiary Era, then, Dartmoor was briefly an island, with wave-cut platforms and reefs cut into its coastal slopes (Fig. 42). Their best remnants are in the southwest of the National Park (where the modern wind and thus wave attack direction were already prevailing). Hanger, Roborough and Plaster Downs are good-sized samples. They recur up the western and right along the north sides, but up the eastern side too, round the embayment at Holne and on up the then 'inlet' of the Bovey Tracey – Moretonhampstead trough. There is a long peninsula extending westward from Okehampton, and small offshore islands like Great Haldon to the east and Kit Hill to the west.

Briefly was the geological word. The sea retreated quite soon under a generally cooling climate and while its level during that retreat oscillated with glacial and interglacial stages of the Great Ice Age, at each of the latter it returned to a lower position than those before. The stages of its withdrawal are well displayed south of Dartmoor throughout the South Hams in a series of horizontal platforms, sometimes with rearward (landward) bluffs most marked at 180, 130, 100, 85, 45, 15, 7.5 and 4 m OD. They are taken to represent pauses, or standstills, in that general, if wobbly, retreat when waves had time to cut the kinds of platform which result from a bandsaw-like attack of limited vertical dimension.

The Dartmoor Pleistocene

For the geomorphic timetable this is perhaps the logical place to re-register a Dartmoor detail. Between the last two cold phases of the Quaternary so far (we are after all, still in that Era now) – the Wolstonian and the Devensian – the interglacial is named the Ipswichian. The Ipswichian climate reached tropical quality and the proto-Dart was leaving Dartmoor though a limestone landscape where Buckfastleigh now stands. Beneath what is now an 83 m OD surface on a spur bearing *inter alia* what is left of Buckfastleigh church (Fig. 43), underground caverns, with sink-holes connecting their roofs to the open air contain the richest collection of Ipswichian mammalian remains in a British cave. The most significant cave is called Joint Mitnor, after the three men who discovered it in the 1950s via a cleft in the side of the abandoned Higher Kiln Quarry. They were Wilf Joint and his colleagues Mitchell and North. They found inside a scree or

FIG 43. The flat-topped spur at 90 m OD, carrying Buckfastleigh church spire and riddled with caves and passages containing Pleistocene fossils in quantity.

talus slope below a shaft, now blocked, containing in its surface layers the bones and teeth of the herbivores: straight-tusked elephant, rhinoceros and hippopotamus, giant red and fallow deer, bison and wild boar. The carnivores: brown bear, hyena, cave lion, wolf, fox and wild cat are also there; and then badger, hare, water vole and field vole for good measure. The interpretation of the situation here is that grazing animals fell in to the natural 'trap' and carnivores attracted by the smell of the dead and dying voluntarily followed and after a long or short gorge were unable to regain the surface.

Apart from the significance of the fossils to the interpretation of the Ipswichian climate and dependent vegetation, it is useful for us to note that the surface containing the sink-holes must have already been well above the river, otherwise the cave would have been full of water and no scree structure formed. Joint Mitnor Cave's talus cone is regarded as one of the best in the world.

The Ipswichian ended some 70,000 years ago and the succeeding Devensian stage lasted more than 52,000 years as a 'full glacial' (the last real periglacial period in Dartmoor for our purposes). It thus brings us to about 18,000 BP but then takes at least another 5,000 years to fizzle out, and see the next chapter to continue the timetable. The retreat of the sea from Dartmoor during the Ice Ages, which the Ipswichian along with other interglacial stages and the Joint Mitnor Cave story clearly interrupted, persisted ultimately beyond the present coastline to somewhere near the present 30-fathom line. So the British Islands and thus Dartmoor were connected to the European mainland before the sea rose again through the Channel to a level close to its present, though still moving, position.

The whole sequence of the Quaternary so far has taken – according to careful examination of North Atlantic deep-sea deposits – a maximum of 1.7 million years. During that short geological time there have been at least 17 cold phases of which 8 or so occurred in only the last 850,000 years. They may not all have been glacial in the accepted sense of the word, and there is still difficulty in correlating what has been most recently calculated from those deep sea deposits with the land-based evidence of glaciations so long used by British and European interpreters. However, Dartmoor, an island at the beginning of the Quaternary Era, has since been part of continental Europe more than once – most recently as little as 6,000 years ago. Only 18,000 years ago it was within 100 kilometres of the edge of the last ice sheet to come south, and not long before that (geologically of course, say 130,000 years) was within 50 kilometres of the southernmost glacial extension over Britain when Irish Sea ice rode up on the shore of the north Devon coast.

Dramatic weather

So, on a landscape blocked out in the arid and tropical Tertiary Era from Palaeozoic and early Mesozoic rocks by riverine and marine action and earth movement, there is a series of final physical attacks by extreme forms of freezing weather and its gravitational consequences. Dartmoor lies during the latter glaciations well within what is known as the periglacial zone, currently best demonstrated in Northern mainland Canada and its Arctic archipelago, Spitzbergen, northern Scandinavia and of course northern Siberia. Vegetation is at most sparse – over large areas there is none.

In such places the earth's crust is frozen to considerable depths – 600 m or more in Spitzbergen still. Whatever else that does it makes the crust watertight.

FIG 44. Sharp Tor: jointed blocks ready to fall as the intense freeze-thaw ceased – now a salutary reminder of the power of expanding ice crystals.

All those joints in the granite are sealed; water that does arrive at the surface cannot descend nor move sideways within the rock. It is a time of long winters and very short summers. Spring (late May) through to autumn (late August) is the active season when some thawing occurs at the surface in the daytime and re-freezing occurs at night. This alternation of expansion and contraction – the freeze-thaw process – generates forces, as ice crystals in cracks grow and melt, or grow and grow on, which split off fragments of all sizes (down to that of silt particles: 0.002–0.06 mm), thus widening joints and levering off the outer blocks of granite from every available face (Fig. 44). That last mode leaves, of course, a new set of 'outer' blocks for the next leverage, maybe the next day. Periglacial weather is windy (cold air sinks over adjacent ice sheets and winds blow outwards from there at strength), snow is picked up and blasted into exposed joints and other fissures where it is packed tight, becomes white ice where otherwise water would not be retained, and adds to the levering potential.

The brief summer daily thawing provides lubrication at the surface, so all the material split away becomes part of a mobile mass of sludge containing all sizes of rock fragment (from silt particles to boulders of considerable tonnage) quite randomly distributed through it – most unlike a waterlain sediment. On any slope, the mass moves. Indeed 'mass movement' is one of those useful generic terms for the processes that include this one – solifluction. Solifluction can be observed in motion on slopes of as little as two degrees. New additons of weight upslope transmit power through the sheet of sludging debris – a boulder falling on to the top end of the sheet causes the toe of it to move instantly forward. In Yarner Wood National Nature reserve (NNR), flanking the valley of the River Bovey in eastern Dartmoor, granite blocks lie now (where they last stopped) on an aureole sub-surface more than half a mile from the solid granite outcrop boundary. Sheets moving down valley sides can coalesce at the bottom and run down the valley. Such streams of rock fragmental mixtures are often called 'rock rivers' or 'rock glaciers' and play their own part in eroding the surfaces over which they move.

It is important however to recognise before we press on with the periglacial story, that when conditions favourable to movement change, such sheets and 'rivers' stop dead in their tracks and become static parts of the scene themselves. The deposit that they have then become is called 'head' – wherever it is in the landscape and whatever rocks provided its parentage. Head is what quarrymen shifted before they got to what they wanted, so Victorian geologists, surveying our rocks for the first time, adopted the term, for at that stage they too were only interested in the solid stuff and all else was in the way. So close in time are we to those periglacial events that head is a significant feature of most of the southern landscapes of Britain – not least on the coastline and in the uplands and its contribution to Dartmoor landscapes is immense. Often unobtrusive where its effect has been to smooth out profiles, sometimes spectacular where its halting has choked a valley or subsequent erosion has exposed its make-up in a modern cliff.

The western coasts and uplands of Britain have had in common for a long time in our geological context, the fact that much rock is already exposed, and thus immediately vulnerable to the kinds of mechanical attack that invest the periglacial time and place. In the case of Dartmoor, as we have seen, the granite had been exposed and chemically corroded for a large part of the Tertiary Era, under warm, damp tropical conditions. Granite had been rotted, joints widened and rock kept bare in that environment. Contemporary granite under those conditions has been studied to check, among other things, the theoretical considerations surrounding historic chemical weathering. Granite 'bosses' and other tor-like features abound in Malaya and Borneo for instance and the processes of chemical change which *inter alia* have render the rock between them friable to some depth are now well understood. All this to underline the fact that the recent periglacial processes did not 'start from scratch', some advantage was offered to them by this long chemical preparation.

To illuminate the Dartmoor situation in these circumstances it is worth contemplating the outcome of the first onset of periglacial conditions. (There must have been at least eight such occurrences and between some of them a reversion to near tropical conditions, so repetitive attacks on the same surfaces alternating with chemical rotting was the norm for nearly a million years.) For our purposes, the arctic weather descends upon a Dartmoor hillside, the soil thaws diurnally in the appropriate season and is made mobile because its parent material remains frozen and sealed against water penetration. The resulting mud slithers off and down every sloping surface. The next thawing sees the parent material itself made mobile. In a normal southwestern granitic situation that material is 'growan', thoroughly rotten granite where the constituent crystals have all been separated but still lie as they did in the solid rock. (Growan is a Cornish miners' term for useless material and has a Germanic origin meaning sand.) The mobile growan thus follows on, and over the mud already downslope. Then the parent of the growan itself, the joint-separated granite, is exposed, blocks are levered away and slither down, then over-top the mud and the growan. There are many observed instances in contemporary periglacial zones of blocks sliding down the frozen surface, on the rollers provided by smaller grains and of course, when it is available, on snow and ice. Remember the Yarner Wood blocks.

Low down our slope there thus occurs a complete inversion of the original sub-surface profile: now it is raw granite on rotten granite on soil. A more

FIG 45. Looking up and across the clitter slope to the pinnacles of Staple Tor.

sophisticated sequence downwards in the lower slope position has been described as boulder head, main head (from a growan origin with contorted streaming lines), disturbed growan, growan *in situ* and back to granite, often exhibiting a platy division sub-parallel with the original surface. Back at the hill top, the summit is narrowing as more blocks are levered away and in extremis it narrows until no more levering is possible for lack of a fulcrum, but perhaps conditions change before such an idealistic climax is reached. Nevertheless most hill tops with decent slopes below them and at the edge of either Dartmoor plateau, or alongside narrow, deep valleys, exhibit the phenomena just described. Hence the Dartmoor tor – and its ancillary 'clitter': the boulder field that slopes away on some or all sides as Staple Tor demonstrates well (Fig. 45).

Tors and clitter

That is the simple story, and for lumpers it will do, but for splitters there is more than one path to tread. Tors occur at spur ends – e.g. Sharp Tor (Fig. 36), Western Beacon, Penn Beacon, Pew, Leather, Vixen (the tallest tor), Crockern and Fur Tor; at the lips of valley sides – e.g. Bench Tor, Hucken, Ger Tor (Fig. 46), Calveslake and Buckland Beacon; on valley sides themselves – Hockinston, Luckey, Sharp (at Drogo), Ravens, and in Wray and Lustleigh

FIG 46. Looking up Tavy Cleave with Ger Tor on the valley lip.

Cleaves: and of course on true summits – Bellever (Fig. 47 – left), Laughter, Rippon, Hay, Saddle, Yar, Great Staple, Sheepstor, Sharpitor, Great Mis Tor (Fig. 47 – right), Belstone and Yes Tor. All these sites have in common at least the fact that they are the most exposed, the most vulnerable positions in our landscape – ripe for weathering and erosional attack. Gravity, the basic ingredient of all non-glacier surface erosion, transport and deposition, is able to offer its most effective contribution at all of them.

FIG 47. Summit tors: (above left) Bellever Tor from the south; (above right) Great Mis Tor overlooking the Walkham.

Tors themselves come in many guises, and inevitably the splitters have attempted to explain the differences and classify them. It is an exercise like crossword puzzle solving, a challenge only if there is nothing else to do. That is not to say that there are not some intriguing and repetitive peculiarities. One of the most challenging is seen in the so-called 'avenue' tors. These are usually in summit sites where two or more rock piles persist separated by a space floored by a smooth, now turfed, surface. The granite blocks making up the piles are clearly still in their original vertical and perhaps horizontal relationships, exhibiting the progression downwards of increased angularity, or the lessened rounding that exemplifies previous underground chemical corrosion. Great Staple Tor above Merrivale in the west, seen in Figure 45, has four corner piles. Hayne Down near Manaton in the east, with the famous but unique single column of Bowerman's Nose on its flanks, exhibits a similar phenomenon at its southern summit, and Hay Tor on the extreme eastern edge not only makes an avenue with Haytor Rocks but classically demonstrates a correlation between closer joints and diminishing upper surface height (Fig. 48). What allowed the abstraction of the intervening granite leaving almost separate tor piles intact is a question still as open as these hill tops themselves. But the density of jointing, and thus variation in vulnerability to physical and chemical weathering, plays some part in the detail as it has already appeared to do at the landscape scale.

FIG 48. The eastern peak of Hay Tor from its western twin across the 'avenue'.

FIG 49. Clitter slopes around the head of Tavy Cleave, where the Rattlebrook joins the Tavy from the north. The foreground is the western slope of Fur Tor.

Below tors there are invariably scatters of granite blocks. In many cases they are literally boulder fields with little or no space, soil or vegetation between the boulders themselves. The solifuction vertical profile that has already been discussed would have them classified as 'upper head', the resting place of the last blocks to be levered away from the summit and the immediate slopes around it. They form the 'clitter' or 'clitters' of local topographic description – and make the approach to some tors difficult, demanding continuous attention to foothold and stride. Clitter appears at first consideration to be much more common, extensive and 'pure' below western tors as Figure 49 suggests. Careful fieldwork in the east however reveals dense boulder distribution where woodland masks it from the casual view from outside. This situation is well expressed in the Dart gorge below Bench Tor, for instance, where the 'pipe track' from Venford Reservoir waterworks offers a splendidly carefree walk along a near contour-like line halfway down the steep valley side. Even more open slopes when traversed on foot exhibit an unexpected population of boulders disguised from above and below by bracken and scattered hawthorn. The Hayne Down slopes are a good example.

Taken altogether therefore there is clitter throughout the Moor. Its exposure and apparently greater significance in visual landscape terms in the west may simply be that that is the 'weather' side of Dartmoor and has been so, ever since the end of the last periglacial period. Under a regime of westerly rain-bearing winds for 10,000 years the postglacial 'fines' (sand, silt and clay particles) which create the mineral frame for soil formation have always been readily washed away downslope; and thus a happy environment for low and tight vegetation to be established has never been achieved. Even in the east and despite the cover there, just described, it is clear that slopes facing the western half of the compass

FIG 50. Staple Tor from Cox Tor; the vestigial 'net' shows at the foot of the tor. In the foreground is the field of 'periglacial goose-pimples' – another variation on the patterned ground theme.

on the whole carry more boulders on the surface, or half buried, than those with other aspects. Down-wash has affected and still affects all such slopes, but best not to forget that in the dying days of the periglacial period these also would have been the sites of most effective thawing in the freeze-thaw phase. The sun strikes slopes more intensely than flats anyway, and strikes these west-facing ones after the day generally has warmed up. As ever, a combination of processes has almost certainly produced the effect in the landscape that we now see.

The flanks of the ridge crowned by Great Staple and Roos Tors bear wonderful examples of almost pure clitter. Viewed for more than a moment from Cox Tor (which is outside the granite) to the west, they can be seen to contain the vestiges of a pattern, or patterns (Fig. 50). Near the summit out of an apparently tumbled mass (the French call it a 'chaos' which is much more telling) there emerges downslope within the chaos a kind of net, and further down the meshes of the net open into strings running down to the bottom of the clitter. It is not a unique site – such 'stone stripes' emerging downwards from nets can be seen looking east from the B3212 across the headwaters of the River Meavy above Burrator Reservoir, and again on the slopes of Leaden the other side of the road (Fig. 51).

'Patterned ground' is a nice generic term for these and other phenomena that characterise most sub-arctic surfaces with little or no vegetation, and fossil versions are not uncommon in the highland zone of the British Isles. There are especially good examples above Applecross in Wester Ross, and on the Carneddau in Snowdonia, but Dartmoor is the repository of the southernmost we have. The physical process that produced the various patterns involved is (like the splitting off of small flakes from rock surfaces and the levering away of large joint-bounded blocks) largely a matter of the effect of expanding ice crystals – their actual formation and subsequent growth. Their expansion is universal in direction, i.e. as significant upwards and downwards as sideways or even more so. So particles from the whole of the clay-to-boulder spectrum can be heaved upwards and outwards and a kind of sorting happens which eventually moves the largest components of a mixture to its outer edge. Given the universality of the process over a flat or gentle slope, a 'best-fit' pattern of polygons is created. Hence the term 'stone polygons' which form the classic sub-arctic patterned ground in a wide variety of rock materials. You can perhaps imagine the different aspect of such phenomena in thinly cleaved slate with slabs lying in the vertical and in bulky granite in which no obvious long axis exists, but the gross pattern is the same in both. Hence also the nets of polygonal mesh on the upper slopes below tors, or even over the whole summit where no adequate tor remains.

FIG 51. Stone net running downslope into stone stripes below Raddick Hill. Cramber Tor is near the right-hand skyline.

FIG 52. The benched hillside of Cox Tor from the south.

Upper Dartmoor physical surface detail, then, is most often a series of fossil periglacial patterns and incidents. On occasion however the fossil detail is reflected and maintained by contemporary vegetation. If after viewing the Great Staple slope the observer walks towards it off Cox Tor he will soon find himself among what appears to be a continuous cover of 30 cm-high closely vegetated anthills touching each other at their bases, and almost as difficult to traverse as the clitter which he is approaching. Here is another periglacial pattern, common in the high arctic where strong winds are the norm blowing outwards from the cold air sump that exists over any ice sheet. Fine wind-borne particles accumulate as tiny dunes and mosses and arctic heather anchor them and grow upwards through the mineral mass trapping more. A cross between a molehill and a tussock emanates and is self-sustaining (Fig. 50 and compare Fig. 66).

If Cox Tor itself was originally approached from the car park to the south then our observer has climbed a series of benches or stair treads perhaps 20 m from front to back and with vertical risers of 10 m (Fig. 52). These 'benched' hillsides recur around the Dartmoor outer edge and are almost all on the aureole rocks. There are five more sets on the west side – at Peek Hill, Smeardon Down, Southerly Down, Lake Down and Sourton Tors. There are more on the north flank of Yes Tor, partly on the granite, and on East Hill above Okehampton. They are on Brent Hill in the southeast and Black Hill near Hay Tor further north.

They appear to be structurally controlled, the treads of the stairways aligned with major weaknesses in the slates, sandstones or dolerites, close to near horizontal pseudo-bedding planes. They first remind us that the periglacial attack is comprehensive, i.e. not confined to the granite or to specific surfaces. Indeed, the finely divided aureole rocks offered to the freeze-thaw process many more tiny cracks on which to work and resulting slaty or slate-like fragments were easily transported across basal platforms developed on those dominant structural lines. Spring-sapping at the foot of each riser is now slowly destroying the benches, which at least confirms their relict status and our privilege in seeing them before they are no more.

That reminder of the universality of the periglacial process is emphasised by the implication already that the tors themselves are not confined to granite. Cox Tor and Sourton Tors have already been mentioned, but elsewhere substantial features occur in the landscape, like Brent Tor in the extreme west, Brent Hill (Figs 7 & 9) and Leigh Tor above New Bridge on the Dart. The latter exists in a reef of quartz-schorl which runs for two miles west to east, crossing the meandering Dart twice and with rock exposed at each of three high points (see Fig. 31). Neither are tors by name confined to Dartmoor, however rare they are elsewhere. The tors of Torbay are in Devonian limestone, Mam Tor in the Peak District is in Millstone Grit and High Tor in the Gower is in Carboniferous limestone, but all have a periglacial past. Origin and etymology nicely coincide – we have already seen that in the place name game physical features, rivers, hills and headlands have the oldest names. Tor is at least Anglo-Saxon, but the 'Anglish', in the highland zone at least, picked up the landscape names of their new hosts and, reminiscent of the Welsh 'twr', the Anglo-Saxon 'tor' meant tower as well as rocky summit.

The tor/clitter combination (with all the variations on patterned ground where visible) dominates the scene where local relief is substantial – hence the earlier reference to the plateau edges as a generic location. The type list of tor sites (see above) tells the more specific tale and almost all are in and alongside valleys. Even a few tors apparently well into the plateau interior, on more careful examination can be seen to relate closely to valley sides. Fur Tor is a classic example (Fig. 53). Perhaps the most remote tor of all (Fur was Vur or 'far' in early Devonian) – but when you are there it is clear that the land falls so steeply from the tor to the north, 120 m in less than 800 m in fact, that this is yet another valley-side site: the plateau edge is more dissected than you thought. Bellever Tor, on the other hand, looming over the central basin from its northern edge in Figure 47, is a summit tor unrelated to any really steep slope. From it, as from the south side of Fur Tor, and as from most plateau summits, long slopes of the

FIG 53. Fur Tor seen on the southern skyline over Bleak House from the Rattlebrook peat works.

'main head' spread and clothe the interfluves, producing the typical 'high land of low relief' that is the basis of the Dartmoor 'wilderness', beloved of so many. Between them are the converse elements of such a landscape: the shallow 'vales' and basins where drainage is now impeded and very poor, and where mire and valley bog thrive, and remember the 'oldlands'.

On the crests and flanks of the interfluves surrounding the central basin there are many shallow pits where commoners have long indulged their right to take gravel and stone for their own domestic use, as have Duchy tenants. Surviving faces in them have demonstrated in the last 50 years (and there are few left as clean exposures now) the once mobile nature of the head, as in Figure 54.

FIG 54. Periglaciation: (above left) Cryoturbation of granite head in a pit on the Cowsic–Black-a-Brook interfluve; (above right) fossil structure of growan dragged by downslope sludging on the side of the West Dart valley at Prince Hall.

FIG 55. Profile from contemporary soil (peaty, gleyed podsol) through head, to frost-split platy granite *in situ*: a pit face on Merripit Hill in the 1960s, now invisible.

Flow lines and 'stirred' involutions are the main symptoms detectable. In some the mixture of flattish granite fragments, crystal gravel and fines could be seen in downward sequence of surface boulder (or upper) head, soil profile, main head, disturbed growan, growan *in situ*, platy granite and blocks in their original positions below that; the now-complicated profile with which we started this periglacial story. Figure 55, taken in 1963 in a pit on Merripit Hill, shows most of the sequence.

In passing, a reminder that Bellever Tor, seen well in Figure 47, despite its present coniferous plantation backcloth, has a profile from the south against the sky reminiscent of the inselberg-and-footslope of the southern African landscape mentioned earlier. Of all the tors it offers most hope to those who remain convinced that tor development is of longer standing than the Pleistocene. It may well be. It is certainly clear from some shallow quarry faces – notably at Two Bridges in the upper Dart basin – that chemical decay via pneumatolysis and weathering can reduce immediately sub-surface well-jointed granite to tor-like shapes consisting of piles of round-cornered blocks increasing in size downwards (Fig. 56). They have been revealed in two dimensions by human

FIG 56. A classic 'buried tor' in the Two Bridges quarry with chemically rotted granite on either side.

excavation but otherwise remaining embedded in the growan and other products of chemical disintegration – in a sense appearing to sit in their own waste. However, it is hard to see such waste surviving the freeze thaw onslaught of the Pleistocene *in situ* in any exposed location, even to imagine pre-existing tors thus formed at the surface staying the same when the scale and intensity of the periglacial attack is so clear.

As is so often the case in the landscape it is as well to accept that all the processes so far observed, described and conceptualised by geomorphologists, have played some part in the achievement of the present surface form. It is reasonable to conclude that, however effective and efficient the final periglacial denudation of the Dartmoor surface, it and its underlying structures had been well prepared for it by the exploitation of their weaknesses by chemical means in interglacials. Much rock and rock waste was lying on that surface innocently waiting to be stirred up and swept downslope. As long as the climatic conditions pertained the processes would persist, exposing more and more rock on hill tops and valley sides to be translated downwards to fill up valley bottoms with gritty mobile sludge.

The final melt, the last big rivers

The critical conditions did of course change, and from sometime just before 14,000 years ago freeze-thaw ceased to be effective. That is a landscape understatement. Whether the change was sudden in our terms or in geological terms, one must try to imagine the effect of the final melting of all those ice crystals. The permafrost had probably penetrated to 600 or 700 m down. It all had to melt, most of it had to exude at the surface and, however briefly, torrential valley discharges were bound to occur. The positions of the tors, on valley sides especially, have one more, simple message for us – they underline the fact that the detailed valley pattern was here *before* the last periglacial phase, indeed before the Ice Age itself. Thus the meltwater at the end of that phase was channelled down the valleys we now see. So, at first each springtime, sluicing out of the valleys began. As the climate continued to warm up torrential rivers, far greater in depth and width than the present occupiers of our valleys, became all-year-round affairs, until there was nothing left to melt even at depth. Then the torrents stopped, whimpered and (metaphorically overnight) shrank to a discharge dependent on the seasonal rainfall regime which the new temperate climate of Northwest Europe dictated. Britain had entered the next period of the Quaternary Era, the Holocene. The next 14 millennia of Dartmoor's history enjoyed a climate similar to that of our, or at least my, childhood with a few simple but significant temperature peaks and troughs.

However, in that geologically short meltwater time valleys were deepened. When ice advances from the poles globally sea level inevitably drops worldwide as seawater is locked up in ice. So, when they start running again long before the general polar ice retreat is complete, rivers have a base level far to seaward and much lower than the coastline that we know now. Their incentive to cut down is thus that much the greater. Remember also that this whole process was repeated at least four times in the Pleistocene Ice Age in the same valleys. For their pattern, as we have seen, was established before the onset of the first glaciation. Sea level, remember, offshore around the southwest peninsula at the peak of the last periglacial period, was at about the present 30-fathom mark. The lowest reaches of the rivers radiating from Dartmoor southward and their last reaches before leaving the plateaux in which their rivers had risen thus both became gorge-like, very narrow and very steep-sided. The former were eventually drowned by rising sea levels – the rias of South Devon. All the rivers that rise in a Dartmoor plateau display the same phenomenon as they leave it (Fig. 57). So much so that a topographer might use the phrase 'tor-and-gorge' to characterise this zone at the Dartmoor plateau edges (see Fig. 58).

74 · DARTMOOR

FIG 57. (above left) The Dart gorge from Sharp Tor – 152 m deep from valley lips at 300 m OD; (above right) looking down the Teign gorge from above Castle Drogo – 170 m deep near centre of view. (T. Eliot-Reep)

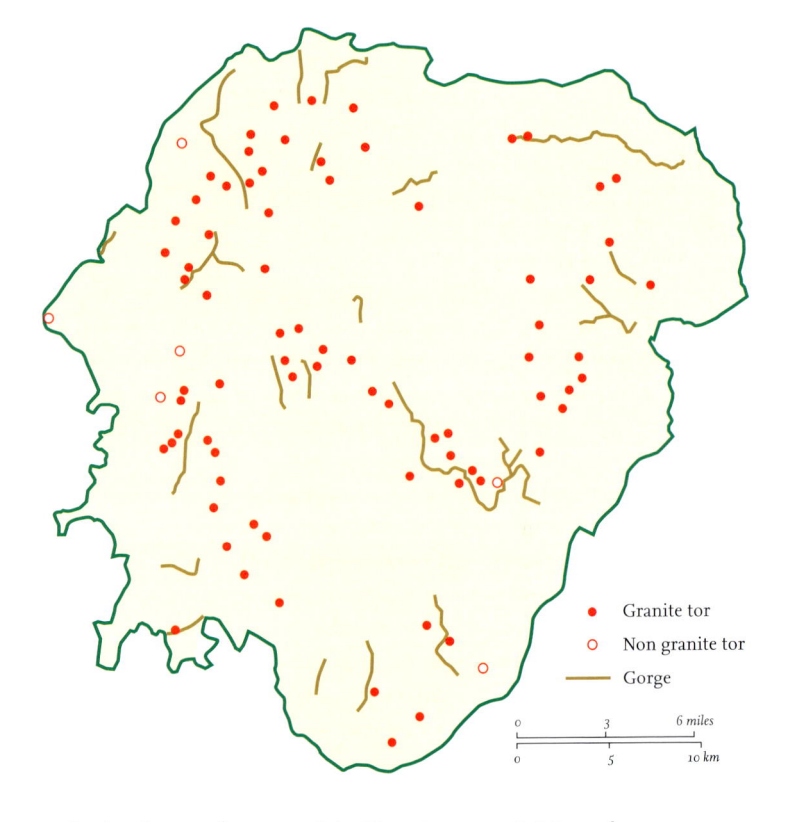

FIG 58. The distribution of gorges and significant tors around plateau edges.

The Dart, the largest stream to leave Dartmoor still, and possessing the largest catchment within it, carries three 'gorges'. The West Dart valley becomes gorge-like below Crow Tor and contains Wistman's Wood. The East Dart's last mile above Hartyland at Postbridge is in a steep-sided north–south slot and enters another just below Babeny. Its West Dart partner does the same below Huccaby House. They combine at Dartmeet and form the Double Dart that continues in the same mode. The whole of that gorge then runs for nearly 12 km to Holne Bridge, seen already in Figure 3, and under Bench Tor has reached 150 m in depth and the fragmented valley floor is still miniscule throughout.

But, when the source for torrential discharge (the melting permafrost) was finally used up, so the load of the moment, fines *and* boulders, was dropped (the load moved by any river is absolutely related to its discharge) and clogged the valley bottom wherever there was a natural sump – a sudden wider stretch of valley floor or the exit from a gorge on to a 'plain' for instance. That Dart gorge exemplifies the situation well. For three-quarters of its 12 km there is no valley floor to speak of, the present river – a puny inheritor of the gorge compared with its last real working occupant – still occupies the whole of the valley bottom. Suddenly, however, as at New Bridge, there is a widening (interestingly just above the point where the Aish to Ausewell schorl reef crosses the Dart for the first time). A small flat, perhaps a mile long, in three 'beads' – below Hannaford, at New Bridge itself and at Deeper Marsh – and never more than 150–175 m at its widest, provides space for human activity, odd tiny enclosures, even a dwelling or two, nowadays a car park and all that goes with it. It also provides, for our purposes here, a more important demonstration. Boulders lie on its surface, protrude through that surface from below and, in section at the modern river's edge, are buried in it. It is clearly a jumbled deposit with none of the graded vertical order of a normal water-lain one. It arrived in a torrent and was dumped when the torrent finally failed.

Such phenomena occur throughout the modern exit gorges of the Dartmoor streams. In extreme cases and in narrower, tighter valleys there can be a complete choke of jumbled boulders as at Becka Falls just before the Becka Brook joins the River Bovey emerging from its own gorge – Lustleigh Cleave (Fig. 59). Here the Brook 'falls' properly sometimes in the winter, but all summer long filters white water through a boulder wall perhaps 12 m high. But everywhere over Dartmoor now, at all grades of downstream slope, the puny contemporary streams flow round the boulders moved into place by their mighty predecessors. Collectively the boulders may form islands or 'aits' – cf. the 'eyots' of more sedate rivers, and *in extremis* text book braiding of the streams occurs. A classic example is in the River Swincombe just below its exit from Foxtor Mire south of Princetown (Fig. 60).

FIG 59. The Becka Falls boulder choke, left when the meltwater torrent finally died.

FIG 60. The braided River Swincombe – just within the Foxtor newtake.

A final related phenomenon is where the torrent of meltwater and the Dartmoor massif parted company cleanly. Here a fan, almost a delta, may mark the exit. The most impressive lies south of Ivybridge, a settlement sited at a classic crossing point-cum-power source on the River Erme. Here the surface slopes gently outwards, fanning away from the moorland edge and now bearing fields, a tight housing estate and the A38 dual carriageway, all of which mask the dense deposit of rounded boulders of the Erme's great parent stream. Before the last quarter of the twentieth century the space was called Newlands, a late enclosure of square fields bounded by walls and massive Devon hedge-banks, the latter typically 2 m thick and 2 m high and clearly faced by rounded granite boulders. Short sections of them are now incorporated into a number of housing estate garden walls. Where the fields still exist for their original function some straightforward single- or double-thickness walls also remain.

Granite core-stones are already rounded by chemical attack as we have seen, but these boulders have clearly been cleaned of anything rotten and further rounded by their transport downstream. They are now hard-surfaced balls. Indeed before 1975 whenever a public utility dug up Ivybridge High Street (the old A38) for one purpose or another, the road and pavement were littered with free-standing one-ton round boulders, for all the world as though a giants' skittles match was in progress. All this to underline the power of the transfer

FIG 61. Wall of rounded boulders near Newlands Cross, south of Ivybridge.

system involved and the distance an unnaturally dense load of boulders, jostling each other the while, was transported. Normal riverine deposits consist of sub-angular fragments of whatever size. That is how they are distinguished, whether still free or lithified in the geological sequence, from marine deposits, where smooth and complete rounding is the norm.

So, the last contribution of the Pleistocene period to the modern Dartmoor landscape was brief, tumultuous and had dramatic effect. In its way it ranks with the other 'spasms' that have characterised the history of this singular bloc of country since the first granite emplacement all those 280 million years ago. Those spasms involve two more granite intrusions, Dearman's 'exhalation' of metalliferous pneumatolysis and kaolinisation, the great faulting and tilting of the Alpine orogeny and even the brief survival as an island in the Plio-Pleistocene sea. They should all be remembered as making their own distinctive and long-lasting gifts to the Dartmoor surface as we know it. But the spasmodic 'periglaciations' at the end of the Pleistocene earn their place in this premier league of dramatic interludes partly because they are so recent and their effects all still so impressive to any contemporary observer.

Fifteen thousand years of soil and vegetation development and the occasional scour and flood of shrinking, and thus weakening, successor streams, and 7,500 years of human interference as the second half of that 15,000, have not seen any real diminution of the sculptural and moulded detail provided by those arctic spasms. Indeed it might be argued that much organic activity has enhanced their scenic effect. The lasting natural large-scale additions from that activity – mires, bogs and valley-side woodlands – have increased the variety at the surface without masking (honourably excepting blanket bog) any of the geomorphological detail. Human manipulation has modified these natural organic contributions somewhat, most dramatically in the alteration of soils and the accidental invention of inland moor and heath after woodland clearance. But despite exploiting something of each of the hard and soft products of the granite face itself, man has left, and still leaves, only incident (pits, quarries, buildings) to punctuate, and thread-like nets (of walls and banks, tracks and lanes) to accentuate, the grand scale of the whole countenance of the high moor.

The rest of this book is about the way all forms of life have worked out their relationship with that physical landscape, and with each other, upon it.

CHAPTER 3

Plants and People Return: Into the Prehistoric

The presence of peat over much of the high ground of Dartmoor has furnished material for paleo-ecological analysis, but it has also very likely obscured many (human) remains of Mesolithic date. Detailed work ... has elucidated the transition from a hazel-dominated woodland at 7,000 BP [Before the Present] to the establishment of true blanket bog ... about a thousand years later.

Ian Simmons, 2003

THERE WAS A MOMENT – in geological time – at the end of the Ice Age proper but before the melt of deep permafrost was complete and while there were still odd cold spells to come, when a casual observer in Dartmoor (a wider-ranging coastal Palaeolithic hunter perhaps) would have perceived only coarse gravel, rock and water. The gravel dominated, and all the gentler slopes appeared smooth but bearing dark streaks and downhill furrows that suggested a flowage of this mantle at the surface, swerving and swaying with the lines of sloping spurs and intervening hollows. The tors were there and obvious, and some clitter would have festooned the gravel glacis surrounding them, so rock emerged from the gravel somewhere in almost every view. But the rivers, while still looking strong in the summer, were already incapable of moving the biggest boulders in their beds. Of all this, for our present purpose, the 'streaks' are the most significant things to note, for they were the lines of persistent dampness where life was already born. The dark lines are colonies of algae, alive and dead, alive attacking weaknesses in the grains of gravel, dead providing the potential mulch in which other organisms might just begin to flourish. The gravel dominates, but it is already accompanied by particles of sand and others down to silt size. With a diameter of 2 μm silt is the smallest grain that can be split off by the freeze-thaw action already described. So, the physical framework of soil is

FIG 62. Furrows in downslope mobile gravel on Somerset Island, Northwest Territories, Canada.

almost there, then the algae reduce chemically appropriate grains such as mica – by organic grip and by swelling in any crack available – to clay platelets and, *hey presto!*, all the standard ingredients of a soil are here. They are the three mineral grain sizes, sand, silt and clay and the algal beginning of the organic quotient. It is here that higher life forms start to settle – in those periglacial furrows and the hollows where they converge and amalgamate, in the sub-arctic gravel (Fig. 62).

THE RECORD IN THE PEAT

The register that tells us of the next moves in the sequential clothing of that gravelly surface is kept in peat – the peat that is still with us. In it is preserved the pollen, the spores, even fragments of plants that dominated the vegetation communities of the surrounding land from 15,000 years BP onwards. This early peat began its own existence in the lowest part of the furrows and hollows already described. The dry, windy conditions, which pertain in the sub-arctic desert because cold air sinking over the solid ice to the north has nowhere to go or blow than outwards or south, gradually gave way to damper weather from other directions as the ice sheet shrank away northward. While rivers may have fluctuated in flow as a result without regaining much power, water from increasing rainfall saturated high-level hollows and in such natural sumps began the anti-decay situation, as oxygen was precluded, from which peat emerged.

Damp, whether as moisture-coated gravel or actual bodies of shallow water, begins its contribution to this story there by catching wind-blown spores and seed, as do crevices between grains and gravel or even those in solid rock surfaces. Water plants germinate and survive in pools, others – especially lichens, mosses and liverworts – find cracks anywhere potential havens for procreation and so the colonisation of the whole surface begins.

Nothing in the natural world is simple and the allegoric geological 'moment' that began this chapter must not be allowed to mask the fact that climatic oscillations occur at the boundaries of perceived major climatic time zones. So, even as life returns to Dartmoor after the (latest) glaciation, there may still be falls in temperature sufficient to set off freeze-thaw and thus solifluction processes again. Such things inevitably disrupted the pollen and other organic relict record held in the peat that we now see. They must, of course, have set back real colonisation by plants and animals for some little time but the resilience of sub-arctic pioneer insects, birds and mammals is more than matched by plants which cannot physically retreat south again, and thus must grin and bear it or succumb. The proof of this pudding lies on the next granite moor to the west. At Hawks Tor on Bodmin Moor's western slope, and roughly on the same latitude as Laughter Tor in Dartmoor's central basin, granite head rests on top of organic matter whose lowest layers are dateable by the measurement of radioactive decay (Carbon-14) to 14,000 BP. So two things arise, first the evidence that southwestern colonisation really was interrupted by cold spells and setbacks did occur, but the c.15,000 BP generalisation for the beginning of that colonisation is nicely confirmed.

But colonisation proceeds. Of course some seeds may have survived the Devensian glaciation. After all, purple saxifrage *Saxifraga oppositifolia* (Fig. 63) appears to have clung on to Snowdon and to Pen-y-Ghent in the Pennines throughout the full glaciation, i.e. with glacial ice all around; so why not here in the periglacial zone where such 'clinging'

FIG 63. Purple saxifrage in full bloom.

82 · DARTMOOR

FIG 64. Scatter of patch-forming plants – the pioneer colonisers of arctic gravel.

must have been marginally easier? Certainly the next 'casual observer' would have seen that gravelly surface of Dartmoor bearing scattered patches of very low plants, looking like so many cow-pats from any distance until they flower (Fig. 64). Purple saxifrage was certainly one such patch-former, mountain avens *Dryas integrifolia* another; thrift *Armeria spp.*, campion *Silene spp.* and, eventually, crowberry *Empetrum spp.* and arctic willow *Salix arctica* (the first woody plants, albeit only 3 or 4 cm high) all contribute to this overall effect. The potential for amalgamation of patches would not escape the observer, and the contribution of all patch-forming plants to the first successful establishment of a continuous cover of flowering plants displayed for all to see, had they been around.

FIG 65. Arctic willow, the first woody shrub of the sub-polar succession.

We should note that 'they' were not far away. We know that Palaeolithic man lived on the South Devon coast during the last three glacials and their interglacial separations. His tools lie in dated deposits in Kent's Cavern in Torquay. He and his colleagues were 'hunters and gatherers' as were their Mesolithic successors who were just beginning to ease into this landscape as warming began and our developing natural cover story started to unfold. Casual observers therefore there may well have been, and after all eskimos hunt and gather in the gravelly landscapes of the sub-arctic still, so a weekend trip from the coast may have allowed a welcome variation in a diet dominated by shellfish.

Continuous cover would first manifest itself in the damper hollows and where snow patches persisted and ironically acted as protection from wind and even from low temperature in spring. But never forget the wind's potential for good as well as its inhibition of vertical growth. It is the bearer of seeds, spores and pollen, even the transporter of broken shoots which might end up as 'cuttings' in the good old arctic-alpine reproduction process well known to rockery gardeners – but also shifter of sand, silt and clay to be trapped by patches of capable plants. In the Dartmoor context, none would be more significant than arctic white heather *Cassiope tetragona* – the marram grass of sub-polar tiny dunes! Well seen near Resolute Bay on Cornwallis Island in the Northwest Territories of Canada (Fig. 66). The successors of those 'dunes' persist. Just east of Cox Tor, as we saw in Chapter 2, is a small mirror image of the fields of such contiguous 30 cm-high humps, or hummocks.

Cover, already containing woody plants, boosted soil development and as the ice to the north retreated and Dartmoor sneaked beyond the effect of the

FIG 66. Periglacial 'dunes' in arctic heather – Resolute Bay, Northwest Territories (see Fig. 50).

strongest out-blowing winds, plants reared up above the 3-cm carpet that had so far been the norm. Suddenly, comparatively, there was small scrub, willows heaved themselves nearly upright, and soon birch trees – admittedly dwarf birch *Betula nana* – began the procession towards a woodland cover, where crouching conifers would soon join their deciduous pioneers and a whole circumpolar forest zone below 500 m established itself. So it was on Dartmoor. For what that Bodmin Hawks Tor site (just 32 km westward) has also revealed is a grass/sedge and herbaceous dominance from 14,000 to 11,500 BP when birch and crowberry pollen emerge in quantity. Just after that, at 11,000 BP or thereabouts, a cold phase known elsewhere as the Loch Lomond Stadial (after a small ice sheet centred there) set in and lasted until 9,500 BP when birch and crowberry with juniper *Juniperus communis* arose again and clothed the gentle slopes around pool-filled hollows. The whole scene was heathy, but in the flattest sites with depressions reminiscent of today's tundra.

Wind strengths continued to reduce, rainfall increased, and forest closed its canopy nearly to the high tops, but up there herbaceous vegetation seems to have fought off the trees. Rain, persistent cloud, fog and mist sustained a continuous surface saturation that inhibited the decomposition of dying vegetation, and more peat was born. This is ombrogenous peat, whose cover plants gain their nutrients solely from the falling rain, cut off as they are from the mineral surface below by the peat itself. It may have been 'born' but peat does not die and disappear under these conditions, it simply accumulates and only the weight of its upward accumulation has any effect upon its lowest layers. They slowly lose recognisable vegetative structures and become an amorphous black bed, still, happily for us, preserving the spores and pollen grains of the plants that contributed material to them and of those which surrounded the site in question. It is those tough capsules of plant genetic material that allow us to make a fair reconstruction of the floral communities that began and eventually fully clothed the gravel surfaces with which the latest phase of Dartmoor's life as a landscape began.

PREHISTORIC TIME, PEOPLE AND PLANTS

The Quaternary Era from then on – even through the Pleistocene/Holocene boundary at about 10,000 BP – is divided into time zones based on climate and vegetation via pollen analysis (numbered I–VIII) and via radiocarbon dating (named Flandrian I, II and III). The diagram at Figure 67 portrays a version of this sequence as simply as possible for our purposes. Because the Era also contains the migration inwards of humans as well as plants and animals – not all for the first time – there must be an attempted correlation between the scientific eco-climatic

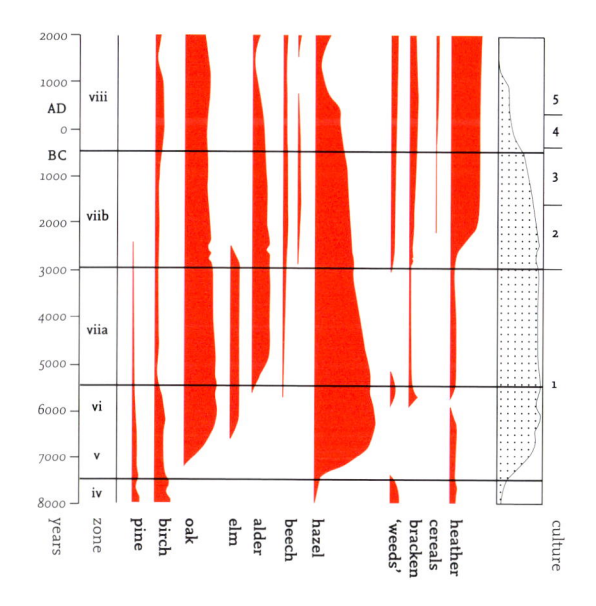

FIG 67. Generalised pollen diagram for high Dartmoor (after Simmons, 1964). The climatic zones are: IV. Late glacial, V. Pre-boreal, VI. Boreal, VIIa. Atlantic, VIIb. Sub-boreal, VIII. Sub-Atlantic; the stipple is total tree cover. Cultures are: 1. Mesolithic; 2. Neolithic; 3. Bronze Age; 4. Iron Age; 5. Historical.

zoning and what our own superiority complex will call 'cultural' ages. They are based primarily on successive exhibitions of human technological prowess, or lack of it, at the time. Technological cultural change was not generally a matter of evolution *in situ*, but rather of infiltration – it was not necessarily by militaristic invasion – and take-over by those with some superior quasi-industrial knowledge or experience, usually involving tools and/or weapons.

As we begin to try to understand the development of the vegetated surface that we actually walk upon today it is clear that accuracy has increased as the availability of techniques by which cross-checking can occur has also increased. Pollen analysis from peat deposits was all that was available in the 1940s to Professor Harry Godwin for instance (*History of the British Flora*, 1956), but this was extended to pollen in podsolised soils, by Dimbleby in the mid-1950s. Soon after that the development of the measurement of radioactive decay as a tool for dating fragmental organic remains, Carbon-14, allowed for much tighter calendars to be produced for the last 70,000 years. In the last decade the measurement of the density of testate *amoeba* in peat has allowed the even more precise registering of wetter and drier phases during the last 4,000 years. (To survive adverse conditions, mainly drought, amoeba can develop a tough complete case called a testa that allows almost infinite survival.) We should, however, also recognise that there is still considerable argument about the validity of the extrapolation of local interpretation conclusions from one site, or even a few sites, to wider areas. How to define the 'catchment' of pollen 'rain' for a given peat deposit or how to compare pollen sequences where the peat deposits in question may have accumulated at different rates at different times are still outstanding questions. But, despite both the technical advances and the remaining problems, each of the many versions of parts of the late Quaternary timetable available now have a contribution to make to our contemporary lay comprehension of the Dartmoor sequence – but none have contradicted the earliest popular generalisation, so Figure 67 reproduces it. It also brings for the first time into this narrative the seminal work of Professor Ian Simmons that effectively triggered Dartmoor vegetation history studies in 1960. They have proceeded at pace since and now rely on sophisticated analysis of many kinds of microfossils in the peat. Simmons's pollen diagram, however, is unchallenged as to its generality and its lack of complication, which makes it especially useful to us here.

We have just seen that Mesolithic folk had begun to move in on their Palaeolithic (Old Stone Age) predecessors almost before the Pleistocene merged with the Holocene at about 10,000 BP. They stayed a long time. While they too were hunter-gatherers, Mesolithic tools and weapons improved enormously during the 7,000 years they held sway and their mark on Dartmoor was probably much more significant than the physical evidence of their presence at the surface suggests. Their long reign lasted through the development of the maximum woodland cover that seems to have driven them as hunters to the coast one way and to the upper edge of the woods the other. One of the best collections of their flint tools on Dartmoor is from a knapping site on Langstone Moor at Peter Tavy Great Common, but there are others right across the Moor as far as Gidleigh Common and at Bridford. Near Postbridge tools and discarded flakes are beneath the peat and so older than its inception there. They also saw the best of the post-Ice-Age weather! That apogee is reached in Atlantic times (Zone VIIa and the end of Flandrian II), say 6,500 to 5,000 BP, and is known as the 'climatic optimum' – though the build-up to it probably began soon after 8,000 BP.

Picking up the fragmental references to the vegetation so far, the pollen record seems to show that the southwestern uplands were dominated by herbaceous plants for at least 2,000 years after the pioneering covering of the gravel and its first primitive soils, with grasses and sedges in the ascendancy in all the hollows however large. Sediments with pollen from pools suggest tundra-like landscapes. Then on drier slopes juniper and crowberry moved in and dominated from about 12,000 BP and sparse tree pollen from pine, dwarf birch and willows is also recorded. Woody plants diminish 'suddenly' just after 11,000 BP as our version of the Loch Lomond Stadial was felt and grasses regained ground even though solifluction once more disturbed many slopes and valley bottoms. As Dartmoor entered the Holocene the juniper/crowberry suite reappeared on slopes, and pioneer woodland from 9,600 to 9,000 BP heralds the beginning of the Flandrian or postglacial time zone. Birch, hazel and oak build on the heathy scrub of the pioneers and dominate the deciduous woodland of the Moor for the next 8,000 years – though their companions vary and the extent of the woodland varies even more.

The precision of this timetable is bolstered by the Carbon-14 dating carried out on some of the Bodmin material. Such tools were not available to Ian Simmons when he constructed Figure 67 from simple but detailed pollen analysis of peat in Blacklane Mire near Caters Beam on the southern plateau in 1960. A return to the site in the late 1970s yielded Carbon-14 data and, in his own word, 'happily' confirmed his original conclusions and timing. He began the Dartmoor work, as we have already noted, and despite many illustrious followers whom he readily acknowledges, was still writing about it in 2003.

His original diagram showed that the oak/birch/hazel troika was joined by elm from 8,700 to 4,700 BP; and by alder – doubtless in the appropriate sites – from 7,500 BP through to the historic mediaeval period. The alder confirms the continuation of dampness as a crucial component of the high Dartmoor scene throughout Flandrian times, and elm, not an upland tree, has been used as a marker of the temperature condition. Elm demands warmth compared with birch and pine, say, and thus is taken to be an indicator of the development and length of what we have seen already as the postglacial 'climatic optimum' (elm declines rapidly across Europe at about 4,500 BP).

It is worth remembering here that until then, 4,500 or so BP, the Britannic-continental 'land bridge' persisted. Sea level, as northern ice melted, was rising in any case from 30 fathoms below present sea level. The lessening weight of ice on the northern two-thirds of the British Isles caused a rocking back towards a pre-glacial equilibrium (which is still proceeding in this century) and thus accelerated the re-adjustment of the relative levels of sea and land along the south coast. There was still, nevertheless, a time lag. The significance of that, the lag and the consequent persistence of the land bridge, is the opportunity it provided for plants and animals to move back into Britain as climates ameliorated and their preferred or optimum nutrients, food supplies and habitats also migrated pole-wards.

Certainly, pollen analyses from across southern England show that oak, elm and hazel migrated back across that land bridge, and rapidly fanned outwards from the bridgehead, between southeast Dorset and the North Foreland. Their longer life allowed them to dominate shorter-lived birch and pine quite soon. Hazel peaked early on Dartmoor but stayed at strength for the whole of the

Flandrian, i.e. into historic time, and there is some evidence that pure hazel woods may have existed within the composite forest cover. Work in the 1990s, on pollen from a peat deposit on the western flanks of Fur Tor at Pinswell, registers a hazel-dominated scene at about 7,000 BP (early Atlantic or VIIa).

The 'tree line'

At this point we should note the altitudes of the pollen-carrying peat sites that have been analysed. They are not in themselves a measure of the height that woodland reached before human interference because of that open question about pollen 'catchments', but they help towards a consensus about it. They also indicate (perhaps 'the obvious') that peat deposits were forming, being maintained and growing contemporaneously with, the woodland, and that a quite complex vegetation mosaic existed close to their altitude. Simmons's first site, at Blacklane Mire, was at 457 m OD. While it is now surrounded by blanket bog spreading up and out from the Mire itself, the present slopes rise to 488 m in the east, and c. 470 m to the northwest, southwest and southeast (Fig. 68). Ryders Hill, the highest point of the southern plateau and only 2.4 km to the east of Blacklane reaches 515 m and woodland may have reached it, particularly when we compare the altitudes of analysed locations in the northern plateau. Fur Tor rises only 112 m above the site where the hazel pollen rained down at 461 m, Little Kneeset rises to 500 m to the northeast of it and across the valley of the Amicombe Brook to the northwest the slopes run gently up to 488 m and then northward up the spur to 570 m and then 580 m above Kitty Tor. So again we see, conservatively, likely wooded slopes up to 550 m or so and well over-topping the southern plateau. Other sites in Britain have yielded tree remains above 500 m, though rarely more than 550 m, and they are all far north of Dartmoor, if the climate of the moment had a bearing on the trees' ascent then Dartmoor was an easy climb. Again we should recall the Atlantic Zone climatic optimum, which is generally regarded as hosting the climax vegetation – deciduous forest – of Britain. The likely altitudinal extent of woodland just referred to is Dartmoor's version of that climax.

But it is also necessary to register here that before the optimum passed and the climate deteriorated from 5,000 BP onwards so another major factor entered the Dartmoor vegetation evolutionary story. Men join in the game, and while comparisons with earlier interglacials (in case we are still in one) show a similar deterioration of woodland and even increases in heath communities in their 'second halves', men certainly were not a factor in vegetation change then. It must be concluded that we cannot entirely separate human activity from natural change from now on – it is a very significant new influence and we may have yet to push the consideration of it back in time a little.

FIG 68. Blacklane Post, looking upstream into Blacklane Mire, Simmons's working site.

Simmons showed that heathers were present on the southern plateau almost throughout the Flandrian – we must consider his one gap quite soon. It seems likely that clearings in the woods and certainly their upper edges bore heather growing on predominantly wet surfaces as the ling *Calluna vulgaris* and cross-leaved heath *Erica tetralix* communities on blanket peat, peaty gleys and peaty gley podsols do today. So a woodland/wet-heath assemblage is easily visualised with peat thickening under the patchy heath a distinct possibility. This must be remembered as the exchange of woodland cover for heath, moor and blanket bog is considered – for opportunity for change is nothing if the wherewithal for replacement is absent.

The 1964 pollen diagram at Figure 67 shows a blip in the oak, hazel and even heather pollen at about 7,600 BP. At the same time pioneer ash and rowan pollen increased and suddenly bracken appears for the first time, accompanied by the return of some of the herbaceous plants recorded before the tree pollen began to dominate. All this adds up to an increase in light, and thus the local loss of shading tree canopy. We have already seen that Simmons's work was carried out at a high altitude, so the change recorded may well have been at or very near the forest edge – its upper edge or, popularly, the 'tree line'. The likely cause of the change, all authoritative workers seem to agree, is fire. They also agree that charcoal in the peat of northern Dartmoor dated at 8,785 BP is almost certainly the result of natural fires, such a record is common across Europe and at all altitudes around that date in the early Holocene. There is however growing evidence for the human use of fire at and around the inferred upper edge of the forest.

In the early 1980s, work in the northern plateau, notably at Blackridge Brook just northwest of Fur Tor this time, demonstrated the possibility of birch/hazel woods on the summits with clearings of heath after 8,700 BP, then an apparent retreat of woodland from the high plateau beginning 1,000 years later. Hazel pollen diminishes, heather and grass pollen increase, and charcoal, ever present in the peat from 8,000 BP, reaches regularly repeated high levels from 7,000 BP on. It looks as though Mesolithic burning suppressed woodland at its upper edge and allowed the beginning of the development of the blanket peat we still see. (At a site in the Black Mountains near Brecon (Waun Fignen Felen), peat and peaty soils sitting on a mineral base have been shown to coincide with Mesolithic artefacts all dated at around 7,500 BP.) By 6,250 BP, or so, an early woodland/moorland balance may have been struck, and it would last until cultural change modified their mutual boundary further. So Simmons, and Caseldine, Maguire and Hatton (who worked later on those Fur Tor slopes) and Charman *et al.* all propose that Mesolithic folk used fire to maintain or possibly extend their best hunting ground by increasing its openness and thus improving grazing for the hunted *and* the spatial hunting potential at the same time. Small quantities of fungal spores, connected with dung, and of grass pollen add to the evidence, but not spectacularly. The food gathering that balanced the Mesolithic diet might also have been facilitated by more clearings even by a more convoluted woodland edge, but speculation that might lead to the attribution of even more sophisticated land management to pre-agricultural people better still be constrained. However the Mesolithic presence has already been recorded, thinly but widespread, right across Dartmoor. In some cases substantial collections of later Mesolithic finer flint points and blades – termed microliths by archaeologists – have been accumulated during professional and amateur searches. The increased sophistication that these weapon and tool 'parts' represent, sits well with the idea that some manipulation of vegetation by men in the interests of their domestic economy was also taking place for the first time. It was after all to be the main shaper of Dartmoor's whole character from then on, and it is important to recognise that what Dartmoor gives to so many folk today, in social, recreational and cultural terms, is the result of a very long history of work by generations of, initially slowly, developing land managers.

The Mesolithic landscape, of woodland with clearings and a convoluted upper boundary, above which heathland sat on the high tops, was beginning to be infiltrated by successor settlers from 6,000 BP, or so, while the climatic optimum persisted. Among them were probably the vanguard of the Neolithic stockmen who would bring about the most dramatic changes in Dartmoor's woodland distribution, though its effect on the spore and pollen record in the peat is not fully evident for around another 2,000 years. The shift from hunting–gathering to the farming of animals and eventually crop growing is the basis of those changes, but its revolutionary effect on the human attitude to land and vegetation cannot be over-played. The Mesolithic people may well have initiated 'management' of Dartmoor to the extent that they used fire as a hunting adjunct, but the behaviour, techniques, plants and animals which the Neolithics brought with them, to all intents and purposes fired a totally new culture across landscapes which had been the scene of only hunting and collecting for more than 10,000 years.

The first farming

The Neolithic culture came to Britain from the Low Countries and from the Bay of Biscay. The land bridge had gone by then but there is a school of thought that proposes calmer seas and less stormy weather around the climatic optimum and beyond it into the Sub-Boreal, so sea-borne immigration may well have been easier then than we might think, even in such boats as were available. Neolithic people probably still hunted, but they brought not only skills in husbandry but also in domestic living – pottery being the obvious example – and a spiritual need exemplified by ritual monuments and the way they dealt with the newly dead.

Simmons describes the presumed Neolithic clearances as small and temporary – from evidence at Postbridge (Gawler Bottom) and Taw Head, partly because he detected woodland regeneration from pollen diagrams at both sites. Work on the Black-a-Brook near Cadover Bridge and nearby at Wotter and on

FIG 69. Peat cliffs on the Black-a-Brook, below Great Trowlesworthy Tor in the Plym valley where Beckett worked.

Lee Moor (more precisely Shaugh Moor) by Stephen Beckett adds to this impression and at the latter site cultivation weed pollen (*Artemesia*) is present. Here also woodland regeneration is registered. However, more recently it has been suggested that these scattered samples of evidence underestimate the extent of Neolithic activity. All the pollen records at the sites concerned straddle the sudden 'elm decline' which is well documented across Europe and is confidently dated close to 5,000 BP. Elm pollen at southern Dartmoor sites is sparse, but in the north, at Taw Head for instance, the onset of the decline is very clear. The date is important for its marking of coincidences, Neolithic clearances – the first for agricultural reasons – are in full swing however local and patchy, the climatic optimum is just over as the Atlantic (VIIa) passes into the Sub-Boreal (VIIb) and ironically, as the warm/wet gives way to the warm/drier, blanket peat begins the new growth which will bring it, in only 2,000 years, to the pattern of cover which we still see today.

At Cholwich Town, not far from Lee Moor and Wotter, is an evidential vignette of the times. Beneath an early Bronze Age stone row lies a soil profile whose pollen analysis revealed to Simmons and Proudfoot agricultural activity involving cereals and arable weeds in a clearing in an oakwood. Even more significantly the pollen diagram indicates moorland development following a 'brief' cultivation. All this happens within 1,000 years – the early Bronze Age, 4,400 to 3,400 BP. Men clear the wood, reap a quick crop and the woodland soil begins to deteriorate as more rain hits the ground and annual leaf fall, for humus replenishment, disappears.

This, in a sense, is the classically understood sequence of events. Neolithics, and early Bronze Age people almost tripping over them, cleared trees and established an agricultural landscape, even if still as clearings in the forest. The clearings were large enough however to allow moor and heath to develop as soils changed after some cultivation amid a largely pastoral system. Beckett's work, only a mile from the Cholwich Town classic, shows this in a series of closely sited analyses across this 'Dartmoor edge' with variations in the upward sequence of the profile. Moor and heath, in the form of acid-tolerant vegetation with woodland fairly close, characterises his 'late neolithic' but also shows that moorland development did not always follow immediately the agricultural pioneering, a scrub phase in some cases intervened. Taken together with evidence from the upper Dart basin and the northern plateau valleys already cited, it does look as though upland pastures were becoming widespread by 4,000 BP, and other archaeological work points to the increasing interest in their status (perhaps even value to personal or group economy) and thus a desire to organise a physical pattern of land use and occupation. Beckett certainly shows that Bronze Age clearance, on Shaugh Moor at least, was promptly accompanied by parcelling up the land and the construction of boundaries – the Saddlesborough Reave in this case.

Settlement proper

Reaves are (now) low stone banks shown to be grouped in 'systems' of parallel lines usually butting against a baseline reave. The systems surround the moor, densest up the east side from Holne Moor to Gidleigh Common, extending in to Dartmeet and Stannon and further into the upper Dart basin, but also round the south from Corringdon Ball to Whitchurch Common, via Bittaford and Shaugh, with more scattered smaller incidents on the north and west. The map of their distribution (Fig. 70) is enhanced by the occurrence of other cultural detail, stone rows and 'prestige' cairns (those over 15 m in diameter) are concentrated in the same peripheral zones. It is proposed that one of *their* functions was the 'marking' of territory and their absence in the central basin may indicate that

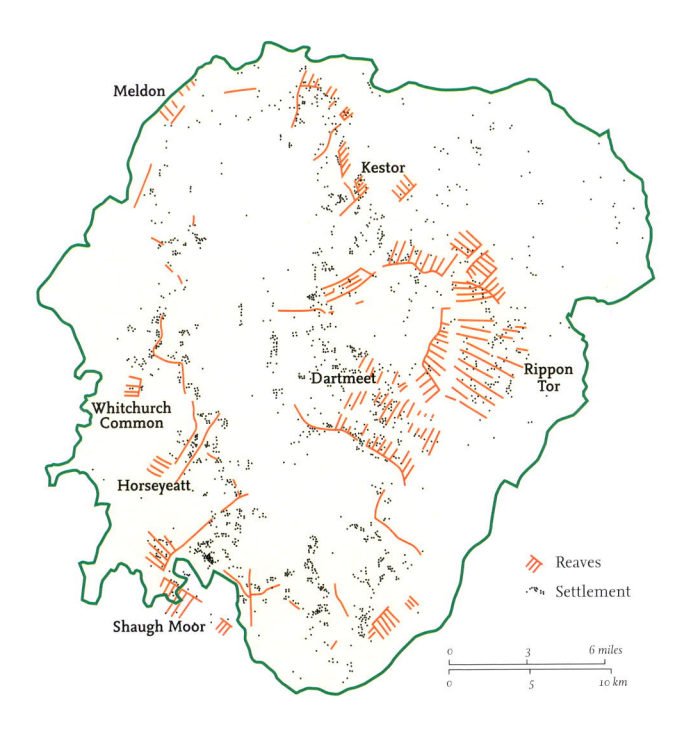

FIG 70. Map of the pattern of reave terrains and Bronze Age settlements right around the Moor. (After Sandy Gerrard, who readily offered this map and those at Figs. 198, 201 and 218)

FIG 71. (above left) Grey Wethers stone circles near Fernworthy Forest; (above) Stone row on the north end of Challacombe Down; (left) Grimspound, the best known of the Bronze Age 'villages' on Dartmoor.

that marking was only needed against the outside world as far as Dartmoor settlers were concerned (Fig. 71). Andrew Fleming has shown that reave systems contain huts or houses, sometimes not far apart, with yards and small fields, and that wooden structures and fences preceded stone ones in some cases (Fig. 72). The whole complex suggests the division of the grazing foothills between groups of people, extended families – if you will, a recognised boundary system and maybe common grazing both between them and upslope beyond the basal reave. It should not surprise us that prehistoric reave patterns merge imperceptibly into later, perhaps mediaeval, field patterns and that enclosed meadows we still have close against the moor appear as an extension of patterns now abandoned, or conversely – and more accurately for now – that our fields have discernible extensions out on to 'the moor'. Fleming, at one point, draws a potential parallel with Welsh *cloddau* which are low stone banks topped by hedges and wonders whether some reaves may have borne hedges or fences and thus been more stockproof than now seems possible. (An extension of that idea towards the evolution of the countywide Devon hedge-bank of historic and contemporary time then arises, but it can be considered when we look at the present in-bye valley landscape.) Before proceeding, we should also note that Fleming's excavations of the Holne Moor system and its detail revealed, as well as the use

FIG 72. Map of the prehistoric remains on Holne Moor showing the reave pattern and its associated huts (DNPA after Fleming).

of wood in the construction of early hut, fence and drying rack, that the mole population was considerably higher than it is now (Fig. 73). Moles mean earthworms, earthworms mean a different soil from the peaty gley podsol that Fleming was excavating. Brown earths were there still when the Bronze Age people were beginning to build their huts and walls, tending their flocks and growing what they could. Woodland had only just gone.

FIG 73. Bronze Age mole runs revealed, below the present soil profile.

FIG 74. Bronze Age boundaries: (left) Reaves on Vag Hill on Spitchwick Common, continuing the Holne Moor lines across the Dart valley; (below left) Line of stakeholes revealed by excavation indicating a wooden fence line parallel with the stone reaves, the quadrat is leaning on the terminal reave; (below) Reave, in the foreground, continued by a 'modern' hedge bank, near Oldsbrim.

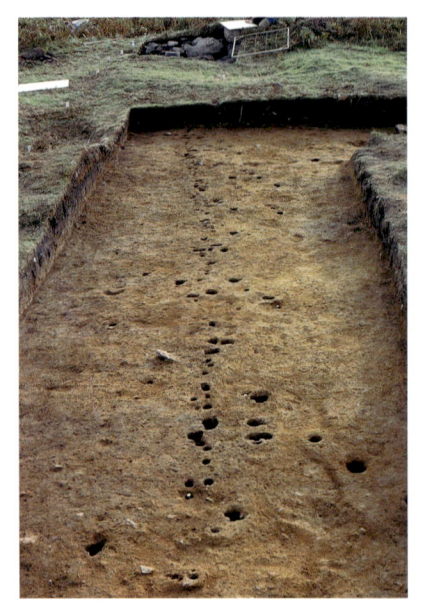

So we see that Ian Simmons's early postulations are all largely confirmed and hugely extended by this later work. Given the evidence made available in the scatter of his and other pollen diagram sites across the whole Moor below the blanket bog, with the density of hut circles, pounds, cairns, stone rows and reave pattern clusters, the fundamental change effected by the Bronze Age people on the Moor's face cannot be gainsaid. With Andrew Fleming's excavations adding in the detail it is clear that in less than 2,000 years they took the largely Mesolithic forest inheritance through pioneering Neolithic cultivations to the pastoralism which still dominates moorland management today, another 2,500 years later. If we look back, we see a concertina-like prehistoric time sequence from the 7,000-year long

Mesolithic huntsmen's reign which tinkered at the edges of the forest near its end, through the 1,500 years of Neolithic scattered clearances, to the 1,000-year Bronze Age in which farmers amalgamated the clearings, created fields, grew what could be grown while climate allowed, grappled with the effect of deteriorating soils and had virtually colonised all the land between 250 m and the edge of the blanket bog, but then abandoned it before 2,500 BP.

The objective downside to all this needs emphasising. Tree clearance produces very significant microclimatic changes. Increased exposure, lower ground temperatures and more rain hitting that ground, all contribute to the soil impoverishment that favours moorland vegetation, which has, whether the Dartmoor aficionado likes it or not, a much less valuable cultural potential than the woodland-with-clearings that preceded it. Whether the Bronze Age folk are wholly to blame for the change is not a resolved question. Postglacial Dartmoor soils, as we have seen, were probably acid in any case, thus with less to leach away and to that extent diminishing the drama of the process. The clearance's microclimatic effect is within a bigger climatic picture. The Sub-Boreal time zone in which Bronze Age men largely lived on Dartmoor is characterised by a more continental-type climatic situation in which higher temperatures and drier conditions prevailed. Less rain, less cold, less leaching, may well have been the state of affairs when they started to finish off the forest of the middle ground, i.e. between the valley gorges and the blanket bog. A 'major' climatic deterioration from 3,400 to 3,150 BP has been determined from testate amoeba evidence from Tor Royal Bog and is supported by evidence elsewhere in England (Amesbury *et al.*, 2008). This coincides with the apparent abandonment of the reave terrains. Which coincidence suggests that cropping was a significant part of the Bronze Age support system, for a wetter/cooler change affects animal husbandry far less than arable farming as our contemporary hill-farmers demonstrate daily. Cloudier wetter periods (with leaching more likely) alternating with better weather is typical of the cyclonic situation that we are still enjoying now. There is also a detectable change in the stratigraphy of the peat itself at this time, from cotton grass to *sphagnum* mosses as dominant peat formers, another indication of increased wetness. The Sub-Boreal gives way to the Sub-Atlantic around 2,500 BP when the Bronze Age merges with the Iron Age at this altitude.

Most researchers agree that Iron Age men, popularly the Celts, settled nearer the present moorland edge than their predecessors on Dartmoor, if not always further down the slope. Simmons suggests renewed clearance of lower woodland to make room, but at Kestor, near Chagford, pollen analysis indicates reclamation of heather moorland for farming and, by extension, not necessarily a woodland barrier between off-moor agriculture and moorland grazing. On northern

FIG 75. Iron Age square fields at Foales Arrishes, on Widecombe Town Common near Hemsworthy Gate, taken in the 1960s.

Dartmoor, cereal pollen appears, but blips in the record of bracken and weeds suggest that human activity was not continuous, on the other hand Dark Age radiocarbon evidence from Okehampton Park demonstrates clearance of long standing. Back on Lee Moor in the extreme southwest, it is clear that weeds go missing and tree and heathland regeneration happens. All this adds up to a much lower Dartmoor population of Iron Age farmers, and except for a cluster between the Plym and the Meavy, their farmsteads and fields are mostly in the Dart valley and up the east side of the northern plateau, all in the rain shadow of the high moor – very wise during the Sub-Atlantic. It seems likely that rough grazing upslope from the farms was still used as summer pasture. Iron Age 'hill forts' circle the whole Moor, intriguingly in the east and the southwest just outside the area where farmstead remains occur, and clearly 'guarding' the Teign, the Dart, the Bovey and the Plym valleys downstream of the farms.

Improved dating techniques, together with more and more surface and sub-surface evidence has brought us thus far. From the Iron Age onwards land use change and vegetation change become so inextricably bound together that the interpretation of pollen analyses becomes increasingly difficult. Evidence for change from now on, for evolution, even for development in land-use terms, is archaeological and eventually documentary. Dealing as we are with upland land use and plant cover, outside the lower valleys, we should recognise that from now on they share a history. Once we have established the basic early historic pattern – admitting oscillations of the boundary between the in-bye (enclosed land) and the moor throughout time after that – we can examine the contemporary vegetation structure and distribution.

INTO THE HISTORIC

But it is necessary first to complete that early history. The Romans, having come to Devon and established Exeter, seem to have skirted Dartmoor to the north. There is no evidence that they made any change worthy of note on the Moor. Anglo-Saxon pioneers pushing off from a crowded Sussex to seek pastures new, made landfall on the 48 km-long stretch of east-facing coast from the mouth of the Exe to Start Point. The string of Saxon names: Shaldon, Paignton, Churston, Brixham, Slapton and Stokenham down that coast lend weight to the idea, and the military arrival in the late seventh and early eighth centuries found the coastlands already settled. Within a century the Saxon settlement of the whole lowland country of the Dumnonii – the Roman name for the Celtic residents – was complete enough for forages into the upland to become necessary. Anglo-Saxons pushed up the main valleys and established farmsteads and vills in them, notably that of the Dart, above the gorges. We have already noted the confinement of 80 per cent of the villages within Dartmoor to the acid brown earths of its eastern half. They are recorded in Domesday Book (1086 AD) as established local economies. They were doubtless then two or three hundred years old, and the basic pattern of settlement and enclosed valleys that we still see was already set down, ready for the imposition of the Norman feudal system on a not dissimilar Saxon precedent.

Three things remain to be emphasised before we can concentrate on the contemporary vegetation pattern. The first is to underline the fluidity of that moorland/in-bye boundary which persisted from the Dark Ages to the twentieth century. We now regulate such change – if we allow it at all – but climate change (fourteenth-century warming), the Black Death and even bracken advance caused substantial changes when the lord of the manor and his courts were the only regulators and the Duchy of Cornwall may alone have had a strategic view. The evidence lies in many places, but the abandonment of the Hound Tor medieval village and its fields (where corn was grown) in the late fourteenth century is one case. Holne Moor, referred to so often already as a laboratory of evidence for much change, is another. There the whole of the present moorland between the Bronze Age basal reave and the Dart valley lip was enclosed at various times between the construction of that reave and the fourteenth century (though there is no evidence of occupation in the Iron Age). Certainly three mediaeval farmsteads were there and their lands linked the present moorland boundaries to east and west, totally enclosing what is now common. This situation helps us to understand the reference to the modern common as 'the waste of the manor'. Through mediaeval history it could be brought into more intensive use when conditions and demand allowed, and let go back to common grazing at others.

A soils resume

The second is to remind ourselves that the pattern of soils we and our plants live with now, described briefly in Chapter 1, was more or less in place by the shift into historic time. Figure 76 is a sketch map of that pattern and Figure 77 has four soil profiles that illustrate its components. Figure 77.1 shows a section in the

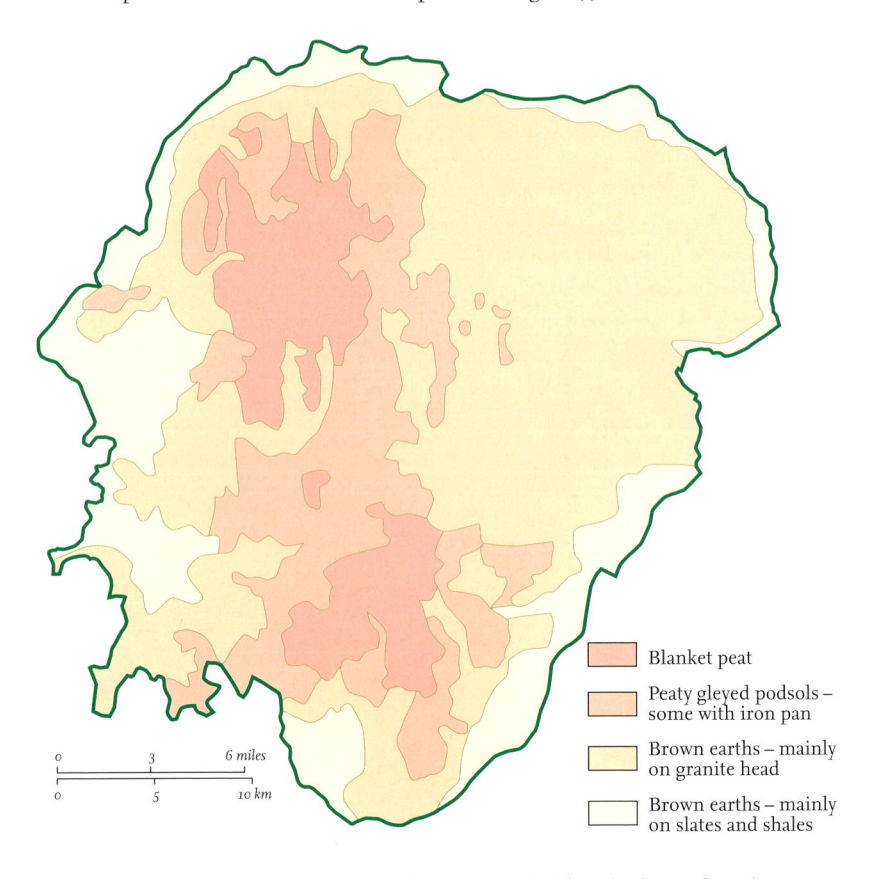

FIG 76. Sketch map of the general pattern of Dartmoor soils (after Clayden et al, 1964).

blanket peat of the southern plateau resting on kaolinised granite at the disused Redlake china clay pit. The pit is just north of Redlake Mire, the source of a short tributary of the River Erme perhaps a 2.5 km below Erme Head. The peat here is a 1.5 m thick, but it reaches more than 4 m in the northern plateau south and east of Cut Hill and in the col where the Taw, the West Okement and the East Dart rise. That thickness helps name the soil associations involved. Crowdy 2 is at Redlake, over the vast area of both plateaux and includes the larger areas of higher-level basin peat such as at Foxtor Mire, and in Tor Royal newtake, which show as islands between the two plateau blankets. Winter Hill is the name for the smaller patches of thickest peat, which do occur on the southern plateau too: on the watershed between the Plym and the Yealm and from the right bank of the Avon up to Greenhill. They are too small to show on Figure 76, which displays the whole area of the blanket peat and with its internal basins in one colour.

The peaty soils shown ringing the blanket peats on that same map and, with 'islands' on Blackdown in the west, on Hameldown and Riddon Ridge, comprise two dominant associations with Dartmoor names (soils like rocks are usually named for the locations where they were first described). The Princetown series usually abuts the blanket peat, has a peaty upper horizon over a grey one merging slowly with the parent material. It is poorly drained and supports wet moorland. The Hexworthy series, shown in Figure 77.2 in a pit dug on Holne Moor, is very closely related but mostly has a thin iron pan at the bottom margin of the grey horizon below which the ochreous colours of a rich iron content are typical. The pan can inhibit root penetration, and be locally watertight causing waterlogging, or gleying, above it. The grey colours in both these soils denote strong leaching of the upper part of the profile, and yellow grey hints at the gleying from the surface water surplus inhibiting oxidation of the iron content. The Hexworthy series also occurs in eastern 'islands' too small to show here. The granite-based Moretonhampstead series, shown in Figure 77.3, and the slate-based brown earth from the aureole in Figure 77.4, are principal examples of the brown earths of the rest of the map at Figure 76 – they are well drained, appear to have been little leached and are the basis of most of Dartmoor's farmland landscape. A companion to the Moretonhampstead series with the same granitic parent material is the Moorgate series that has, if anything, a more humose top horizon, and lies closest all round the northern plateau edge with a big island running south from Manaton to Buckland-in-the-Moor. Both these soils are punctuated by relatively tiny patches of the Laployd series – another Dartmoor name – which are waterlogged from below. They are usually associated with the margins of valley mires, and wet pasture. Beyond the granite there are mostly thin silty soils derived from slates and shales, but they are still brown earths to the soil scientist and the farmer.

FIG 77. Four contemporary soil profiles: **1 – top left** blanket peat over rotten granite at Redlake pit on the southern plateau; **2 – top right** peaty gley, sometimes podsolised with an iron pan, as here (the Hexworthy series) and sometimes not (the Princetown series); **3 – above left** a granite brown earth under bracken (Moretonhampstead series); **4 – above right** a brown earth on aureole Devonian slates near Ivybridge.

The third idea to take into a viewing of contemporary Dartmoor vegetation is to register the havoc the early tinners wreaked on the moorland valley floors. These men were not yet miners proper as we shall see in more detail later, but won and marketed the tin ore they found in granite pebbles in the 'fossil' beds of the periglacial streams, by now forming the floors of all the valleys. This ore harvest was available right down the river valleys, even off Dartmoor as far as the heads of the South Devon estuaries and some miles downstream in the Okement and the Taw. The visible physical effects of it all will be described in Chapter 7. The now invisible effect, however, is revealed by pollen diagrams, just before the point where they are too close to us in time to remain useful in historic interpretation. Alder pollen crashes right at the top of such diagrams. Alders alongside streams and in groves in wet places must have been: a) in the way of tinners' endeavours and b) a splendid source of charcoal – alder is the best charcoal wood in the country. Excavation of ore was accompanied by smelting in 'blowing houses' (or blast furnaces) close to the source, if value was to be added to the extraction effort. Charcoal was the smelting fuel to hand, and thus alders were felled with gay abandon. The diagram displaying the alder crash also suggests that birch, beech and hazel may have contributed to the charcoal demand. Dark Age tinners, as Simmons noted, completed the deforestation of high Dartmoor, begun some 8,000 years earlier by Mesolithic hunters.

CHAPTER 4

Dartmoor Vegetation in the Last Millennium

The whole surface of Dartmoor, including the rocks, consists of two characters, the one a wet peaty moor or vegetable mould, but affording good sheep and bullock pasture during the summer season. The other an inveterate swamp absolutely inaccessible to the lightest and most active quadriped [sic] that may traverse the sounder parts of the forest.

The most elevated part of the forest … consists of one continued chain of morass answering in every respect the character of a red Irish bog. This annually teems with a luxuriant growth of the purple melic grass, rush cotton grass, flags, rushes and a variety of other aquatic plants.

The depasturable parts of the forest whose spontaneous vegetation, among many other herbs and grasses consisted of the purple melic grass, mat grass, downy oat grass, bristle leaved bent, eye-bright, bulbous rooted rush, common termentel, smooth heath bedstraw, common bone binder, cross-leaved heath, common heath or ling (dwarf), milkwort, dwarf dock and the agrostis vulgaris in very large quantities. The disturbing of this herbage however inferior it may appear to the refined agriculturalist is on no account whatever to be recommended or permitted.

Charles Vancouver, 1808

Vancouver was reporting to the Board of Agriculture 800 years into the millennium of the chapter heading, and speaks of 'the forest' as though encompassing all the moorland out of a deliberate deference to its owner. But his observation of the surface, its plants and its agricultural use or potential would not go amiss today, and could probably stand for a few hundred years before he set it down. After all, he was writing when the 'Little Ice Age' was still running so the flora he lists was clearly surviving it, and there is no evidence that the relative warmth of the fourteenth century had changed the moorland character in the general sense. What is underlined here is the persistent interaction of human activity and even the highest moorland, a relationship begun in the Mesolithic, nearly 10,000 years before him and still, just, going on today. Clearly man did not stop manipulating the vegetation of Dartmoor when the tinners felled the last high moorland alder. Throughout historic time, under a series of economic, environmental and often repetitive pressures, hill-farming man has moved the moorland boundary up and down. He has sometimes enclosed and ploughed moorland for an exclusive use and let some of it go to 'waste' again, not literally but as 'waste of the manor'. He has intensified and then relaxed the 'improvement' of moor and meadow, inserted plantations into moorland enclosures and valley-side broad-leaved woods and planted new deciduous copses again. In the very early twenty-first century the advocacies for livestock production and the protection of 'semi-natural' things may be being reconciled for the first time. While that means that the effort on both sides may be halting and the agreed formulae still in the test-bed stage, farmers, ecologists and their shared political masters are rubbing shoulders after more than 50 years of, to underplay the situation, hostility. The national park status of Dartmoor, locally unpopular still in some parts, has in the end become a catalyst for this convergence of quasi-scientific thinking and traditional irreplaceable skill, as will be steadily revealed. At the beginning of the twenty-first century dedicated Dartmoor moormen are, in a real sense, ahead of the game.

    The prehistoric process had blocked out the general ecological pattern of the landscape within the National Park boundary by the clearance of woodland from all the upper lands of subdued relief and inadvertently created moorland. The Dark Age Saxon immigration completed the clearance of, and enclosed, the broader valley floors and gentler lower slopes, as the Domesday survey shows. Almost all the present-day parish names appear in the Domesday Book as manors, many with subsidiary manors still identifiable within them. So a second sophisticated land-use pattern and land-tenure system had been imposed on the whole Dartmoor landscape by 1,000 AD. Mediaeval men consolidated the general arrangement which left most of the woodland confined to the steepest and rockiest valley sides, indeed in some parishes the dimensions of woodland recorded in the Domesday Book accord very closely with the broad-leaved woodland standing today, largely because of that land use and terrain correlation (Fig. 78). Thus was the gross pattern of the vegetated landscape for the next 1,000 years established.

    That pattern has three major components on which the distribution of the Dartmoor flora is based: the open and newtake moorland, the steep valley-side oakwoods, and the network of fields, walls, banks and lanes that comprise the farmland, or in-bye proper, which extends well upstream of the gorges in the

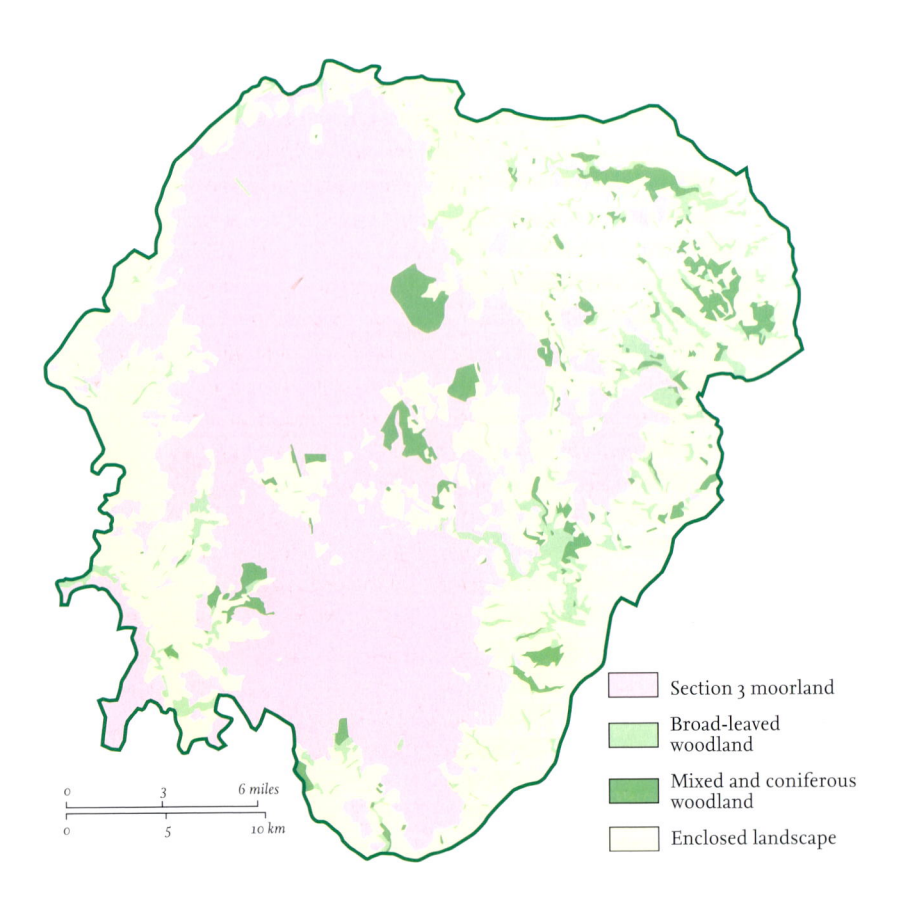

FIG 78. A four-fold division of the landcover of the National Park (after DNPA).

valleys of the Dart, the Bovey and the Teign. In the case of the Dart and its tributary headwaters this includes a broad spread across the central basin of Dartmoor as far upstream as Princetown, Postbridge and beyond Widecombe. Princetown became the base of an island of new nineteenth-century in-bye. A second near-island centred on Postbridge includes at least seven Ancient Tenements (see below) but has eighteenth- and nineteenth-century extensions which create tenuous links with the West Webburn and the Wallabrook valleys. In one sense they are paralleled by the larger conifer plantations at Bellever, Soussons, Beardown and Fernworthy, which as woodland 'islands' have been lately inserted into that mediaeval and Victorian mosaic.

Otherwise, the original woodland is the most clearly defined and to that extent the purest of the three gross eco-geographical elements of Dartmoor despite a few coniferous insertions, of which more anon. For as we have already seen the lower, eastern farmland, even that in the central basin, has within its compass islands of hill-top moorland of variable size, long narrow valley mires and bogs historically not worth the draining, and copses sustained through time at the occupiers' whim. 'Moorland', too, is a generalisation masking a substantial variety of soils and plant communities. None of them individually of hugely rich biodiversity but taken together so different from lowland man's day-to-day experience, that the complex forms a wonderful but unlikely raised oasis in the intensely cultivated 'desert' that is lowland England, even lowland Devon. From high blanket bog to spur-end heath the continuum of perceived open expanse, because the vegetation is properly below knee height, is the greatest delight that Dartmoor moorland offers to both the farmer at his newtake gate and to the Dutch tourist – there are a vast horde of visitors, local and distant, in between those two extremes. The tors that punctuate the edge of that open expanse also occur throughout the woodland and field landscapes, often so small that they pass unnoticed. In each of the three they provide a habitat variation all of their own for plants and animals.

We have already seen that the quotations from Vancouver's survey at the head of this chapter, which are closely allied in his 'Dartmoor Forest' text (clearly currying favour with the Prince of Wales of the day), describe a flora we can recognise now. They also show that, although in one sense he almost over-generalised – did he merge blanket bog and valley mire in his 'morass' for instance? – in another he recognised subtle distinctions on the surface which we still see. He sought the little vertical exposures that showed him the deep peat of his 'morass' and the soil profiles under his 'wet peaty moor' as in Figure 77.1. He was clear that the high morass – or blanket bog – was still growing and he talks nowhere of eroded peat, except when dramatically describing 'slope failure' at the edge of that blanket bog. Some 200 years on, that may be the only discernible difference between our perception of the general state of the moorland and his. Elsewhere, just to complete the two-century comparison, Vancouver recognises the singularity of eastern Dartmoor, even making it a separate agricultural 'district' in his breakdown of Devon for survey purposes. It has, he says, 'a grey loam lying on a coarse rubbly clay and granite gravel' where cultivated, and moist peaty earth on a reddish brown clay where not. He noted also that the light-brown mould of many parts (of the district) 'by judicious cultivation produced excellent turnips, barley, clover, wheat, oats and where too strong for permanent pasture, beans and pease'. The mixed farming that this statement implies, was still the farmstead base from which hill farming was conducted into the second half of the twentieth century.

THE MOORLAND

In the last 40 years there have been three attempts to portray the whole upland vegetation pattern comprehensively at a reasonable mapping scale. In 1970 the then Nature Conservancy decided to do some research into the effects of contemporary grazing and burning on Dartmoor and realised that a map of the vegetation was a necessary pre-requisite for that work. (A nice comparison springs to mind, with the need, at exactly the same time, to find out what was happening to bird predators vis-à-vis pesticides, which led to the need for a national common bird census.) The research team, led by Stephen Ward, then at Bangor, after that with Scottish Natural Heritage, used a combination of ground survey, on the basis of a systematic but random sample, and the analysis of aerial photographs in colour specially flown for the purpose to extend the survey, with follow-up 'ground truthing' of the photogrammetric analytical results. The vegetation was then subjected to an association-analysis separating vegetation types by the presence or absence of indicator species. The result was a 'one-inch' map of the open moorland superimposed on an uncoloured Ordnance Survey base and published by the Field Studies Council in 1972 (Fig. 79a). The survey itself had recognised nine vegetation types (one transitional between heath and grassland and not mapped separately in the end). It was also decided that while the heather/purple moor grass type was readily distinguished from blanket bog in the field it could not be safely interpreted as different from aerial photographs. Its mature version was thus lumped with blanket bog and its 'over-burnt' state with grass or heath. So the final map shows seven vegetation types: blanket bog, heath, bilberry moorland, grassland, grassland invaded by bracken, grassland with gorse, and valley bog. Ward made it clear that the identification of 'communities' would involve a more detailed analysis of each 'type', and also pointed out that the result could be described as a map 'of vegetation potential' which relates it well to the latest attempt published in 2005 (see below).

In 1994, the Agricultural Development Advisory Service (ADAS) – still then part of Ministry of Agriculture, Fisheries and Food (MAFF) – given the prospect of financial agreements with hill-farmers and commoners' associations involving vegetation management under the designation of Dartmoor as an Environmentally Sensitive Area (ESA), made a 'land-cover' map of the whole national park (Fig. 79b). The mapping extended on to the east side of the Teign valley, in the northwest between Sourton and Lydford, south and southeast of Tavistock and in the extreme southwest to envelop the china clay workings at Lee Moor, the whole reflecting the Dartmoor Natural Area rather than just the

National Park. It did not attempt to show blanket bog as a separate category of land cover, the whole of the 'blanket' was subsumed under grass moorland or heather moorland, which echoes Ward's difficulty but chooses the opposite outcome. Not really surprising given that the target was a grazing regime. This map, too, was made from aerial photographs. The only other category which falls under our moorland heading is 'bracken and scrub' largely confined to the eastern fringes of the moorland all the way from north to south and in the southwest, especially on Lee Moor proper, east of Burrator reservoir woodland and the northern half of Roborough Down. There is no reference to gorse of any kind.

It has to be noted here that between the 1970 (Ward *et al*) and the 1994 (ADAS) dates, in 1983, the Soil Survey published a map at a ¼ inch to the mile of the 'Soils of South West England' whose contribution to this list is its portrayal of blanket peat. Given the difficulties revealed, or soft options taken (!), by ecologists, perhaps the soil scientists' mapping of deep peat will give us the best approximation of the true boundary of the blanket bog at a small scale (see Fig. 76).

In 2003, farming commoners' muttering about the confusion (my translation of their view) caused by different government agencies bringing different messages about moorland management to their kitchen tables, triggered in the minds of the National Park Authority (NPA) the thought that convergence in that advice might be brought about by facilitating debate first amongst the agencies and then between the agencies and the commoners. The NPA had already set up a Hill Farm Project and had recruited to it one John Waldon, who set about getting all the local representatives of English Nature, English Heritage, the Environment Agency, the Duchy of Cornwall, the Ministry of Defence, the Rural Development Service of the Department for Environment, Food and Rural Affairs (DEFRA) and the NPA together and persuading them that they ought to be able to agree a map of the vegetation pattern they could share as a vision for Dartmoor 25 years hence. In 2005 that map (or properly, cartogram, for its divisional boundaries are not precisely transferable to the ground) was published (Fig. 79c).

The map – entitled 'A Vision for Moorland Dartmoor' – is by a broader brush than the Nature Conservancy had used 35 years earlier, and ended up with five vegetation categories: blanket bog, heather moorland, western heath, (selectively) mires of high ecological quality and naturally regenerated woodland. The fact that it is a visionary map may explain the last category, and the area of woodland 'invasion' on it is tiny, but its existence probably satisfies some 're-wilding' purists. More significant is the fact that three of Ward's vegetation types are rolled up into 'western heath' on the 'Vision' map and they were all grassland variations in his analysis, although in his text he says of them 'heather is always present'. It is a matter for conjecture whether or not the 'Vision' group see pure grassland – or

110 · DARTMOOR

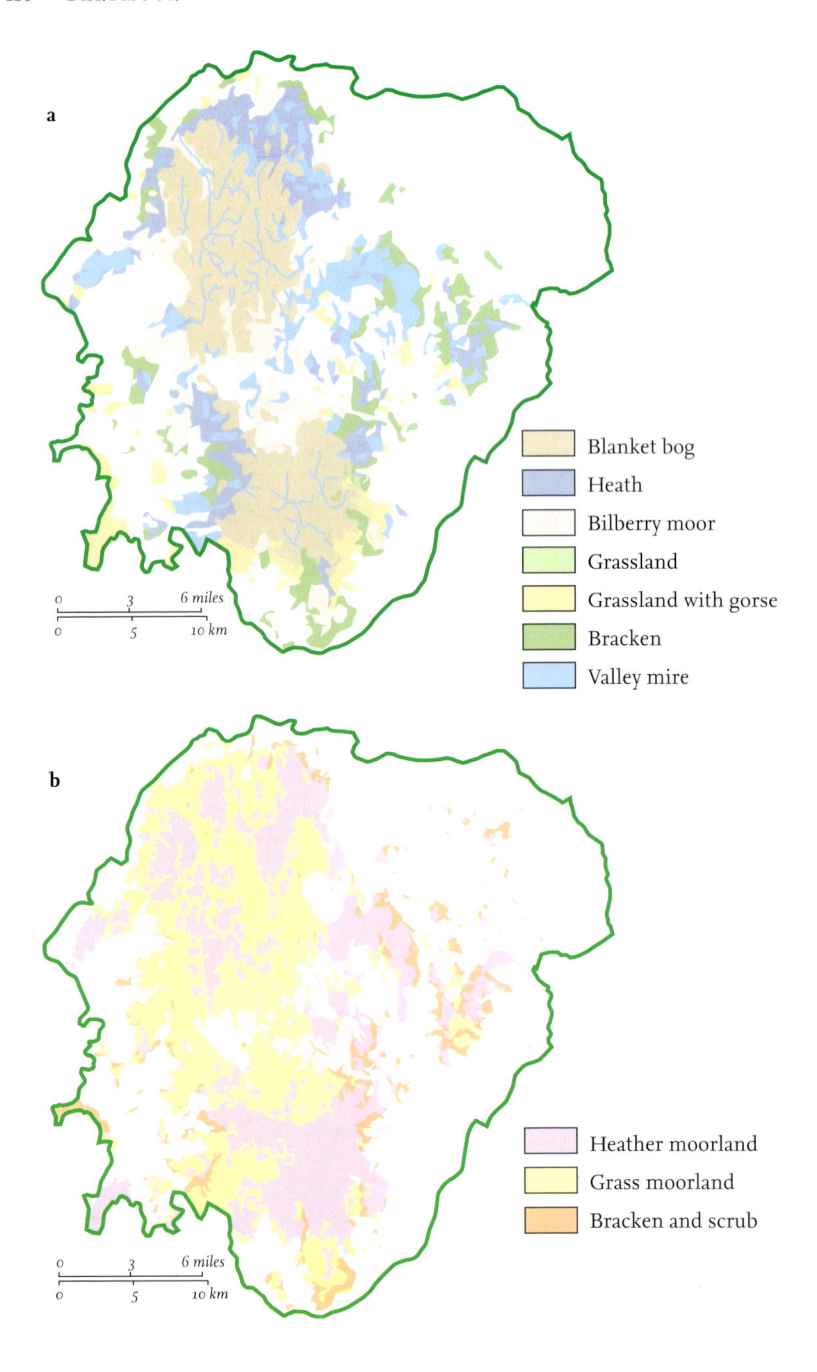

a

Blanket bog
Heath
Bilberry moor
Grassland
Grassland with gorse
Bracken
Valley mire

b

Heather moorland
Grass moorland
Bracken and scrub

c

- Blanket bog
- Heather moorland
- Western heath
- Quality mires
- New woodland

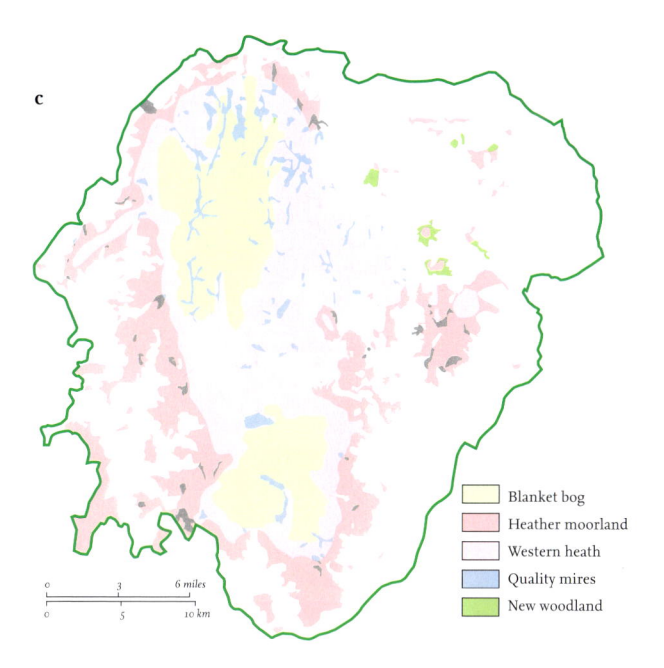

FIG 79. Three attempts to map the open land, made with different motives over 33 years – for comparative purposes only. **(a)** – The Vegetation of Dartmoor (after Ward *et al*, NERC/FSC, 1972). **(b)** – Landcover (after ADAS, 1994). **(c)** – 'The Vision for 2030' map (vegetation only, after DNPA, 2005). For the complete 'Vision' map see Figure 25.

even grass moor – as a less than desirable component of the Dartmoor scene in the future. Most moorland travellers now would point to a much greater hectarage of apparently grass-dominated space than that clearly dominated by any other, while all can also point to more confined areas they see as dominated by heather (properly ling *Calluna vulgaris*) – Bush Down say (Fig. 80); bracken – Green Coombe as in Figure 95; or gorse – Whitchurch Down (Fig. 81). The 'Vision Group' seem not to have had the same difficulty as Ward in identifying heather moorland – for their own purposes admittedly – which probably also accounts for the size variation in areas of blanket bog between the two maps. Ling, usually called heather in this context, it is fair to say, has become a symbolic plant in much 'conservation specialist' thinking. Thus its restoration is now a target and a measure of success for lonely 'official' fieldworkers, especially when they meet. Yet

FIG 80. Ling in flower on Bush Down in Chagford Common, 2008.

FIG 81. European gorse and short-cropped grass on Whitchurch Down (see also Fig. 7).

many ecologists will point to heather-dominated stands of vegetation as among the least species rich. Like the whole of Dartmoor's moorland it is the contribution it makes to overall southwestern biodiversity that matters.

'Western heath' was not a name used by Ward, but it is clear that the current visionaries wish it to be a mosaic of heathers, western furze *Ulex gallii*, grassland and a gradation between wet and dry heath each with its own indicator plants, all under this single heading. Suffice it to say that, as ever, for the purpose of appreciating the present organisation of plant communities one should extract from these three maps – produced after very different motivation – whatever is most helpful. Ward had his critics, and many a local botanist thought that he extended the blanket bog too far down some slopes and made continuous mires where in reality the relevant valley floor contained a chain of separate ones. Such is the difficulty of interpreting even good colour aerial photographs at a 1:10,000 scale – and to be fair to Ward, he points out that his ground sampling grid of quadrats was never going to 'catch' a representative set of examples of linear features such as the valley mires.

There are now of course satellite images of Dartmoor in colour, of which those in infra-red form are most helpful. Despite their reproduction scale, even the sites of individual recent fires can be identified within heather moorland for instance because ironically they are 'cooler' than the heather itself. This gives an idea of the potential for picking out some detail, though the coincidence of the 'temperature' colour of pure heather stands and conifer plantations, say, indicates the limits of that potential for someone who doesn't know the ground.

In the same time frame – roughly the last quarter of the twentieth century – the National Vegetation Classification (NVC) – a comprehensive attempt to classify and describe British vegetation – was conceived, gestated and born. The fieldwork began in 1975, was published in five volumes between 1991 and 2000, and is now widely accepted as the standard system for the classification of plant cover in Great Britain. It forms the important background, for our purposes, to *An Illustrated Guide to British Upland Vegetation* published by the Joint Nature Conservation Committee in 2004. That single volume reveals that Dartmoor has 30 of the NVC upland open vegetation types at the community and sub-community level. These two levels are grouped into mires (M) – subsuming bog in all its forms – of which Dartmoor has 16 of the national 38; of heaths (H) 5 of 22; and of acid grasslands and montane communities (U and MG) Dartmoor has 9 of 21. There is also listed a bracken-with-bramble 'underscrub' (W25) that might be said to be developing now on some of our moorland fringes.

At this point it is important to reflect that all those upland vegetation surveyors concede that there is a general 'natural' simple sequence upward of woodland, dwarf shrub heath, grassland and blanket bog, and that the last three are all punctuated by small bogs on level ground and mires wherever water is at the surface more than temporarily. They also seem to concur that, despite the origin of the middle two members, the sequence has been distorted by grazing and burning activity in the last 50 years. The special effect of this has been to insert grassland of variable character among the heath, lower down the altitudinal sequence than its natural position. Burning – or 'swaling' on Dartmoor – is also the partial explanation of Ward's difficulty over the separation of heather/purple moor grass moorland from blanket bog at the latter's edges, from the air. When this community is burnt or perhaps burnt too often or too slowly, its two prime distant visual characteristics are destroyed. The dark (all the year round) heather may be totally burnt away, and the white raffia-like purple moor grass (winter) litter certainly is. The tiller buds of the grass are almost fireproof deep in the bases of last year's tussocks, so the green of young shoots dominates the distant prospect of a winter-burn site in spring, and then their rapid growth may shade out or otherwise setback stump shoots or seedlings of the heather.

All this explains why the greatest concern for moorland vegetation managers and their mentors now, and whatever *their* motive, is to try to reduce the burning of this heather/purple moor grass community over time whether it is overlapping the blanket bog edge or not. The same set of motives all point to an increase in

FIG **82.** Infant heather on Bush Down after a fire in 1983.

cattle grazing in spring and summer to reduce grass dominance if the renovation of the dwarf shrub component of the community is an ambition (Fig. 82).

The good thing that emerges from a simple examination of the mapping exercises and the descriptions and the classification of the upland vegetation referred to so far is the general accord between them about the Dartmoor pattern. Moreover Ward points out that his map does not depart in any degree from the 'verbal description' of the vegetation by Harvey and St Leger Gordon in the predecessor volume of this book in the New Naturalist series published in 1953. Further, it is possible to fit the NVC types into Ward's association analysis – the scientists of the Vision Group could readily tell you where those types sit on their map, and the farmers will still describe the main community of the blanket bog in Vancouver's terms with a nod towards Harvey if necessary. Even so it is as well to remember, in the words of the authors of that *Illustrated Guide to British Upland Vegetation*: 'just as a map is not the territory it represents, a vegetation classification is not the vegetation itself. Vegetation does not fall neatly into man-devised sub-communities, but varies through space and time. The boundaries that seem obvious to us may mean less to other animals or indeed to the plants themselves.' However, for the layman enjoying the Dartmoor scene, some degree of perceptible organisation of the plants on the surface can only enhance that enjoyment and make the questions that surround contemporary management somewhat easier to grasp. Hence the discussion so far, now some detail.

The blanket bog

The bog surface of high Dartmoor's two plateaux is now quite variable physically, and even at its smoothest somewhat threadbare. From the air a strikingly dense net of sheep tracks takes the eye (Fig. 83), and there are two kinds of micro-relief. First, where erosion is clearly taking place, and although diminishing rainfall may slow down or stop peat development there are still storms, and gully erosion is more easily initiated in drying peat. Burning of bog vegetation if poorly managed, vandalistic or carried out under the wrong wind conditions, may dry or even burn the peat, and thus aid and abet such erosion. (The wind itself may move dry peat fragments on occasion in a kind of organic dust storm.) This gullying process can leave a set of mini-canyons separating small plateau-like blocks or 'haggs' that stand up to two metres above the gully bottom, around Cranmere Pool for instance. The other kind of micro-relief is artificial and arises from man's use of the peat mainly for its qualities as a fuel. Peat digging for domestic purposes has been a right of common for at least 1,000 years and the evidence for it lies in small faces of peat where natural erosion is unlikely. They are often apparently irregularly distributed, as on Crane Hill and Great Gnats

FIG 83. Northern plateau surface after a wildfire in 1990.

FIG 84. Blanket bog surface, cotton grass, sphagnum and rushes; the formal lines of the Rattlebrook peat diggings can be seen on the far slope.

FIG 85. Bog asphodel.

Head. The odd attempt at commercial exploitation of peat on the Forest in the nineteenth century, before it was legally a common, has left a rather formal pattern of parallel trenches in places, notably around the head of the Rattlebrook, itself a headwater of the Tavy (Fig. 84).

Gullies and trenches obviously aid the drying of the blocks that they neighbour. Their near-vertical sides are often bare of flowering plants and the relative dryness of the upper surface of the blocks may not be readily indicated by the plant cover. Ward talks of 'constant species' and certainly deer grass *Trichophorum caespitosum*, cotton grasses *Eriphorum angustifolium* and Sphagnum moss species are just that, but so are ling, cross-leaved heath *Erica tetralix* and of course purple moor grass *Molinia caerulea*. Indeed the 'easy' separation of this blanket bog vegetation (NVC M17) from the heather moorland (H10) on the ground depends upon the disappearance of deer grass and cotton grasses as one walks across the boundary. Another cotton grass – harestail *E. vaginatum*, tormentil *Potentilla erecta*, milkwort *Polygala serpyllifolia* and heath rush *Juncus squarrosus* can be common, and in wetter depressions bog asphodel *Narthecium ossifraga* (Fig. 85) and sundew *Drosera spp.* will show (Fig. 86). Some depressions may be the site of bog pools, even collections of them, sometimes covered by blankets of floating sphagnum with odd spikes of some of the flowering plants

FIG 86. Careless damselflies caught by oblong-leaved sundew. (C. Tyler)

FIG 87. Typical pool in blanket bog surface.

piercing the moss surface. In the occasional hollow sedges, especially beak sedge *Carex rostrata*, may dominate to the apparent exclusion of other plants, giving the site the appearance of a field of unripe corn as the sedge leaves wave processionally in the wind. The NVC classifies bog pools as M1 (Fig. 87), collections of them as M2 and sedge 'meadows' as M4.

On the gentler slopes of valley sides within the general plateau of blanket bog apparently pure stands of purple moor grass can occur – they are not pure, but the

FIG 88. Rank sward of purple moor grass on Gidleigh Common – result of substantial under-grazing.

grass is so dominant that that is the clear impression even when the observer is very close to or within the community. The upper Cowsic, the northeast slopes of Amicombe Hill, White Hill on the northern edge of the Willsworthy ranges, the middle reaches of the upper West Okement, Tavy Head and Chagford Common close to Fernworthy Forest bear such stands in the northern plateau (Fig. 88). Slopes above Fox Tor, and Cramber Tor and the plateau right across from Crane Hill to Ryders Hill in the south are similar. That list is not exhaustive but it shows how widespread is the phenomenon. Even some central newtakes are white with purple moor grass tussock and litter all winter – Muddilake, a valley mire in the angle of the 'scissor roads' immediately east of Two Bridges, is a good example (Fig. 89). In all, purple moor grass recognised from the air in 1970 covered 14,000 hectares, or around 35 per cent of the common land and higher level newtakes – including valley mire as well as blanket bog, and even some of Ward's inscrutable 'heather moorland'. On many a hillside clothed in darker vegetation such as ling the almost white winter grass will define a very shallow gully as though it were itself a stream flowing down the slope.

As has been noted already, burning too often, usually in March – to get rid of the purple moor grass litter and so expose new shoots soon after for spring cattle grazing – is one of the reasons for such extensive 'fields' of the grass within, and at the edge of, the blanket bog. The nature conservators' mantra is that if cattle grazing could be intensified as a substitute for much of the burning, then the dwarf shrub members of the community would do better. But there is some evidence that stock relish purple moor grass less after midsummer (though cattle may return to it in the late autumn, however reluctantly, out of necessity), and only intense grazing in the latter half of the year will really affect the amount of 'raffia' present in the winter. Equally, the system that allows a hill-farmer to

FIG 89. Muddilake newtake with purple moor grass in winter, white 'raffia' on mire surface.

maintain a good enough herd of the hardy stock and of the right number all the year round, to be profitable *and* to follow current nature conservation thinking about a regime for blanket bog vegetation management has yet to be devised. It is exercising the Vision Group as I write.

Grasslands and heath

Ward's map demonstrates that in 1970 on some radial walks out of the blanket bog, grasslands would appear in their rightful altitudinal position – adjacent to it. This was especially the case on the southerly arc of the northern plateau's edge from say Lydford Inner Common round to Great Stannon Newtake immediately west of Fernworthy Forest. But from Bridestowe and Sourton Common round the northern edge to Watern Tor on the outer boundary of Gidleigh Common, with the exception of the West Okement valley, no grassland intervened between blanket bog and heath. Interestingly, grassy islands occurred beyond the heath on Belstone and Throwleigh Commons. The grassland adjacent to the southern plateau blanket bog was then a very patchy fringe – most extensive in and around Foxtor newtake south of Princetown, and eastwards nearly to Hexworthy, with a little on Penn Moor near the head of the Yealm. Otherwise, through the Plym and Meavy headwater valleys and on Shaugh Moor, heath butted up against the blanket peat, as it did on Holne Moor to the east. As in the north there were significant islands of grassy moor at lower levels, some wholly detached like the south end of Roborough Down, Wigford Down and Hanger Down, others like the southern ends of Walkhampton, Harford, and Ugborough Commons were separated from the blanket bog by heath and bilberry *Vaccinium myrtillis* moor.

The 'heath' of the 1972 map was dominantly dry heath, with ling in the ascendancy then and cross-leaved heath and bell heather *Erica cinerea* present in the damper and the drier places respectively. Grasses were and are always present (a nice mirror image of the grassland types on the same map where 'heather is always present'), especially bristle bent *Agrostis curtisii*. Bristle bent – bristle because of its thin wiry leaves – is a distinctive basally tufted but long-stemmed grass with a noticeably compact straw-coloured flower-head appearing to dominate the sward in June and July. The significance of bristle bent is that Dartmoor is near the northern limit of its range and while it occurs sparsely in South Wales, on the Quantocks and Bodmin Moor has some hectares of it, here it is much more widespread on gentler slopes of the drier peaty soils. Dartmoor is its British stronghold (Fig. 90). A mosaic of patches with different characteristic grasses, sheep's fescue *Festuca ovina*, wavy hair grass *Deschampsia flexuosa* and common bent *Agrostis tenuis* for instance, among the dwarf shrub dominants, occurs on this dry heath as it does on the grasslands of the same map. It is in these patches and especially where they amalgamate into lawn-like areas that

FIG 90. Bristle bent covering the long slope of Rippon Tor with scattered western furze bushes.

FIG 91. Vigur's eyebright, parasitic on western furze on Lydford High Down. (DNPA)

rarities like the purple Vigur's eyebright *Euphrasia vigursii* occur. Vigur's is a likely stable hybrid among the semi-parasitic eyebrights and only grows in the southwest peninsula, Dartmoor is again a stronghold and Lydford High Down the citadel within it. The grassy elements of this heath are almost certainly more dominant now than they were in 1972. It is suggested by contemporary upland ecologists that too intense burning and the mixture of grazers after the burn – sheep, cattle and ponies as well as rabbits – keep the dwarf shrubs at bay for longer. Interestingly the toughness of bristle bent tufts in the face of fire seems to be reflected in their avoidance by grazing stock. It is important to register that, as well as the heathers, western furze is a senior member of the dwarf shrub community on this heath, and that combination is now what the 'visionaries' 30 years on call western heath.

Just as Ward blurred the boundary between blanket bog and heather moorland, so the 2005 Vision Group, taking its map and brief text together, blurs in a different way the boundary between heather moorland and western heath – a phrase neither Ward nor the NVC used. But no one should be surprised that grazed habitats evolve, even in 30 years. Everyone agrees that ling characterises heather moorland on Dartmoor, though all the dwarf shrubs and moorland grasses may be present. Bilberry *Vaccinium myrtilis* is quite common and crowberry *Empetrum nigrum* grows near the summit of Ryders Hill where it may well have grown 15,000 years ago. Western heath has all three heathers though bell heather is regarded as symbolic, but with more extensive areas of short-cropped grassland and with western furze almost as a distinctive companion. Where the dwarf shrubs are in clear domination, to the apparent exclusion of all else at a distance, and they flower, as they all do together suddenly in late summer, they create one of the most colourful and thus memorable communities of plants to be seen within the National Park (Fig. 92). This remarkable sudden colouring of patches on the middle altitude Dartmoor slopes, a dense mixture of bright yellow and magenta with variable shades of mauve and pink, provides a splendid context for the personal

FIG 92. The bright mixture of ling, bell heather and western furze in August alongside the road between Cold East Cross and Hemsworthy Gate.

FIG 93. Tall European gorse on Holne Moor.

harvesting of bilberries, either for consumption on the spot or retrieval for pie-making at home. There are extensive such stands on Trendlebeare Down, on Haytor Down, in the Rippon Tor newtake southwest of Haytor and on Wittaburrow and Buckland Common south of that, also on Buckfastleigh Moor, Penn Beacon and parts of Roborough and Plaster Downs, but hardly any on similar slopes in the northern moor. European gorse *Ulex europeaus* may also be present at the edges of these sites. It is the well-known leggy shrub characteristic of walls, hedge-banks and verges throughout the British Isles and can dominate such lines here on Dartmoor and spread from them to form extensive shrubberies in enclosures and on commons – Holne Moor's northeastern corner is a classic example of that. It flowers all the year round (hence the traditional country saying, 'when the gorse is not in flower kissing's out of fashion') but does have its own climax in April and May on Dartmoor when the heavy coconut-like scent intoxicates those getting out of the wind behind a good clump of it (Fig. 93).

The 'western heath' of 2005 then, in part picks up the 1972 map's 'heath' and 'grassland-with-gorse'. Some of the 1972 'heath' is heather moorland in Vision terms – notably on Chagford Common and the adjacent parts of the Forest: Bush Down, Headland Warren and Coombe Down Common (Fig. 94).

FIG 94. Is this 'heather moorland' or 'western heath' on Chagford Common?

Bracken

Bracken is part of the grassland and heath story, but its vigour, and thus its contribution to the landscape and effect on access alone warrant its own special treatment here. The bracken plant *Pteridium aquilinum* is a dense network of underground rhizome(s) that annually sends stalked and branched leafy shoots above ground often forming dense and extensive stands covering whole hillsides. In 1972 and 1994 bracken invasion warranted a special category even on the maps. Its spores, of course, have been present in the peat-protected record since 8,000 BP, or so, and at a fairly constant density from 3,500 BP to the present, with a slight increase during the Dark Ages. Intriguingly none of the eighteenth-century observers mention bracken, but Worth in 1933 and Harvey 20 years later thought it important enough to register. By the latter date its invasive tendency was attributed to the successful survival underground of the main plant in the swaling season – October to March. Its fronds show where it is alive when they protrude for annual reproductive purposes and to boost the energy of the whole clone with some opportunist photosynthesis from May to October. Bracken is also a choosy plant and not a bad indicator of a good depth of acid-to-neutral well-drained soil, as witness its ready take-over of once-cultivated ground given

FIG 95. Dominant winter bracken straddling Green Coombe; the 'Far East' beyond.

the opportunity. Its mapped concentration at the outer edges of the whole moorland block and throughout the middle-eastern brown earth area demonstrates its rampant success in the right conditions (Fig. 95).

The Dartmoor Commoners' Association in its submission to the Royal Commission on Common Land in 1956 suggested that bracken had begun to spread as commoners cut less and less for bedding – but many longstanding hill-farmers also pointed to a reduction in cattle grazing in their lifetime, and thus far less trampling in recent decades. When intense summer grazing was more the norm, heavier lowland cattle like South Devons were brought up, especially from the South Hams, and as many as three such herds would regularly work the lower western slopes of Hameldown where bracken is now dominant. Apart from spraying with Asulam, a commercial herbicide which kills the next year's growing points below ground, crushing bracken at the 'fiddle-head' stage in early summer is the acknowledged best form of controlling it. Boulders hidden from the tractor driver's eye by the bracken itself are an inhibition for both economic spraying and mechanical crushing attempted too late in the season. Aerial spraying is efficient and on the face of it well tailored to landscape sensitivities because its work is brief and the effect is not seen until next year and is then wholly positive. But it is expensive, hedged around with health and safety difficulties and unpopular in many quarters –

those of principle and those protecting holiday-season wanderers among them (ideal timing is late July when the fronds are at fullest spread). The Vision commentary rightly points up bracken's ecological value and thus its acceptability 'in some places', especially as habitat host to high brown fritillaries *Argynnis adippe* and much of the whinchat *Saxicola rubetra* population.

But it is universally accepted that bracken is, and always was, a problem plant. Some archaeologists believe it defeated high-level farmers in the late Middle Ages and that whole villages were abandoned because of it. In the twenty-first century as we have just seen, it hides boulders from ramblers, prehistoric remains from their seekers, fire-break making swipe operators and would-be sprayers of it, from itself. Its rhizomes are regarded by archaeologists as a damaging agent for the same remains. Its preference for particular soils and dryness means that scrub and woodland development are likely successors to it, especially adjacent to existing tree seed sources. Its spores are carcinogenic to mammals, among the few invertebrates it harbours are the ticks that transmit louping ill (Ovine Encephalomyelitis) to farm stock and birds, and it can wet you to the armpits as you try to get through it. The dead fronds smother other struggling vegetation and accumulate in dense beds except where swaling finds them. On the other hand it provides the summer shade necessary for bluebell *Hyacinthoides non-scripta* survival if the trees have gone (Fig. 96) and violets

FIG 96. Sheets of bluebells in the open in Okehampton Park.

FIG 97. Violets flowering among last year's bracken litter.

Viola spp. for fritillaries (Fig. 97); and from November newly dead bracken provides one of Dartmoor's richer colours when many other communities have become drab and before the ling/purple moor grass light and dark contrasts are as striking as they can be from mid-winter on, as Figure 95 showed.

The final moorland argument

'Grassland invaded by bracken' is one of the 1972 map's three grassland categories (and by implication a fourth, courtesy of purple moor grass, might now be added) and they still form a useful concept. The acceptance that ling is present in all four and that grasses are always present in the heath means that there is no great conflict between the 1972 interpretation and the 2006 vision, with that of 1994 sitting comfortably on the fence. The simplification of the Vision's map is understandable when one considers its original purpose and that the process of its achievement is almost more valuable than its expression on paper. About grassland – carefully labelled 'acid' – the Vision, which does not map it, expects it to be reduced in total area by 2030. It acknowledges, however, that extensive tracts of it must be retained for the conservation of a few rare plants: Vigur's eyebright, and wax caps for instance, some insects, field grasshoppers *Chorthippus spp.*, dor beetles *Geotrupes stercorarius* and hornet robber flies *Asilus crabroniformis* which prey on both. Ground nesting birds, especially lapwings *Vanellus vanellus* also need short-cropped grassland especially for feeding. Nevertheless western heath must, even if by default, include all that grassland and it would be a pity if it became interpreted in the future as a sort of Dartmoor ecological dustbin, attempting to contain too much and an easy way out of an identification dilemma.

The NVC needs to be referred to again. Purple moor grass tends to dominate the damper end of the grassland spectrum (M25) and bristle bent the drier (U3). Cotton grass will emphasise the former and heath bedstraw *Galium saxatile* the latter, but tormentil is present throughout that spectrum – taller with the purple moor grass and short and supine among the bristle bent tufts and in the short-cropped sward where its four bright yellow petals make it the star of that particular show. Near the dry end, and especially on the acid brown earths and simple podsols, a shorter turf mainly of sheep's fescue *Festuca ovina* commonly occurs, common bent and sweet vernal grass *Oenanthe odoratum*, with heath bedstraw and tormentil always there (U4). It forms the common sheep pasture of Dartmoor's eastern slopes and summits, but as we have seen a candidate for bracken invasion when only sheep are left to graze it.

So, Ward's heath and four grasslands often form a mosaic in detail that the present visionaries wish to call western heath, and for 'management-by-agreement' purposes that may be perfectly practicable. As the last commentary on this particular discussion: when Ward extended his association analysis from the original ground transects by reference to the aerial photographs, the significance of a ninth vegetation type was underlined, and he called it grass-heath. 'The stands appeared to be a fairly heterogeneous collection in terms of their physiognomy, but they did have in common the fact that they were all transitional between heath and grassland.' Some were grass swards where isolated bushes of ling, western furze and bilberry still remained, while others had the three shrubs finely mixed with the grasses but with a very low percentage cover of each. Constant species are ling, tormentil and two mosses, but common bent, carnation and pill sedge *Carex panicea* and *C. pilulifera*, red fescue *Festuca rubra* , heath bedstraw and heath grass *Sieglingia decumbens* were common; and bristle bent, sheep's fescue, purple moor grass, matt grass *Nardus stricta* and western furze occurred in more than half the samples. The whole list is reproduced just to emphasise the complexity of the stands. Ward says: 'due to the extremely variable appearance of this vegetation, it would not have been possible to define suitable criteria by which to recognise it (presumably from the air). In practice such stands have been classed in either grassland, heath or grassland with gorse.' It seems to say it all.

Valley bogs and mires

After that complexity, this last of the vegetation types of the open moorland has no such problems of recognition or classification. All are agreed that it normally expresses itself as a relatively narrow, linear pattern along valley floors and sometimes in more steeply graded downslope depressions often from the edge of the blanket bog. But as we have seen when discussing peat deposits there are notable examples of broader bogs in shallow, wide valley basins often when headwaters meet. Classic sites are Taw Marsh and Raybarrow Pool in the northeast of the northern plateau, Redlake near the head of the Erme, Foxtor Mire from which the Swincombe emerges. Its extent is seen in Figure 98 and it was the probable inspiration for 'Grimpen Mire' in *The Hound of the Baskervilles* – Conan Doyle stayed in Princetown while writing some of the story. Muddilake in Spaders Newtake draining to the Cherry Brook was seen in Figure 89. The two last named are within large enclosures, and of course there are long and narrow valley bogs among the more elderly and smaller enclosures of the middle-eastern valleys, especially along the East and West Webburn. Near the head of the latter at Challacombe (Fig. 99) the peat accumulation is such that the bog is raised in the strict sense of the term, there are others below Crockern Tor and above Statts Bridge, both close to the B3212. Even further east there are important valley mires at Blackslade, which is a Site of Special Scientific Interest southeast of Widecombe, and in Bagtor and Halshanger Newtakes either side of Rippon

FIG 98. Foxtor Mire sunlit in the middle distance. Whiteworks buildings can be seen beyond the mire on the right, with Nun's Cross farmhouse further left. Fox Tor itself is on the extreme left.

FIG 99. Challacombe raised bog surface.

Tor. The last named occupies a broad and shallow basin at the head of the River Ashburn and is easily overseen from Cold East Cross on the Widecombe to Ashburton road. It is pictured in Figure 16.

Valley bogs differ substantially from blanket bog because of their physical context whose significant effect is water movement. The water within a valley bog distributes chemical goodies for plants laterally throughout the site. Mineral material is continuously washed in from the valley sides and on to the bog surface however gentle and limited in height those slopes may be, providing nutrients denied to the plants on a summit blanket bog whose surface is sealed off from the underlying rock by thick peat.

So, unsurprisingly, we have on these wet valley floors the richest flora available in one site within Dartmoor, indeed as acid mires go these are as good as they get in upland England. While the floristic colour combination may not compete for

FIG 100. Bog bean flowering in Challacombe bog; its trifoliate leaves in left foreground.

intensity with the August western furze-with-heathers of the heathy slopes, its variety and the mosaic of small patches within a polka-dot pattern of single flower-heads has its own charm. All the plants have both formations. Cotton grasses and bog asphodel are often in patches of white and yellow, but can equally punctuate the green base in an even scatter. Yellow marsh St John's wort *Hypericum elodes*, the small white towers of bog bean *Menianthes trifoliata*, red rattle or marsh lousewort *Pedicularis palustris* and lesser spearwort *Ranunculus flammula* have similar distributive patterns. Wetter places, especially the arterial slow streams, have water crowfoot *Ranunculus aquatilis* and pondweeds *Potamogetons*; bare peaty muddy surfaces carry greater birdsfoot trefoil *Lotus pedunculatus*, marsh pennywort *Hydrocotyle vulgaris*, bog pimpernel *Anagallis tenella*, marsh bedstraw *Galium palustre* and marsh violet *Viola palustris*. Such surfaces also support pale butterwort *Pinguicula lusitanica* quite often (Fig. 101) and its grosser cousin *P. grandiflora* very rarely (there is a fair collection near East Bovey Head, while their fellow insectivores, round-leaved sundew and its narrow-

FIG 101. Pale butterwort in surface scrape.

or oblong-leaved cousin *D. intermedia*, may prefer closer association with mosses. Sphagnum species are everywhere, often forming tussocks which higher plants pierce from below. Rushes are similarly widespread and their tussocks may bear one's weight – early and late in the season they appear to dominate whole bog surfaces, and in some cases they really do, but they do the same in very wet meadows. Tall, magenta ragged robin *Lychnis flos-cuculi* early and shorter, blue devil's bit scabious *Succisa pratensis* late, are mire-edge plants and splendid less common flowers will sometimes leap out at the sharp observer from that edge, southern marsh orchid *Dactylorhiza praetermissa* (Fig. 102) and ivy-leaved bellflower *Wahlenbergia hederacea* among them. In one place in western Dartmoor drooping Irish lady's tresses *Spiranthes romanzoffiana* hangs on by the skin of its teeth, in the face of unfettered grazing.

The Vision map draws attention to the fact that 'all mires are not shown' but that all 'internationally important' ones will be retained and managed by grazing, while 10 per cent will be allowed to 'scrub up' into willow and alder in the first

FIG 102. Southern marsh orchid near Cator.

instance. The cartogrammetric nature of the Vision map means that the representation of a habitat as finely drawn in reality as long, narrow valley bogs, cannot be expected to be very accurate. Ward, as we have seen, was criticised for over-playing the valley bog network. Despite both these commentaries, valley mires extend into the enclosed landscape, often close to roads, a flavour of precious wildness among fields that is quintessentially lower Dartmoor.

THE ENCLOSED LANDSCAPE

The valley bogs and mires clearly straddle the boundary, and the distinction, between open moorland and total enclosure and ease the transition into our second vegetation suite in their own right. Because they are often bordered by damp pastures of purple moor grass and rushes whose Welsh name 'rhos' has been adopted even by European convention (Devon, Wales and Eire have more of it than the rest of Europe together) their influence for us is widened. Such wet fields penetrate a complex pattern of fields and walls, lanes and hedge-banks, which landscape embroidery contains knots of buildings ranging from single farmsteads to full-blown villages. Isolated single buildings do occur but not as in the consistent pattern of the field barns of the Yorkshire Dales.

There are, in this landscape, two types of enclosure to consider. Large, walled spaces called newtakes sprawl across the central basin of Dartmoor closely associated with the two turnpikes – Moretonhampstead to Tavistock and Ashburton to Princetown and on to Yelverton and Plymouth, mostly 'taken' from the Forest in the late eighteenth and early nineteenth centuries by authority of the Duchy of Cornwall, Muddilake in Figure 89 is in one. There are also odd ones at the outer edges of the original moorland north and east of Widecombe and up the west side from Merrivale to Sourton, largely as a result of successful applications under the Enclosure Acts. Most of these later newtakes still consist of 'moorland' or at least grass moor and dwarf shrub communities even though some were occasionally and patchily limed up to the mid-twentieth century. An exclusive enclosure of moorland for those still having suckler cattle herds is very valuable. 'That's my hay', said one knowing farmer explaining to the innocent what newtakes were for. He let it grow all summer and put his hardy hill cattle from the common into it for the winter. Another worked out how much winter ling equalled a bale of hay, and the trace elements that the ling contained which were not available from his hay meadow.

But newtakes have a longer history. Sometime between Domesday Book (for there is no reference to them there) and the late fourteenth century, the administrators of the Forest encouraged the establishment of farms within it, probably to ensure that controlled grazing maintained some open land for the Forest's prime purpose – hunting (remember the Mesolithic hunter/manager!). It also meant that there was a labour force readily available on the spot for all those tasks that were ancillary to that purpose. The farms established then are still known as the 'Ancient Tenements' and are not all separate holdings, or holdings at all now. They are crowded together, but in two blocks north and south of Riddon Ridge at the centre of the eastern edge of the Forest. They were thus an extension westward and upward of the Saxon pattern of farms and commons already well established in the vales of the Dart catchment. The southern block lies between Prince Hall and Huccaby in the south and up to Riddon on the Wallabrook; the northern block stretches from Bellever to Walna, whose remains are near the Warren House Inn, in the north, with an outlier at Postbridge called Hartland (see more detail about them in Chapter 7). The tenants of these farms were allowed to enclose land in about 3.25-ha plots according to certain rules, one of which was the speed with which the enclosure could be completed. The result is that these more elderly smaller newtakes often do not have right-angle corners – it was quicker to keep building the dry-stone wall on a curve. Many have been subdivided at later times, often when original single farmsteads became hamlets of three or four smallholdings and good fields were shared between them. Thus right angles may have re-entered the pattern at that time although the curved boundaries are still obvious on the maps of farms like Babeny and Hexworthy. These smaller but still high-level fields are usually no longer heathy. Most are permanent grass that has been limed and the driest have become hay meadows, 'shut up' from March or April to July.

In parallel with the Duchy, perhaps much earlier in some cases, Saxon or Norman lords of the manor also allowed, even encouraged, the creation of farmsteads in the waste-of-the-manor. Holne Moor's 4,000-year spread of enclosure remains has already been registered as incorporating prehistoric, Saxon and mediaeval patterns, some seen in Figure 75, but at the northeastern edge of the present common are a string of farms – West Stoke, Seale's Stoke, Middle Stoke and Fore Stoke. The Stoke element implies an Anglo-Saxon stock farm with a dwelling and such places were often set up as ancillary holdings to a main farmstead in good economic times. Their fields are thus of great age, and their pattern is physically extended by the observable remains of banks out on the common although the present outer boundary is undoubtedly a 'cornditch' against the common. They are 300 m above sea level, small and with sheltering walls and banks which offer yet another habitat possibility or variation on the high meadow theme. Similar small fields reach 400 m at the Merripit farms once a single Ancient Tenement northeast of Postbridge.

FIG 103. Hay meadow flowers. (DNPA)

As Vancouver noted all these fields played their part in a mixed – once self-sufficient – local farming system. They may well have been ploughed, re-seeded, limed and manured many times in their 1,000-year-plus lives. Their twenty-first-century biodiversity depends almost certainly on how long it is since the last time their surface was broken or enriched, in farming terms. Management agreements have been made with the occupiers of many of them – initially by the NPA in the 1980s, and continued under Environmentally Sensitive Area schemes by MAFF and then DEFRA – which is some commentary on their contemporary richness and biodiversity value (Fig. 103). Meadow and bulbous buttercups *Ranunculus arvensis* and *R. bulbosus*, black knapweed *Centaurea nigra*, self heal *Prunella vulgaris*, spear thistle *Cirsium vulgare* and creeping thistle *C. arvense*, sheeps bit *Jasione montana* in drier parts and devil's bit scabious *Succisa pratensis* in lower-lying fields and in the damper corners, yellow rattle *Rhianthus minor* and greater butterfly orchid *Platanthera chlorantha* (Fig. 104), along with the grasses: sweet vernal *Anthoxanthum odorata*, crested dogstail *Cynosurus cristatus*, common bent *Agrostis tenuis*, cocksfoot *Dactylis glomeratus*, red fescue and Yorkshire fog *Holcus lanatus* all tell of that richness on the ground.

Apart from these select flower-rich hay meadows and the best of the rhos pastures, within the enclosed landscape it is the roadside verges and the unmetalled wider driftways that offer the only other open feral habitats not being heath or moor.

FIG 104. Greater butterfly orchid in Dunnabridge meadow. (DNPA)

Driftways are winding avenues between fields for stock to be driven from farmyards and linhays to the open common and back (Fig. 105). Decent lengths of continuous verge are really confined to the turnpikes – the 'scissor roads' B3212 and B3557, and the A382 and the A386 – and although historically young, at least they can be dated and represent an unequivocally unlimed, un-fertilised and largely unmanured sample of permanent grassland. Otherwise there are little beads of verge on the more important inter-village lanes of the middle east and more importantly the outer edges of those driftways. The latter have been well manured during their long history as frequent nettle beds proclaim, but their soil remains neutral to acid and they have certainly never been ploughed.

FIG 105. Field pattern on the east flank of Cosdon. Two driftways intersect the fields, both emerging on to the common at the left-hand side of the block.

FIG 106. Devon bank with the bluebell, stitchwort, red campion combination that follows the primroses. Some lesser celandines linger at the bank foot.

In these open linear sites the early bright yellows of lesser celandine *Ranunculus ficaria* and paler primrose *Primula vulgaris* are followed by the patchy but patriotic red, white and blue of campion *Silene dioica*, stitchwort *Stellaria holostea* and bluebell, the latter usually indicating the shade of bracken to come (Fig. 106). Early purple orchids *Orchis mascula* punctuate these generalities in many places as does betony *Betonica officinalis* later on. As spring progresses a white floral domination develops as stitchwort is joined by cow parsley *Anthriscus sylvestris*, upright bedstraw *Galium mollugo* and ox-eye daisy *Chrysanthemum leucanthemum*, which then give way to the summery cream of hogweed *Heraclium sphondylium* and meadowsweet *Filipendula ulmaria*. Yellow reappears strongly in June and the scatter of hawkbits *Leontodon spp.*, hawkweeds *Hieracium spp.*, cat's ears *Hypochoeris spp.* and hawk's beards *Crepis spp.* persists until September, having been joined by tansy *Chrysanthemum vulgare* in mid-August, and in the shorter grass under the highway authority's flail there are always dandelions *Taraxacum officinale*. Foxgloves *Digitalis purpurea* (Fig. 107) leap up and over-top all else in July on many a verge and willowherb *Chamaenarion angustifolium* and hemp agrimony *Eupatorium cannabinum* continue the pink-to-puce theme well into August (Fig. 108).

FIG 107. Foxglove on Blackaton roadside.

FIG 108. Hemp agrimony often dominates the August banks.

These last three creep up from the verges wherever proper Devon banks give a toehold. Better drainage and slight leaching may be the motivator, but the foxglove seed bank must be full and of long standing, for when a bank or wall is rebuilt they are always the first big plants to appear in the new crevices. These banks, in the Dartmoor lower landscape all round the high moor, are of course a habitat in themselves, as may be the double-skinned dry-stone wall variation which often supersedes them up the granite slope. Most of the plants listed for verges just now cling also to them and find their special niches. Lesser celandine likes the damper base, primroses like to be up away from the road edge and foxgloves, when their turn comes, prefer the top.

Devon banks are vast structures, a late-eighteenth-century recipe says that they should be 9 ft (2.75 m) across at the base and 4 ft (1.22 m) across the top and stand 7 ft (2.1 m) high, then be stoned to 4 ft (1.22 m) high on either side. They were to be topped with cuttings and seedlings of a large number of shrubs and trees at a specified number per unit-length. Off Dartmoor their origin almost certainly lies in the lack of good stone for wall building in Anglo-Saxon times except in odd places where limestone or schist outcropped (Torbay and

FIG 109. Dartmoor hybrid between South Devon bank and granite dry-stone wall at Welstor above Ashburton. Beech has been planted on the crest.

FIG 110. The significance of hedgerow trees in the farmland downstream from Widecombe.

Plymouth hinterlands, patchily from Chudleigh southwest to Buckfastleigh and between Start and Bolt Tail) and no formal hedging tradition. The only precedent was the low earth banks separating strips in the open field. If you 'suddenly' needed to contain stock or keep it out, why not simply enlarge the low bank. There is also the suggestion that adjacent landowners, or in the Dark Ages probably long-leaseholders, digging a boundary ditch between them side-by-side, throwing the earth and stone out on their own side, created by chance a strip of no-man's-land between crude banks. The strip became a passage and then a hollow lane whose bottom became rich enough over time from the passage of cattle to warrant digging out and spreading on the fields, thus increasing the hollow characteristic. Such banks and their attendant lanes creep up into the National Park, but there, as we have seen, the abundance of granite boulders at the surface must have made wall building a logical alternative which the prolific prehistoric precedents demonstrated to the Anglo-Saxon settler. Banks and walls both provide important, well-drained sites for plants and animals as variations on the open verge. Banks particularly provide good footholds, while walls have their own specialists – wall pennywort and ivy-leaved toadflax on the sides and more than one stonecrop species on the top, hard fern and harts tongue providing a shiny green accompaniment often from the base of the wall or halfway up the bank on the shady side (Fig. 109). Both wall and bank happen to support trees, the Dartmoor version of the hedgerow tree of lowland landscapes, and they give as particular a character to the fringe farming landscape here as they do to the Vale of Pewsey or the Weald (Fig. 110).

DARTMOOR'S WOODLAND

The single tree is one thing, the wood quite another. The word 'dart', as Chapter 1 hinted, is a derivative of the British 'daerwint' (and 'derw' is oak), and means oak tree river in the Celtic languages that almost always gave the British landscape its original names for physical features. The River Dart's valley sides from Dartmouth to Totnes and from Buckfast into Dartmoor as far as Dartmeet are clothed in oakwoods still. Much further into the moor is a small oak copse, Wistman's Wood (Fig. 111), well up the West Dart above Two Bridges. It has two analogues, Piles Copse above Harford on the Erme and Black-a-Tor Beare on the West Okement that, reaching 450 m OD, is the highest broad-leaved wood in the national park. We shall consider them at greater length in due time. But it seems somewhat ironic that the first element of the name of this great hill is about woodland which covered most of it before man intervened, rather than the moorland of the second element which man now reveres for its relative rarity in

FIG 111. The site of Wistman's Wood on the left bank of the West Dart above Two Bridges.

FIG 112. Looking up the East Dart valley, Brimpts Farm is at the top of the left-hand middle-ground, with plantation still surrounding fields.

the southern part of this island and the scope it offers to him for recreation in all its forms. That irony apart, the whole of contemporary Dartmoor's tree cover falls first into two equal parts by area: long-established deciduous woods, which will complete and dominate this account, and new-ish conifer plantations.

Coniferous plantings

The creation of plantations on hitherto open moorland newtakes was begun by Duchy of Cornwall leaseholders near the end of the eighteenth century at Beardown, Prince Hall and Tor Royal – none were then very successful, but at Beardown and Tor Royal the idea, at least, persisted and a plantation still sits at the former and a shelter belt along a third of the length of the road from Tor Royal to Whiteworks. But, developing a story begun in Chapter 1, from 1862 onwards at Brimpts above Dartmeet the Duchy's land steward who happened to live there, planted 40,000 trees (Fig. 112). The first crop was felled early, and transferred to Princetown by aerial ropeway, because of the demand generated by the First World War. That seems to have inspired the then Duke (later briefly Edward VIII) to investigate the potential of other newtakes with the fledgling Forestry Commission after that war. He began the planting but eventually leased land at Brimpts, Beardown, Fernworthy and Bellever to the Commission, which completed the largest and highest plantations we still see (Fernworthy's western edge reaches 500 m and sadly, in scenic terms, over-tops the skyline from Postbridge and other parts west). Soussons Farm, across the road from Fernworthy and only a mile from Bellever, was added to the Commission's estate at the end of the Second World War, bringing the total area to 1,500 ha. All these separate blocks are currently going through their first harvest, providing, however temporarily, a new set of habitats as clearings, and scope for enterprising species like nightjar *Caprimulgus europaeus* and grasshopper warbler *Locustella naevia* to linger and breed. After its early habit the Commission created smallholdings at Bellever and the retained Soussons, for the retention of part-time forest workers who farmed for themselves in their own time. At Bellever houses were also built to house foresters and woodmen.

Four other plantations of varying size but on high-level moorland and adjacent fields were created in this same time span. Plymouth City Council planted the biggest – 280 ha of high-level fields in the closer catchment of its Burrator Reservoir – soon after the First World War. Convicts planted, first, northwest of Princetown around the prison quarry and on both sides of the Princetown–Rundlestone Road. Then a little later they created Long Plantation, well north of the prison, from the B3357 to the southern boundary of the military Merrivale Range to provide shelter from the northeast for the most exposed part of the Prison Farm.

(Exposure can be a problem for the plantings themselves, as Chapter 6 will tell.) Finally, a southwestern newtake, Hawns and Dendles Waste, occupying a ridge between the River Yealm and Broadall Lake, was planted in the 1950s.

These four have been more significant for their presence in the landscape than for any internal, intrinsic value. Burrator, apart from Brimpts, the oldest of these conifer woods, makes the central Meavy valley as it leaves the moor proper, a discrete 'lake-in-forest' vignette. Despite that unity from within it is, from anywhere outside, in huge contrast with the moorland above and around it and with the fields and broad-leaved woods of Sheepstor and Meavy parishes immediately downstream of the reservoir's dam. Nevertheless, good management of the Burrator woods over some 80 years now has produced a very reasonable density of stems and enough light reaches the forest floor to maintain a green lawn of a grass/moss mixture that walkers and trespassing sheep enjoy in about equal parts. The many walls remaining from the predecessor fields within the forest now bear a dense crop of mosses and scattered ferns varying with the aspect of the wall side and light penetration. Lanes, for instance, with two walls, create a wider slot in the canopy. The popularity of the site with very local and Plymouth-based visitors has led to much effort to provide clearings and sustain broad-leaved trees as well as many parking places, walking, riding and cycling routes, sometimes utilising the Devonport Leat side and the bed of the Plymouth to Princetown railway, both of which pass through the forest.

The Hawns and Dendles Waste ridge is lower than those to east and west of it so no 'wider landscape' problem really attached to its site. Nevertheless its planting, by private investors, was far from popular with moorland protectors if only because of its intrusion into the southern plateau, as any map shows. In the last decade of the twentieth century it was bought, after clear-felling, by the NPA which spent much energy – and cash – clearing stumps and brash so that moorland could re-develop on an uncluttered soil surface. The prison plantings are strictly functional in origin, Long Plantation strangely complements Beardown when one is between them in the Cowsic valley, but there is tangible relief for the walker on emerging upstream from that skyline 'avenue'. The Princetown sheltering woods took a greater beating than others in the great storm of 25 January 1990 and their replacement includes a much higher percentage of broad-leaved trees.

All this had been paralleled within the enclosed landscape by smaller conifer plantings notably above Ashburton on Ausewell Common, at adjacent Buckland, up the Webburn valleys and further north at Frenchbeer – another Duchy holding – quite early (Fig. 113). Torquay Urban District Council planted much of the small catchment of its Tottiford reservoir complex (in the far east) in the

FIG 113. Conifers inserted into an oakwood landscape – here on a spur between the Webburn and Ruddycleave Water.

early 1930s. Later, Kingswood and Dean Wood west and southwest of Buckfastleigh were converted to conifers and from the end of the 1920s so was the woodland of the middle Teign valley. The Dartington Hall trustees, whose inspired benevolent despot Leonard Elmhirst had rural economic regeneration ambitions for South Devon which included afforestation and sawmilling, purchased nearly three miles (4.8 km) of the right-bank valley side. It was clear felled and planted with Sitka and Norway spruce, Douglas fir and European larch and a sawmill built at Moretonhampstead, where Elmhirst's planters and woodmen still lived in the late twentieth century. Smaller plantations were developed in the upper West Webburn valley around Heathercombe, on the eastern flank of Easdon and in the Wray valley at Steward and Sanduck Woods around the same time. In the last case the woods on the western valley side adjoining the railway line had been felled in both World Wars because of the ease with which the timber could be taken away. Dartington stepped in here too and planted some hectares of larch and Douglas fir after 1945. Sanduck Wood now belongs to the NPA along with neighbouring broad-leaved woods.

It is important in the contexts of both biodiversity ambition and landscape change to note that this addition of the first new and very visible habitat to the Dartmoor suite for perhaps 2,000 years took only 200 years to run its course. It started when only a few conifer species were available – Scots pine, European larch and Norway spruce – which were often at the outset mixed with oak, beech and sycamore. Only after the First World War were the western hemisphere Douglas fir, very far eastern Sitka spruce, and Japanese larch brought to the high Dartmoor plantations. But it was their positioning in the scene, apparent obliteration of ancient monuments and finally coincidence with national park designation, that roused so much opposition that new planting extending the area of coniferous cover on the high moor is no longer contemplated. In one case just mentioned – Hawns and Dendles – wholesale removal of a living eyesore (to moorland devotees) has happened at public expense but with the Heritage Lottery Fund playing a considerable part in the exercise.

Broad-leaved woodland

It will be necessary to return to the plantation as animal habitat, but the other half (2,000 ha) of the Dartmoor National Park's woodland must first be described. There are essentially four types of broad-leaved wooded landscape within the park: valley-side woods, parkland, wet woodland and orchards. By far the most extensive is the first of those, the old original valley-side successor-without-a-break remnant of the pre-Bronze Age forest. The gorge sections of the Dart and the Teign carry the longest stretches, but the Bovey, the Wray, the Ashburn, the Erme, the Yealm, the Plym and the Meavy, the Walkham, the Tavy, the Lyd and both Okements all bear their share. All carry oakwood dominated by the sessile oak *Quercus petrea*, but with some English oak *Q. robur* and their hybrids present, a sprinkling of ash, beech and sycamore and a thin understorey of hazel, rowan and holly, often localised and sometimes absent over substantial areas within any particularly extensive wood. Not only are these woods *in loco filii* to their postglacial predecessors on sites which have never seen anything but a tree cover, but they are classic British upland oakwoods, albeit with a southwestern and oceanic gloss. In most valleys they straddle the granite/metamorphic-aureole boundary with good lengths on both sets of rock, and the character of the woodland floor varies markedly on each side of the line if only because of the boulder density on the granite side. Within this woodland type must of course be those three high-level oak copses already listed and deserving their own treatment, but each does occupy a low-valley-side slope or narrow valley floor against the stream.

Parkland

There are places where the lower-level valley woods merge with, or abut, the second broad-leaved woodland type – the parks, where man's more recent but still historic hand is visible, where, at the extreme, scattered venerable trees punctuate a grazed grassland, as in Okehampton Deer Park, Whiddon Deer Park near Castle Drogo, Blatchford near Cornwood, Woodtown near Sampford Spiney, Holne Park and Parke at Bovey Tracey (Fig. 114). But more often 200-year-old estate management of the otherwise ancient semi-natural woods is recognised by the insertion of specimens and groups of larch, more beech, even some sweet chestnut (for estate fencing) into the oak-dominated woodland context. Such management has also tolerated the rarity or the idiosyncratic. In Holne Chase, a 200 ha domed wood in the biggest meander of the Double Dart, small-leaved lime and wild service trees occur, the former in a large pure stand (Fig. 115).

FIG 114. The National Trust parkland at Parke takes centre stage in the landscape between Bovey Tracey and Haytor Down (on the skyline). Parke House, pale grey and at the right-hand end of the park in this picture, is the headquarters of the National Park Authority.

FIG 115. Holne Chase – 200 ha of oakwood filling the huge meander of the Double Dart – seen from Buckland Beacon. The southern plateau forms the skyline.

Wet woodland (carr)

Both valley-side ancient oakwood and parkland may join with, or contain, the third broad-leaved tree habitat and addition to the scene – wet woodland. Avenues of willows and alders can mark low-gradient stream sides wherever there is room in the valley bottom. Low groves of willow can develop in and around valley mires and in the valleys of the middle east are some of the most extensive and richest with good epiphytic beard lichens *Usnea spp.* and tree lungwort *Lobaria pulmonaria*, all proclaiming cleaner air. Goat and grey willow *Salix caprea* and *S. cinerea* respectively, with some alder *Alnus glutinosa*, provide the main canopy and clumps of marsh marigold *Caltha palustris* may vie with tussock sedge *Carex paniculata* in the eye-catching stakes. Throughout the enclosed landscape tiny wet plots of woodland recur as though ignored for centuries since alder and willow provided clogs, broom heads and basket materials. Remote from the wooded valleys, very small groups of willow appear high on the moorland, especially around old mineral workings where men manipulated water channels, often increasing their density on the ground adding leats to streams, and in abandonment leaving a happy site for all life that

FIG 116. Carr developing in a valley mire near Cator.

regards water as a breeding ground, a refuge or just critical to good rooting and feeding. At the highest level, 535 m OD, upstream of Bleak House on the Rattlebrook for instance, the distinctive ferns, horsetails *Equisetum spp.* thrive in such a site and at the opposite end of the height spectrum the royal fern *Osmunda regalis* is not uncommon in the miry woodland alongside the Double Dart at 90 m or so.

Single trees and orchards

Isolated willow bushes at high levels punctuate wilder landscapes and encourage reed buntings for instance to hang around, even breed, and despite its sub-title this section would be less than adequate if it didn't repeat the reference to the significance of the single tree separated from its peers in 'Enclosed landscapes' above. The willow example is often remote from other trees or scrub, but those not far apart, in hedges, on banks and in parkland provide important habitats in their own right and contribute greatly to the scene, especially in wider valleys such as the upper East Webburn. The most formal of sites in this connection is the fourth woodland type, the orchard, and there are still some 460 of them within the national park though only 10 per cent of those are currently managed. Map analysis suggests that maybe 300

FIG 117. Elderly orchard in winter near Wolleigh Cross.

orchards have been grubbed up in the last 50 years. Like other collections of 'separated trees' they offer different opportunities for a range of organisms from lichens to mistletoe and goldfinches.

Valley oakwood variations

Returning to the main body of the national park's woodland and given the apparent uniformity of the tree species distribution across the spectrum of the downstream valley woods it is variations in the age of stems and more especially in the nature of the woodland floor that give different woods different characters. The former arises for three reasons. Estate planting was of its fashionable age – eighteenth into early nineteenth century – when Evelyn's work and the ideas of Capability Brown penetrated this far west, and many woods not now seen to be parts of estates were clearly so when a species check is carried out. Thus the age of the trees planted and cared for then may well give us our oldest standing stems. Secondly, the two World Wars generated a demand for timber which took its toll of woods with the easiest extraction access in the first half of the last century and the unaided and largely unmanaged re-growth gives us a canopy now between 60 and 80 years old. But the third, and by far the most widespread, influence on even contemporary appearances is the fact that over centuries and up to the 1930s, the prime function of these woods was to provide, first bark for tanning and second the rest of the tree (useless without bark) for charcoal and domestic firewood. Up to and into the twentieth century, every market town had its tannery and there was a guaranteed and steady demand for oak bark for each one. Dartmoor is ringed by markets, in the classic exchange-between-two-economies siting. Store cattle and lambs, wool and metal ores came one way; fruit and wine, cloth, tools, flour and leather went the other. So the woods of the Dart, the Bovey and the Teign provided bark for Bovey Tracey, Ashburton and Buckfastleigh and almost certainly Newton Abbot, the Okements for Okehampton, the Tavy for Tavistock and so on. Charcoal, in a coal-less county, was also in similar demand for the knap mills and forges that turned out the edge tools and horseshoes which every part of the quasi-industrial sector of each town and even some villages had to have. Dartmoor farmers and miners in their turn needed leather and wrought iron and were glad to provide the raw materials for their production.

The appropriate woods were therefore thoroughly coppiced and the girth of stems in the early twenty-first century depends to a large extent on when the last coppicing exercise took place. It seems clear that that was, like the wartime extraction, necessarily nearest to the easiest exit. So the collection of slimmest oaks in White Wood under Bench Tor is close to the north end of the Tor with a cleared path through the clitter up to the open common, those on the right bank of the upper Teign are close to the Steps Bridge gate. Within the steepest woods a network of zig-zag packhorse tracks up and down the slope, from which a pony-width of boulders have been cleared, is a relic of the functional system, and as might be expected a set of charcoal hearths, half-moon-shaped 'ledges' in the hillside, are the nodes of that network (Fig. 118). There was often a family extraction operation. Father and mother stripped bark from the stem as far up as they could reach, then father felled the tree while mother bundled the bark and loaded the pony. Children stripped the worthwhile branches while dad began cutting up the stripped stem into logs for the home fire or for the charcoal burner. The White Wood just named is part of Holne Common so in that case there would be arrangements made in the Manor Court if the logs were for other than domestic use. The coppicing process went on until at least the 1930s and witnesses 50 years later described a quasi-industrial scene in which smoke and ringing axes played a major part – they also thought that on the whole a coppiced hillside then was not as attractive as a closed woodland canopy is now! Nowadays we would probably claim that rotational coppice was, in biodiversity terms, richer than a standard wood at this altitude, if only because of the presence of sheltered clearings and the increase in 'edge effect' which they automatically provide. While considering coppice as a system it would be remiss not to refer to the hazel version. Pre-nineteenth-century buildings in Dartmoor were normally thatched and hazel is the main source of thatching 'spars' used to tie down the bundles of reed or straw ('farm reed') on the roof. There are plots of pure hazel within some woods and adjacent to many more but all are now derelict in the coppice rotation sense. They remain nonetheless a prized habitat for dormice, especially when honeysuckle accompanies the coppice stools. Hurdle-making also needs hazel, and popular landscape gardening has recognised the new demand for hurdles. Perhaps thatchers

FIG 118. Management relics: (top) Long-abandoned charcoal burner's hearth; (above) long-untended hazel coppice on the Wray valley side.

and hurdle-makers will begin to invest in hazel coppice. It would pay them in the end, for we currently import hazel from Eastern Europe, along with thatching reed. Ecologists ought to be a third ally given the biodiversity value of coppice and the coppicing routine – and remember that hazel may well have been Dartmoor's postglacial true woodland pioneer.

As far as the woodland floors are concerned the most spectacular variations are between those on the granite and those on metamorphic rocks. Those on the former are boulder-strewn throughout and in extreme cases the clitter is often without visible space between the rocks, which are then often covered by a dense population of bryophytes – mosses and liverworts. *Rhytidiadelphus undulatum*, *Dicranum scoparium*, *Plagiothecium undulatum* and *Isothecium myosuroides* are common in this situation, the last of these often swarming up the trees growing between the boulders to almost 0.5 m. The lasting impression is of a strangely lumpy lime-green blanket, well seen where White Wood turns into the Venford Brook valley side from that of the Dart itself (Fig. 119). Where the boulders are more scattered there is room for a flowering plant carpet, and great hairy woodrush *Lusula sylvatica*, bluebell and bilberry can each so dominate in different places as to present an apparent monoculture. On the slates and other

FIG 119. Moss blanket on clitter and swarming up coppice oak in White Wood, Holne.

FIG 120. (top) Wild daffodills in Dunsford Wood; (above) bluebells where they are expected in Wray Cleave.

metamorphic rocks, similar cover-plant communities occur on smooth soil surfaces with a complete absence of boulders. Dog's mercury *Mercurialis perennis* and wild garlic *Allium ursinum* join the monocultural potential where the soils on the aureole are slightly less acid. Enchanter's nightshade *Circaea lutetiana*, cow wheat *Melampyrum pratense*, woodruff *Galium odoratum* and more than one St John's wort *Hypericum spp.* sometimes break up these otherwise continuous carpets. One of the latter, the flax-leaved St John's wort *H. linariifolium* only occurs in the Teign valley but in more than one wood, and includes about 90 per cent of the English population. In Dunsford Woods, wholly on the slates of the left bank of the upper Teign, a spectacular wild daffodil community is a target for early spring local (human) visitors (Fig. 120). Until the 1960s coach excursions were specifically organised to Steps Bridge to pick daffodils and only an intensive campaign by the Devon Trust for Nature Conservation, as it then was, aided and abetted by Dunsford Women's Institute patrols, brought the habit to a halt.

In deeper shade in all the woods away from the dense clitter there are patches of the floor apparently devoid or partly devoid of ground vegetation – rather like the norm elsewhere under a pure beech canopy. Some are bare all the year round, others are seasonally so – as when bluebells, having got the important part of their year over early while the sun can still strike the woodland floor through a leafless canopy, die back and their leaves flop down the slope and then, combed by gravity and rain-wash, give the surface a pale straw colour. Often at the outer edges of these open patches conspicuous mosses like *Polytrichum formosum*, *Thuidium tamariscinum* and *Mnium hornum* occur and may infiltrate adjacent stands of bilberry and woodrush from there. A variation on the theme is where ferns scattered in individual crowns or clumps dominate the otherwise naked scene, for they are often unaccompanied by other plants. They range from the comparatively neat glossy straps of harts-tongue *Phyllitis scolopendrium* to the almost blowsy three-dimensional fans or inverted cones of broad buckler fern *Dryopteris dilatata* with hard fern *Blechnum spicant*, golden scale male fern *Dryopteris affinis*, male *Dryopteris felix mas* and lady *Athyrium felix femina* ferns sitting somewhere in the structural spectrum. Common polypody *Polypodium vulgare* is on almost every lying log, happy too on rocks and quite high up trees in forks and on horizontal branches (Fig. 121). Bracken fronds can totally dominate lighter areas of the woods, especially those younger, less dense plantings of, say, the early nineteenth century where the bracken underground stock may even predate the trees. Its winter debris accumulates steadily and despite the slowness of its breakdown, produces a thick body of humus sought by some as the best medium in which to propagate rhododendrons and azaleas. These very different winter (humus) and summer (frond spread) density characteristics of bracken can exclude almost all

FIG 121. Rotting log with polypody and moss population.

other plants, though in some places as we have seen bracken plays an important role, even if at arms length, in the success of animal species as varied as whinchats and purple hairstreak butterflies *Neozephyrus quercus*.

At the lower ends of the steeper slopes, even in granite, soils can be slightly enriched by the downwash of nutrients and other mosses will be happier there if wetness in such sites doesn't overpower the enrichment. Where it does sheets of golden saxifrage *Chrysosplenium oppositifolium* may exclude most other plants (Fig. 122). Its cousin *C. alternifolium* also occurs, but sparsely, and some mosses such as *Sphagnum spp.* and *Hookeria lucens* can also hold there own here. Good examples may be stumbled upon wherever there is a little flat between the bottom of the slope and the river, especially in narrower tributary valleys of the Dart, in the middle Walkham below Vixen Tor and places like Lustleigh Cleave.

FIG 122. Golden saxifrage at the foot of a wooded slope near North Bovey.

Woods, tors and lichens

At the top of such slopes and where there is no man-made boundary to the wood, which is rare, is the opposite end of a dampness spectrum. Here light and relative dryness are the significant factors affecting plants and the canopy is provided by pioneer trees like rowan and silver birch with odd light-demanding ashes, and bracken, bramble and moorland dwarf shrubs creep in under them. Here too, at the valley lip, are tors and the most recent rock falls so that the real pioneers of rock surfaces, lichens, come into their own. The dappled shade of what canopy exists, coupled with that in rock crevices of varying depth, means that a huge variety of lichens can survive. Sixty species on a single tor is not uncommon, and 96 were recorded on Black Tor in 1990. Bench Tor, overlooking White Wood and the Dart valley crossing from granite to aureole, is a splendid site from which all this top-of-the-wood-with-tor habitat complex can be examined in short order. The thin canopy of birch and rowan below the observer can be almost transparent, and the welter of crevices on all rays of the compass guarantee a moss and lichen festival.

Lichens are long-lived survivors and withstand extremes unacceptable to any other plants in hot and cold deserts, mountains tops and specific zones of very exposed rocky shores. Systematic study has revealed that communities of lichens can be uniform over wide areas and lichenologists have developed names for the principal ones – *Lobarion, Graphidion, Usnion* and *Xanthorion*. Dormancy is the lichens' main armour but they do need moisture to photosynthesise let alone reproduce, hence the relativity of the dryness referred to as a factor on these woodland upper edges. Indeed the comparative richness of the lichen flora on Dartmoor's tors, walls, tree trunks, heather twigs and ground surface is in any case partly attributable to its southwestern position and the concomitant oceanic (Atlantic, Lusitanian – what you will!) influence upon it. That fact is relevant on many sides of the general consideration of Dartmoor's uniqueness. Crustaceous lichens inevitably appear to dominate drier natural granite surfaces, as on walls and roofs in farmsteads and villages, and they include *Lecanora* and *Ophioparma* species, *Fuscidea cyathoides* and the map lichen *Rhizocarpon geographicum,* but fruticose and foliose species are all there on appropriate faces. The *Umbilicaria* of the last of those three general growth forms may be the most spectacular plants present on the highest, most remote and thus more pristine tors like High Willhays and Fur Tor. At the Bench Tor level on the dampest faces the 'rock tripes' *Lasallia pustulata* whose convoluted glutinous grey-brown splodges are less than attractive to many, but catch the eye. Lichens, especially the Usnion community, are notoriously

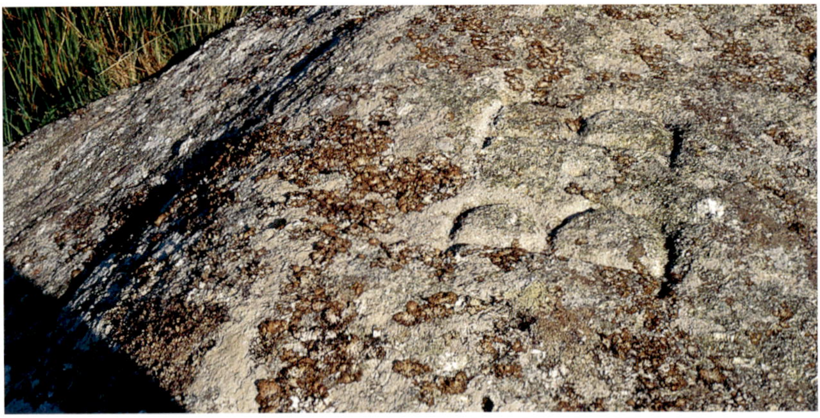

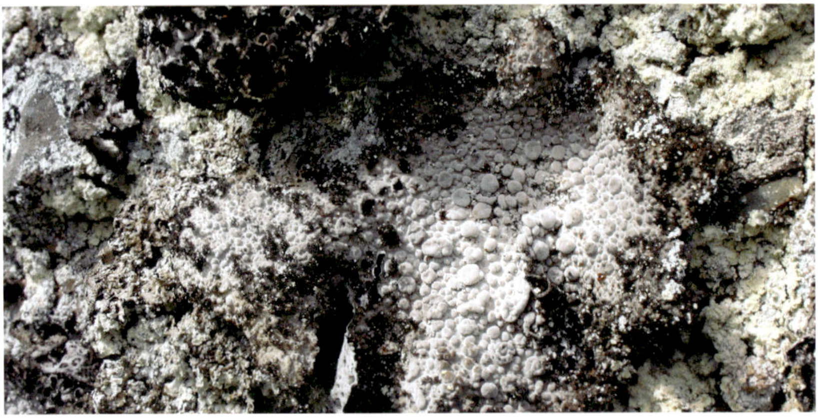

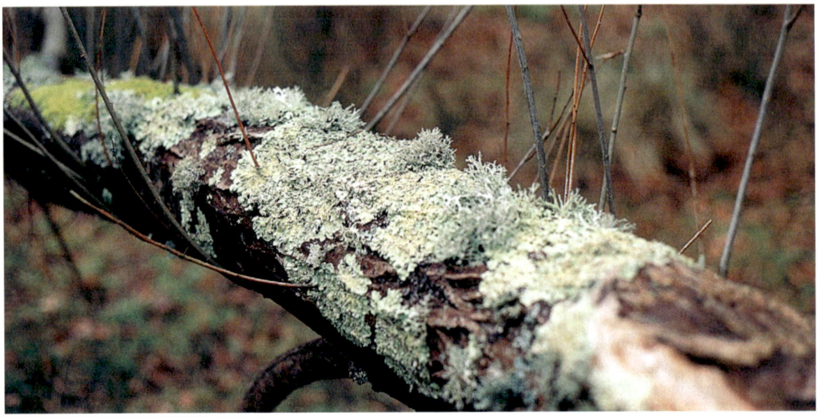

FIG 123. Lichen habitats: (facing top) Granite boulder – Broad Rock, on the southern forest boundary; (facing middle) rock tripe on Hay Tor (DNPA); (facing bottom) horizontal bough of tree in Whiddon Park; (left) *Usnea*-festooned hedgerow tree above Dartmeet.

sensitive to atmospheric pollution and while a southwestern position in these islands helps greatly in that respect there is a faint 'plume' of gases and particulate pollution northeastwards from Plymouth city, lying close to the southwest of Dartmoor, and feeble though it may be by industrial conurbation standards, it has its effect. Northern and eastern Dartmoor are most remote from it and thus most favoured. Places like Okehampton and Whiddon Deer Parks, whose ancient trees are home to as good a collection of lichens as in any English park, demonstrate the certain benefits of their geographical position. Whiddon Park has 163 species on its trees, the Lobarion and Usnion communities dominating.

High-level oakwoods

The high point of any survey of Dartmoor's woodland even of its oakwoods, in more senses than one, has to be the consideration of the three small woods referred to in the first paragraph of this section. Wistman's Wood is the best known and the most easily accessible – about 1.6 km on a public footpath from Two Bridges. Black-a-Tor Beare (or Copse), on the West Okement, is the highest and biggest – perhaps four times bigger than Wistman's at some 14 ha compared with 3.5 ha – and reaching 450 m OD. Piles Copse on the Erme in the extreme south is the lowest – its downstream end is only 260 m above sea level – but taking the whole area of each wood they overlap each other on an altitudinal scale. Nevertheless they are still well below the best guess at a maximum tree line in the postglacial period referred to in Chapter 3, and it is fair to point out that a number of other oakwoods reach the height in the landscape covered by the lower end of their range. Not far downstream of Blach-a-Tor Beare a tiny wood on the Isle of Rocks and Halstock Wood in the next valley, the East Okement, are the nearest to it reaching that height.

The historic written record, such as it is, describes Wistman's Wood's trees as low, stunted and contorted and to an extent that is still the impression given to a first-time visitor (Fig. 124). It is also a reasonable description of the trees at the

FIG 124. Contorted oaks in Wistman's Wood. (C. Tyler)

FIG 125. Interior of Piles Copse; much straighter stems than in Wistman's Wood.

upstream and upslope edges of the other two, but most of their trees are not so low (average height in Black-a-Tor is 8.5 m, and is Piles 7.5 m, compared with a Wistman's average of 4 m). Neither are they so stunted or contorted (Fig. 125), and some in Wistman's are straighter and slightly taller now than were seen in the nineteenth century for instance. Wistman's and Black-a-Tor are on steep slopes, in a dense clitter of very large boulders but with substantial amounts of humus between the boulders and on some of their level surfaces – while Piles Copse is on the valley floor with fewer rocks. All are on the west- or southwest-facing side of their respective valleys and all are close to good-sized streams – in the Dartmoor context. All have rich moss, liverwort, lichen and fern ground and epiphytic flora, though Wistman's is the richest, and all have at least one understorey shrub – rowan. Wistman's and Piles have holly too, and Wistman's boasts a few willows.

All have rich moss, liverwort, lichen and fern ground and epiphytic flora, though Wistman's is the richest. Dominating the boulders are the mosses already listed but with *Thuidium tamariscinum* and the leafy liverwort *Scaparia gracilis* joining them. Amongst all this are spectacular cushions of the fruticose lichen *Sphaerophorus globosus* and on steeper faces long pendant branches of the beard lichen *Usnea flammea*. Prominent on the tree trunks is the large foliose lichen *Hypotrachyna* (=*Palmelia*) *laevigata* confined to high rainfall areas of western British uplands. The branches of the oaks are equally eye-catching, draped with long festoons of another beard lichen *Usnea articulata* like strings of grey sausages. This rich epiphytic growth has been described by many botanical visitors and H. N. Dixon described a spectacular moss *Antitrichia curtipendula* 'as growing nowhere more finely in our islands than in Wistman's Wood, Dartmoor, where it clothes the limbs of old and stunted oaks with large masses, hanging down to a length of a foot or more and producing fruit in abundance'. The moss has not been seen for at least 20 years, and the explanation may well be something to do with atmospheric pollution even up here. The 'plume' from Plymouth under the southwest wind has Wistman's right in its track. A similar fate seems to have befallen the 'hair' lichen *Bryoria smithii* (a Red Data Book entry), though it still hangs on in Black-a-Tor Beare.

Apart from their intriguing appearance and atmosphere of mystery to the lay visitor for centuries – even the name 'Wistman' implies that – they present more enquiring observers now with more than one problem. The most obvious one is about their isolation, involving ancillary questions about origin and survival, and that is made more complicated by the second, which is the fact that they share a single species of oak, the English oak, as their sole canopy tree. In all the other oakwoods in the national park although the English oak is present, the sessile oak and hybrids between the two share dominancy, and other tree species are present. Black-a-Tor Beare is the closest of our three to the 'edge' woodland, and the Isle of Rocks, already mentioned and less 1.5 km downstream from it, has the English oak at its upper end, the sessile oak at its lower and hybrids in between (Fig. 126). Perhaps significantly, it also straddles the granite/aureole boundary, and one question has to be: does the sessile oak do better than the English oak on the slightly less acid metamorphic rocks?

As to origin and survival it is only possible to rehearse the obvious theories. The three woods may be remnants of the original woodland cover in successional terms. It was at its likely greatest extent at 6,000 BC according to the pollen record but sadly it is not possible to separate the pollen of the two oak species, so there is no confirmation through species presence of the remnant theory. The fact that two are in dense and massive clitter is suggested as the answer to survival in the face of, first, prehistoric and historic clearance (for tin smelting purposes) – i.e. why bother? Why take the risk of broken limbs that far? And second, sheep grazing of seedlings and browsing of saplings more recently. There is of course equally dense clitter on other west-facing slopes without trees at all, and sheep do browse seedlings now in all three woods. Piles Copse would have to be the exception that proves the rule in any case. The idea that they may have had some religio-ceremonial function or a sacred quality connected with their peculiarity and remoteness, given survival thus far, partly revolves round the name Wistman or Whishtman, both Anglo-Saxon references to the Devil or at least the supernatural – but what then of the other two? It has even been suggested that they may have been planted, for cover in a hunting chase early in

FIG 126. Black-a-Tor Beare alongside the West Okement; the Isle of Rocks is discernible downstream.

historic time, or on a landscaping whim when sessile oak was out of fashion at the turn of the eighteenth and nineteenth centuries, with which such ring counts as have been made on Wistman's timber strangely coincide. The Duke of Cornwall still owns two of them – his early predecessors were the huntsmen. Later a Duke or his bailiff may have been whimsical enough to want to add to the scene and there are records elsewhere of nineteenth-century landowners having trees planted in extremely rocky sites at altitude at what must have been relatively great cost, at Malham Tarn House in the West Riding for instance. But it seems a thin argument in all three sites, thinner for Black-a-tor Beare and Piles than for Wistman's, given its proximity to the heart of the Duchy's Dartmoor fiefdom and its nineteenth-century headquarters. In one case, Black-a-Tor Beare, there are written references to the extraction of timber and underwood in the sixteenth century. Although they refer in part to a fine for illegal activity in the Forest they must be something of a counter to a fearful characteristic in what was still a hugely superstitious time.

Ian Simmons, to whom reference has already been made, points out that all three woods are within extensive, but also isolated, stands of bracken. We have already seen that bracken is a choosy plant as far as soils go, and Simmons wonders whether the bracken is an indicator of the earlier extent of the woodland under which acid brown earths would be developed. There is photographic evidence, just to complicate the story further, that Wistman's Wood had begun to extend itself in the twentieth century and that that may be a resurrection of extension in receptive soils under, say, reduced grazing pressure at other times, rather than a new phenomenon (Procter, 1980).

Simmons also points out that modern evidence suggests that the English oak is just a bit hardier than the sessile oak, and may have arrived earlier in what was to become Britain in the postglacial period. Certainly oak arrived here very soon after hazel and uniquely before other forest trees, it could well be that the relative proximity of the glacial refuges of the two oaks determined the status of the pioneer. That *Quercus robur* is present in the Pays Basque and northern Spain leads to the suggestion that it may have had periglacial refuges nearer to Dartmoor, even in more oceanic west Cornwall or in what is now an offshore location below modern sea level.

Whatever the real explanation of the origin and continuing existence of these three remote and tiny woods their story so far serves to remind us that Dartmoor, along with much English upland, has not always been the moorland oasis that now earns it its status in national landscape or public access terms, or its ecological status in Europe. In another sense they point up the relative immensity of that moorland space, add targets to its recreational qualities and certainly supplement the biodiversity of the whole complex that is the National Park's heartland.

CHAPTER 5

The Dartmoor Fauna in the Twenty-First Century

It is true that many moors are dominated by one or two, or even a single species of plant, and this inevitably restricts the numbers and diversity of animals in the community ... But the resident animals, interesting in themselves, are reinforced by others of widely ranging habits which cross or visit the moors.

L. A. Harvey, Dartmoor, 1953

Professor Harvey's discipline was zoology and while his authorship of the first New Naturalist volume about Dartmoor (from which this quotation is taken) demonstrated his impressive status as a rounded naturalist and Dartmoor devotee, his commentaries on the fauna of the 1950s must carry even more weight. He also readily acknowledges the aid he received in observation terms from well-known local mammal men of the day like H. G. Hurrell and all-rounders like Malcolm Spooner and his wife Molly. While he makes no generalisation about the other divisions of the landscape portrayed in this book's previous chapter as he does for the moorland quoted above, he spends enough time on the woodland fauna, especially the birds, to show how rich that collection of habitats is compared with the wide open spaces. His references to farmland are thin but he was deliberately concentrating, as most writers did then, on what was, quite properly, perceived as the individuality of Dartmoor – its moorland and remnant woods. It is certainly the case that the valley, and the National Park fringe, farmscape is less individual as a set of animal habitats when compared with the land abutting the Park and to that extent will take up only the space here that its unique structural features and their denizens justify. This book, nevertheless, is about the whole rural space that is the modern National Park in which all units of the landscape have a place, a scenic and ecological role to play and thus a fauna to be accounted for – man within it.

That of course sets its own challenge. How comprehensive can such a description be? The total species list for a 953 sq km-space in any part of the English countryside, if known, would fill a bigger book than this. What assumptions, therefore, must be made? About selection; about significance; about the proper contribution made by any one animal community to the immediate ecosystem in which it sits and to the wider ecosystem that encompasses that?

That last is part of the methodological answer to the challenge. The community is more important than the individual. Its ecosystem – that which provides it with a home, a range and many living relationships – may be revealed to us as a significant component of a whole habitat. The habitat is itself a distinctive contributor to our perception of the place where we are standing in the Dartmoor landscape. Some characteristics of that animal community may hit us in the face, others will appear as we silently stand; but we may have to sit or kneel and scratch about to put more of the jigsaw together. So, we will proceed on the basis that the last chapter gave us the structural frameworks for Dartmoor animal habitats; and that there is still a 'pyramid of numbers', or at least of volume in biomass terms. Like Davis's age-old geomorphological truth, that pyramid is an ecologically old-fashioned but an unashamedly useful way of organising our thinking about any ecosystem. In that pyramid, plants provide the huge ground floor, the grazers or vegetarians the very large first floor and *their* controlling carnivores and omnivores the next. The top carnivores deal with them, and they are joined by top omnivores (because we have to count ourselves in the grand ecosystem) who affect all of the layers, both occupying the peak of the pyramid. Then we have a formula for looking at the animals of Dartmoor with due economy but not missing anything that matters in these days of local, national and international biodiversity policy and its action plans.

As with plants, what matters to many in that context is, of course, any distinctively Dartmoor species, and especially those rare in both the local and the national scenes. Rarity, as a measure of effort to be expended by the conservator, can be a worrying concept especially at the edge of an animal's range. What is rarity when applied near the south coast of an offshore island, if the species involved, say red-backed shrike or Cetti's warbler, is common across the strip of water separating that island from the mainland? Perhaps, if science really does consist simply of physics and stamp collecting, rarity is only the proper interest

FIG 127. (above left) High brown fritillary; (above right) caterpillar depends on violets and thus bracken and pony trampling. (C. Tyler)

of the collector. But biodiversity, in the quasi-political sense at least, must encompass the rare, and the welfare of the rare may well become an indicator of success or otherwise in a nature conservation world. There is also much to be said for the premise that if conditions continue to favour the rarity, they are likely to be favourable for all its natural companions too, though beware innocent habitat management moves that have not calculated every potential consequence in advance. If the predators of ground-nesting birds' chicks are also controlling baby rabbit numbers the conservator may have a dilemma to resolve about the structure of the habitat, if resolvable it is.

All this is important before attempting the faunal overview of Dartmoor in the twenty-first century because in this landscape man's touch on the moorland, since its Bronze Age creation, has been of the lightest in the whole spectrum of agricultural activity. That touch still maintains what is to many the habitat framework that personifies Dartmoor – the complex that is the whole moorland – and therefore man and his animals must be included in the Dartmoor pyramid of numbers and in the analysis of the gross ecosystem. The habitat for the high brown fritillary *Argynnis adippe* may be an accident as far as the grazing motive of the hill-farmer is concerned, but their (farmer and motive) relationship may be a key factor in sustaining that population of butterflies among the sheep, cattle and ponies and the rest of the resident wildlife (Fig. 127). The number of cowpats determines the numbers of beetles that are key components of the diet of foxes, starlings and kestrels at particular times of the year. The scrape of a pony's hoof at the edge of a mire gives a pale butterwort seed a chance it might not otherwise get and there will lie the fate of many an insect – the wool of a Scotch Blackfaced ewe on a rubbing rock can end up as readily in a wheatear's nest as in that of a raven.

THE MOORLAND ANIMALS

The grazers or biters of heather occupy a huge range. It runs from tiny heather beetle larvae *Lochmaea suturalis*, through red grouse and lambs in spring, cattle in any winter, to ponies in hard winters when heather pokes through the snow while grass lies under it. Within that spectrum are more spectacular beasts like emperor moths and their caterpillars. The emperor moth *Saturnia pavonia* is somehow the symbolic insect of heather moorland, the caterpillars start out small, black and orange but develop into large bright-green animals with black rings bearing orange knobs both warty and bristly. Its parents are also large for open country moths, having fawn-grey wings with large dark 'eyes' on both pairs, though the male's underwing may be largely orange, as may the tips of its forewings (Fig. 128). Male emperor moths fly by day and rapidly, and that is how they are commonly seen in mid-summer. They can detect a female's 'scent' or pheromone up to 2 km away, but the females in their turn are not very strong fliers and are more active at night. Despite the bright colours of the caterpillar and the size and striking patterns of the adults, neither is seen easily at rest and the caterpillar inevitably skulks low in the heather for fear especially of cuckoos *Cuculus canorus* for whom caterpillars are a favourite food in the time off from parasitising meadow pipits

FIG 128. Emperor moths mating. (C. Tyler)

FIG 129. Meadow pipit feeding cuckoo fledgling. (C. Tyler)

Anthus pratensis. Professor Harvey's description of the emperor moth's cocoon is worth quoting for its own sake but also as a sample of his own writing:

> the cocoon is spun in the cover beneath the heather tops, and is an elaborate affair of closely woven brown silk and incorporating bits of heather twig and leaf. One end is left open for the emergence of the imago, but the opening is guarded by a cheval de frise of stiff silken points which converge outwards to form a conical valve easily enough pushed aside from the interior but firmly closed to intruders from the outside.

The gingery brown fox moth *Macrothylacia rubi* is more common than the emperor, but smaller, less patterned (though with two pale stripes parallel with the trailing edge of the wing at rest) and thus less conspicuous than its close cousin, the slightly larger oak eggar *Lasiocampa quercus*. The larvae of both feed on heather but the latter ranges more widely and its 'woolly' size means that it is often seen crossing paths with a humping gait at a fair speed. The larvae of a number of micro-moths live on grass stems, biting them near ground level and living their larval lives in tunnels in basal tussocks. The grass moths *Crambus pratella* and *Caleptris pinella* are common, the latter quite liking cotton grass as

FIG 130. Marsh fritillary on southern marsh orchid. (C. Tyler)

well as the real grasses around it. The caterpillars of a number of butterflies are also grass feeders on the moorland, meadow brown *Maniola jurtina*, hedge brown (or gatekeeper) *Pyronia tithonus* and small heath *Coenonympha pamphilus* are commonest. Marsh fritillary *Eurodryas aurinia* caterpillars feeding colonially on devil's bit scabious, in and at the edges of damper sites, represent one of the species most threatened nationally and for which Dartmoor is one of the few remaining happy places (Fig. 130) The narrow-bordered bee hawk moth *Hemaris tityus* is in a similarly precarious position in the same sites and intriguingly its larvae also feed on devil's bit scabious (Fig. 131). Have we a race to the finish here? Two butterflies which do not yet cause alarm in biodiversity camps are the grayling *Hipparchia semele* and the green hairstreak *Callophrys rubi* both of which prefer drier ground (Fig. 132), the latter especially favours those carrying bilberry stands; perhaps their status and their preferences are connected.

FIG 131. (above left) Narrow-bordered bee hawk moth; (above right) caterpillar feeds on devil's bit scabious and thus potentially competes with marsh fritillary caterpillars. (C. Tyler)

FIG 132. Green hairstreak, enjoys bilberry stands on drier slopes. (C. Tyler)

The most significant other insect biter of heather after the emperor moth caterpillar is the tiny grub of the heather beetle. Recent experience suggests that there are population explosions of heather beetles the causes of which are not yet entirely clear. A high infestation of the larvae shows itself first by its effect on heather plants in early to mid-summer, the fronds appear to turn wholly to a rusty orange-brown colour, though careful examination will reveal some green still evident close to main stems. When widespread, as it was on Dartmoor in 2006 and again in 2008, the rusty colour is seen to be concentrated along road and path sides and round the edges of mature heather stands where they are adjacent to recent fire sites for instance. It seems that female heather beetles are weak fliers (is this a common female insect attribute on moorland?) and choose as open a flight path as possible. They can then penetrate the 'thicket' only so far. There they lay their eggs and so the hatchlings, lazier and even less agile than mother, feed on the heather shoots immediately available. In the process shootlets are ringed and thus starved of the stuff of green life, hence the very obvious colour change. The area affected in 2006, right across the moor, and up to 550 m OD on Great Links Tor for instance, was great enough to cause concern to commoners at the loss of winter feed, visits by the Heather Trust from its base in Dumfries and Galloway, and meetings devoted to the problem. A splendidly named ladybird *Coccinella hieroglyphica* feeds on the larvae (one a day), and a parasitic wasp *Asecodes mento* lays its eggs in them – in a 'good year' in almost every one. It is the best controller of heather beetles as pests that we have.

More invertebrate grazers exist on the moorland, though 'the whole insect fauna is not conspicuous for its variety' (Harvey) and none is so spectacular as the emperor moth, nor has such an obvious and immediate visual effect on the vegetation as the heather beetle. However, walking through heather and grassland habitats triggers the avoiding action of grasshoppers, almost spraying away from ones path, and that is likely to be the best evidence that plant biting is going on. The meadow grasshopper *Chorhippus parallelus* is the commonest shorthorn grasshopper of the drier grass moor, though a number of its cousins may also be around, and it is almost replaced on thicker peat with more sparse vegetation, as in recovering swaling sites, by the mottled grasshopper *Myrmeleotettix maculatus*.

The acid ambience of the open moorland means that shelled snail grazers are in short supply but the large black slug *Arion ater* is common enough in short-cropped grassland. While it varies in colour across its range it seems to be always black in the hills. Its close relation *Arion lusitanicus* is also present.

Of the smaller herbivorous mammals on moorland the short-tailed, or field vole *Microtus agrestis* (Fig. 133) is the commonest and certainly the most

FIG 133. (above left) Field vole ; (above right) long-tailed field mouse. (C. Tyler)

significant grass feeder, though it also eats the bark of dwarf shrubs and very young trees, it may also develop a taste for the roots of sedges and rushes, notably *Juncus squarrosus*. Its known altitudinal range in Britain over-tops Dartmoor but purple moor grass moorland is its highest comfortable habitat and although it prefers to feed on the basal stems of softer grasses it seems to survive where coarse stuff may be the only choice. It makes runways through dense grassland on and just below the surface, and is a serious component of the diet of all the open-ground bird predators and of foxes. Both bank voles *Clethrionomys glareolus* and long-tailed field mice (or wood mice) *Apodemus sylvaticus* share the edges of the short-tailed vole's general territory, especially at woodland/moorland boundaries and particularly where the latter is dominated by heather or other dwarf shrubs and bracken (Fig. 133). Bank voles also make surface runways but burrow more than short-tailed voles. Light snow often reveals the tracks and thus footprints of these small animals, and those of wood mice have been found on the high moor well away from their more favoured habitat. All these small mammal species appear to have a three- or four-year population cycle, with a steady increase in numbers to a climax followed by a crash as food supplies are overtaken. As the climax builds so predator numbers also increase, though there is little evidence that buzzards *Buteo buteo* (Fig. 134) and kestrels *Falco tinniunculus*, the only ones using our moorland consistently, lessen their territorial area at such times, allowing room for more pairs. In contrast, the passing harriers and short-eared owls may linger longer in spring and autumn in climax years. Hen harriers have at least one winter roost in the heather on the north side of Merripit Hill and their numbers may follow the small mammal ones upwards as even the off-season food supply grows.

Omnivores are not as rare among the small birds as one might suppose, and the skylark *Alauda arvensis*, the second most common breeding bird on the

FIG 134. Buzzard on the edge of White Wood. (C. Tyler)

moorland (more than 13,000 pairs in 2000 AD) is known to consume up to 45 per cent vegetable matter. While insects and other invertebrates are preferred when available and chicks are almost exclusively fed on animal material, still the fact that much of the plant matter is seeds means that the effect of these small birds on the vegetation mustn't be discounted (Fig. 135). The commonest breeder, the meadow pipit, eats fewer seeds but as autumn proceeds so they become a more significant part of the whole diet. Linnets *Carduelis cannabina* are the most common finches on the moorland proper, and like most seed-eaters eat insect larvae at times themselves and especially feed them to their nestlings and fledglings as exclusively protein-rich animal fare. Small flocks of starlings *Sturnus vulgaris* patrol the open moor from Whitsuntide onwards out of the

FIG 135. Skylark. (DNPA)

villages, but the flocks build in size as the season progresses and substantial roosts develop in small plantations, notably in 2006 within the military compound above Okehampton (Fig. 136). The omnivorous starling has a taste for the beetle larvae growing up happily in cowpats and performs a valuable manure scattering function as it deals with the mature to elderly pat.

FIG 136. Starlings over a popular roosting site near Okehampton. (C. Tyler)

FIG 137. Male wheatear. (DNPA)

Wheatears *Oenanthe oenanthe*, whinchats *Saxicola rubetra* and stonechats *S. torquata* are insectivores *par excellence* and take the range of adults and larvae that are within their handling capability. Dartmoor is the wheatear stronghold of southern Britain, the density of breeding pairs outweighing other uplands south of the Pennines by three or four times. Wheatears like rock to be around, especially on steep slopes, and often nest in holes in dry-stone walls and among clitter (Fig. 137). They range here from 213 m to 579 m in altitude, so on the western slopes of the northern moorland block with that densest of clitter, the population rises to 3.66 pairs per sq km. RSPB surveys on the whole north Moor (north of the scissor roads) in 2006, estimated a figure of 2.6 pairs per sq km. The total number of pairs revealed by a DNPA/RSPB survey in 1979 was 1,182; in 2006, the estimate for the north Moor was 550. Overall, all moorland

FIG 138. Whinchat. (C. Tyler)

insectivorous bird species have declined somewhat in the last 25 years. Whinchats seem to prefer sites with some bracken, though gorse can perform the 'lookout' function too (Fig. 138). Scattered bushes increase the attractiveness of the territory, but the combination explains to some extent the localised nature of the breeding population. Clusters occur in the Erme and Avon valleys, on Buckfastleigh and eastern Holne Moor, and at the head of the West Webburn below Birch Tor, so there is almost an eastern bias to the distribution. Stonechats reach higher numbers than whinchats, perhaps 1,500 pairs in good years compared with an estimate of 577 for their cousins, and the proportions are the same now. Stonechats are spread all around the lower slopes of the moorland block with a marked concentration on the commons around Widecombe and Haytor (Fig. 139).

FIG 139. Stonechat. (C. Tyler)

In many ways the most mysterious of our moorland edge insectivores is the nightjar *Caprimulgus europaeus*, long known in plantation clearings, now increasingly nesting in heather and under bracken notably on Holne Moor and clearly the scourge of moorland moths (Fig. 140).

Swifts *Apus apus*, swallows *Hirunda rustica* and sand martins *Riparia riparia* use the uncluttered sky-ways over moorland as good feeding spaces and obviously take a huge number of adult insects. Swallows and swifts need buildings to nest in, but the sand martin lives up to its scientific name on Dartmoor and, despite the lowness of the vertical banks on the outside of moorland stream meanders it has used them on the East and West Dart, at Postbridge, Bellever, Dartmeet and at Prince Hall; on the Cherry Brook and at Cadover Bridge on the Plym. When Duchy tenants used their roadside pits in the growan, and thus kept their faces sheer-sided, up to the 1990s say, sand martins found them reasonable nesting sites, but neglect of their old purpose and the increase in their new use as car parking places seems to have put paid to that. On a different scale a decent-sized colony has long used the abandoned faces of china clay pits at Lee Moor.

Up the bird size scale slightly, mistle thrushes *Turdus viscivorus* feed on the moorland edge, they too are omnivorous and take beetles, their larvae and those

FIG 140. Nightjar on Holne Moor. (C. Tyler)

of others, as well as the seeds and fruit that all the thrushes consume. In autumn and winter, fieldfare *T. pilaris* and redwing *T. iliacus* flocks join them and rowan and hawthorn berries are a staple as long as they last. But *the* breeding thrush of the moorland is of course the ring ousel *T. torquatus*, the large black thrush with a white bib. Its breeding on Dartmoor is now very localised – rocks, ruinous buildings and walls have a magnetic attraction for ring ousels. They appear to thrive in the steeper-sided moorland valleys, especially on the West Okement and in Steeperton gorge on the Upper Taw in the north, in Tavy Cleave and at Vitifer in the abandoned mining girts (deep, narrow vegetated excavations) and ruins just a little further south. A small population shared Merrivale Quarry with the quarrymen in the 1970s.

Taking together this specialised interest of ring ousels in steep slopes, cliffs and mining relics, sand martins in growan and china clay pits and wheatears in clitter, the ecological connection back to Dartmoor's geological, geomorphological and land-use evolutionary detail is as telling as the general link between the granite's altitude and acidity and its moorland cover. It is in its way as important to the Dartmoor story as the connections between the grazing of dwarf shrubs and rambling and military manoeuvres (long sight and easy walking), between short-cropped grassland and car parking and

FIG 141. Above Dartmeet; boulder density and ruins allow strenuous enjoyment.

picnicking, and those implied by the outdoor gymnasium provided by boulder-filled streams and ruined clapper bridges (Fig. 141).

But we must return to the animals. In any discussion of the 'lesser' carnivore level of the pyramid of numbers on the moorland the reptiles and amphibians must be included. Adders *Vipera berus* inevitably top this particular list and take invertebrates as well as their infamous predation of the eggs and

FIG 142. Adders mating – the male is bright grey. (DNPA)

young of ground-nesting birds. They will consume vole offspring if a nest offers them up. They are summer creatures and favour bracken and gorsey slopes facing south (Fig. 142). Frogs *Rana temporaria* are found all over the moorland and well into the blanket bog, they are common in mires and valley bogs and surprisingly large numbers are stumbled on well away from standing water. Their part in the control of invertebrate numbers must be a useful one. The common lizard *Lacerta vivipara* also has a complete altitudinal range as far as Dartmoor is concerned and deals competently with the smaller insects, adult and young.

A few waders still breed on the open moorland, but in the last 100 years Dartmoor has never been the kind of popular breeding ground where they would play a large part in the food chain that is the basis of this chapter. A very small number of golden plover *Pluvialis apricaria* and more dunlin *Calidris alpina* have bred on the blanket bog between Cranmere Pool and Cut Hill up to the present, some 14 pairs of the former and 10 of the latter were there in 1979 (Fig. 143). By 2000, golden plover had dropped to five territories but dunlin occupied 15, and reached 24 in 2007. At lower levels, curlew *Numenius arquata*, lapwing *Vanellus vanellus* and snipe *Gallinago gallinago* share the honours but numbers of the first two species have fallen dramatically in the last 50 years (Fig. 144). While such a decline has been countrywide and habitat loss in the in-country the usual guess at the reason, that cannot be the case to the same degree on Dartmoor. Curlew and lapwing were to be heard in most extensive valley bogs and mires in the 1960s, even if at the rate of only one pair each per bog, but now they seem to be confined to extreme eastern mires as at Halsanger and Bagtor newtakes. Despite the fact that moorland wader habitats have not been actually lost, there is some evidence that vegetation height may be just getting to, and

FIG 143. Golden plover (centre frame).

FIG 144. Curlew photographed in the 1960s – new nestling.

staying at, a level that discourages wader movement and feeding potential, at least on the higher moor. Although work done by the Duchy of Cornwall, to encourage lapwing particularly, on the Prison Farm and in Spaders Newtake by mowing and making wet scrapes has so far had little success, at least it has revealed winter roosting of lapwing flocks, a phenomenon not recorded before. Lapwing traffic between Princetown and the Teign estuary seems to be a feature of the winter season.

All these four species are largely invertebrate feeders, and although most of us know them from winter sightings on estuaries and thus of their mud-feeding techniques those bills, long or short, are sensitive tools and pick up the available larvae and adult beetles and grasshoppers quite easily. Snipe, again, have an eastern bias with clusters around Raybarrow Pool, on Gidleigh and Throwleigh Commons, around Vitifer, in Muddilake, along the Swincombe in the central basin and in those eastern mires again including Blackslade. In 2000, numbers surveyed were above the 1979 figures (120) at somewhere closing on 200 pairs, with more than ten different males heard drumming over Foxtor Mire in that year. So the snipe story is different from that of the other waders, snipe appear to be holding their own, and they of course feed entirely on animals. Perhaps they are more 'at home' the year round inland, and not, as with golden plover and dunlin at least, at the edge of their breeding range where rarity and annual variation is inevitable.

Moving up the size scale again, and back with the grazers, rabbits *Oryctolagus cuniculus* and red grouse *Lagopus lagopus* must come next (Fig. 145). Rabbits were encouraged historically by men from the early Middle Ages onwards, on Dartmoor by the building of warrens – usually long, low mounds of rocks and soil, and the trapping of their mammalian predators around those warrens. Warreners managed the construction, protection and harvesting of the rabbit colonies and place-name reference to the activity is widespread across the Moor, from Ditsworthy Warren and others in the Plym valley to Headland Warren below Birch Tor. The whole industry will be referred to again in Chapter 7. Short-cropped grassland is the rabbits' favourite location and indeed partly of their making, certainly their maintenance. While the dense rabbit population of most of Devon crashed in the mid-1950s as *myxomatosis* took its toll, that of Dartmoor's open moorland held up remarkably and it was suggested that the better ventilated homes whether in artificial warren or tor-and-clitter may have at least inhibited the transmission of the disease through the population. Young rabbits are a favourite food of buzzards and foxes, and badgers will dig out nests of the very young, so perhaps those predatorial populations benefited also from the 'healthier rabbits' of this moorland

FIG 145. Red grouse nest in purple moor grass in the 1970s.

terrain. Warrening is no longer, but rabbits are caught for human consumption still, sometimes by long netting involving a few people's co-operation, more often as a solo operation. Before the *myxomatosis* outbreak rabbit was a serious component of the human diet. The Plym valley warreners certainly had a ready market in Plymouth from the seventeenth century on, and evacuees from the South East in Second-World-War Moretonhampstead complained of its regularity on their menu, being a meat they had not met before. Closely related brown hares *Lepus capensis* are not common on Dartmoor perhaps because they prefer the juicier stuff of man's crops rather than coarse vegetable matter from upslope acid soils. Sightings of hares tend to be at the fringe of the moorland as though out for exercise from a farmland base rather than for serious grazing.

The staple food of red grouse is young heather shoots so without heather there will be no grouse. Numbers on Dartmoor have never been high since the introduction of the birds in the early nineteenth century, and no serious organisation of shooting has ever taken place, despite more than one release of 100 pairs (each time) in the first half of the twentieth century. A number of those surveys of birds of the high moorland from 1979 to 2000, referred to already, yielded numbers of pairs between 57, of which 24 were confirmed as breeding in 1979, and 30 territories in 2000, but scattered over probably 50 different localities, of which a dozen were in the southern plateau and the rest well into the northern moor except one pair under Birch Tor where a cock was calling in 2006. In the same year, a party of 11 birds were flushed by the author near Ockerton Court, near Cranmere Pool, in mid-summer – so breeding is still going on. Black grouse *Tetrao tetrix* on the other hand, although considered to be native, were thought to be declining as long ago as the eighteenth century. Despite the afforestation expansion of the 1920s – giving them more ideal conditions of shelter and food (young conifer shoots) – and the release of some new stock, numbers continued to decline and the species is now thought to be extinct on Dartmoor. Leks, or breeding male displaying sites, existed on Assycombe Hill at the edge of Fernworthy plantation, Merripit Hill and near Bellever within the last century, the last being active until the end of the 1940s. Blackcock were regularly seen at the head of the Plym in the same time span, sometimes moving around to take in Nun's Cross and Foxtor newtake. Single sightings have been made at a wide scatter of localities right up to the late 1990s, which at least suggests that there are still some mysteries attached to the occurrence of these grazing birds. Grouse bird predators are not breeding on Dartmoor now, but foxes almost certainly take some chicks. Men, as miners, probably poached black grouse, and as foresters tried to protect the youngest shoots of their new spruces by shooting the last of the central Dartmoor population.

FIG 146. Fox cubs outside lair in abandoned tin workings.

Foxes and badgers are the only mammal predators other than buzzards and us. Foxes are seen regularly, usually in lone sightings. They breed right across the moorland – tors, clitter and miners' excavations offering numerous ideal sites for lairs (Fig. 146). The 'countries' of five hunts converge on Two Bridges, but since the ban on normal fox control a good idea of numbers is hard to come by. Some farmers claim to see more foxes together now, rather than the traditional loner of 1,000 years' observation. The omnivorous badger is not a moorland resident of any widespread status, but ranges well out on to the moor from woodland and farmland setts, and is adept at digging out rabbit and smaller mammal nests as well as taking eggs and chicks from ground birds' nests stumbled across.

And so we come to the major moorland grazers, the big mammals, without whom there would probably be little or no moorland – a fact we should remember as this tale goes on. The vast majority of the numbers involved belongs to, and is cared for, by hill-farmers. Until the last few decades that caring was not an altruistic operation. It was admittedly a way of life if it was to be successful, ever since softer agricultural alternatives were developed in lower country, say 2,000 years ago. But its industrial psychology was based on an economic exercise, bolstered in social terms since 1946 by ever-evolving public support: from the hill cow subsidy of that year to the Hill Farming Allowance (HFA) which in 2008 is being reviewed, probably for the last time. We must

FIG 147. Cattle are important grazers of all Dartmoor's moorland components; here black cattle tackling a grass mosaic on Dunnabridge Common.

FIG 148. South Devons and Belted Galloways concentrate on a recent fire site – Scotch Blackfaced sheep and ponies prefer the short-cropped grass.

consider that in a deeper discussion about agriculture not long hence, but it explains the continuing existence in this century of a breed of men and women living at altitude as graziers and ensuring that the grazers, their stock, are still there in some numbers, though much diminished from those in the 1980s. Sheep, cattle and ponies graze, between them, all the vegetation types that have been described in the last chapter except pure bracken stands, though there are records of animals developing a penchant for very young bracken shoots with unhappy consequences. Grass invaded by bracken often provides a small store of palatable grass, useable as the bracken fronds die in the autumn having been difficult to access when the bracken was at full spread, which may account for heavier densities of grazing observed in that community on some occasions. Cattle, especially the real upland breeds – Galloways and Highland Cattle, and sheep wander up on to the blanket bog in high summer but ponies do not necessarily follow them in numbers. Happily however, the three species do complement each other's favourite feeding in early summer, and as a last resort in hard winters. They are jointly responsible therefore not only for the generality of 'moorland' in which nothing of any significance except bracken and gorse is much above knee height and a good deal well below that, but also for the maintenance of the fascinating mosaic of plant communities with which that generality is vested. That we can walk in short order from close-cropped turf starred with tormentil into tussocky bristle bent, and out the other side into almost exclusive heather or equally singular western furze, then downslope into a sea of purple moor grass through which to slide into a valley mire edge of rushes and sedges is, from day to day, a grazing phenomenon. On the mid-altitude slopes Scotch Blackface ewes and lambs jockey with Belted Galloways and big ginger-brown South Devon cows (Fig. 148), ignoring the Dartmoor Hill ponies a pace or two away, all selectively biting their choice of the season. The sheep like the already-short stuff but are equally responsible for the fact that a huge number of 1 m-high gorse bushes are pruned in the winter into a mediaeval bee skep shape, something like a wigwam, all over this level of the moorland. From June onwards purple moor grass tussocks appear to have been sheared by the best Sheffield could offer as cattle bite them so tidily, and ponies bite the heart out of every matt grass tuft having yanked the rest of the matt itself out and discarded it, for us to find as scattered tiny bundles of thin straw with right-angle bends.

 It is incredibly difficult to make estimates of the numbers of the three species actually grazing open moorland in 2008, let alone attach much credibility to historic figures. The latter were probably informed guesses or extrapolations from samples counted out there, or given to the 'recorder' by farmers in different

FIG 149. Close-pruned western furze on Merripit Hill.

parts of the Moor. In modern times many farmers still regard their actual stock numbers as their business alone, and the demands of government and European Union 'agri-environment' schemes involving grazing densities only serve to confuse matters. At the simplest level of confusion non-grazing farmers, who nevertheless have a right to graze, have been entitled to participate in such schemes and be compensated for not grazing (which they weren't anyway). The numbers of relevant stock, whether grazing or not, thus appear in totals kept by official bodies and are even published. To compound the problem of calculation further, many rights were registered under the 1965 Commons Registration Act as for the grazing of 'livestock units' in which one cow or bullock, one pony, but five sheep each equalled one unit. While useful for calculations of ideal grazing densities, such a formula conveniently hides the numbers of the three species involved for the owner, to the despair of the analyst of their ideal combination for maintenance of a particular plant-cover mosaic.

In 1808, Vancouver reported that 'on the commons belonging to the parish of Widdecombe [sic] (and Buckland) in the month of October last there were estimated by gentlemen residing in the neighbourhood to be no less than 14,000 sheep, beside the usual proportion of horned cattle'. Those commons now total some 1,032 ha, so the sheep alone would have provided two livestock units per hectare. What 'the usual proportion (of horned cattle)' involves is anyone's guess and although then most cattle were probably only there from May to October, they would certainly have increased the grazing density substantially in a year-round count. Vancouver admits there and then that:

> the number of sheep summered and kept all the year round upon Dartmoor, the depasturable parts of which in a dry summer is one of the best sheepwalks in the kingdom, is not easy to ascertain, but if any inference can be drawn from Widdecombe and Buckland in the Moor, their numbers must be very considerable indeed.

In 1963, during the latter part of a notoriously hard winter, the numbers for 'Dartmoor' were estimated by MAFF as 40,000 sheep, 5,000 cattle and 2,000 ponies – and the spokesman claimed that that indicated a grazing density of one livestock unit to eight acres (3.2 ha), which suggests that MAFF was counting moorland newtakes as well as common land in its density calculation. It was of course the condition of ponies that made the news at that moment and although those figures were announced in Parliament, three estimates for pony numbers had been published locally only a fortnight earlier (Fig. 150). The Dartmoor Commoners' Association said 2,000, the RSPCA estimated 3,000 to 4,000 and the Horses and Ponies Protection Association thought 6,000. That MAFF and the Commoners agreed may be significant, and charities have to boost their story in any case to stay in business.

FIG 150. Dartmoor hill ponies above the Cowsic.

In 1997 the Agricultural Development Advisory Service (ADAS) produced some figures that suggested that there had been a substantial increase in the cattle herd and the sheep flock on Dartmoor between 1952 and 1996 – thus straddling the 1963 statement just quoted. In 1996 it was estimated that there were just over 20,000 beef cattle and 130,000 ewes on the moor and that these represented nearly ten-fold increases over the period which, by counting back, indicates fairly low figures for the 1950s, even compared with Vancouver at the turn of the eighteenth century. But they also suggest a rapid rise into the 1960s presumably as support for farming continued to improve, if the 1963 numbers are valid. Even then, that sheep numbers more than trebled and cattle headage quadrupled in the next 30 years suggests that fairly important changes in the vegetation would have been triggered. The 1996 figures equal 46,000 livestock units and thus 1.3 units per hectare or nearly three times the grazing density 33 years earlier. Pony numbers are not included, such numbers were estimated again at 2,000 in the early 1980s for the NPA, and thought to be nearer 1,500 in 2006, when fortunately the pony trade started to pick up, and there was every hope that the population of true hill ponies would follow that trend.

Those still administering the Environmentally Sensitive Area (ESA) scheme in Dartmoor in the early part of the present century work on the basis of 0.225 units per hectare in the summer and 0.17 in the winter on dwarf shrub stands, and 0.365 in the summer and 0.23 in the winter on acid grassland as ideal densities for the maintenance of vegetation already in a healthy state, with lower densities for those areas where 'restoration' is the priority. They also estimate that only 9,000 livestock units of sheep and cattle were present in 2006 together with the 1,500 ponies already mentioned. A fall from 46,000 to 9,000 in ten years can only be described as a crash in animal population terms and not only reflects ESA formulaic dictat but also the ravages of the stock farming situation through those years in Britain as we shall see in Chapter 8.

The effect of the crash in stock numbers is already exercising those charged with managing the agri-environment schemes that are the medium for farmers in their turn to manage the moorland. Cattle numbers are currently too low to keep purple moor grass in proper check, and in the heathland mixtures or at the mutual edges of heath and grassland stands, heather is being suppressed by grasses. Short-cropped grassland, shared by the remaining sheep and the vast majority of human visitors, especially close to the road, is diminishing in area. A significant side effect of all this is the increase in fire risk in the winter or very dry summers, which are predicted to become the norm. While fire is a valuable tool in moorland management when properly used, in 'wildfire' terms it can do enormous damage immediately in the visual and biodiversity senses (Fig. 151). It

FIG 151. The morning after a wildfire above East Bovey Head in 1984. It ran from the Challacombe road across to the B3212. The wisps of smoke are because the arsonist tried again on his way to work – he was caught. One of the purest stands of ling on Dartmoor developed over the next decade.

can undo years of work geared to the restoration of some dwarf shrub communities, damage blanket bog irreparably if the fire gets into the peat, and sear the surface – even the sphagnum – of any valley mire in its path.

The other big mammals that graze Dartmoor moorland, though very occasionally, are deer. It is generally assumed that red deer *Cervus elaphus* arrive here having filtered southward across the lower Culm landscape from their southwestern stronghold in Exmoor, and some may drift across the Teign valley from Great Haldon and reach eastern islands of moor and perhaps the head of that valley. Moorland vegetation is not necessarily their favoured food, but root crops and kale are not common on high Dartmoor, woodland cover is thin except in the big plantations, but there edible shrubbery and grasses are confined to internal edges of clearings, at streamsides and along rides. Nevertheless odd stags and hinds are seen grazing in newtakes and have been accosted well out in open moorland, though then usually travelling to some purpose. Other species, notably fallow *Dama dama* and roe *Capreolus capreolus*, wander out of their valley woodland territories on occasion where moorland abuts the wood, but never go far from easy escape to cover.

FIG 152. Raven at nest full of fledglings. (Devon Wildlife Trust)

The large feral mammal adults, recently (2006) joined by wild boar *Sus scrofa*, escapees but breeding, have no predators but man. Their offspring, at least very young fawns, like lambs, are somewhat vulnerable to foxes whose diet also ranges down to earthworms (in short supply in peaty soils) and beetles, and to dogs out of control, which includes farm dogs that have gone native. Carrion, especially on roads and in early summer, is dealt with by crows *Corvus corone cornis* – and magpies *Pica pica* closer to enclosed land. Ravens *Corvus corax* too, do some clearing up and specialise, to the extent of timing their nestling development, in the after-birth left by ewes after lambing (Fig. 152). They nested on many of the remoter tors until the middle of the last century but are now mostly confined to woodland and scattered tree sites largely at the edge of the moor proper. Buzzards, already mentioned, will also consume carrion and the placentas of sheep and ponies. In latter years peregrine falcons *Falco peregrinus* have re-established themselves in abandoned quarries around the Dartmoor edge from which they range far and wide over the Moor, taking wood pigeons *Columba palumbus* and jackdaws *Corvus monedula* in flight as they find them, though they will take anything of that size and smaller that moves in the air and on the ground if it is foolish enough to expose itself.

THE ENCLOSED LANDSCAPE

The moorland edge, taken as the cornditch against the common and the inner wall of rough grazing newtakes where appropriate, abuts many more small fields than woods. Even counting the big plantations the physical length of that moor/field abutment is much greater than the wooded one.

The animal traffic across the mutual boundary is likely to be one way, not very dense, and from bases within the farmland. The cornditches were designed to ensure no hindrance to game returning to the Forest and a one-way direction as far as domestic mammals were concerned with their sheer stone face to the common and a ramped earthen slope up from the field surface. Farmers didn't really mind their own animals getting on to the Forest, but needed to prevent its domestic grazers entering their fields. Where it still exists that inner ramp of course has become a ready site for rabbit and badger excavation, and the whole thing lost its original commons boundary stock-holding efficacy when Scotch Blackfaced sheep were introduced in the nineteenth century. Their leaping ability (or 'saltatory propensity', as a judge in Okehampton County Court once described it when faced with a decision about responsibility for trespassing sheep from the common) demanded posts and wire on the cornditch summit if the age-old rule that any sole occupier of adjacent land had to fence 'against the common' was to be sustained (Fig. 153).

FIG 153. Cornditch above Moretonhampstead Moorgate on Shapley Common. The profile of the cornditch is clear inside the right-hand field. The modern need for a fence atop the bank as proof against the common is well shown.

Sheep or rabbit, the grazing is better in the small field than on the moor, the soil is considerably more accommodating of invertebrates than the peaty soil outside even if that improvement is only due to 1,000 years or more of enrichment by concentrated stock and application of lime, manure from the yard and occasional aeration by their overseers. The fields vary, as we have seen, and the two permanent grassland extremes – given that the arable acreage has shrunk to a few hundred hectares of kale, roots and a little grain near the edge of the national park – are hay meadows and the rush-and-purple moor grass pastures adjacent to valley mires and on some western wet slopes. The former, as must be expected, have the richer collection of plant eaters from the larvae of the butterflies and moths that relish the flowers in due season through the abundant grasshoppers to the small mammals, all well protected from their predators by the developing height of the grass-for-hay crop as the summer progresses. The

FIG 154. Barn owl. (C. Tyler)

latter, the rhos pastures of the conservation vocabulary, are also described in the biodiversity literature as species-rich and in season they will seem so, but a strict botanical or zoological comparison between the best neutral hay meadow and best wet pasture does not yet exist. Given the decline of many wet meadow invertebrates in southern England, Dartmoor rhos pastures have assumed a new significance as strongholds for once much more widespread species. Chief among these are the marsh fritillary in Figure 130, a butterfly with over 40 colonies in Dartmoor sites or a fifth of the total known in England, the narrow-bordered bee hawk moth in Figure 131 and the double line moths *Mythimna turca*, the common blue *Enallagam cyathigerum* and the southern *Coenagrion mercuriale* damselflies and the mud snail *Lymnea glabra*. The snails and the larvae of all the moths and butterflies are the smallest grazers of rhos pastures, and themselves are prey to snipe, woodcock and now much-rarer lapwing, as well as birds from adjacent scrub like reed buntings, when feeding nestlings. Where purple moor grass is dominant the vegetarian vole population attracts barn owls *Tyto alba* all year round (Fig. 154), and short-eared owls *Asio flammeus* very occasionally pause to hunt over such stands on late summer and autumn passage.

The adult flying insects over both rhos pastures and hay meadows are prey to insectivorous birds if the field is close to the moorland or woodland edge and the moths especially are vulnerable to bats, of which the greater horseshoe bat

FIG 155. Grid over entrance to cave at Buckfastleigh allowing greater horseshoe bats in and out but denying cavers.

Rhinolophus ferrumequinum is by far the most significant in biodiversity assessment terms. Its Dartmoor breeding colony is based in caves at Buckfastleigh and feeding is fairly local (perhaps a 4-km radius) and thus confined to the farmed landscape in and outside the Park (Fig. 155).

Close to the same edge of the National Park two other rare omnivores occur: a few pairs of cirl buntings *Emberiza cirlus*, common until the mid-1960s, but now very scattered through South Devon, breed in the arc of farmland between Chagford and South Brent and while seeds constitute the bulk of the autumn and winter diet, insects, particularly grasshoppers, are relished and fed almost exclusively to the nestlings. Woodlarks *Lullula arborea* have the same recent history and share the same kind of territory, appearing to need a combination of grassland, bare ground and scattered trees. Insects dominate their feeding, caterpillars being the favourite food of the chicks, but seeds, commonly smaller than those the buntings prefer, have to be the staple of the back end of the year. The woodlark's song once heard is never forgotten and for many never bettered – nightingales shout in comparison. It is poured out from ground and tree, but characteristically continuous in a low circular slow orbit it is a real joy. With very short tails and a strenuous fluttering flight, woodlarks give an impression of feathered butterflies as they patrol their territory not far above one's head. Seen close to, the striking feature is a pale 'eye-stripe' that runs right round the head separating the crown and crest from the face and neck.

There is of course the expected population of farmland birds in this landscape, less now than of old, but most species still represented. The year round seed-eaters – yellow hammers *Emberiza citronella*, all the common finches including siskins *Carduelis spinus* in increasing numbers this century, are joined by bramblings *Fringilla montifringilla* in the winter just as the fieldfares and redwings join the resident thrushes in the hawthorns and rowans at the roadside. Robins *Erithacus rubecula*, wrens *Trogdolytes trogdolytes* and dunnocks *Prunella modularis* keep the low-level insects at bay, while great, blue, marsh, willow and long-tailed tits *Parus spp.* deal with the higher-hedge and hedgerow-tree populations. The scattered trees of the farmscape of the eastern half of the national park and its western fringes are patrolled by green and great spotted woodpeckers *Picus viridis* and *Dendrocupus major* and many nuthatches *Sitta europea*, but treecreepers *Certha familiaris* (Fig. 156) and lesser spotted woodpeckers *D. minor* are few and far between now compared with the numbers seen in the middle of the last century. Any of these birds may be prey to hedge-hopping sparrowhawks *Accipiter nisus* if they are unlucky enough to be in the wrong place at the wrong time, and the growing number of peregrines will take some, though the bigger vegetarians and omnivores, primarily wood pigeons and

FIG 156. Treecreeper. (C. Tyler)

jackdaws, even the odd pheasant *Phasisnus colchicus*, are more their style. There are still breeding stock doves *Columba oenas* on most farms, joined by eastern birds in the winter, and as many collared doves *Streptopelia decaocto* as anywhere else round buildings. Crows and magpies take their share of eggs and nestlings in farmland in season while scavenging generally the rest of the year.

Shrews *Sorex spp.* and hedgehogs *Erinaceus europaeus* are the commonest mammalian insectivores, mopping up beetles and innumerable larvae. The mole *Talpa europaeus* population is high and along with foxes, badgers and buzzards, regards earthworms as the most important protein easily available. While it 'mines' for them, the rest find them on the surface of well-grazed meadows during the night (the mammals) and in very early morning light, when all three species can be seen quartering the short grass at the right moment. As on

FIG 157. Roe deer fawn lying where mother told it to stay. (C. Tyler)

moorland, these three top carnivores all take young rabbits and dig out shallow hedgerow nests of blind babies – omnivorous badgers probably only manage a rabbit supper that way.

The biggest wild mammals of this walled and hedged countryside, as of the other components of Dartmoor's cover, are deer. Roe are seen in the open in the daytime more than any other, but fallow and increasingly muntjac and sika browse the brambles and the meadow grasses close to cover, very early and very late in the day. All need woodland to lie up in and will rarely be seen far from it (Fig. 157).

THE DARTMOOR WOODLAND FAUNA

The mutual boundaries between stands of vegetation are usually richer in animal life than the hearts of either stand, for two populations intermingle here and others specialise in the 'edge' location, sheltering on one side and feeding on the other for instance. The same is true at the component landscape scale, and the function and richness of the edge is enhanced by the mobility of its dependants in any one place. Thus walking around or along the edge of a woodland block allows a glimpse of a loose community of species different from that observable within the wood or well away from its edge outside it. We will deal with the animals in the order used in the descriptions of the woods themselves.

The conifer plantations' animals

The point about the edge community just made is almost more significant in the case of conifer woodland. For the outer edges, it is also complicated slightly by the fact that most plantations, even most woodland blocks in Dartmoor, have constructed boundaries. The high plantations especially were created in large existing newtakes whose original boundaries were granite dry-stone walls, and planting went right up to the wall. This has two effects, the edge is very sharp and the wall itself adds another potential dimension to the available habitat. Wrens for instance are great devotees of walls, almost confined to them in landscapes with no other shelter or cover, their mode of travel around and through them involving little apparent flight has led to the name *mousebrodir*, or mouse-brother, in bleak spaces like that of much of the Faroes. So even though the maturing plantation is not attractive to wrens they occur as sentinels of their linear territories at regular spacing along the boundary. Only under Bellever and Laughter Tors and well within the newtake plantation limits are there conifer edges without human interference between tree domination and grassland or heath. Here the Forestry Commission paused in its original planting, respecting the immediate setting of the tors and elsewhere of prehistoric artefacts.

Some plantation edges have lines of deciduous trees, often beech and thus decried as just as alien as the conifers by afforestation critics, but offering up a different population of insects as bird food and thus enhancing the edge community slightly. Many internal 'edges' also exist in the four biggest high plantations, and the ride sides and valley bottoms of Fernworthy and Burrator for instance have high rowan, sallow and alder numbers as avenues and groves. They, too, are now being carefully conserved by the forest managers, as they go through their first main harvest of pine, spruce and fir and then replacement planting, along with the encouragement of self-regeneration by at least the spruces. The sallows and alders especially are home to, and thus bitten by, a bigger variety of insects than the conifers. The sheltered position of these shrubs and small trees within the coniferous 'compound' adds yet one more quality to the high relative humidity of this habitat from the flying insect point of view. Not having to contend with the wind makes the feeding and courting of the lighter butterflies, moths, lacewings, damselflies, stoneflies, mayflies and caddis much easier (Fig. 158). Even the stronger dragonflies and the real heavyweights like longhorn and stag beetles, some of which are happy in both conifers and willows, find their, always spectacular, flights encouraged in this quiet air. Both Burrator and Fernworthy plantations wrap round the heads of substantial reservoirs (by Dartmoor standards) and in each case at least six streams flow

FIG 158. (above left) Damselfly; (above right) Black darter dragonfly. (C. Tyler)

through the wooded slopes. Each also has a considerable length of leat – the famous Devonport Leat in the Burrator case – and a long one from the East Dart towards the Warren House, or more likely to the Ancient Tenement of Walna, originally and then to the Vitifer tin workings. Woods always contain more humid air than the space immediately outside them, but this density of water in channels within and large bodies of it just down valley much enhances the whole habitat and accounts for both the alder/sallow groves and the high insect population, much of which depends upon water, running or still, for its larval stages. Bellever, having the East Dart briefly alongside and Soussons, flanked by a small tributary of the West Webburn, and each having only one tiny tributary within the respective wood are arid by comparison. In both, sallows are confined to the banks of the two rivers. Water and its contained life, comes to the fore in the next chapter but its role, especially imparting another dimension to the fauna of the woods, demands its reference here.

The larvae of the terrestrial insects in these sheltered sites within the plantations are mostly vegetarian and their chewing ranges from the leaves of the shrubs and small trees to the herbaceous plants and even the lichens, relatively abundant in the southwestern clean air. They sometimes reach pest proportions in the sallow thickets. They are preyed upon by other larvae and adult beetles and of course the birds. The aquatic larvae are all carnivorous, and

FIG 159. Golden-ringed dragonfly. (C. Tyler)

deal with their smaller cousins and much that falls in from the overhanging shrubbery. The dragonfly adults, such as the golden-ringed *Cordulegaster boltonii* (Fig. 159) catch other flying insects on the wing whether hawking on patrol or darting from vantage points (hawkers and darters are dragonfly groupings based on hunting technique) while damselflies who fly much less strongly tend to pluck resting prey off streamside vegetation. The snail and slug population grazes as efficiently here as out in the open, and the beetles try to keep them under control. Small insectivorous birds are relatively numerous in these special sites within the plantations; the ubiquitous robins and blue and great tits are rarely absent and their coal tit cousins and goldcrests *Regulus regulus*, both happier in the conifers, come down to help out with the scrubby insect crop; blackcaps *Sylvia atricapilla* and willow warblers *Phylloscopus trochilus* join them for the long season. Grey wagtails *Motacilla cinerea* stick close to the streamsides and swallows and sand martins skim along the sallow and alder fringe overhanging the reservoir and larger river edges taking anything on offer but certainly the adult mayflies and stoneflies emerging from the water surface.

Reference has already been made to the current state of the plantation cycle and it should be clear that this is the time when the long dull maturing of the conifer crop is replaced by relative excitement for the animals as large sheltered clearings are made, soil is disturbed and, among the newly planted crop, ground vegetation burgeons. Weed pioneers move in first, other wind-borne seeds arrive – and seed stored since the first conifer canopy closed warms up and germinates. Ling seed, for instance, can wait easily for a conifer cycle to run its course. So, those birds already listed suddenly have a potential expansion of territory from their damper oases, and are inevitably joined by other insect seekers such as grasshopper warblers *Locustella laevia* who really do like the combination of coarse grassy vegetation and low sapling tree-top perches in young plantation sites for its own sake. Others stay because the already much-vaunted edge effect is greatly increased while the wind is still kept out, so spotted flycatchers *Muscicapa striata* may hold territory from mid-May round many new plantings. The slightly bigger insectivore that revels in these new clearings, however, is the nightjar already seen to be a moorland-edge predator. The moth population is high, the wind is less and these exciting birds are rewarding birdwatching targets on a late summer evening. If grasshopper warblers and nightjars inhabit the same area, then anglers' reeling noises can last nearly all of the 24 hours.

It must now be clear that the irony of the plantations' contribution to the faunal characteristics of Dartmoor is largely to do with secondary considerations. So far we have only dealt with the spin-offs from the plantation structure and it is the case that conifer woods of the planted kind from the moment the low canopy closes through to maturity are not rich in animals. Three bird species, however, are almost certainly only breeding in this National Park because these plantations exist. Crossbills *Loxia curvirostra* and lesser redpolls *Carduelis flammea caberet* are vegetarians (Fig. 160). Crossbills are normally resident further north and east but after a good breeding season and then a poor spruce cone crop at home, the population irrupts and often lands in Dartmoor (and many other southwestern forests) in numbers, sightings of up to 200 have been not uncommon since the high Dartmoor plantations began to bear cones. If the crop

FIG 160. Lesser redpoll. (C. Tyler)

here then holds the birds, breeding often ensues in the next season because crossbills mate and build very early, from mid-winter through to early spring. Records of certain breeding are sparse not least because crossbills nest very high up in the densely needled canopy, and thus much more is suspected than is proven in most years. But in 1997 crossbills bred in Burrator, Soussons and Fernworthy and probably in Bellever. They are regularly encountered in the smaller conifer woods around the Kennick, Tottiford and Trenchford reservoirs, and at King's Wood and Dean Wood near Buckfastleigh. Lesser redpolls are much smaller birds (even smaller in Britain than in their Scandinavian stronghold) and devoted to middle-aged conifers for breeding, but happy feeding on alder and willow catkins as well as conifer seed. They were first recorded on Dartmoor in the 1950s, perhaps because the big plantations were then at their redpoll optimum. Up to ten pairs bred in Bellever at the height of the species' stay. When the conifers grow on redpolls abandon them and move, so there is almost a nomadic pattern that looks for different stages in the plantation cycle at different sites.

The third and very different and (almost exclusively) plantation breeder is the goshawk *Accipiter gentilis*, bigger cousin of the sparrowhawk and having nearly the length and wingspan (over 1 m) of a buzzard. Goshawks are still rare enough here to have nest sites protected by deliberate lack of publication, but since 1990 a small number of territories have been established. These secretive birds nest at least 10 m off the ground, well into the dense cover on offer, though the total area of the tree block involved may not be vast and often involves deciduous trees at its edge. The Dartmoor goshawks take mainly middle-sized birds as prey, omnivorous crows, magpies, jays and vegetarian woodpigeons primarily, but rabbit and grey squirrel remains have been found at local nest sites too.

Coal tits and goldcrests have already been noted as sharing the sallow lines and thickets from their preferred conifer bases. Their insect fodder in their favourite trees is in the canopy and along the edges, where light is best, and the other tits will help them out quite often. Aphids are their staple, especially *Adelges spp.* on pine and fir and *Elatobium abietinum* on Sitka spruce, all of which damage their tree hosts but rarely to excess. An occasional great spotted woodpecker may use rare nest holes in mature pines, spruces and tall-enough dead stumps near the edge, and feed on pine weevil larvae *Hylobius abietis* under the bark of such stumps and broken limbs. Mistle thrushes seem to like the geometry of the plantation edge pines for nest foundation, and the lookout/singing post which the prominent evergreen often provides, but feeding demands short-cropped grass close at hand. In the clearings and new plantings after harvest the vegetarian field vole and wood mouse populations quickly establish themselves and get into their familiar four-year boom-and-bust cycle. Tawny owls *Strix aluco* often then seize the chance, move in and settle for the

FIG 161. Tawny owl. (C. Tyler)

time being (Fig. 161). Old crow's nests can prove perfectly adequate for their breeding for what may not be a very long stay.

The deer species already identified as crossing and re-crossing moorland and fields may all spend long daylight hours lying up in the plantations and thus become the biggest animals in the forests. They, especially the fallow and red deer, will browse the brambles on the fringes and in the new clearings where they may not only bite the growing shoots of the little spruces but use the occasional sapling for territorial marking by 'fraying', scraping the bark with antlers so that it hangs off in strips. Roe stags often chase their latest hind in such tight circles that paths are worn in and around the clearings which they have adopted, quite distinct from the 'racks' or paths of their routine movements. Man is their only true predator and while there is no organised recreational shooting of deer on Dartmoor, the damage done proclaims populations which need management, and fallow especially are the subject of culling by stalkers working for and with deer control societies.

The denizens of the broad-leaved woods

Ninety per cent of the area of the native woods of the National Park is on steep and often rocky slopes and as we have seen that relationship is of very long standing, such that no other cover has intruded on the slope in question for a few thousand years. Thus the ground surface has only been disturbed by natural processes – downslope wash, tree fall and animal activity, except where man has made the odd track or platform or built a wall but, crucially, has never ploughed. Here is a shallow soil profile but with a thin tripartite zonation at the surface. Fresh autumnal leaf fall produces the litter layer (L), it is quickly attacked from below, bitten and eaten by mites, springtails and woodlice – which are themselves eaten by pseudo-scorpions, centipedes, millipedes, harvestmen, hunting spiders and others – and becomes the feeding layer of leaf fragments (F). The droppings of all those processors form the true humus layer (H). Earthworms move material from all three layers downwards and so the A horizon of the soil proper, the admixture of mineral and organic particles which hosts the seeds of all the woodland plants, is constructed. Since coppicing ceased, management of these woods has been minimal to non-existent and their floors are strewn with fallen trunks and branches in all stages of decay. The quarter of the British fauna that lives in rotting wood includes many species of the insects already named but all the slugs known in Britain are in these woods, many of them in this fallen timber and are prey to beetles and birds (see Fig. 121).

Bugs, their larvae and more slugs also contribute to the dismantling of the leaf litter and beetles and their larvae prey upon them. Of the woodland beetles,

FIG 162. Blue ground beetle (DNPA).

the blue ground beetle *Carabus intricatus* is by far the most rare – only eight populations are known in Britain and five of them are in Dartmoor (Fig. 162), placing a real responsibility on those bodies who have shared its Biodiversity Action Plan (2001). The habits and ecology of the beetle are not well understood. It seems to be confined to ancient oakwood sites of the damper kind where the moss carpet and tree-trunk wrapping is widespread and it is most active in dampest times and at night. It feeds mostly on caterpillars and climbs – despite its name – high into trees to find them, as do other woodland beetles. Two or three species of bush cricket or great green grasshoppers *Tettigonidae* (Fig. 163) which also eat other insects can occur in these woods and in one site in the Teign valley a true cricket colony, of the omnivorous wood cricket *Nemobius syvestris*, has been identified, fortunately in a nature reserve.

While blue ground beetles and crickets are not going to leap out at even the careful observer, wood ants *Formica rufa* almost trip you up. They transport a vast volume of leaf fragments out of the litter to the preferred site of their colonial home, a tall dome built entirely of vegetable matter, often at the edge of the wood or alongside paths or rides, where some of the sun's light and heat may penetrate (Fig. 164). Wood ants are large compared with other ant species, have an unmistakable red 'waist' and no one can miss the long lines of worker ants moving steadily to or from the nest. Most moving towards it will be carrying material for the apparently ever-necessary maintenance, but every now and then

FIG 163. Great green bush cricket. (C. Tyler)

FIG 164. Infant wood ants' nest, at path side on Trendlebeare Down against Yarner Wood.

there will be one dragging a caterpillar, beetle larva or even an adult insect. They are omnivorous with a bias towards animal food and play their part both in cleaning up the woodland floor and keeping down the populations of other insects, some of which reach pest proportions on the continent. This last function gives these ants protected status in some countries. When you accost a wood ant by stooping towards it you would not think it needed any protection, for, despite your size, it will get up on its hind legs and threaten you. The workers have no sting but can spray formic acid from the rear end. Some birds, notably starlings, indulge in 'anting', landing on a nest they will pick up ants and put them under their own wings where the ants by spraying acid or eating lice do a pest control job for the bird. Professor Harvey, in the predecessor volume to this one, tells of a local Dartmoor belief that wood ants and adders do not co-exist (his wife, who relayed the story to him, was brought up in Moretonhampstead, where I have lived for some 30 years). One of the significant effects of this folk tale was that it was felt safe to pick bilberries in woodland sites, but not out on the open moor – where ironically the 'whorts' are sweeter given their greater exposure to sunlight.

Off the floor of the valley-side woods the insect fauna is as rich as that in the litter if only because by the nature of their siting these woods are adjacent to rivers and streams so the terrestrial flying insects and their larvae are joined by aquatic adults even if high leaves and twigs are only, for them, places to sit in the sun. Higher relative humidity in any case is desirable for most insects. So, caddis, stone, alder and mayflies, midges and mosquitoes, all of which start life in the water, extend the total population. It is however already large, and the vegetarians are either bugs, notably aphids and leafhoppers, or the caterpillars of butterflies and moths. The latter, loopers like the winter moth *Operophtera brumata* and micro-moths, especially the green oak tortrix *Tortrix viridana*, can reach epidemic proportions and reduce the oak tree canopy from a distance to an autumnal state in early summer when their biting removes the leaves or rolls them up and damages them to the extent that they turn brown over large areas. The phenomenon, when it occurs, is best seen where there is a complete overview of the canopy; Bench Tor above the Double Dart upstream from New Bridge offers such a lookout.

Of the butterflies, the speckled wood *Pararge aegeria*, brown, purple and green hairstreaks, *Thecla betulae*, *Quercusia quercus* and *Callophris rubi* respectively, and silver-washed fritillary *Argynnis paphia* are present in glades and along trackways in most of the eastern oakwoods (Fig. 165). White admirals *Limenitis cammila* have recently increased their numbers, as Harvey predicted they would, having hung on in Buckland Woods since the 1960s. High brown *Argynnis adippe*

FIG 165. (above left) Silver-washed fritillary, Hembury woods; (above right) Brown hairstreak (C. Tyler).

and pearl-bordered fritillaries *Boloria euphrosyne* also haunt the lighter parts of the northeastern woods and the Double Dart valley (Fig. 166). There are outpost colonies in the East Okement and the Tavy valleys, but their larvae both need violets whose own preferred place is under a light shade provided by bracken cover so good-sized clearings or sites sheltered by close woods are needed for breeding. Some of the woods of the Teign valley offer such combinations. The Dartmoor locations of the high brown represent a third of the UK recorded sites and those for the pearl-bordered fritillary are a fifth of them. Like the blue ground beetle they represent another significant challenge for twenty-first-century conservators.

FIG 166. Pearl-bordered fritillary, New Bridge. (C. Tyler)

FIG 167. Dormouse.

While the insects occupy a large part of the 'grazing' layer of the woodland pyramid many of their species sit in the next one up and the omnivores straddle both. They are joined by small mammals, and the birds on the ground and in the shrubs and trees. Wood mice and bank voles are here as well as in the fields, and dormice, while present in other landscapes, come into their own in the oakwoods with hazel under-storeys (Fig. 167). They are right round the eastern and northern boundary of the National Park from South Brent as far as Okehampton and occupy woods and copses throughout the far eastern block. But they are almost entirely absent from the west, nor are they recorded from Wistman's Wood or Black-a-Tor Beare. It is thought that there may be a sensitive level of relative humidity that influences their desire whether or not to stay in otherwise well-equipped woods. Even in the small compass of Dartmoor the physical pattern of the surface in altitudinal terms and the Lusitanian context exert pressure on the distribution of life forms. Shrews and hedgehogs represent the insectivores at the woodland edge, especially where a Devon bank provides the boundary rather than a stone wall. Adders and common lizards are not unknown under the better lit, low canopy and they both deal in insect food while the adders will take eggs and nestlings of ground-nesting birds and small mammals and their young.

The commonest ground-nesting birds in these woods are three of the warblers: chiff chaffs *Phylloscopus collybita* and willow warblers at the edges of the

FIG 168. Wood warbler singing at its nest, Holne Moor. (C. Tyler)

woods, and wood warblers *P. sibilatrix* throughout them. All three feed in the canopy on aphids and caterpillars, and nest on the ground in the shelter of a tussock of greater woodrush, a stump or a boulder, sometimes within a stand of bilberry, woodruff or cow-wheat – bluebells don't last long enough or upright enough to offer sufficient cover. Wood warblers are heavier than their commoner cousins and have a very yellow tinge in the pale-brown standard warbler plumage (Fig. 168), as well as a yellow breast and belly. The male sticks very steadfastly to his columnar territory from ground to canopy, not to be dislodged by birdwatching visitors, and produces a two-part song, a tuneless extended rattle (tuneless because it's above our hearing range) and quite separately a falling scale of long drawn-out notes whose music we can appreciate to the full. The two parts are not only separate but not necessarily strictly alternate either. Common redstarts *Phoenicurus phoenicurus* nest in holes in trees, rock piles or walls often close enough to the ground for an adder, say, to find the nest (Fig. 169). They too prefer the woodland margin that extends further inwards as a zone when the light does the same, either because of holes in the canopy caused by tree fall or because the edge is occupied by silver birch or ash both of which offer only a light shade. Redstarts appear to feed at all levels in the trees and on the ground but the males usually sing from the canopy top, more easily seen therefore than their companions because of the usual steeply sloping sites which one can often scan from above or from within through the nearer trees. Redstarts are

FIG 169. Common redstart at low-level nest hole, White Wood. (C. Tyler)

insectivorous, as are the pied flycatchers *Ficedeula hypoleuca* who complete, with the wood warblers, the triumvirate of British upland oakwood indicator birds. The arrival of all three is eagerly awaited on Dartmoor every April.

Like the wood warblers, pied flycatchers may be present throughout the wood and while hole-nesting they rarely occupy holes close to the ground (Fig. 170). The story of their settlement of Dartmoor woods is an intriguing one. They were known to pass through, on the way to their then southernmost breeding location in the Forest of Dean, in the 1940s and when the Nature Conservancy acquired Yarner Wood, near Bovey Tracey, in the early 1950s a pattern of nest boxes was emplaced which enchanted the passing birds to the extent that they stayed, multiplied and have since spread right round the Moor's wooded valleys with and without the aid of artificial nesting sites. The whole original scheme was the brainchild of Bruce Campbell, enthusiastically supported by birdwatching Max Nicholson, the director general of the Nature Conservancy of the day. Every nestling born in a Yarner nest-box has been ringed and so the history of the

FIG 170. Male pied flycatcher at nest, White Wood. (C. Tyler)

generations and of the rate of returning to breed is entirely documented over some 50 years. The success of the experiment inspired more nest box provision and numbers have been set up in bigger woods all around the moorland edge – notably dense in the Teign valley and that of East Okement but also in the Dart, the Avon, the Yealm and the Erme valleys, and a fair population returns each summer to the Meavy valley near the Burrator dam. The birds have shown that, while nest-boxes help with the invitation to stay, they can also find more natural holes than were thought to be available, and in White Wood under Bench Tor, all the 2006 breeding pairs were in such sites.

Spotted flycatchers arrive later, often not until mid-May and seem never to have been so prolific even in the edges of the woods. They do have a penchant for buildings and gardens as nest sites, even unoccupied ones, and so may only just qualify as woodland birds in any case. Robins, wrens and goldcrests mop up insects at lower levels throughout most woods and of course all the tits help the specialists just described in the canopy. All these are flexibly omnivorous but protein seems to dominate their shopping list, so if the insects are there that's what keeps them happy. The least common insect eater high up in the trees is the lesser spotted woodpecker *Dendrocopus minor*, sparrow size and stripey across the back where its greater cousin has two solidly white, shoulder blade-like, patches. It is still seen well upstream in the lower valley woods but usually

FIG 171. Tree number 81 of the Yarner Wood nest box experiment (taken in 1971).

alone so breeding is rarely proven. The small vegetarians – given a need for an insect diet for nestlings at first – are also mainly round the edges of the valley woods. Chaffinches are most common as almost everywhere, but greenfinches are here too and siskins like the bottom edge where alders and willows close to the water keep them happy the year round. Willow tits, which are no longer common, show a preference for the damper edges, whereas marsh tits can be heard throughout these valley woods. Having got to the riverside it is necessary to note that common sandpipers *Actitis hypoleucos* do patrol the rivers below Dartmoor woods in most years and the Double Dart and the Bovey have yielded birds regularly in the breeding season in recent times. Breeding is not proven in these sites, but sandpipers nest on the ground in waterside woods often some distance from the river or lake whose shallows clearly provide the bulk of their food. The other woodland 'wader' is the woodcock *Scolopax rusticola*, a winter visitor to Dartmoor woods, where rummaging in damp litter and damper ditches especially for earthworms is its normal habit. It is not uncommon to put up more than one of these delightful 'brown ghosts' during a winter woodland walk east of the main moor.

We have moved up the size scale and in the woods the omnivores dominate the next level. Blackbirds are here all the year round, though summer birds often go south in the autumn and northern ones replace them. They divide their winters between foraging in the litter for invertebrates and taking any berries on hand, mistle thrushes and song thrushes also breed here and all three commute between wood and short-cropped grass wherever possible. Wood pigeons, our only big vegetarians, nest and shelter within the woods but feed in the fields, often miles away. The bigger insectivores are the green and great spotted woodpeckers which are heard laughing and drumming respectively throughout the woods from January until mid-summer and are not difficult to see in spring before the leaves are fully stretched. Both eat a great deal of the larvae of wood-boring insects, but pick up much on the surface of the bark they are traversing. Green woodpeckers very often feed on the ground but usually outside the wood and preferably where ants are available. Both also need sites for nests capable of excavation, in dead and thus softer wood, but the greater spotted male needs dead branches still hard enough to resonate to its drumming territorial declaration, and often finds those with different notes not far apart. Its presence is given away for the rest of the year most often by its staccato but slightly fuzzy single note alarm 'shout'. The long-standing un-managed state of most of Dartmoor's valley woods offers both these birds a profusion of nest hole potential and territorial sounding posts.

These rich woods, like the plantations, are home to sparrowhawks and tawny owls; as the more common top carnivores in the trees, the former will take any of the birds we have so far listed while the latter concentrates on the small mammals. Goshawks are here as well, as long as the cover is thick enough a few metres up, but the biggest breeder in size and numbers is the common buzzard and, like others we have listed, it tends to use the wood as a sheltered and protected nest site and ranges far away from the trees in search of the menu that varies from rabbit to earthworm. Numbers in the air in one place can be high in spring and autumn as local birds are briefly joined, in a better updraught, by those passing through. The handover to some northern birds who winter here while some of our breeders prepare to move south in the autumn, and the reverse process in the spring, also temporarily boost numbers when high small mammal populations prolong the stopover. The estimate of the breeding population of buzzards in the National Park in 2000 AD was in excess of 300 pairs and may well have reached 350 – so, with not much more than 2.6 sq km per territory, the living must be good and the nesting sites more widely distributed than just in the woods.

Most of the small insectivorous birds listed so far occur in all three of the remote high-level oakwoods, including wood warbler and redstart, though not pied flycatchers. All three woods have grey wagtails patrolling their streamside edges and Black-a-Tor Beare boasts tree pipits which haunt the outer edges of most of the woods which border moor or heath.

The big mammals complete this woodland animal selection – accepting that the grey squirrel *Sciurus carolinensis* is included here, not large, but bigger than the mice and voles. Fallow deer are the commonest grazers, as long as there are brambles about. Roe will lie up in the woods and the odd sika must be the biggest animal present. Badgers are undoubtedly the biggest omnivores and, as we have already seen, more likely to travel out of a woodland home into the fields than on to the moor. Foxes may be seen on woodland rides and paths but also tend to hunt most nights outside the woods. Woodland boundaries are very variable in quality and penetration by domestic stock, especially Scotch blackface sheep, is not uncommon. Sheep probably have more to do with the inhibition of natural regeneration in Dartmoor woodland than any other single factor. An NPA experiment in White Wood in the 1980s demonstrated the impossibility of coppicing and expecting re-growth unless sheep were excluded. But under many Dartmoor ESA and Countryside Stewardship contracts still running (see Chapter 8 for more detail) boundary reinstatement and improvement has proceeded apace across the National Park and thus in places around the woods. Thus man, having introduced the Scotch blackface, has finally got round at least corporately to try to deal with those 'saltatory propensities' recognised so early in its Dartmoor stay, more than 100 years ago.

Indeed man, the biggest omnivore of them all, but specifically management man, now has to show whether or not he can cope with the wonderful Dartmoor complex in a changing economic climate, a changing real climate and a set of changed public attitudes. There is in this new century a new public and political demand for better care for the wildlife just described. That places a complex responsibility on administrators and advisers, authorities and agents where their tasks may have been almost fairly singular until now. But it is man the hill-farmer, him with the 5,000-year-old pedigree, who actually has to take on this new more complex job on the ground, and it is for the rest of us as this twenty-first century unfolds, to aid and abet him while extracting our enjoyment, or in a few cases a living too, from this still very much alive Moor. The schedule of natural complexities will be completed once we have looked at Dartmoor's weather and its water. Then we shall return to the evolution of man's management, its current state and what the future might hold for it.

CHAPTER 6

Weather and Living Water

All the patterns of soils and land cover (of moorland) have developed within the framework of a highly seasonal climate ... a regime of low temperatures, severe wind exposure, very high precipitation, cloud and humidity, persistent winter frost and snow cover, a lack of sunshine, continual ground wetness from low evaporation rates, and often poor visibility.
Ian Simmons, The Moorlands of England and Wales, 2003

LATER, IN THE SAME BOOK, Simmons quotes John Hooker who wrote in the sixteenth century of Dartmoor specifically, 'and this one thing is to be observed that all the yere through out commonly it raineth or it is fowle wether in that more or desert [sic]'. Both quotations have their drawbacks, but taken together they provide a summary of the Dartmoor climate – its 'sum-total of weather conditions'. In Hooker's favour the twentieth-century Dartmoor farming year was still 'three months' winter and nine months' wet weather' – and that was only a partial joke. Simmons was generalising about moorland early in his book and most farmers on Dartmoor in the twenty-first century would quibble with the word 'persistent' describing frost and snow, of which latter precipitation there has been no remarkable persistence for some years. But 'continual ground wetness' rings a bell, even if it makes the odd dry summer all the more singular. Hooker's use of the word 'desert' is a perception of its time, presumably a comparison with settled, enclosed and apparent productive landscapes in the lowland about the Moor, but it also chimes with those modern ecologists who regard heather moorland particularly as a biodiversity desert. Harvey, the zoologist, hinted at it in 1953 but some contemporary plantsmen agree with him when faced with heather's apparent popularity and its use as a measure of success in the 'favourable condition' stakes beloved of present-day conservation administrators.

To return to the climate, everyone seems to be clear, in the twenty-first century's first decade, that it is changing. But it always has. We should remember in any relevant early discussion, that we are not as far in time from the end of the last glaciation as halfway through the last significant interglacial. I have already rehearsed prehistoric climatic change on the broad scale as far as we can discern it from the Dartmoor evidence to hand. But as a reminder, using immediately BC timing and building on it a little into historic time: from 1,900 BC there was a short drying, but at each of 1,500, 900 and 280 BC dates there were shifts to wetter conditions. The bulk of the Roman period was warmer and drier but deterioration ran from 300 AD until 700 and there was a wet phase late in the ninth century after which drying started and lasted until 980 AD or so. According to pollen, spores and wood fragments from the north of England it was wet in the twelfth century and became warmer but variable with noticeable dryness throughout the fourteenth, testate amoeba from Northumberland and Dartmoor however suggest wetter conditions developing towards the end of that same century. They also hint that a brief dry stage occurred in the sixteenth century and then wetter conditions set in until the twentieth. That last proposal may put all these variations into some sort of qualitative scale for the more senior reader. Our childhood was 'wetter' than much of the time from the mediaeval period until the sixteenth century despite the collective memory that all our school summer holidays were continuously hot and dry except when we went to the seaside. It is worth noting too that the 'Little Ice Age' began in 1500 and lasted until 1800 or so. We may have been in wetter times in the 1930s than 130 before, but we were also a bit warmer and that warmth seems now, to some, to be increasing.

Dartmoor's extreme southwestern position, as far as British moorlands are concerned, is a major factor in any climatic consideration of it. Exposure to wind and weather directly off the Atlantic surface and to which the Moor offers the first real orographic uplift, brings it some relative warmth early and late and thus a longer growing season than northern moors. But, more significantly, those winds carry much moisture, and, given that uplift (Fig. 172), good reason for high precipitation on to western-facing slopes and the high tops. The average annual rainfall for the last decade of the last century at Cut Hill, as near the heart of the northern plateau as may be and 603 m OD, was 2,496 mm, but it reached 3,049 mm in 1994. As 1995 and 1996 were both dry years, which dragged the mean figure down, one might assume that 2,540 mm (100 inches) is a fair mean for the whole high plateau. Cut Hill after all is only 18 m lower than High Willhays, the peak of the plateau and the whole Moor and, with Hangingstone Hill, one of the two highest points of the main north–south watershed. That important line runs

FIG 172. Typical rain-bearing cloud mass, after Atlantic air rises over the northern plateau of Dartmoor.

south-southwestward from Cosdon through Hound Tor (the northern one) and Wild Tor to Hangingstone Hill, and then through the tiny triangular col between Taw Head, East Dart Head and Cranmere Pool. Here it turns due south to Black Hill and on to Cut Hill, a mile south of which it swings southwestward to Great Mis Tor, back to North Hessary Tor and on south through Nun's Cross to the southern plateau. Then it picks up an eastward line through Crane Hill, Caters Beam to Ryders Hill, the summit of that plateau (after a diversion northward to round Avon or Aune Head), and finally southeastward through Pupers Hill to Dean Moor. This line cleanly separates the Teign and the Dart catchments which both exit the Moor eastwards, from all else, which flows, the Taw and the Okements excepted, west and south. It is worth underlining for the record that the Dartmoor summit, the High Willhays–Yes Tor ridge (Fig. 173), lies well within the moorland catchment of the two Okement rivers which join off the Moor, and that the very small moorland Taw basin, too, lies west of the watershed just described. For the moment, the more significant consideration is that that line on the whole separates the windward, orographic rainfall receptor from the rain shadow of eastern Dartmoor. Exceptionally, but quite close to it, even if still westerly, at Taw Head in the lee of Great Kneeset the rainfall is 150 mm below the mean and 60 mm below Cut Hill's maximum. Well eastward of the line, at

FIG 173. The unmistakable saddle-like profile of the High Willhays–Yes Tor ridge, seen in the centre of the skyline from the far east (Pepperdon Down). Despite being the Dartmoor summit, it lies well west of the main north–south watershed whose northern end is on Cosdon at the right-hand end of the skyline here.

FIG 174. Low cloud enveloping Hameldown – here its base is seen beyond Bonehill Rocks.

Moretonhampstead (15 km), the average for the 1990s was 1,223 mm and at Yarner Wood above Bovey Tracey it was 1,202 mm, less than half of that only 17.5 km away to the west. The altitude of the rain gauges in each of these easterly sites is close to 200 m OD.

The Taw Head observation is nevertheless important because it is still high enough to show that, watersheds apart, the rivers which drain the plateau, and all their head-streams, are amply provided for by the rainfall – the 2,540 mm just quoted. That rainfall, and the lack of evaporation from the surface that goes with it and its parent low clouds (Fig. 174), have formed and still (just) maintain the blanket peat that stores the water from continuing rain and condensation and thus sustains the flow of 'water-in-channels' which feeds Dartmoor's myriad rivers. We have seen already that those channels are shadows of their former selves, but they still occupy narrow meandering lines in the floors of valleys which were created some millions of years earlier by their forebear rivers. They were scoured by torrents of meltwater perhaps only 25,000 years ago when, momentarily in geological time, bare ground was the norm, and little or no vegetation and certainly no peat existed. But blanket peat began to form 7,000 years ago and now the East Dart, the Taw and the West Okement rise within a few hundred metres of each other in the extensive bog mostly just west of Hangingstone Hill but straddling the great watershed. The West Dart, the Tavy and the Cowsic rise within a few hundred metres of that line and from the same plateau blanket a little further south. The bog is their source now – if their valleys are as old as they seem to be, there has been at least the same rainfall as now, and perhaps a bog too, on a number of earlier geological occasions.

In addition to the rivers and their main headwaters met so far in this book, 11 all told, the northern blanket bog gives rise (literally) to 25 more named streams and some unnamed ones as well. The southern bog has 22 leaving its edge as well as its five main rivers. The stream pattern is dense, the norm over much of the land below the blanket bog boundary fits with the global temperate zone statistic of one kilometre of stream to one square kilometre of surface. But it is the long-profiles of the streams, their width, their volumetric discharge and the variability of all three that matter to the lives of all aquatic organisms and their predators. The same three characteristics offer to men scope for re-distribution of the water itself via leats (see above). The long-profile upstream detail of alternating riffles and pools proclaims habitat variation for all life up to salmon size and, as a spin-off, variations in current speed that accommodate more plant and animal species than would otherwise be the case. Greater gradient changes lower down, often marked by aits or islands, give scope for energy production, as does the general rapid fall from source to departure from the Dartmoor boundary. The leats

FIG 175. Goat (or Goadstone) Pond alongside the B3212 under Sharpitor.

involved in that and those just mentioned as distributors have an ecological significance that has to be part of this chapter too.

But we also have to register that there are no natural 'wide places in rivers' within this National Park. That description of lakes is a nice one, but Dartmoor has never experienced the over-deepening of valleys by glaciers nor the dumping of their scourings as morainic dams that produced most of the natural upland lakes in Britain. Within the moorland, its 'lakes' are Devonian streams and its natural named 'Pools' – Cranmere and Raybarrow for instance – are actually bogs with time-limited water-filled central depressions. Its biggest ponds, Goat (or Goadstone) Pond near Sharpitor, Big Pond above the Black-a-Brook

FIG 176. Dew pond on the east side of Dunnabridge Common by the Two Bridges–Ashburton turnpike.

(the one that flows into the Plym just above Cadover Bridge) providing the head for the water monitors within the china clay pits, Harford Reservoir, a small domestic supplier on the Butterbrook, and the Wheal Jewel reservoir on Mary Tavy Common (now storing the energy for Mary Tavy (hydro-electric) Power Station) are the biggest deliberately made to hold water – in fact for four different purposes. Like the first of them (Fig. 175), there are many tiny unnamed ones, usually man-made, that would be called dew ponds on drier hills elsewhere. Most are close to roads, draught horses needed to drink as well as grazing sheep and cattle, like that on the summit of Merripit Hill, or the six on Dunnabridge Common (Fig. 176). Then there are water bodies in working china clay pits on Lee Moor, a number in the abandoned granite quarries – Blackingstone, Merrivale, Foggintor and Haytor – and small cleaner ones in the long-defunct clay pits at Brisworthy, Redlake, Leftlake and Petre's Pit on the southern plateau. There, too, old holding ponds for mine workings at Crazywell (Clasiwell) and Cramber Pools also sit. Their northern parallels exist in tiny form at Vitifer near the Warren House, and Ockerton Court on the side of Okement Hill. Near Lydord there is a flooded abandoned railway line that supports the small red *Ceriagrion tenellum* and scarce blue-tailed *Ischneura pumilio* damselflies, both are nationally rare but

FIG 177. Haytor Quarry pool – a partial exception to normal quarry pool sterility. (C. Tyler)

also happy at the Brisworthy ponds. The 'Lydford Railway Ponds' are notified as a Site of Special Scientific Interest (SSSI) on their account. The water bodies of the longest-abandoned pits are usually the richest in the ecological sense, the active china clay pits and most of their smaller inactive cousins suffer from dense physical pollution of clay in suspension, though the Brisworthy ones have cleared and are home to a fair selection of aquatic plants and animals as well as the rare damselflies just listed. The hard-rock quarry pools are, on the whole, vertical-sided and offer no scope for marginal emergent vegetation, their depth, too, inhibits plants with rooted footholds but floating leaves (Fig. 177). The (dew) ponds are cleanest and, if sheltered enough, harbour some water plants and accompanying invertebrates, Goat Pond is bleak and rarely without waves but even there floating sweet grass *Glyceria fluitans* persists.

Off the moor itself there are a small number of private pools, some with landscape garden lake-like pretentions, as at Blatchford near Cornwood, Canonteign near Hennock, below Bovey Castle off the B3212 and Bradford Pool near Shilstone in Drewsteignton parish, which also has flooded quarries at Blackaller. There are more of the latter near Christow, one at Scatter Rock alongside Christow Common and one at the old mine above Christow Bridge, two in South Tawton parish and one between the Meldon dam and Meldon Viaduct. None of these quarries are in the granite, some even have limestone associations and thus a higher pH with scope for different plants and animals.

FIG 178. Venford Reservoir on Holne Moor – opened in 1907 for Paignton UDC.

To complete the set of still-water bodies within the national park we have to turn to the major modern exploitation of Dartmoor's deep, steep-sided, mid-course valleys which has been the construction of reservoirs for water storage for human consumption, most now off the open moor. Burrator was the first, in 1898, constructed by Plymouth's city fathers in farmland in the upper Meavy catchment. Then the Kennick, Tottiford and Trenchford complex was build by Torquay Borough Council, followed by Venford on Holne Moor for Paignton Urban District in 1907 (Fig. 178). Torquay came back to build Fernworthy, starting in 1936 but finishing after some difficulties in 1942. The Avon was dammed above Shipley Bridge in 1956 and finally at Meldon on the West Okement, begun by the North Devon Water Board, and completed by the South West Water Authority in 1972 (Fig. 179). The last attempt at damming a Dartmoor river, on the Swincombe south of Princetown, was beaten off in Parliament by an alliance of amenity bodies and the National Park Committee of the day in the late 1960s. It would have been much bigger in area than either Venford or the Avon elsewhere in the southern plateau – wholly flooding Foxtor Mire, now an SSSI – and sapping further the other headwaters of the West Dart by doubling the width of the Devonport Leat already taking water across the main watershed. That alone would have diminished the Black-a-Brook, Cowsic and high West Dart discharges even more and created an unleapable barrier for livestock, their herdsmen, their shepherds and everyone else who walked that part of the Moor.

FIG 179. Looking into Meldon Reservoir from Longstone Hill in 1988. The steep sides of the West Okement gorge with scattered hawthorns plunge into the reservoir. The island nature reserve negotiated during dam-building by the Devon Wildlife Trust is clearly visible, as are the ruts caused by the carriage of fodder to stock on the common – now banned.

These reservoirs were clearly built with off-moor money and still largely supply the communities for which and by whom they were created. Most Dartmoor residents, whose original benefit was simply the price of the land (often including the catchment) to the lord of the manor or other landowner and perhaps some temporary labouring work, at least now draw their own water from their nearest water treatment works. These are associated with Meldon, at Prewley near Sourton, with Tottiford below its dam and Venford the same; the Avon has a treatment works above Shipley Bridge and one at Dousland treats Burrator water. Respectively these works supply the northern fringe of the Park, the east including Widecombe, Venford supplies the southeast around Ashburton and Buckfastleigh and the Avon feeds the extreme south. The west of the National Park including Princetown is all fed from Dousland. Fernworthy water is treated at Tottiford but also at a small works at North Bovey supplying the villages around it. The Taw contributes water from extractors in Taw Marsh, which at least avoided creation of another reservoir; and the Dart, whose whole moorland catchment has escaped any more dams since Venford, is tapped through its floodplain gravels just above the tidal limit at Totnes, well off the Moor. The meagre benefit referred to above was in some cases more than matched by disbenefits. Displacement for some, from home and fields, and for greater numbers from loss of common grazing especially at Burrator where the commoners were bought out of the entire catchment which then ceased to be common land and where the grazing is now let on a commercial basis.

Burrator, on the Meavy, is the lowest of these reservoirs in the landscape and the Avon the highest at 340 m OD, seen near the top of Figure 205, Fernworthy and Venford are at 290 m, Meldon 280 m and the Kennick, Tottiford and Trenchford complex's lowest dam is almost level with Burrator at 220 m. Six of the eight have all the disadvantages for aquatic life that high-level, steeply shelving and annually oscillating shorelines plunging quickly to considerable depth ensure. Of Meldon in the West Okement gorge – the last to be completed – it was said, early after flooding, that the side slopes above the water are so steep 'even sheep fall in'. Only at the inflow ends of such 'lakes' can emergent plants and light-demanding submerged life find a foothold. But Burrator and Fernworthy have some less steep-to shores and the draw down of very dry summers reveals swards of shore weed *Littorella uniflora* extending out from the winter water mark (Fig. 180), joined quickly by terrestrial annuals and creeping perennials as the water level goes down. All but the Avon and Meldon sheets of water now have surfaces sheltered from prevailing winds, at least in some places, by the kind of tree planting (a conifer and rhododendron combination) that was

FIG 180. Burrator Reservoir in high summer (1976) with a *littorella* sward high and dry among the boulders.

fashionable among water companies when they were built. Odd breaks in the screen, and their dam-ends especially, still let breezes through when in the right direction. Avon and Meldon remain bleak, the latter's host valley providing a funnel for the prevailing wind that can pin boats against its dam for long periods. One of the continuing effects on the highest-level water surfaces of exposure to the wind is the massing of 'froth' on the leeward shore produced from the fatty acids released from eroding peat anywhere around the circumference of the lake and often mistaken for detergent!

Burrator and other early twentieth-century reservoirs have been stocked at some time, primarily with rainbow trout, and thus there must be an invertebrate and small fish food supply available despite the ecological disadvantages already listed. Little work has been done on the invertebrates but copepods such as *Cyclops* and *Canthocampus, Daphnia,* mites and *Oligochaete* worms have been recorded in filters after extraction as the water is prepared for human consumption. The fish subsisting on these and doubtless more species are themselves preyed upon by herons *Ardea cinerea*, which have nested alongside Burrator and Venford in the recent past, by cormorants *Phalacrocorax carbo* and by wintering goosander *Mergus merganser* which now breed regularly on the West Dart and the Double Dart rivers in a number of places, a family is seen in Figure 181. In the last two decades breeding has also been proven on the Tavy and at Burrator. Goosander nest in holes usually in trees, and even tried a nest-box

FIG 181. Female goosander and chicks on the Dart just above New Bridge. (C. Tyler)

FIG 182. The Devonport Leat at Princetown, passing below the Prison whose own leat is crossing below the quarry on the top right skyline.

(designed for an owl!) in Yarner Wood. Many other waterfowl call in at the older reservoirs, especially during dispersal after the breeding season, little grebe *Tachybaptus ruficollis* (carnivores) and coot *Fulica atra* (vegetarians) among them. Both suggest that on Burrator and Fernworthy at least the inflow ends provide available food in high summer. Moorhen *Gallinula chloropus* figures are very low but breeding on Fernworthy is fairly regular. Mallard *Anas platyrhynchus* inevitably breed here and are present all the year round. They are omnivorous and graze ashore, but need shallows as far as dabbling is concerned so also tend to feed at the upstream ends of the more mature lakes.

It is important to note that as well as the two variations on the extraction theme already mentioned, reservoir output itself is augmented direct from some rivers within the Park. At Prewley, water from the West Okement (the intake is near the Isle of Rocks) is also treated and in the south extractions are made from the Erme and the Yealm. Burrator water is supplemented by the Devonport Leat, which as we have already seen is fed by the headwaters of the West Dart (Fig. 182).

The rivers then are Dartmoor's dominant natural water habitats and each for ecological consideration incorporates the whole channel system of its catchment including the leats within it. The granite ground source and the peat over most of that in all its forms – from thick blanket through valley mires to peaty

FIG 183. The infant Bovey below Challacombe Cross.

horizons in much of the soil cover – suggests an acid environment for their water source. Despite that, its pH regime is remarkably close to neutral at the highest altitudinal levels of recording within the last two decades. That being said there are recognisable variations among the main rivers and fairly low readings at the other end of the scale. In that time frame the biggest mean range has been recorded on the Plym at Cadover Bridge (pH 7.7. to 4.7, which last is very low), the Teign's three main headwaters ranged from 7.9 to 5.8, the Bovey 7.7 to 6.8, the West Dart 7.5 to 5.3, East Dart (at Postbridge) 6.8 to 5.0 and the Tavy (at Denham Bridge in the latitude of Yelverton, but outside the Park) 8 to 7. Of those, the Bovey has tightest range or, if you like, varies least, and is the only one which does not rise in blanket bog (Fig. 183). The Tavy, with almost as tight a range,

FIG 184. The middle course of the Tavy flowing through the metamorphic aureole and much dolerite on the boundary of Mary Tavy and Peter Tavy parishes.

leaves the granite 24 km or so before it reaches Denham Bridge and half of that distance is through or alongside dolerite (near the basic end of the igneous rock spectrum) and its immediate catchment over the whole 24 km is peppered with outcrops of the same rock see the map at Figure 28, which may help account for its high mean pH (Fig. 184). The Plym's lower readings may well be associated with china clay in suspension, which also has other effects on the fauna under the general pollution heading. The records from 1991 to the present also show a slight increase in acidity over time in all the rivers except the Teign (looking at the mean highest records per year) and the Plym (in the lowest records). Perhaps this last hints at a slight reduction in kaolin pollution since reduced working in the Whitehill Yeo Pit began in the last few years.

FIG 185. The very young West Webburn below Grimspound.

All the raw data, held by the Environment Agency, is based on monthly and sometimes bi-monthly readings over the last two decades, but the analysis, such as it is, is my own. The Agency has also registered pH readings in the past as low as 3.5 on the Okements when heavy storms after long dry periods appear to have flushed out water that has been held in the highest peat for longer periods and thus become, it is assumed, more acid than usual. The passage downstream of such acid water, however, temporary has dramatic results, fish kill is the most obvious symptom but the invertebrate fauna is also affected. Such incidents have been rare so far (since recording began) but if summers do get hotter and drier and more storms accompany that scenario then such flushing might become more common. Otherwise there is not enough evidence from these general figures to come to more concrete conclusions or establish firmer trends.

FIG 186. Bog pondweed, common in 'eyes' and other tiny water bodies.

Together, the water chemistry and the physical nature of the tiniest headwaters of all Dartmoor streams provide an environment that encourages aquatic flowering plants not at all. Gradient, frequent torrential spate and a boulder/cobble/pebble bed mean that only algae and some tough mosses, notably *Fontinalis*, survive, providing little food and less shelter from the torrent for invertebrates. On the other hand the muddy seepages at the edge of bogs and mires and from 'eyes' and springs on gentle slopes carry starwort, *Callitriche stagnalis* with small leaves and white flowers, and where there is enough of a seep the bronze-green leaves of bog pondweed *Potamogeton polygonifolius* can cover the mud/water mixture (Fig. 186). Both these plants are common over Dartmoor's shallowest waters and float off the mud when any water surface is provided. Aground or afloat they provide cover for some of the more rare insects such as the southern damselfly *Coenagrion mercuriale* which occurs at the downslope end of some seepages of the northwestern slopes of the plateau in the aureole where a higher pH seems to be the norm (Fig. 187). Both starwort and bog pondweed will inhabit some smaller leats provided they are shallow and slow enough. Many of the flowering plants of bogs, already listed in Chapter 5, will join these two widespread plants where conditions encourage them.

FIG 187. Southern damselflies mating. (DNPA)

In the slacker currents between the riffles of the growing streams even where submerged and floating vegetation may still be absent a thin invertebrate fauna may be found. Mites *Hydracarinae*, shrimps *Gammaridae*, and the larvae of many 'flies': mayflies *Baetis spp.*, stoneflies *Plecoptera*, a number of caseless caddis *Rhyacophilidae goeridae* and *Hydropsyche* among them, blackfly *Simulium spp.* and non-biting midges *Chironomidae* are here. Some water-surface bugs such as skaters *Gerridae* and beetles whirligigs *Gyrinus spp.* occur and odd flatworms *Planarians* and *Polycelis* lurk under some stones. Most of these taxa occur throughout the length of streams and rivers within the National Park and are joined by others or increase their own local membership as conditions ameliorate downstream.

Moving in that direction, the first real change in invertebrate and plant niches occurs when currents are slackened to the extent of allowing finer material – of the calibre of most growan particles – to dominate the bed for at least some metres. Upstream from here there may well be small 'beaches' and shoals between the boulders, and such a mixture can recur right down the largest rivers especially where their gradient steepens and where stationary boulders of late periglacial dumping recur as dominant features of the channel, in the Dart near New Bridge and in the Teign at Fingle for instance. The washed growan provides a sub-angular gravel mostly under 2 cm in diameter which may be accompanied by pebbles up to 15 cm or so, but the mixture offers rootholds for a very dark olive-green, almost black, water milfoil *Myrriophyllum alterniflorum* and a very much brighter green water starwort *Callitriche brutia*. This pair of totally submerged plants, of such contrasted shades of green, stream along the bed with the flow, always close together, as though offering a drowning Ophelia a choice of wig, and they dominate all the streams with the same gravely substrate. The emergent hemlock water dropwort *Oenanthe crocata* can dominate the shallowest shoals and tower upwards as long as it survives felling by spate and driftwood. All three afford shelter for invertebrate larvae and the latter 'ladders' for their metamorphosed adults. In really slack water and at the edges of channels the acid-loving moorland water crowfoot *Ranunculus omiophyllus* will grow, its floating carpet of leaves and white flowers making a real change at the surface. Here pond skaters can be seen in 'flocks' in almost every backwater and on the downstream side of biggish boulders. Below such surfaces the water boatmen bugs *Notonecta glauca* and lesser water boatmen *Corixidae* occur. The former is carnivorous as is the pond skater, which takes other insects on the surface, particularly the terrestrial ones who miss their footing or whose uncontrolled leaps end up in, or on, an alien medium. I once saw a pond skater on Ruddycleave Water take a struggling froghopper *Aphrophoridae spp.* only to be snatched down itself by a water boatman in seconds. Lesser water boatmen are vegetarian and vulnerable to their big cousins if unwary.

Below some near channel-wide aits and weirs purposefully just downstream of leat intakes, much finer substrates of sand silt and clay verging on mud in places, may accumulate and here the populations of *Oligochaete* worms and the variety of leeches including *Helobdella stagnalis* increase substantially. The biggest of these river 'pools' are well downstream near the National Park boundary and here there are more species of mayflies, stoneflies and caddis. The black fly and *Chironomid* species populations also have their grand climax here as far as Dartmoor's rivers are concerned. Although pools low on the Swincombe and the Black-a-Brook have yielded counts in samples in the last two decades of up to 2,000 individual *Chironomids* compared with 1,300 mayflies, 20 to 30 uncased caddis and 200 to 750 *Oligochaetes* at the same sites. Harvey, describing the pool above Steps Bridge on the Teign in the 1950s refers to the burrowing freshwater pearl mussel *Margaritifera margaritifera* and it was certainly seen up to the 1980s, but then only below the weir. The Dartmoor Biodiversity Action Plan (BAP) claims that it is probably extinct in the Natural Area which is a pity, for numbers of mollusc species are not common in these neutral-to-acid streams, though some small bivalves burrow in the finer substrates and the freshwater limpet *Ancylastrum fluviatilis* grazes the algal film on the downstream- and under-sides of boulders in the lowest reaches of tributaries and particularly in the main rivers. Here, as we saw on the Tavy, passage through some metamorphic rocks lessens the acidity and shell formation for molluscs may be just that bit easier.

The invertebrate population occupies more than one layer near the base of the freshwater pyramid of numbers, for the bigger carnivorous dragonfly larvae and adult beetles prey upon free-swimming and burrowing vegetarian larvae, worms, water fleas and the like. All of the population is potential food for fish, and despite the easily observed circular ripples of brown trout taking emerging mayflies in early summer, that is not their main feeding method. Brown trout, grayling, loach and bullheads take all or any invertebrates from the bottom all the year round and also feed on 'drift', especially in the spring and the autumn. Drift comprises all those organisms that find themselves floating downstream in mid-water having been dislodged from their safer niches by small changes in flow due to rain, say, or because they essayed a move too far of their own accord, or because, like my froghopper, fell in from a terrestrial loss of footing. Some will drift on the surface having mistimed their own attempt to lay eggs there or never properly emerged on metamorphosis. Even given this tripartite larder, acid-to-neutral streams do not produce huge volumetric amounts of food. Analyses of trout stomach contents, taken in bigger tributaries of the Dart like the Walla Brook, show all-age fish taking more stoneflies and caddis than anything else in winter and mayfly and *Diptera* in summer. But in a sample area of the channel an average of 300 first-year fish will have reduced to one or two in four years – the biggest loss being between the alevins and the yearlings, but still another substantial drop in numbers in the second year. Through this time of course the fish are themselves easy prey to others and even to big invertebrates. The survivors to the fourth year will not normally have tripled their length, whereas in a chalk stream the same brown trout will have tripled their length in three years. The actual measurements are more telling: 7.2 cm in the first year to 18.5 cm in the fourth in the Dartmoor stream; 11.3 cm in the first year to 38.8 cm in the fourth in the Kennet (chalky tributary of the Thames). Young brown trout in Dartmoor often find their way into the leats which are still running where physical hazards may be fewer and food as easy to come by, though the heron that finds a leat may have a field day if too many trout have followed each other in there.

Salmon *Salmo salar* also use Dartmoor's rivers for spawning and thus breeding another carnivorous contributor to the pyramid. The adults feed little during their excursion into these river systems from the sea, but their progeny may stay in the river in which they hatch for up to two years, thus occupying a position in the food chain alongside the brown trout. Both species need similar stream-bed conditions to spawn though salmon on the whole deal in much coarser pebbly gravel. All the headstreams of the Dart provide good spawning grounds somewhere. At least 27 km of 'redds' or suitable gravel beds occur in total from the Black-a-Brook in the west to the East Webburn and including the Swincombe. Just above Dartmeet and below Huccaby Bridge on the West Dart are the downstream limits of these redds. They are the scene of much vigorous activity near the end of the year when females plough furrows with their lower abdomen and tail and release eggs into them as the attendant males release sperm. The pair then moves just upstream and repeats the process, which has the added bonus of sending gravel downstream to cover the earlier deposit. The Dart is known as a 'spring' river because the adults run up from the estuary then and wait around in pools until the late autumn to spawn. The Plym's salmon enter the river as late as December, charge straight upstream, spawn and return while there is enough winter rainwater to allow that. It is suggested that abstraction on the Moor (in the case of the Plym system for both china clay working and human consumption on the Meavy) has reduced summer depths downstream over time to such an extent that only this early winter routine will work for the big fish. The Teign's fish appear to do both, having spring and autumn 'runs' upstream. Salmon hatched and educated in the Dart return to it after their marine excursion, with all its adventure and good food, to attempt to spawn in the tributary where they were born, and this instinct seems to include memory of the seasonal routine, hence the particular reputation of any river. However artificial enhancement of the stock by game fishermen by the seeding of developing eggs into redds obviously may introduce fish genetically programmed differently from the true natives; and it is thought that this may account for mixed situations like that found on the Teign.

Fish are not the only exploiters of the invertebrate fauna of the Dartmoor rivers; two such are the birds which have normally characterised all the streams in their gorge mode – the dipper (Fig. 188) and the grey wagtail (Fig. 189) – and they have both penetrated upstream, especially through the enclosed landscapes of the middle Dart system, the Bovey and the Teign and the bigger streams of the western fringe. Both are almost wholly carnivorous, the dipper feeds mainly

FIG 188. (top) Dipper feeding one of its fledglings on the edge of the Dart below Holne Woods; (above) Grey wagtail. (C. Tyler)

below the water surface, walking on the bottom and using wings like hydroplanes to stay down there, sometimes appearing to swim in search of any of the larvae already listed. Grey wagtails feed off the surface itself and snatch adult insects from emergent stones and vegetation, but seem to be tied as closely to the waterside and the line of the stream as the slightly more specialised dipper. The latter needs shallow swift water, tends always to be close to riffles and rapids and is often first seen resting on pebbles on the edge of midstream shoals or those at the inside of the bend. Always look as far up and as far downstream as possible when you come to a stream bank, for 'their working eyes will see you long before your leisure ones sees them' (I adapt Alasdair Maclean). Fortunately their territories are linear and no wider than the channel so a dipper driven to the end of its territory will fly up and turn back over the 'driver's' head. That territory is usually not more than a kilometre in length on rich feeding streams – which means that on acid waters it may be a little longer, though studies of the Plym and the Meavy and of the Dart have produced figures of 1.5 pairs of dipper per km. The latter, in the mid-1990s, revealed 43 pairs on 65 km of the East and West Dart. Dippers have a strong instinct to nest within the sound of rushing water – in the extreme behind waterfalls, but also close above spate level over rapids. The moss-built nest is like that of a wren, domed with a side entrance but big enough for a blackbird, which is the size of a dipper though it is shorter and thus appears plump by comparison, and as often as not under some other shelter or overhang, which is why bridges provide many a nesting site. There are of course exceptions and exotic dippers have nested under eaves – at what was once the Angler's Rest at Fingle Bridge – and in trees – near Postbridge. Numbers on the upper Bovey have declined in recent years, late-winter attempts at territorial establishment failing to run the full breeding course.

Grey wagtails also have a stable population on Dartmoor streams, and a similar density as dippers, about a pair per km across all the river systems. Their nests are open shallow cups so that shelter from above may be more important for them than for dippers; holes in walls and any other available cavity may be used. Their one advantage is their more catholic food source, they will include many terrestrial insects and larvae especially small caterpillars in their own and their nestlings' diet and so are spared the difficulties experienced by dippers in times of persistent spate for instance.

The fish in their turn have their own predators, both mammals and birds. Otters have survived and seem to be increasing on Dartmoor streams – they may well move down as far as the coast in hard winters. They are well protected, but well out-numbered by mink. The Dartmoor mink were originally escapees from mink farms in the Teign valley established in the 1930s but now breeding away

FIG 189. Kingfisher with bullhead, River Dart. (C. Tyler)

on all the National Park's rivers. They will prey upon waterside birds as well as fish, so dippers and grey wagtails suffer their presence less than gladly, indeed it is suggested that the dipper population of the West Webburn was decimated by the arrival of the mink in the third quarter of the twentieth century. Herons have found sufficient fish food in the recent past to nest alongside the West Dart at Beardown and the Venford Reservoir, they still do at Buckfast and in Lustleigh Cleave. Cranery Brook at Postbridge suggests that they were once there too. They nested at Archerton just northwest of Postbridge until the 1980s but their whole wood was blown down in the great storm of Burn's Night 1990. As on the reservoirs they have been joined, as predators, by cormorants in winter on the longer pools of the Dart and the Teign and now by the handsome goosander which breeds on the Dart (see Fig. 181) in at least three places, causing game fishermen great consternation. 'They fish in line, abreast, steaming upstream and cleaning out the river,' said one in a meeting to discuss emerging biodiversity conservation difficulties for anglers. Herons, like grey wagtails, have the advantage of a greater range of food on offer and, if spate precludes an easy fish, resort to the bog where the same rain will have enlivened the frogs.

This chapter began with the weather, and the symptoms of accelerating climate change may of course modify the content of this account of water's direct

FIG 190. Hawthorns near Combestone Tor 'pruned' by the westerly winds.

contribution to the wildlife of Dartmoor within the next decade or so. One set of those symptoms proposed is an increase in episodes of violent weather, and some think we have had more storminess that is not seasonally defined. Wind of course has always been a factor in wilder Dartmoor landscapes, as most exposed hawthorns will show (Fig. 190). But the extremely high-wind incidents in 1987 and 1990 have not been repeated in the intervening 18 years. The latter pure windstorm, there was no rain, laid low many Dartmoor trees, some like the Archerton drive beech avenue in spectacular fashion as Figure 191 shows. Princetown's western sheltering plantation was also devastated. Chimneys came down in many villages and their entrance roads all blocked, however temporarily, by fallen trees. As always these events force re-thinking on land managers about what should now best replace what has been removed before its time, and in its way that is the kind if adaptation we have to contemplate in the face of any of the facets of weather change we may experience.

I hinted at casual observation of milder change at the outset, certainly winters seem less cold up here, if no less damp. Snow has been rare over the last decade though it seemed common enough up to the end of the 1980s (Fig. 192) – and *pace* a short dump in February 2009 – and frost days are apparently diminishing. Drier summers are still a laughable idea in moormen's minds

FIG 191. Near Postbridge – the drive to Archerton, its beech avenue laid low by the windstorm of 25 January 1990.

(2008 being the wettest for decades), but higher average temperatures may just be beginning to affect Dartmoor, already earlier flowering of ling and western furze has been noticed in successive high summers. On the other hand the heather beetle attack of 2006 was evidenced by hectares of dead heather canopy, as the 2007 summer began, in Dartmoor's most vigorous stand on Bush Down. Increasing dryness favours the beetle, say the Heather Trust. It also favours the arsonist and makes legitimate swaling a more complicated and burdensome business. Just outside the Dartmoor agreed date for ending swaling (31 March) in 2007 a fire began, or was begun, just east of Quintin's Man 2 km west of Fernworthy Forest and burnt, thankfully swiftly in front of an east wind, across to Amicombe taking 1,552 ha of surface vegetation with it. A symptom of dryness, its speed meant that the peat, for this was mainly over blanket bog, was untouched by fire but the sphagnum in the wettest places was singed. By June the site was bright green with soon to be rampant purple moor grass. The Dartmoor Forest Commoners' Association, recently trained and properly equipped for fighting wildfire, did a sterling job and contained the western front of the fire in due time but the whole burn perimeter was 31 km. This is probably the biggest fire on the Forest since 1984, seen in Figure 151, but it goes to show how what a persistent

FIG 192. Four scenes that were common in Dartmoor winters until the 1990s (top to bottom): looking northwest from Merripit Hill in 1979, the southern edge of the north plateau, at the skyline, under a real blanket; ponies scraping snow off potential feed in what shelter can be found; snow-covered fields around Widecombe – there is clearly more grazing available on the moor than in the in-bye; Cold East Cross living up to its name in February 1986.

spring and summer temperature increase might mean, and fire, or its risk, apart, it has implications for the solidity of the blanket bog, its volume and thus its water- and carbon-storage capacity. Re-wetting the bog, a formula for attempting to address those potential ills and already begun by Defence Estates and the Dartmoor Wildlife Action Group, will itself become more difficult if evaporation increases.

Winter rainwater may of course balance the equation for reservoirs and human needs but the side issues are obvious. Regulations about residual water below take-off points and over or through dams to keep streams and rivers in good fettle will be put under pressure. 'Dew' ponds and eyes have already dried out in recent springs, as have abandoned but still, until now, wet leats, for the first time in many local memories. It has happened before in historic time, if the available record is anything to go by, but the abandonment of villages in the late fourteenth century, Houndtor, Challacombe and Blackaton for instance, was not just a Black Death matter. Bracken galloped across fields, crops failed and the temperature had risen. Global trade and European and national governments' inability to stabilise the purchase of public goods at a sensible price in the hills may yet be disastrous for the hill-farmer, but the predicted winter/summer changes will not help either. The combination could see an even less attractive scene and a duller habitat covering for the hill develop even more quickly. The attractiveness scale is as much a measure of an animal and plant combination, of a healthy ecosystem, as it is one of human delight. Both need to enjoy the present climatic regime while they may, even if the change proves to be temporary in geological terms.

CHAPTER 7

Working the Landscape: Dartmoor Men and Their Masters Through Historic Time

The villeins, bordars and serfs mentioned in the Domesday (Book) must have been clearing their lord's waste lands for settlement at a very early period. Of these shadowy people nothing is known except that it was their toil and their industry that formed the landscape ... They were the forbears of the present owners and occupiers of the farms whose ancestors have lived in the district 'time out of mind' ... and can have known little or nothing of their overlords ... or the complication of several holders between ... the King and the actual occupier.

C. D. Linehan, 1962

All the subjects of the parts of the 'natural' Dartmoor story that have gone before in this book have become intimately involved with men at work at some time since their own inception. Indeed reference has had to be made to that work, as some components of the natural history of the Moor have been portrayed, to complete that part of the picture. It is the landscape effects of the work that provide the theme for this chapter. The surface, the rocks from which it is fashioned, the water running on it and off it, that that grows on it and the soils developed from their relationship, even the interplay between them all that has come to characterise the uniqueness of Dartmoor, have at some time offered livelihoods, satisfactions and profit to men. The slope, the flat, the height, the aspect, the channel, the boulder, the gravel, the ore, the clay, the peat, the heather, the grasses, the gorse, even the bracken, have been jointly and severally exploited – mostly in the nicest, though occasionally the most selfish, of ways. Much of that exploitation has gone on throughout the last 4,000 to 5,000 years and most of it persisted through nearly all of the last 1,000. In just a little more than the last 100, the subject of the next chapter, new incomers have planted commercial softwood crops, stored water for distribution to half a million people elsewhere or have crawled or yomped from one firing point to another, all because there was this space, at this height and with this climate. All, except perhaps the soldiers, or the miners and quarrymen on occasion, have 'quietly enjoyed', as the tenancy law has it, their moiety of that space for their life and work. In about that same length of recent time, ramblers (of different kinds) have walked and horsemen have ridden over the moorland and between the fields for a new kind of enjoyment and some others have even profited from that.

A PREHISTORIC REMINDER

It has thus been inevitable that, since that moment in Quaternary time rehearsed at the beginning of Chapter 3, men and women have been drawn into the developing story of the evolution of what we now know Dartmoor to be. They, as animals, hold a place in any pyramid of numbers and in the relevant natural food chains, even if humans are neither 'top carnivores' in the pyramid nor much of a link until the end of the chain. But the postglacial evolution of the vegetation cover has to include man as more than an animal. Mesolithic men, as we have seen, improved their hunting and gathering grounds and, DNA studies suggest, were the founding fathers of a succession that has persisted in western Britain at least throughout prehistoric and maybe all of historic time too. They thus began a vegetation management process, and modified it as new cultural ideas, skills, experience and practices were brought to Dartmoor by 'new men', probably up the Atlantic coast and across the Western Approaches. Our well-worked archaeological cultural time zones are still very important reference phases but increasingly the evidence is that cultural change was a handover matter rather than a displacement of whole peoples by newcomers. So, in Neolithic time, the making of better glades and grazing for game and thus easier hunting of the Mesolithic was integrated into a short-term and very nomadic clearing for some growing of crops and penning of animals, but still with 'hunting and gathering' as part of the lifestyle.

By the Bronze Age the 'agricultural' part of that formula had clearly taken over and the comprehensive clearance of the high-level forest, which might by then in any case have come to resemble savannah, was rapidly followed by the need to organise the first widespread enclosure on the gentler slopes and flats above the gorges as Figure 72 showed. This pattern will be examined more thoroughly before this chapter ends, but men were, by then and into the Iron

Age, influencing the mosaic of surface plant cover and turning a good deal of it into a fairly dense system of human land use. Doubtless each of the phases of evolving culture contained masters and men, and corporate activity demanding leadership is implied on more than one front. From Roman writing we know of British masters. Before that the Bronze Age ceremonial structures and burials we have identified do not constitute a large enough 'graveyard' for the total population calculable from the hut circles still on the ground however carefully the generation factor is fed into the equation (i.e. not all the huts were occupied at the same time and a rate of one new hut per group per generation has been suggested). Those community structures must have been the celebrations and graves – whatever their other territorial functions – of the 'masters'. The hut groups and pounds like Grimspound and Riders Rings proclaim village communities that have throughout time bred leaders (Fig. 193). Those leaders surely decided who did what, who specialised and who laboured day to day. In crises like defence of the territory when threatened and necessary communal

FIG 193. Riders Rings looking south: a large and complex Bronze Age settlement on the lip above the Avon valley (the road to the reservoir dam runs alongside the river in the top left-hand corner). Here, both huts or roundhouses and rectalinear 'yards' are attached to the outer wall of the pound. A nineteenth-century leat runs in an arc above the settlement on the right.

routine such as the earliest drifting of stock, both requiring 'all hands to the pumps', someone had to be in charge. We shall see that organisation (and the implication of possession of, and defence of, the territory) has persisted as time has passed as a prime motive in Dartmoor management.

Most recent interpretation from the ground alone suggests that Iron Age people did not take over the whole of Bronze Age Dartmoor, and that fits with the new thinking that cultural change is not effected simply by 'mass inward migration'. The surface legacy of the late first millennium BC is of some nine 'hill forts' at the edges of the moor and a dozen other settlements. The so-called forts on summits and spur ends are crowded on the east and northeast and Holne Chase, closely related to the Dart 'entrance', is notionally the furthest in, or moorward. The same structures occur at Hunters Tor at the north end of Lustleigh Cleave, at Prestonbury, Wooston and Cranbrook either side of the Teign's gorge; then on East Hill near Okehampton and on Brentor down the west side. There is then a big gap on the anti-clockwise ring until Brent Hill overlooking the Avon and Hembury Castle above Buckfast and thus not far from Holne Chase. They may have had little or no military significance despite their popular description, for 11 'other' Iron Age settlements, involving fields, are inside (in the Dartmoor sense) the fort circle which might otherwise have been interpreted as an Iron Age frontier, and apart from Leigh Tor, across the river from Holne Chase, are not closely related to any of the forts. They all pose problems in precise dating terms and to a layman most hint at occupation which may begin in the late Bronze Age and recur in mediaeval times. It should surprise no one that any site might yield the same potential to new subsistence farming settlers (whatever else they did) after gaps in occupation. At Foales Arrishes, below Top Tor, Metherall and Kestor either side of the South Teign west of Chagford and on Shaugh Moor there are huts and small fields. At Kestor iron was smelted and wrought but exactly when is less than clear, and pollen analysis suggests that this site was occupied at the same time as a Late Bronze Age one on Dean Moor in the southeast. The fort-like 'tor enclosures' at the Dewerstone above the Plym and Whittor above Peter Tavy are only separated from 'forts' by their complexity, and in both cases occupation (or construction) may extend back to before the Bronze Age. Iron currency bars from Holne Chase, pottery in sites already named and at Smallacombe near Haytor, and two Greek coins of 92 BC at Holne are all within the concentric rings of the forts and the more workaday settlements. So, it seems clear that the last 500 years BC saw a withering of settlement at the heart of the Moor but a clear zone of Iron Age development around its outer edges; and we know that the climate had deteriorated during that same time.

The Romans, as far as we can tell, by-passed the Dartmoor mass close to its northern flank. A mile and a half south of North Tawton and close above the River Taw is a Roman signal station, earlier a staging post, with some three miles of the course of a Roman road leading to it from the east as though from Exeter, the only substantial Romano-British settlement so far west. The suggestion is that there was Roman traffic to Cornwall where metal was the probable prize, making the Dartmoor avoidance a small mystery. Maybe no one told them there was tin, copper and iron up there; maybe it was rainy enough to make lower coastal sites further west a more attractive proposition despite the distance; maybe we haven't found the evidence yet. Perhaps the proto-Cornish were better traders than the highland Dumnonii (the tribal name the Romans learnt, or gave, to the native British they found in Devon). The Dumnonii did not defend their territory but made some peaceful arrangement with the Romans. Exeter was already a British settlement and became a Romanised tribal centre where British masters and their men learnt about city life. But having been walled properly in about 200 AD it had been thoroughly neglected and abandoned, by the masters at least, at the end of the fourth century. Whether this whole interlude was much of a distraction from Dartmoor management and development is not clear. Dartmoor people had perhaps already begun to keep themselves to themselves.

THE SAXON LEGACY

Quite soon 'formal' Saxon newcomers penetrated beyond the inward-facing Dartmoor frontier of the British natives they overtook, whether peacefully or by military advance. Those alternatives arise because we know that Anglo-Saxons from earlier settlements up-Channel had landed on and settled the east-facing coast that stretches southward from Exmouth to Start, before the military advance of the west Saxons had reached east Devon. The Frontispiece map shows that coastline well. Stokenham, Slapton, Brixham, Goodrington, Paignton, Shaldon, all proclaim this early Saxon settlement. They may have ousted the Britons fairly gently at first from the coastlands. At Slapton, in the extreme south of the South Hams, Wallaton Cross on the present inland parish boundary suggests that Slaptonian Saxons in their 'slippery place' lived alongside 'the place of the natives'. The equable South Hams was named by farming Saxons – an extant charter of 846 AD (in which Aethelwulf, Alfred's father, conveyed land to himself from that which he held for the people) confirms that. But the Dart, which crosses that landscape, bears a British name almost certainly related to those lower reaches of the river's course, at least half of whose length is tidal, between continuously oakwood-clad valley sides. What is clear is that the main

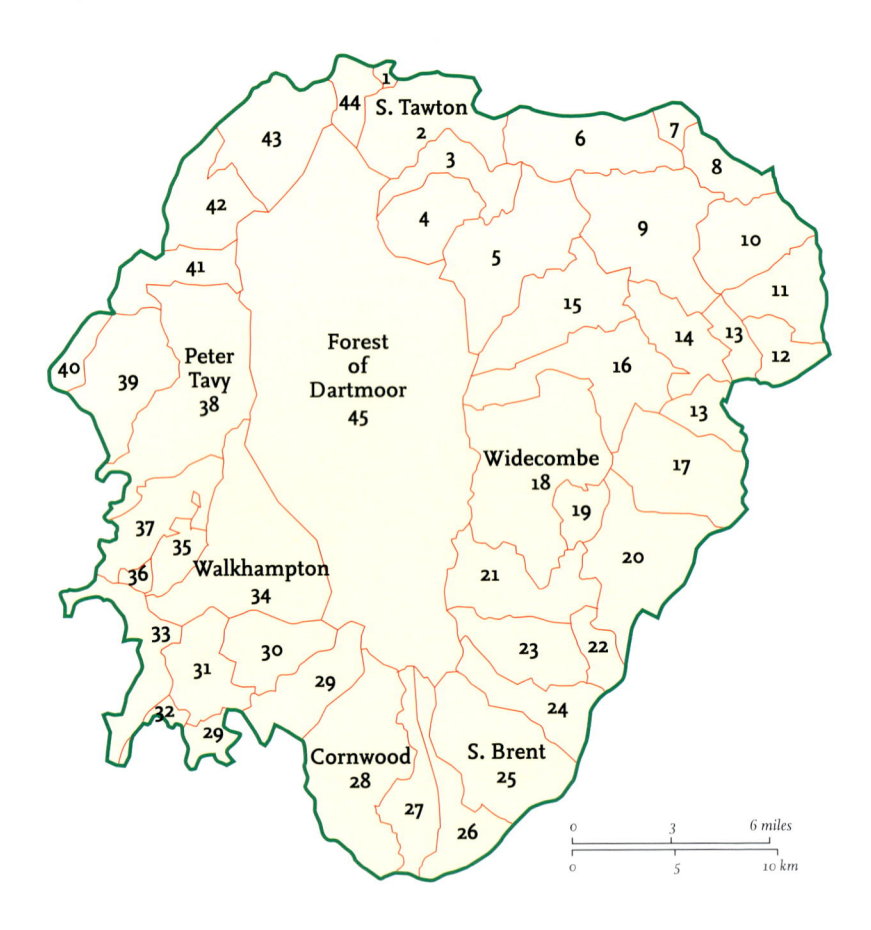

FIG 194. The modern map of Dartmoor parishes (those with tiny areas within the National Park boundary are not identified). All but six are identifiable in the Domesday Book, though not always by name. KEY TO PARISHES: Seven are named on the map and all are numbered: 1. Sticklepath; 3. Throwleigh; 4. Gidleigh; 5. Chagford; 6. Drewsteignton; 7. Cheriton Bishop; 8. Dunsford; 9. Moretonhampstead; 10. Bridford; 11. Christow; 12. Hennock; 13. Bovey Tracey; 14. Lustleigh; 15. North Bovey; 16. Manaton; 17. Ilsington; 19. Buckland-in-the-Moor; 20. Ashburton; 21. Holne; 22. Buckfastleigh; 23. West Buckfastleigh; 24. Dean Prior; 26. Ugborough; 27. Harford; 29. Shaugh Prior; 30. Sheepstor; 31. Meavy; 32. Bickleigh; 33. Buckland Monachorum; 34. Walkhampton; 35. Sampford Spiney; 36. Horrabridge; 37. Whitchurch; 39. Mary Tavy; 40. Brentor; 41. Lydford; 42. Sourton (and lands common with Bridestowe); 43. Okehampton Hamlets; 44. Belstone.

WORKING THE LANDSCAPE · 251

Saxon penetration of what we call Dartmoor was via the upper valley system of the Dart and they, it may be, who transferred the coastal river valley name to the moorland of the river's birth.

The Saxons had completed their colonisation of the lower end of the central basin of the Moor and the middle east well before 1000 AD, for almost every twenty-first-century village and parish here, and many a manor still lending its name to a smaller settlement, is entered in the Domesday Book and thus had some value in land-use terms by 1000 AD (Fig. 194), and to their holders (to distinguish them from the actual occupiers) long before that. Some other Saxon essays into the Dark Age moorland/woodland complex must also have taken place, but only from the eastern side, up the valleys of the upper Teign, the Bovey and the Wray and through the cols between them. Otherwise Saxon settlement is confined to a zone outside the moor, though some like Gidleigh and Throwleigh (classic secondary or pioneering woodland clearing names), Mary Tavy, Shaugh Prior and Harford are close to its frontier. South Tawton and Sourton, and from Lydford through Peter Tavy to Whitchurch, Sampford Spiney, Walkhampton, and on to Cornwood, South Brent and Dean Prior are all a step away from the moor but had connections with it in Domesday.

The Domesday Book records more Saxon villages unlikely to have been settled by a Dart basin approach. There is a string of interestingly high-level settlements: Hennock, Bridford, Drewsteignton, Moretonhampstead, North Bovey and Manaton in the northeast, and Belstone isolated in the north, all above 200 m OD (Fig. 195). Belstone and Manaton are well above that and both

FIG 195. The view out to the east from high-level hillside Hennock across the Teign valley to Great Haldon – Teign village is the one-street settlement down below.

252 · DARTMOOR

are closer to the moor itself. Well off Dartmoor proper and lower but close enough to influence the land use of its margins, are Christow, Dunsford, Okehampton, Bridestowe, Tavistock and Yelverton round the north and western arc and Buckfastleigh, Buckfast, Ashburton, in the lowest part of the Dart catchment, and Bovey Tracey all on the south and southeast.

As we saw at the outset of this twenty-first-century version of the whole Dartmoor story, the Domesday record adds up to a demonstration that the people of the Dark Ages laid out the agricultural enclosed landscapes up to 300 m OD more or less as we know them today. Their contribution to the scene has lasted at least as long as that of the Bronze Age folk did at higher levels in their day. Between them this pair of developer cultures produced two topographically overlapping patterns that, under their separate climatic regimes, cover the ground below the blanket bog. The overlap is evident in both directions. Bronze Age reaves persist in lines within the fields of the valleys of the upper Dart system, and Saxon and mediaeval enclosures, dwellings and plough marks are discoverable out among the reave patterns on the open moor (Fig. 196). No culture from 3,000 BP has neglected or discarded any earlier pattern, wall or shelter that it has found useful and much subsequent work has respected, as archaeologists put it, what it found at the

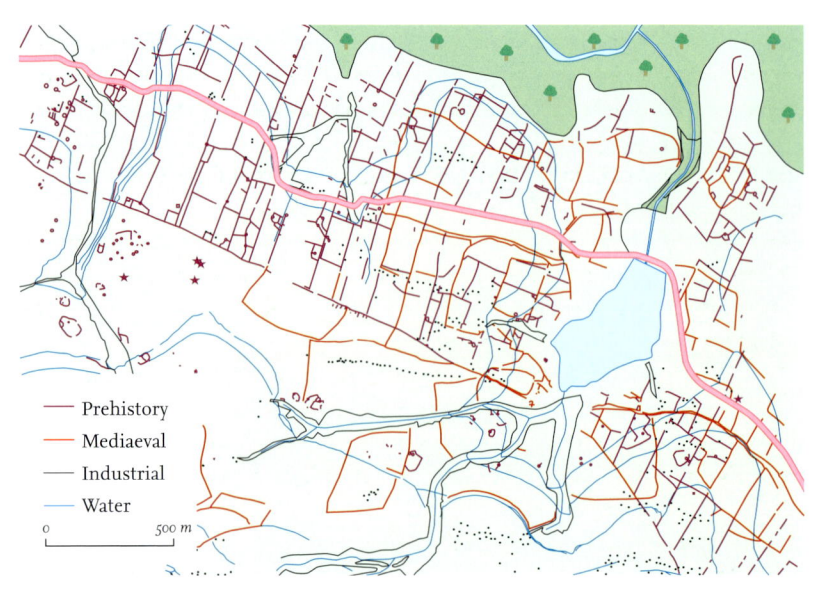

FIG 196. The Holne Moor palimpsest, mediaeval remains and tin workings, superimposed on the prehistoric pattern of Figure 72 (after DNPA).

surface. Only new technique or climatic *force majeure* has caused older lines to be slighted. However, while many Domesday manors have survived in some form, many also ceased to operate wholly as early as the fourteenth century, and some farmsteads and bigger settlements first recorded in the thirteenth and fourteenth centuries have not lasted until now as the map at Figure 218 *inter alia* indicates.

Conversely, towards the end of the eighteenth century and into the nineteenth there were additions to those two grand patterns – notably within the 'Forest' – and thus involving what many still regard as intrusions into the 'pasture' which both pattern-makers had protected, even if only by default. The Duchy of Cornwall, the archetypal 'master' of this chapter's heading, promoted the development of Princetown from scratch and to a lesser extent of Postbridge beyond its Ancient Tenements. The enclosure of the large newtakes from the open moor between those two places and beyond, and the creation of some leasehold small estates on which among other things the first attempts at afforestation were made completed the Duchy's most energetic 100 years. Outside the Forest the same period saw the initiation of granite quarries and of large-scale clay mining. The building of the turnpikes straddled the Forest, which was clearly meant to benefit from their passing through, but their planners, their take-offs and their targets were outside it. To them we must return.

Dartmoor as a place or even as a concept is not referred to in the Domesday Book. But as it, the Book, was recording land use and land-use potential and thus value, that need not surprise us. The Moor was a 'royal' hunting ground in Saxon times and thus belonged to the Crown. Its value was to the monarch and his court alone as a place of recreation and perhaps source of a change of meat in a dominantly meaty diet, so had no calculable price nor was one seen to be necessary by the inheriting monarch's own surveyors (quite clearly in Devon organised and briefed by a Saxon administration of clerics who knew how the land-holding system worked and had managed royal lands before the Conquest). We shall have to refer to 1086 AD again

Because, despite our frustration at the things the Domesday survey doesn't say and especially that lack of help about the whole moorland extent, its timing is a convenient marker in assessing men at work in any landscape. Convenient, partly because of its reference back in most entries to very early 1066, before the last great imposition of power change on the English happened, and partly because it is so close to the beginning of the second millennium AD. That is, about halfway through historic time so far and from whence an increasing amount of documentary evidence has helped Dartmoor historic scholars, just as it has helped their peers all over England. There are many of them, their writings are mostly still easily available and those prior to 1992 fill a 363-page published bibliography. Most began as specialists, but many eventually generalised. It is not the purpose of this chapter (or this book!) to emulate any of them, simply to draw on their work, to add another interpretation here and there perhaps, and hopefully prompt the reader to seek out the more specialised contributions if more breadth and depth in any particular area is sought.

INTO THE MIDDLE AGES

Throughout this last millennium, and never forgetting the specialist tradesman, those niche marketeers who set out to satisfy local needs for moorstone, quarried stone, wrought metal, gravel, peat, wood-fuel and structural timber, two occupations have dominated Dartmoor's working scene. Farming and the working of tin have produced more widespread and lasting landscape detail than any other work. Prehistoric farming, as we have seen, can claim to have created the present cover of at least half the surface of what is now a national park and by their grazing and burning historic hill farmers have inadvertently sustained it. They and their close neighbours have more deliberately maintained the enclosed remainder. The tin workers' etching of the moorland, lying uphill from the enclosures is still very clear to any thoughtful observer. We have already seen that the junction of those two terrains, open and enclosed, has been a blurred zone throughout human time here. The precise position of the boundary at any one time and in any one place depended upon the fortunes of agriculture locally, regionally and even nationally. The intensity of tin working also varied across the centuries, equally dependent upon trading beyond the Exe and beyond the coast. That also meant that at its economic peaks the legally privileged tinner could cross the same boundary, between moorland and farmland, but downhill.

Whilst farming and tinning and their surface effects must be traced through historic time it is important to register first that they were not always separate or exclusive. It is clear that farmers sometimes worked tin, and that quasi full-time tinners grew crops and kept stock. There was doubtless a great variation in range of time spent, by either individual tradesman on the other's specialism, and this dual part-time work is typical of most historic metal-mining areas. There is also plenty of evidence that men and their masters were engaged in both industries. Tin working had its shareholders and its 'waged tinners'. Farmers forever have been landlords, tenants and free labourers or hinds (hired hands in Devon). Some farm workers, even beyond the first millennium had no independent status at all. The slaves and serfs still recorded in Domesday had existed since the Iron Age, the 'landless' are recorded for a few centuries more in rent and tax surveys and some mine workers as late as the nineteenth century were rewarded with tokens they could 'spend' only in their employer's store. There were degrees of shade among all of Linehan's 'shadowy people' throughout the millennium. But it is they who did the work that left us with the rich tapestry that geology and climate had invited them to embroider across the Dartmoor surface.

MINERAL WORKING AND THE LANDSCAPE

The working of tin

No evidence on the ground to prove prehistoric working of tin on Dartmoor has yet been discovered, though it is assumed by many. Dartmoor Bronze Age men had bronze articles, and scrap bronze from elsewhere was available to them (bronze is an alloy of copper and tin). Smelted metal has been found inside huts but rarely alone or with only other Bronze Age artefacts. A hut on Dean Moor (where the Avon reservoir is now) yielded a 'drop' of tin and some tinstone, but most similar finds have been accompanied by at least mediaeval ones, implying that the hut's structural remains proved useful shelter for later workers. The earlier reference to the Kestor hut with iron-smelting and iron-working evidence, but doubt as to the date of the work, supports this principle. We can only imagine that Bronze Age folk found pebbles containing tin as readily as their many successors, but we have no idea how sizeable were their individual 'works' on the ground or how widespread they were over the moor. This appears to leave the landscape contribution field clear for the tin workers of the historic period, at least for the time being. More intensive research and new techniques may change that perception at any time.

FIG 197. Tinners' hut in the side of a streamwork trench – Beckamoor Combe on Whitchurch Common.

It is the extraction of tin by at least three different processes that has left the most significant set of features in the moorland landscape associated with the whole industry, collectively known as tinworks. Structures, such as shelters, tool stores, blowing houses (smelters) and tin mills are also scattered over the moorland and within the enclosed landscape, but even compared with prehistoric hut circles their surface legacy is small in scale (Fig. 197). Shelters, as one would expect, are usually where extraction took place, but the remains of buildings associated with processing the ore may be some distance away, for some processors probably collected and dealt with raw material from a number of scattered sites.

Tin occurs in lodes (to a miner), veins or collections of veins to a geologist. Lodes run through the granite and now and then outcrop at the surface where streams may erode them along with all else that lies in their course. Thus downstream of the outcrop mixtures of fine and coarse debris have been deposited including tin crystals as fine as the accompanying sand, and pebbles of various sizes containing tin. Such deposits, forming 'tin ground', occur alongside most moorland streams and may lie in and on the floodplains and beds of the larger rivers well off the Moor where they have also been worth working in the past. That work could involve quite elaborate channel creation to divert the river while working through its bed, well seen in the Dart below Dartbridge at Buckfastleigh.

The extractive tinworks on the moorland have also been divided by archaeologists into streamworks and mines, and both types, themselves, subdivided. The surface legacy of streamworks is by far the most widespread over the whole Dartmoor surface, and individual sites are much more extensive than either mines, which includes opencast working, or the relatively tiny (in landscape terms) exploration pits associated with prospecting for tin-bearing lodes. The majority of streamworks are alluvial, or as that adjective implies, in the bottoms of valleys however shallow. The others extend up gentle hillsides, and for the tin ground to be worked demanded that flowing water was brought to the favoured site to assist in the separation of tin crystals (as ore) from sand, silt, clay and other material of coarser calibre which may also contain tin. The water was brought by leats, which have been referred to already in more than one context, and often stored temporarily in small reservoir pools above the working site to allow sensitive control of the discharge as needed. The flow had to be just right to shift the lighter fraction of the alluvium but not sweep away the tin crystals which are heavier and thus can settle out given exactly the right conditions. Early on of course primitive searches for the metal depended upon the fact that a pebble containing tin weighs more heavily in the hand than a similar sized one without any such ore.

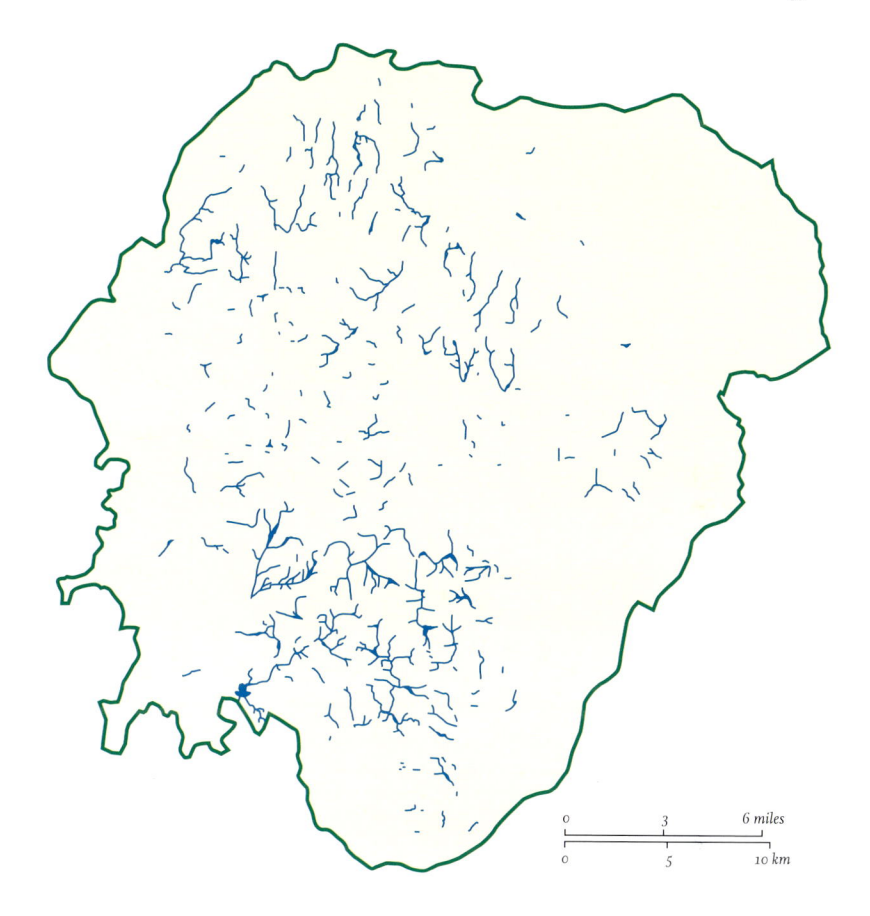

FIG 198. The streamwork contribution to the moorland landscape (after Gerrard, 1997).

Streamworks are especially dense over the southern plateau – there is hardly a square kilometre without such modification of the surface (Fig. 198). In the north a zone of lengthy excavations stretches southeastwards from a Cosdon to Great Links Tor baseline to Hameldown. Both these areas demonstrate that blanket peat did not deter the early miners but there is a discernible area in the southern half of the northern plateau bearing only short lengths of valley bottom tinning scattered more thinly though consistently across the surface. The Haytor block of moorland lives up to its reputation for modelling the gross patterns of the Moor on a small scale with a sequence of lengthy valley-floor works lying in line with the northern zone just identified. The density and distribution of

FIG 199. Streamworks: (left) the lower reach of Beckamoor looking towards Vixen Tor, below the centre skyline; (below left) the floor of the upper East Okement filled by tinners' waste heaps.

streamworks is of course itself a commentary on the density and pattern of tin-bearing lodes within the granite.

These sites are immediately obvious to any observer walking across their terrain. The alluvial tin ground, as we find it now, tends to have outer boundaries that are themselves very steep little slopes a few metres high cut into the bottom of the valley side and representing the outer extremity of digging (Fig. 199). Within the 'trench' so defined there will often be a pattern or patterns of mounds each with a definite long axis, often so close together as to suggest that their upstream edges are overlapped by the next waste dump (the miners worked upstream to save covering unexplored ground with waste). Where the mounds lie across the general slope of the valley floor their shape in section depends upon their origin. When wheelbarrows were in use there is a distinctly gentler slope facing upstream, where they are symmetrical it would appear that only a Devon shovel (long handled, with a shield-shaped blade) was used to turn over the ground. Easily accessible good examples of streamworks are in the upper valleys of the Meavy and its headwaters upstream from the Burrator Reservoir forest and below the B3212 road from Princetwon to Yelverton; in Beckamoor Combe above and below the B3357 between Merrivale and Pork Hill, and in the whole length of the East Okement valley floor upstream from Cullever Steps. Hillside streamworks have similar patterns of spoil dumps but water-flow regulation demanded their secondary use as gradient determinants by their angle across the slope. The steeper the slope the nearer to the contour is the axis of the mound. In some cases short walls have been constructed to hold waste on the upstream side of the dump and prevent it from falling into new working ground – the opposite of the streamwork system. There is a particularly good example on the western flank of Cosdon where the tin ground is some 200 m long and 120 m wide, with parallel curvelinear mounds themselves more than 100 m long.

All these 'cliffs' and mounds offer a variation from the valley floor for plants and animals, they are better drained and provide some shelter on their leeward side, those who have time to wander among them may come across habitat microcosms not found on the more open moorland around the site. Stagshorn club moss *Lycopodium clavatum* clearly prefers the slopes of such mounds. Figure 200 shows the plant near Vitifer. There are some valley-floor tin grounds where

FIG 200. Stagshorn club moss on the slope of a tinners' waste mound at Vitifer.

few if any dumps within the boundary 'cliffs' are apparent, as though little waste was generated or there was later infilling of the spaces between the mounds by waste flushed out from more work upstream.

Of the mines, the so-called openworks, or beamworks, have the greatest effect upon the moorland scene, though less extensively than the streamworks (Fig. 201). Openworks were essentially created by the quarrying of a tin-bearing lode within reach of the surface and as far as its extent lengthways and downwards could be dug by hand. It seems that openworks were already an extension of streamworks in the fifteenth century and had probably been superseded by adit and shaft mining by the early eighteenth. The result in the landscape is a deep, usually

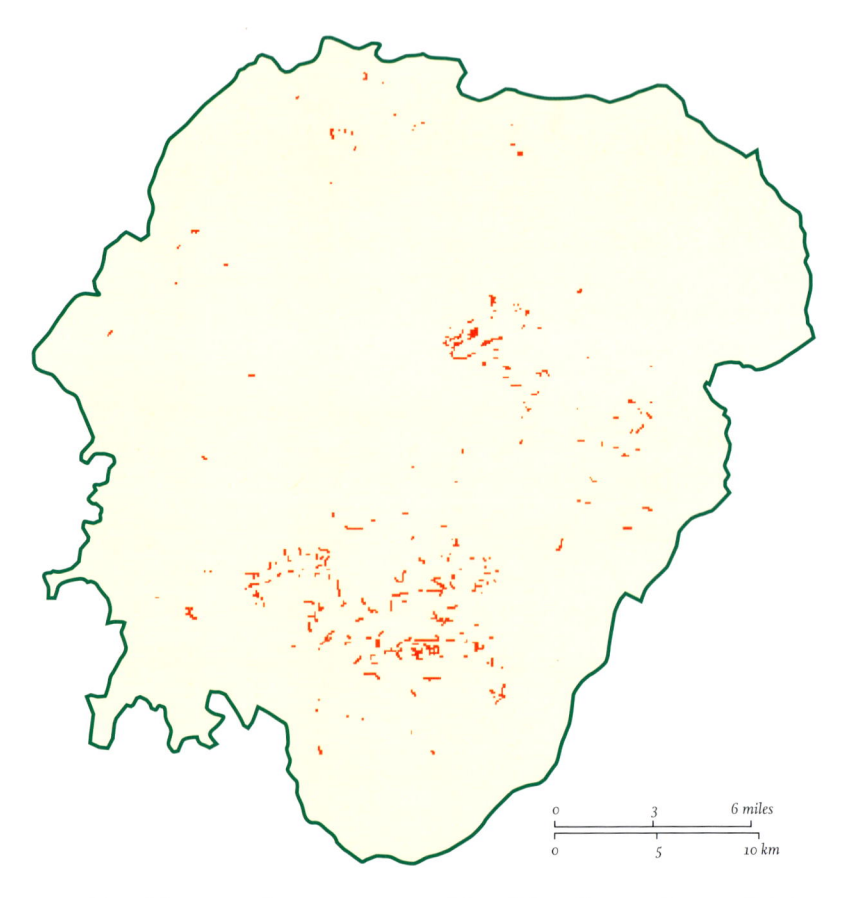

FIG 201. Map of the openworks, more concentrated than their predecessor streamworks but still making a substantial impact on the surface (after Gerrard, 1997).

FIG 202. View from the B3212 across to Grimspound – openworks are carved into the nearer north end of Soussons Down, the col south of Headland Warren and below Grimspound. The ruins of the Ancient Tenement Walna are in the foreground.

narrow, cleft in the surface unrelated to natural features. Most are now V-shaped in section and thoroughly vegetated, though there are still weathered vertical rock faces in some instances. There is a very dense collection of openworks stretching from below Hookney Tor next door to Grimspound through the col above Headland Warren across a headstream of the West Webburn and on to the unforested summit of the Soussons Down ridge (Fig. 202). The collection includes vegetated V-shaped slots especially below Hookney and Birch Tors and rock-sided trenches up to 6 m in depth between Soussons plantation and the Warren House Inn. These are part of a very dense collection of tin-working landscape relics including leats and streamworks and many late-industrial details such as wheel-pits, building foundations for miners' barracks, a blacksmith's shop, miners' walled enclosures for gardens or stock, associated eventually with the Birch Tor and Vitifer mines. The openworks' successor shaft and adit mines were worked here into the twentieth century and there are photographs of work in progress. This complex of tin-working features is much visited because it is so near the B3212 and the Warren House Inn and because it forms such richly concentrated evidence of one of Dartmoor's two long-time staple industries. It provides a more extensive set of variations on the moorland surface than a simple collection of waste dumps, and provides an oasis of shelter for plants and animals and a spectrum of drainage variation that suits a greater range of organisms than that available on the smooth, or rocky, slopes around it, untouched by digging. Until 2005, ring ousels made the site one of their strongholds, they are very attached to ruinous walls and rock faces, but their numbers have thinned all over the moor since then. Wheatears and redstarts actually use the walls and rocks for nesting. Willow warblers and reed buntings find the sallows around the leats and pools to their liking and it is rare not to see cuckoos there, though their hosts are the meadow pipits who share the heather and bracken of the openwork sides and the flats in between them with whinchats and skylarks. Robins, tits, wrens and blackbirds are in sufficient numbers to proclaim this an oasis in the moorland for them and a hint at human companions only recently departed.

There are two other kinds of mine and their spatial surface impact is fairly limited. The most elderly is the lode-back mine which consisted of a short vertical shaft to exploit the lode unreachable by opencast methods, and work persisted along the lode from the shaft bottom as long as it was safe, rather like the bell-pits of the smaller coal fields of the Welsh Border, but shaped in section more like the Duke of Wellington's hat. Such shafts remain at the surface as funnel-shaped holes with waste dumps alongside them. They often occur in procession following a lode already identified, sometimes continuing the line of a streamwork, or an openwork. There are two parallel lines of such mines across the small abandoned fields just opposite the remaining inhabited cottages at Whiteworks south of Princetown, spectacularly seen from the air. They are distinguishable from prospecting pits by their size and shape, the latter are usually rectangular with a long axis across the presumed line of a lode. Finally there are true mines, whose shaft entrances and those of related adits are the only evidence at the surface of their existence. Where most of what has been described so far was indulged on Dartmoor from the Dark Ages onwards, the timing of the origins of shaft mining is still unclear. There are references to 'underground' working and the works of the 'old men' being rediscovered in newer mines in the sixteenth and seventeenth centuries. At Vitifer 13 shafts and three different levels are described at the end of the eighteenth century which implies considerable life before that. It was worked from then, even if intermittently, until the 1930s and accounts for the bulk of the complex of surface remains in that valley head. Its impact on the wider landscape is necessarily very limited but, as photographs from those 1930s show, at the time of the mines' (to include Golden Dagger) peak performances the ancillary surface activity created an industrial scene to rival small sections of the Black Country. Shaft-head structures and large waterwheels protruded upwards where only church towers had ever done that before in the Dartmoor scene. We should accept that smoke and noise must have been a feature of even the smallest tin mine site from early mediaeval times on.

The performance of the whole industry through the period for which there are scattered records was variable. There was clearly a very high peak in the decade-and-a-half beginning with 1515 AD, and in 1523 the 'coinage' at 630,000 pounds (286,350 kg) weight, doubled the output of the best of the 65 years before that. (We have no figures before 1450 AD.) There was a considerable slump during the middle of the seventeenth century (Civil War and Commonwealth dampened all trade) with a slight recovery as tin production moved into the eighteenth with a peak of 125,000 pounds (56,800 kg) in 1706. That was still less than a fifth of the output of Henry VIII's best year and only a half of the mean production figures for the fifteenth century. The last recorded Court of the Stannaries, which will be explained almost immediately, was held in 1786 at Moretonhampstead, when the boundaries of the stannaries were rehearsed. Stannary law, by which miners, their masters and their men had worked for 700 years or more was rendered effectively powerless in 1836 and abolished in 1896. The last tin was shipped from the Vitifer waste tips to South Wales in 1939 for smelting and it represented the end of an industry begun before the twelfth century.

Dartmoor's socio-economic landscape had been divided for most of that time into four stannaries whose production was 'coined' at Ashburton, Chagford, Tavistock and Plympton. No tin could be sold until it had been through the

FIG 203. Crockern Tor close to the B3212, from the south. It is close to the conjunction of the four stannaries, and is where the tinners' Great Parliament met.

coinage process. It was a combination of assay, marking and 'duty' collection. The tin was then often sold on the same day at the same place, so there was in effect a 'tin market' attached to those four towns. The four stannaries, named after the stannary towns, were required by a writ of 1198 AD to send jurors or jurates to a central court – often called since a Great Court or Parliament – which was held at Crockern Tor near Two Bridges, roughly equidistant from the four stannary towns (Fig. 203). The court was under the jurisdiction of the Lord Warden of the Stannaries, a post created in 1197 and first held by William de Wrotham. It still exists in the hierarchy of the Duchy of Cornwall, though of course all this was going on before the Duchy existed and was thus done then in the name of the King. The Court was to be chaired by the Lord Warden or his representative the vice-warden who was usually local. The writ of 1198 was issued by Richard I's chief minister, Hubert Walter, to 'declare the law and practice relating to the coinage' which implies recognition of the need to clarify mining operation and administration for which no earlier written record has yet been discovered. The Great Court dealt with disputes between miners and between mine-owners, and more importantly reviewed the law to date and made presentments establishing new laws or revoking existing ones as was deemed necessary at the time.

It seems likely that the Normans, as they did in many other areas of social and economic activity, 'tolerated and absorbed' whatever Saxon systems existed in this respect, but now felt the need to crystallise them. From before Domesday until the sixteenth century, it was 'lawful for every man to dig tin everywhere in the county where tin is found' and only in 1574 did the tinners' Great Court find it necessary to forbid miners to dig 'in or under meadows, orchards, gardens, mansions, houses and their curtilages, arable land [defined as until two years since the last crop had been harvested] or to take more than twenty timber trees from any wood or coppice'. So, throughout the mediaeval period miners and their processes were very privileged, and their freedom to work ground must be a commentary on the value to society generally of metals in all their forms, prolonged of course by the taxable value of the output to the King. The corporate view may be philosophically sound, but as has always been the case, it does not necessarily help the individual in his own immediate circumstance deal with his difficulties with the privilege of the few. The 1574 'presentment' had effectively confined new entrepreneurial tin working to moorland, where it had always been most intensive. We have already seen how that intensity has affected the moorland surface and produced many local variations in microclimate and habitat. The need for the organisation and regulation of tin working just summarised is in part explained by that intensity and thus a symptom of a nice relationship between the working men, their masters and their shared landscape.

Other metals

Ninety nine per cent of the mines in or on the granite are for tin, but around the metamorphic aureole and just into the fringes of the granite copper, lead, iron, arsenic and even silver have all been mined by shaft or adit. The landscape effect of this mining is not great. An isolated chimney stack at Ramsley above South Zeal represents the six copper mines that stretched in an arc from there to Bridestowe, there were six more, four on the west and southwest and two near Ashburton all without scenic impact now. Lead was worked in three mines between Mary Tavy and Bridestowe the southernmost of which, Wheal Betsy, has left to us the only Dartmoor example of the kind of tall engine house so familiar in the Cornish landscape not far to the west (Fig. 204). Wheal Betsy produced lead and silver from the late eighteenth century well into the nineteenth. Iron proper was only sought in two places, Smallacombe near Haytor and at Shaugh Prior, but into the twentieth century 'shiny ore' or micaceous haematite was worked at numerous small mines on the edges of the far east because it was an essential ingredient of rust-proofing paint. Kelly Mine near Lustleigh is a good and partly restored example of the scale of working in these later stages of the industry. South of Wheal Betsy the Wheal, or Devon, Friendship mine at Mary Tavy was the richest of those copper mines

FIG 204. Wheal Betsy, the only Cornish-type engine house on Dartmoor. It sits by the A386 as it rises out of Mary Tavy on to Blackdown; Cox Tor is on the right-hand skyline.

referred to above. It worked continuously from the late eighteenth century until 1925 (a longer history of continuous working than any other mine in the southwest peninsula) and reduced the Mary Tavy landscape to a real desert in that time. Arsenic, often alongside copper, was a lately valued mineral mined in the northwest and the southeast and up the Teign valley where, even later, barytes or 'heavy spar', a gangue (or 'containing') mineral thrown away earlier, was re-worked well into the twentieth century for a great range of modern uses from paper-filling and paint making, to barium meals to assist radiography. It is said that the Ramsley waste tips which contain arsenic, yield a path-clearing weedkiller to rival any garden centre offering of the twenty-first century. Fascinating though the story of this other-than-tin metal-mining is, bar the two structures and waste tips I have cited it does not contribute overtly to the landscape we find before us now, but, and especially in full, it is a proper part of Dartmoor's whole economic history. That history is not over. It is proposed, as the first decade of the twenty-first century comes towards its end, to mine wolfram for tungsten production at Hemerdon Ball, the southernmost outpost of the industrial moorland about to be described. Planning permission to excavate a low percentage ore has existed for some time, but the world price has not justified working until now.

China clay

The other ancillary economic mineral of the granite pluton and its subsequent geologic history is kaolinite, and its extraction since the early nineteenth century has also yielded by-products such as building sand and brick-making material. Kaolin has been sought and briefly worked in the Erme and Avon moorland valleys, with small pits and waste heaps still evident at the sites (Fig. 205). The line of a railway from Redlake to Bittaford and erstwhile treatment buildings at Bittaford and Shipley Bridge are still standing as landscape memorials to the nineteenth-century effort. But at Lee and Shaugh Moors, stretching from Cholwich Town to Wotter, and inwards to Cadover Bridge and just beyond, the whole landscape is dominated by the symptoms of the extraction of china clay and its aftermath (Fig. 206). It has involved huge pits and waste tips (remodelled from the classic cones after the Aberfan disaster in South Wales), nineteenth-century industrial housing, leat and reservoir creation; road closure and diversion and 'landscaping' in the late twentieth century (Fig. 207). The whole area involved is a rough triangle nearly three miles across its base from Quick Bridge to Wotter, and two and a half miles from base to apex, Wotter to Cadover Bridge on the Plym. It can be overlooked well from the east at Shell Top and Penn Beacon, but there are significant viewpoints within the complex just bounded. There is more to the south: mica dams and treatment works (Fig. 208), well beyond the National Park

FIG 205. Aerial view of the southern plateau looking east from above Plym Head. The Redlake pit and its conical waste tip are on the left of the middle-ground and the Avon reservoir can be seen over the watershed beyond.

FIG 206. The Lee Moor clay workings of English China Clays in the 1960s: (above left) pit and associated 'sand' waste tip, the foreground and the road it carried then have long been excavated; (above right) the ancillary industrial landscape south of the pit also no longer a public view.

boundary but within the 'Natural Area' and, not before the moorland finally runs out, at Headon and Crown Hill Downs. Here is an industrial landscape to match any. Lee Moor and Wotter are, at their hearts, tiny china clay workmens' villages with nineteenth-century back-to-back cottage rows or terraces, a Working Mens' Institute, library and chapels. They shrink to nothing in the landscape compared with their *raisons d'être*, the vast spatial impact of the pits and tips. The three

268 · DARTMOOR

FIG 207. The pits and tips of Watts, Blake and Bearne at the north end of the kaolinite deposit seen from above Cadover Bridge in the mid-1970s. The Plym runs across the foreground; its visitors not deterred by the background vista.

FIG 208. The waste slurry is captured in so-called mica dams downstream of the working site.

FIG 209. Shaugh Moor, archaeologically rich and now permanently saved from the waste deposition which came so close.

originally separate Whitehill Yeo, Lee Moor and Shaugh pits were amalgamated with planning permission in the last 35 years and their concomitant waste tips stretch to the west and the southeast of them with a smaller area of tip and mica dam at the Cadover Bridge apex. Here is a landscape white-out, bridging the boundary between moorland and farmland, bringing the granitic origin of Dartmoor to the surface in the most dramatic fashion, and spilling that geological influence into the valleys off the moorland. In 2000 AD it still provided work for a thousand people, though the world price of kaolin since then has changed that. The planning inquiry in 1971 that settled the pit-merging deal between two different operators, left applications to tip on the remainder of Shaugh Moor and in the Black-a-Brook valley alongside it (Areas 'Y' and 'Z' in the planning jargon of the time) to be settled later. In the late 1990s the clay companies made the magnanimous gesture to the landscape, and to archaeologists, of forgoing any potential tipping of waste on Shaugh Moor. There, as we have already seen, excavation has revealed much about Bronze Age developments on Dartmoor subsequent to the 1970s decision. So, there remains there a microcosm of Bronze Age detail of settlement and land boundaries. It is well worth examination by anyone intrigued by that first organisation of a land-use pattern to replace open moorland on Dartmoor, but who can ignore the pale grey surround (Fig. 209).

Just north of Cadover Bridge lie some pools in long-abandoned and small-scale china clay workings at Brisworthy, that are now clear and providing a habitat already listed in Chapter 6. The stronghold of the scarce blue-tailed damselfly is here and the species features strongly in the Dartmoor Biodiversity Action Plan, where the fear for natural colonisation of the pools ousting the damselfly is registered and close monitoring of change is proposed.

Stone quarries

The quarrying of granite itself, of other rocks in the metamorphic aureole and even beyond it, is the last remaining landscape effect of men at work seeking mineral matter that remains to be considered. We have already concluded that with so much rock lying on the surface the need to quarry beneath it emerged very late in historic time. This has to be a consequence of demand, largely in the south east of England, for large quantities of building stone of handsome strength in sizeable blocks, and in short order, for largely public and national purposes in the late eighteenth and early nineteenth centuries. Even the fourteenth-century parish churches of the Domesday manors, grand and towering though some of them are, appear to have been built with well-hewn moorstone. But when London Bridge and Nelson's Column loom as market leaders there is suddenly a need for excavation on the grand scale (in its day) and the production of large blocks to architectural specification in quantity and on time. Quarrying granite, and effective transportation systems to get it off Dartmoor, are born. Despite that, quarries in the granite are few in number: Foggintor a mile and a half due west of Princetown, the Haytor complex and Merrivale on the Tavistock–Princetown road, remain the largest (Fig. 210). Each has had a specific public building recipe as its origin or sustaining influence:

FIG 210. Granite quarrying late in time: (above left) Merrivale Quarry below Staple Tor – still working in the mid-1970s – New Scotland Yard was clad with stone from here; (above right) Foggintor Quarry's waste heaps – where Nelson's Column was cut .

FIG 211. Points in the Haytor granite tramway as it runs down Haytor Down, to carry the blocks for London Bridge to the canal and estuary for Teignmouth. (DNPA)

Nelson's Column, London Bridge and New Scotland Yard were the respective deals. The fact that the quasi-horizontal joints were wider apart as one descended into the granite, allowing bigger blocks to be raised and dressed was as good a reason as any for quarrying into the hill rather than searching for the block that would do, by wandering about the clitter. That, once started, the hole would yield a quantity of such blocks in one place was an obvious additional close advantage. Merrivale was on the turnpike to Tavistock, Foggintor a short distance on the contour from the same road, though soon nearer the Princetown–Plymouth railway line. Well-worked architectural building components, mullions and coping stones still lie there awaiting collection. A granite tramway was built from Haytor to the Stover canal which floated granite blocks on barges to Teignmouth via the Teign estuary (Fig. 211).

The tramway guided wooden-wheeled flatbed trucks partly horse-drawn and partly gravitationally propelled by a devious route down the eastern flank of the Moor still to be followed on foot as the Templer Way, named for the man who conceived the whole project, and who lived at Stover House between Bovey Tracey and Newton Abbot. None of these three major quarries is currently at work, though Merrivale only closed in the 1990s. It was working its own granite well into the 1970s with an extensive suite of cutting and polishing equipment alongside the hand-tool production of gravestones and farm rollers which it had

FIG 212. Inside the Merrivale complex in the 1960s – the domestic trade persisted alongside the large-scale contracts such as that for New Scotland Yard.

produced since it opened (Fig. 212). The men producing these locally needed artefacts in three-sided shelters with a wooden 'anvil' in the centre of the floor, always had small heaps of uranium ore at the back of the 'shed' to excite students and any other visitor who gained entry. Such was the investment in the finishing machinery at Merrivale by the splendidly named Anselm and Odling, that it went on importing a variety of exotic stones for just that – finishing – into the 1990s, and one can still pick up fragments of Norwegian gabbro, Italian marble and other exotic rocks alongside the track into the quarry.

There are a considerable number of smaller granite quarries scattered among the settlements round the edge of the great pluton, nearly all abandoned now. One of the larger ones is Blackingstone above Doccombe, close to Blackingstone Rock, one of the outermost tors of the granite, where a dark almost green-grey stone was worked intermittently right up until this century. The stone is common in Moretonhampstead buildings and alongside the A382. Almost due south of it is a quarry in the Wray valley side buried in woodland above East Wrey, which bears the same name, this time associated with Blackingstone Farm. Close to the Haytor Quarry already registered, there are additional, smaller pits, the biggest below Holwell Tor, and another just north of Saddle Tor. Near to Foggintor are quarries alongside Sweltor and Ingra Tor, both of which had easy access to the Princetown–Plymouth railway line that ran for some 75 years from 1878. Great Trowlesworthy Tor, in a very pink granite, was itself quarried and a half-finished millstone still lies there. There was of course a small quarry at the prison at Princetown and even smaller ones at Harford and below Western Beacon in the extreme south.

In contrast there is a welter of quarries all round the Dartmoor fringe in the metamorphic aureole and beyond, exploiting the virtues of various rocks. The biggest by far, and like the china clay pits still in production, is the large quarry complex at Meldon just southwest of Okehampton and south of the A30. For many years the quarry belonged to railway companies and their successors, and there is still a remnant of the old Southern Region line from Waterloo to Plymouth, now a branch line from Exeter to the quarry, carrying stone away for use as ballast on lines all over the southern part of Britain. Local demand for road metal is carried away by lorry. The main stone is Meldon Chert of Carboniferous age crushing to sharply angular fragments ideal for 'road' making of all kinds and visible in Figure 31. It turned out in the 1960s to be the only non-limestone rock to which British Rail had access in the south of England. Limestone is not the ideal railway ballast because of its water-retaining properties, hence the longevity of this quarry and the branch line to it. It is a major feature in the local landscape though more visible from outside the National Park than from the moorland. Between it and the Meldon dam are small abandoned quarries in 'granulite', one exposing a branched aplite dyke which runs with the chert from Sourton Tors for nearly 3 km east-northeastward.

Trusham Quarry in the east is the not as big as the Meldon complex. It is just against the National Park boundary at the near right angle it makes to leave the Teign valley and pass north of Bovey Tracey. It is also still working, extracting roadstone and aggregate for concrete block making from the dolerite. It is perhaps under half the size of Meldon but also more visible from outside the Park. Ryecroft Quarry two miles to the north and also adjacent to the boundary is out of use, as are a number of smaller pits upstream and on the shoulders of the valley at Christow Common, Scatter Rock and below Bridford in all of which Teign Chert and dolerite were worked. A recent application to modify the access to Ryecroft Quarry attracted much opposition and was refused in 2001.

On the southeast, alongside the A38 and inside the Park, Linhay Quarry in Devonian limestone is bigger than Trusham in area and also still working, though remarkably invisible from almost anywhere. Bulley Cleave and Higher Kiln quarries at Buckfastleigh (the former in Figure 29) are now long disused, though Bulley Cleave was working into the 1970s. Higher Kiln contains the entrances to the underground chambers whose collections of interglacial mammal remains and contemporary greater horseshoe bat colonies give it Site of Special Scientific Interest (SSSI) status. They too exploited the Devonian limestone. The

FIG 213. Powder Mills near Postbridge; the highest of the deliberately isolated pairs of mills (with shared central waterwheel) all driven by the same leat is seen on the right. Sadly this 'gun powder' factory for the mining industry was built only ten years before the invention of dynamite.

Carboniferous limestone has also been worked just north and northeast of South Tawton, where defunct quarries are visible from the A30, and in which Bill Dearman demonstrated the intense folding that suggested a northward push by the Dartmoor granite pluton at the time of its emplacement within the country rock. At Drewsteignton, the same limestone was moved out of Blackaller Quarry right up until the 1990s. Around Tavistock a number of quarries worked until quite recently. Mostly they dealt in 'Tavistock slate', a dark green to black, coarse slate popularly used for facing parts of new dwellings to meet early planning design demands, sadly often looking like vertical crazy paving up chimneys. Some did exploit the dolerite intruded into the Carboniferous slates and shales and now exposed in a great swathe from Tavistock northeastward to Willsworthy, taking in Peter Tavy and Mary Tavy on the way.

Otherwise most tiny pits in the National Park were excavated for specific building projects, even single buildings, throughout the last three centuries. The odd one of them, at Yennadon near Dousland for instance, has persisted as a one-man, small-scale production site for retail stone – the kind of enterprise which the NPA, as planning authority, tolerates for its contribution to the detail of modern domestic development. Their impact on the landscape is minimal but exposes what lies beneath the surface and helps in interpreting it. The same historic principle of a quarry for a single project of course extends to the major civil engineering works of Dartmoor's last century or so, primarily the reservoir dams. Avon, Burrator, Fernworthy, Trenchford and Venford all have attendant excavations solely for the purpose of immediate construction, now hidden from view or dwarfed by their structural successor. Meldon, obviously, had material already to hand.

Finally, it would be a blatant omission in this catalogue of excavation for construction in its widest sense, if reference was not made to the roadside pits which pepper the verges of the turnpikes across the moor, their companion roads on the fringes and the 'tributary' lanes of either (Fig. 214). The pits have usually been excavated on the horizontal from the road surface into the hill, though the quarry bottom has sometimes sagged; one or two still have vertical faces at their back ends but scree is quickly mounting them. Sadly their geological observational value disappears with that process, and sand martins are denied the low cliffs in which they sometimes nested. Even into the last quarter of the last century, as Chapter 2 tells, there were good exposures of periglacial solifluxion on Merripit Hill on the B3212, on the Cowsic–Black-a-Brook interfluve off the road alongside Long Plantation, where Beckamoor Combe abuts the B3257 and on the road to Moorlands Farm past Prince Hall. All, too, saved soil surveyors the labour

FIG 214. Roadside pit for extraction of gravel by commoners and tenants – one of many on the turnpikes alone, this one on Dunnabridge Common also housed sand martins until the 1980s.

of digging a sample pit. Their initial excavation was almost certainly associated with the road-making itself, their longevity was because Duchy tenants, and most commoners elsewhere, had the right or the privilege to take sand, gravel and stone for their own domestic use. In the 1960s a mini swing-shovel sat permanently in the pit above the bridge to Moorlands across the West Dart, such was the demand for rutted track repairs. These pits are in many ways the most obvious symptom of men at work among raw materials on the moorland surface to the road-bound traveller across Dartmoor. He may even be encouraged to park in them, for they hide the winking sunlit windscreen from many sides, or he may illicitly spend the night there in his camper van. They are also a reminder of the less common of common rights deployable on the moor, compared with the grazing right that is obvious all around. The right 'in the soil' to take stone and gravel, of turbary (to take turf or peat), of estovers (to take firewood and ferns for bedding) are all only for domestic use. Within the Forest, Duchy tenants join commoners in this corporate satisfying of need and so the pits also remind the thoughtful of the continued presence of benevolent landlords.

FARMERS, FARMING AND THE HISTORIC LANDSCAPE

The tinners' dense and still obvious marking of the moorland is now all vegetated except for the standing remains of some buildings. We have just seen that even the roadside growan pits have few bare faces left. As abandonment happened new plant microhabitats were on offer and most of them available to grazing animals. Of course the whole spectrum of plant cover from wet to dry, on original smooth or rocky slope or on the new faces of waste heap and excavators' ditch, has been grazed by stock and burnt by stockmen throughout the 5,000 years that tin ore has been sought, and farmers have farmed Dartmoor. That grazing and burning has created and sustained the vegetation mosaic already described, and over the years has demanded the development of that special set of skills that separates the moorland farmer from his lowland compatriot and sometime client. The clientele of history had two contributions to make to the hill-farmers' economy through time – it bought hill-bred stock in the autumn to fatten and finish downslope and it sent, or brought, its own stock up to the hill for the summer to rest some of the lowland fields, make hay in others and allow yet more to be ploughed to grow winter feed and domestic crops. The annual process of transhumance, for that is what it was, came at a price to the lowlander. Dartmoor men kept a hill man's eye on the lowland stock, reported failings and generally ensured that it thrived, its owners paid those men or their masters for the service and the privilege.

The pre-eminent landlord

The thirteenth- to sixteenth-century records of the Duchy of Cornwall, master of masters on central Dartmoor for nearly 700 years now, nicely demonstrate the business relationships involved then. The Duchy received a 'three ha'pence fee' per beast for summer grazing on the Forest in 1345 from its own agister. (Agisting is the allowing of stock to be grazed on, in this case, the Forest for a fee. 'Agiste' is an Anglo-Norman word meaning lodging.) The agister made his own percentage, and may also have paid others to perform or share his duties to the lowland stock. So the South Hams or mid-Devon cattleman paid more than the 'penny-ha'penny' per beast into the hill economy and in 1400 AD paid it for 10,500 'bovines' to the Duchy's agisters alone. That was the peak of agistment income in this late mediaeval period, numbers varied from 5,000 in 1290 AD to 6,500 in 1300, and fell back to 5,000 immediately after the Black Death (1348). Then it rose but from the 1400 climax there was a steady decline to 8,000 in 1500 AD. Harold Fox, who extracted these figures from the Duchy records, points out that these stock numbers are very large for their time and yet they are minimum grazing figures, for they are only for the Forest and perhaps the Duchy's other commons, but therefore not even for the whole of the Commons of Devon, those which abut the Forest. Neither do they reveal figures for the manorial commons – those outside the Commons of Devon ring, animals not paid for, nor those of the Dartmoor farmers themselves grazing this and other moorland. Nor do they tell us anything about sheep.

That numbers rose so rapidly after the Black Death suggests that with many fewer mouths to be fed the demand for animal products – meat and leather especially – outstripped that for grain, which traditionally feeds the multitude. That of course would be a county-wide if not a country-wide phenomenon, but it points up here a substantial fourteenth-century shift towards livestock farming in Devon (never to be reversed), and the regard lowland Devon farmers then developed for Dartmoor moorland as a summer grazing resource despite their own general climatic advantage in grass growing. Though after all that, we should not ignore the fact that cattle numbers fell again through the fifteenth century and that may even hint at a diminution of grazing value after that peak of pressure in 1400. That is the first-ever suggestion of over-grazing on the moor, an accusatory claim that has been thrown at Dartmoor's farmers at intervals right up to the latter part of the twentieth century.

Fox makes the further point that 'three ha'pence' was a paltry sum throughout this time compared with the value of the beast. An ox was worth ten shillings even in the middle of the thirteenth century, so probably more in the early 1400s. Oxen, whether for fattening and butchering or as beasts of burden and the drawing of ploughs, needed all-the-year-round feeding, so the summer bargain suited the lowland cattle men well. It was quite a good deal for Duchy tenants too, for they coincidentally paid the same figure per acre in rent (three ha'pence) for their in-bye land at this time. Other agisters, and of course the lords of the manor who owned the Commons of Devon or the parcels of manorial waste, their foremen, reeves and commoners, all had a slice of the action, overseeing lowland visiting stock alongside their own. A recipe for potential over-grazing at least in summer is easily perceived, and while Vancouver registered it again in the last decade of the eighteenth century on Widecombe Town Commons, it was only a summer event, the grazing was recorded as knee-high by the time the lowland cattle returned in May. What is seasonal over-grazing to one is balanced routine to another.

The Duchy of Cornwall was to all intents and purposes the lord of the manor of Lydford, in which parish the whole Forest lay until the 1980s when the Boundary Commission made it a parish of its own centred on Princetown. The Duchy also owned Bridestowe and Sourton, Okehampton Hamlets, Belstone, South Tawton and Peter Tavy Commons and, despite the dis-afforestation of 1204, Duchy officers claimed the right to drive stock off the other Commons of Devon when they thought it necessary at various times in the following centuries. So 'lord and master' fitted the Duchy well, and yet as an institution (invented by Edward III in 1337 to support the eldest son of the monarch when there was one) rather than just a family, its records are continuous and thus more valuable than those of other lords in investigating Dartmoor and its farming history. The chief officer of the Duchy, which persists even when there is no Duke, and when the net income all goes to the Exchequer, is still called the Secretary and Keeper of the Records.

The Ancient Tenements and other Duchy farms

At the forefront of the kind of summer stock management we have just noted were the occupiers of the Ancient Tenements within the Forest, described first in Chapter 4, and of other farms against the moorland edge. Again we know more about the Ancient Tenements than the others because of the Duchy's record keeping. They are all first mentioned between 1260 (Babeny and Pizwell) and 1560 (Brownberry) though ten of the 17 mediaeval sites are recorded in the first century of that 300-year span (Fig. 215). 'Sites', because there was almost always more than one farm holding at the named place. The record shows, as well as the three ha'pence an acre rent collected, tax paid for landless souls, presumably labourers or slaves, and a number of places 'paying no rent' in 1350, doubtless empty after the

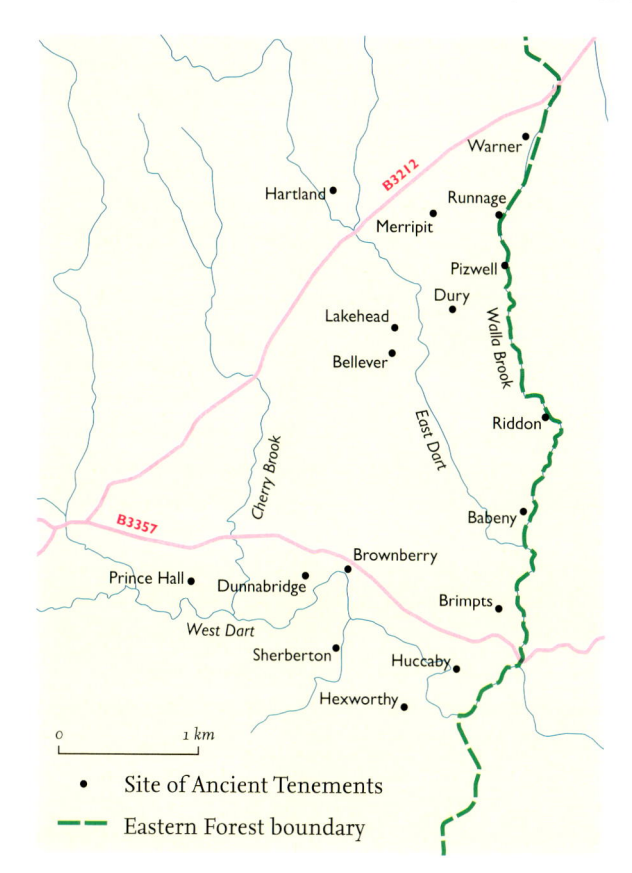

FIG 215. Map of the Ancient Tenements (the modern roads are to aid location). The 17 sites accommodated 34 separate holdings at the peak of their occupation.

Black Death. The reference to Babeny and Pizwell in 1260 (predating the invention of the dukedom, but after the earldom had reverted to the crown), is because the men of those two places petitioned the Bishop of Exeter to allow them to use Widecombe church rather than trek all across the Moor to Lydford for their Sunday obligations and all their other spiritual needs, which traffic the Lych Way (through Bellever and Postbridge, Powder Mills and Willsworthy) still represents. Babeny and Pizwell are right against the eastern boundary of the Forest at either end of Riddon Ridge and the incident suggests that had the other Tenements in like position existed then they would have joined in the petition (Fig. 216).

By extrapolation therefore we can see the first extension of the enclosed farmland landscape, since its Saxon consolidation in the Webburn valleys, up the West and East Dart and the Walla Brook from the mid-thirteenth century onwards. We know less about the origins of farms whose occupiers might also be regarded

FIG 216. The Ancient Tenement landscape: (left) the site of Babeny, its driftway to Riddon Ridge runs up the left-hand side of the middle-ground; (below left) the view from Yar Tor across Sherril, past Babeny and Riddon Ridge to the Warren House Inn (the white building near the central skyline) which sits just above the northernmost Tenement, Walna. Pizwell lies below it.

as likely overseers of summer visiting stock outside the Forest. But such 'moormen' almost certainly occupied sites like Teigncombe west of Chagford; Moortown at Gidleigh; Clannaborough near Throwleigh; Horndon in Mary Tavy; Moortown at Whitchurch; Stanlake above Burrator; Greenwell (mentioned in a pipe roll in 1181 AD) near Meavy; Cholwichtown and Yadsworthy in Cornwood; Skerraton in Dean Prior, Bowden near Cross Furzes; Fore Stoke at Holne; and Bagtor under Haytor. Those farms, as manors themselves or the manors in which they lie are all recorded in the century beginning in 1086, most in that year itself. Other Duchy tenancies, apart from the Ancient Tenements, like Yardworthy and Great Frenchbeer near Chagford, must also have played their part at some time in this upper end of the Devon version of a transhumance system, which Fox believed was well established before the eleventh century. All those 'moormen' were hill-farmers in their own right and traded their own crop of steers, calves, foals and lambs with the 'finishers' off the moor. That lower ground may not have been so far away. For while the base of any historic hill farm was a compact collection of fields yielding some hay, some oats or rye and some roots in a sensible rotation for home consumption and winter feed, there were within the Dart basin and close around the outer fringes of the moorland, mixed farms whose rough grazing was minimal but whose fattening potential was not to be dismissed.

The Ancient Tenements were largely copyhold (a copy of the lease was held by both the Duchy and the family) and succession was allowed for a financial consideration which was thus not far from freehold and thus from family security. While the farms grouped on sites like Babeny or Dunnabridge may have been individually occupied, the present field pattern suggests a degree of corporate activity almost certainly inherited from an open field-type operation. The written record shows that Dunnabridge was 'assarted', or taken from the Forest in 1305, by five men – one being Hamlin de Sherwell (now Sherrill?) – who paid 15 shillings between them as an entry 'fine' for taking in from the 'King's waste at Dunnabridge' three 'ferlings' or 39 ha, and that they had 7.9 ha each. They paid seven shillings and sixpence for the first year's rent of the whole and had to manure it all by the end of 1306, implying that it was by then ready for cultivation. The whole enterprise could only have been achieved corporately. The long, narrow fields closer to the farmstead at Babeny are similar to the 'bundled' strips that still offered fair shares of soil quality, slope and aspect to the then slightly freer farmers. Some of the narrow enclosures are now subdivisions of larger round-cornered outlines of still earlier newtakes and even bear personal names in the genitive to this day ('Hicks's Yonder', 'Hicks's Homer' and so on).

That reference to open fields inevitably drives us back in time. While the first 300 years of the Duchy record has given an insight into the latter part of the mediaeval working of Dartmoor's highest hill farms and their communing within the core of the Park, we have to go back to the Domesday survey nearly two centuries earlier to set the baseline for farming the landscape outside the Forest. Then we shall see how, like the tinners, the farmers also left their physical marks on what we now see as moorland. The Domesday Book also gives us some idea of the stage the Saxon organisation of lower Dartmoor land use had reached before Harold messed up the defence of the realm.

The build-up to Domesday

Just as the Normans 'tolerated and absorbed' Saxon arrangements, patterns and doubtless labour (they became Anglicised; after all we don't speak French!), so it is reasonable to suppose that the Saxons had been there before, though they may have enslaved Britons 500 years earlier in a somewhat less 'tolerant' mode. One step back, Fleming's proposal reported in Chapter 3 that the 18 or so Bronze Age coaxial reave systems, scattered right round the moorland core as Figure 70 demonstrated, reflect what he calls 'large terrains' under at least corporate management, need not contradict the apparent distribution of Iron Age (British) settlement and farming. If the larger Bronze Age settlements fit strategically with the basal reaves then similar status may be applied to the Iron Age 'forts'. The very short planning and construction time for the establishment of the reave systems implies authority, communal or 'masterful', and most likely large terrain by large terrain rather than because there was some central Dartmoor overview. Fleming also proposes putative common grazing above and below the enclosure systems altitudinally, or inside and outside in Dartmoor plan terms. He even suggests that the outer, 'common' grazing was used by 'outsiders' against whom the large terrain farmers needed a defence. So perhaps Dartmoor transhumance is that old. There is no reason yet discovered or archaeologically conceived, why the land-use reflection of such a negotiated, or at least defended, system shouldn't have simply been picked up by the British of the Iron Age. They, folk and systems, seem to have survived through the Roman period and lay ready, even if only in a state of subsistence farming, for Saxon absorption. The large terrains were sometimes bigger sometimes smaller than their successor Saxon manors, and the Normans were probably not the first to bundle some manors into larger estates. The (probably remote) lord of such a bundle, as the Linehan quotation at the head of this chapter suggests, was probably less interested in how things actually worked on the ground than in whatever his or her dues were from those there, whether agents or farmers.

Thus, Fleming's ideas allow the last prehistoric pattern of 'land-holding' to be slipped easily into the eleventh-century one through more than a thousand years, and we have already seen how the relics of those patterns still mark the mid-height moorland. His innermost and higher common grazing becomes the Saxon royal hunting forest extending outwards over the modern Commons of Devon, associated with the large terrains. The outer Bronze Age unenclosed grazing land becomes the Saxon, then Norman and finally the mediaeval manorial waste. Two principles: the valley system as the basis for more intensive land use organisation and the large terrain or 'estate' as the management division of that land use, had persisted, I will claim, for more than 2,000 years *before* William decided to have them described, assessed and valued. Some would say it persisted for nearly another 1,000 after that. Certainly the unique Domesday record demonstrates a Dartmoor Saxon pattern we can still recognise on the ground. Even the thirteenth-century consolidation of the Forest, the initiating of the Ancient Tenements and the information from the Duchy records only reflects that pattern, adds to it but doesn't change it.

Dartmoor Domesday

For our purposes the record shows that 34 of Dartmoor's present villages or small towns were manors in 1066, because each entry in 1086 refers back to the day when King Edward the Confessor was 'alive and dead', i.e. in January of that year (William, for obvious reasons, had no truck with Harold as 'King'). Thirty-nine other manors are still on the map and nearly all their names remain the same, but they range from hamlets like Harbourneford, Dunstone and Sigford to single farms like Lowton in Moretonhampstead parish and Wringworthy near Peter Tavy. One or two names have to be traced forwards until they bear the modern name, a classic being Dewdons, a sizeable manor in 1086, whose name evolves into Jordan, southwest of Widecombe and by no means as sizeable, by 1724. A Jordan family had occupied parts of the hamlet in the seventeenth century during which the manor, long held by Hamlyns who also held Holne in 1086 (and remember Sherrill; Hamlyn is still a common name in southeast Dartmoor). Dewdons passed by marriage to Mallets from Somerset (Shepton Mallet?) at the end of the thirteenth century, was broken up and sold largely to adjoining holdings. But the exact moment of name-change of part of the original manor to Jordan is not yet discovered.

Of the identified Dartmoor manors the King directly held an interesting scatter largely simply assumed from Saxon royal or quasi-royal ownership. Walkhampton and Lydford (one of Alfred's four Devonian boroughs) were pre-empted because Edward held them, Spitchwick and Moretonhampstead because 'Earl Harold' held them and South Tawton because Gytha, Harold's mother, held it. In contrast Baldwin the Sheriff – the King's man in Devon – held a large block of land stretching from Okehampton, where he began building a castle, eastwards to Clifford on the Teign and then south to Hennock and across to Manaton, then to Shapley and Beetor, north of Hameldown, and on to Middlecott, near Chagford. There were obviously islands in the block, for Moretonhampstead has already been accounted for, Osbern held Parford, Shilstone and Lambert, all east of Chagford. Gerald the Chaplain held Shapley but let three manors there to Saxon thanes, and others held manors from Baldwin. But the 'large terrain' emerges again as a management concept. Baldwin's southern boundary butted against the lands of the Bishop of Coutances who, based at Bovey Tracey, held a block from there north to Elsford and across to Scobitor – in Widecombe parish now. Baldwin had an interest in Holne, and the Bishop in Chagford, so 'estate blocks with outliers' is a variation on the theme. Groups of manors under one lord occur all round Dartmoor as at Dean Prior, Mary Tavy and Tavistock, and of course many of them extended well outside what we now see as the Dartmoor boundary.

From the point of view of land-use management succession the most interesting record may be that the last list in the Devon part of the Domesday Book is headed 'Lands of the King's Thanes', i.e. Saxons. Colwin is the first listed and we know that he looked after Queen Edith's affairs in Exeter before 1066 (she was the wife of Edward the Confessor). Colwin held seven manors in 1086, had held two of them before 1066 and four more which Godric had held before then, too. Colwin was obviously one of the Saxon administrators trusted to remain or become one of the Norman King's thanes, and getting a Saxon's lion's share of the available spoils. Godwin, of similar ilk no doubt, held Wray (now part of Lustleigh), Cheriton Bishop and Lambert; and Adred held Manaton. In all, nine Dartmoor manors were held by Saxons in 1086 which goes some way to confirming the Oppenheimer principle set out in the *Origins of the British* (2004), of the easy successive transition of land-holding and working on the ground, almost by infiltration, and well below the level of the change from one ruling culture to another whether that was by invasion, military conquest or other means.

The Domesday records for the manors that fringe the Forest confirm the mixed farming set-up at the turn of the first millennium AD. It was a kind of communal subsistence with some surplus from which dues were paid, metal and leather bought and community specialists, smiths, weavers and quarrymen supported. The model entry gives the dimension of woodland and pasture, an estimate of the arable potential and in most cases the extent to which that was currently realised by reference to 'land for 'x' ploughs ... and there are 'y' plough teams'. 'Meadow' is assumed to be enclosed grassland and 'pasture' to be what we would now call rough grazing. In many cases the appropriate dimensions appear to coincide with the size of the common and woodland we know now (Moretonhampstead's woodland measures the same now as in 1086, the slope determination of gross land use persists!), though sometimes too much or too little for such an easy comparison. Holne, to which I have often referred, has in Holne Moor about the same amount of pasture as now, one league by one league (6.5 sq km), but the woodland may be underestimated at the same area, given that the manor included Holne Chase and Holne Park as far as we can tell. It had ploughland for 12 ploughs but only six existed. One packhorse is listed (a rare thing in the local Domesday record) but it will be recalled that coppice produce was still being extracted by packhorse from White Wood in Holne in the twentieth century, perhaps here is a hint of a 1,000 years of coppicing.

South Tawton, a large parish still, had land for 50 ploughs and the lordship had eight while the 'fifty villagers and thirty smallholders' had 36 ploughs, so only six ploughlands were unused in 1086 (Fig. 217). Along with that arable went

FIG 217. South Tawton village centre, the church and Church House persist since the late mediaeval period and their sites may go back to Domesday. (DNPA)

60 acres (24.3 ha) of meadow and 4 square leagues of woodland, but 16 square leagues (93 sq km) of pasture. There are possibly 9 sq km of Dartmoor moorland in the parish now (mostly on Cosdon) and there might have been a little more rough grazing on the Culm clay in the north in 1086, but the whole modern parish is only about 67 sq km. So, either there is a surveyor's or a scribe's miscalculation based perhaps on a local opinion, off the cuff, never having been asked for before, or South Tawton had a greater status in 1066 than that of a simple manor. It is suggested that it may have been regarded as a minor 100 rather than just a manor in Gytha's day (1066), and perhaps for 20 more years at least. So then it may have administered other places whose pasture was added in by the surveyors. Gidleigh is certainly one possibility, but Throwleigh had been a royal holding in Canute's time and Chagford, which has a big common now, had no pasture, wood or meadow recorded in 1086. Putting all these together a block of moorland of substantial proportions southeast of South Tawton (parish) emerges with another bit of evidence for a Saxon large terrain. Each of these manors, or collections of them, had a good acreage of ploughland, and so the mixed farming (close to subsistence) principle persists, but remember that moorland 'pasture' was within the system.

Early mediaeval land use

Post Domesday, and before the Duchy records give us written evidence for land use and variations in it, we have to rely on odd documented events like the dis-afforestation up to the new forest boundary of 1204; pipe rolls and other local records, and of course what can be deduced from observation of the surface and from excavation. There are at least 130 abandoned mediaeval settlement sites on

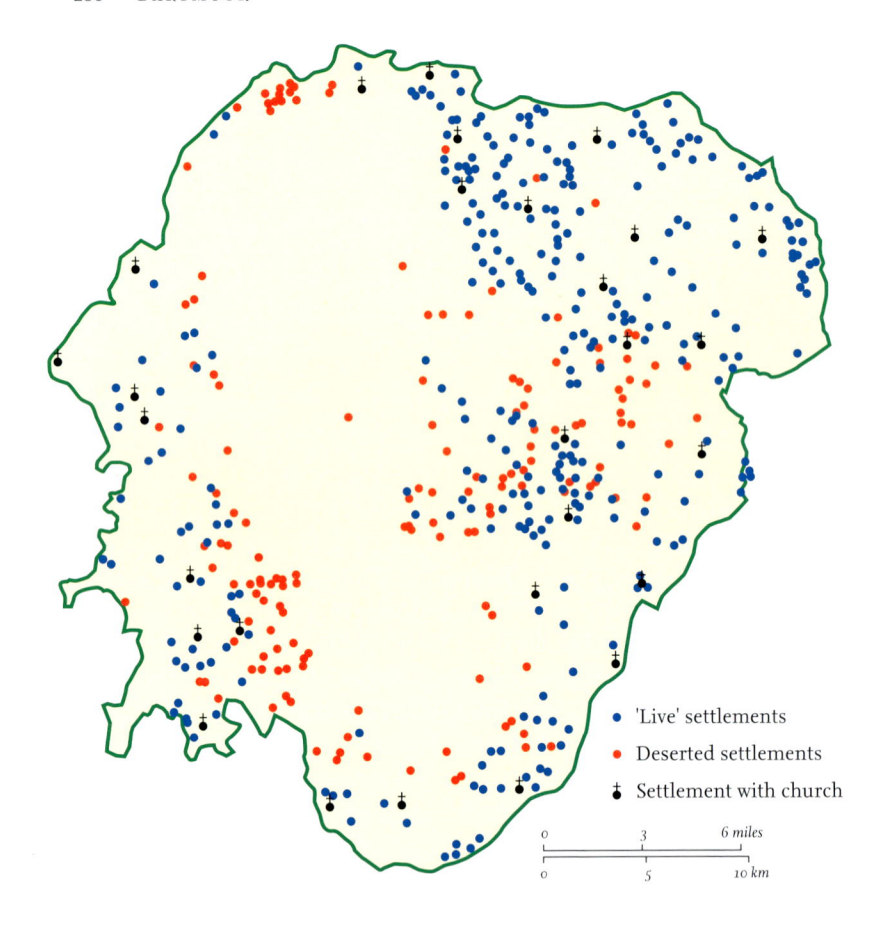

FIG 218. Mediaeval settlement: the survivors and the remains of others (after Gerrard, 1997).

present-day moorland and in the enclosed landscape within the National Park (Fig. 218). They are widespread all around the high moorland core, with concentrations in the Webburns' joint catchment, and that of the Plym–Meavy. The sites range from 'villages' such as the 11 buildings clustered between Houndtor and Greator Rocks on Houndtor common in Manaton parish (Fig. 219), to hamlets in Okehampton Deer Park where lanes connect farmsteads; and to single dwellings like Dinna Clerks in Widecombe whose occupation ended dramatically with a fire, the occupiers leaving so rapidly they left a Henry III penny on the threshold. Nicely, the northern Houndtor hamlet re-uses a

WORKING THE LANDSCAPE · 287

FIG 219. The site of the Houndtor mediaeval village from the Tor itself, looking south.

FIG 220. The fields of the mediaeval village of Blackaton revealed by 1960s ploughing.

FIG 221. The Challacombe lynchets – the biggest scheduled ancient monument in the Moor.

prehistoric pound wall. Nearly all are credited with abandonment in the fourteenth century. Most have associated fields, some still very obvious as those with Challacombe and Blackaton deserted villages in the upper West Webburn valley (Fig. 220). The Challacombe ones form a stairway of lynchets up the east side of the down almost opposite Grimspound (Fig. 221). There are other patterns sufficiently far from known dwellings to be regarded as 'outfields' in the agrarian historical sense, to which more attention must be paid in due course. The remains of many can be seen, in low morning or evening sun, from roads like the B3212 not far west of Moretonhampstead Moorgate, southward from the B3357 above Huccaby, or looking west across the valley of the Venford Brook below the reservoir dam on Holne Moor. From the air such patterns can be even more striking, and aerial photographs offer a cheaper alternative than hiring your own plane for the purpose.

The buildings of settlements like Houndtor demonstrate the popularity and practicality of the longstanding plan of the Dartmoor longhouse (Fig. 223). It was traditionally built up and down the slope with the human space above the cross passage and the cattle below it. Heat rose all winter from the cows to the living quarters, drainage is in the opposite direction downslope and out at the bottom of the lower wall in which was the hatch through which manure was shovelled towards the midden. This pattern was established at least by the eleventh century though there is no evidence of human occupation of any excavated site before that. It lasted as the standard Dartmoor farmhouse until the eighteenth century when new building fashions began to spread westwards from metropolitan England. Pottery from excavation, and more recently the dating of structural timber from standing longhouses in which whole tree trunks (with their tree rings countable) had been used, all help determine the beginning of occupation. The pottery recovered from longhouse foundations all round the Moor tells of living homes or *liviers* from the early thirteenth century on (mid-thirteenth to late fourteenth at Dinna Clerks for instance). Then the population had begun to rise significantly, farms increased in number and the demand for food and animal feed was reflected in a widespread but local increase in arable farming. This in turn put pressure on the moorland edge and *inter alia* on the status of the whole Devon countryside as royal Forest. But by the early fourteenth century the universality of mixed farming, as we have seen, was beginning to decline and there seems to have been a shift to livestock dominance with a concomitant reduction in arable operations. Thus, well before the Black Death changes were taking place in the nature and distribution of agricultural settlements. Hamlets were reduced to single farmsteads, land and dwellings elsewhere were abandoned totally, some steadings fell into disuse and their land was attached to that of near or distant erstwhile neighbours. While this was a pan-Devon phenomenon, Dartmoor stands out because the remains of forsaken farms, hamlets and infields and outfields have survived in a subsequent moorland context. Their walls and boundaries would have been removed and recycled in intensively farmed lower country. Even on the moor, of course, many such settlements have survived as single farmsteads to the present day with little or no evidence of the former nucleations of which they were once only part.

The timing of the longhouses' occupation and the patterns of infield development go well together, suggesting a series of vigorous generations pushing farming moorwards from about 1175 through to 1340. Cornditches round newly 'taken' moorland were necessary until about 1240, but only against the 'new' Forest after that. Symmetrical hedge-banks, even if mini versions of the standard Devon bank with the three-metre base, were used on the land between them and the old cornditches at the outer boundary of the Saxon valley fields when that space was subdivided. This demonstrable local energy allows Fleming to postulate a very rapid phase of settlement and infield creation in the first two generations of the thirteenth century and outfield development for three or more beyond that, and note the coincidence with the earliest Ancient Tenements. His evidence is in 'whole farm' patterns on Holne Moor (Holne was held by

FIG 222. Mediaeval outfield in Greencombe, north of the B3212 west of Challacombe Cross.

FIG 223. The classic Devon longhouse seen at Uppacott, Poundsgate, now owned by the DNPA. The porch is a later whimsy.

Hamlyn the Harper at this time – whose predecessors once held Dewdons as already reported). There the archaeologist's 'north lobe' infield, northwest of the Venford dam, has a strip cultivation pattern which fits 1200 AD or so and the southern outfield fits a mid-thirteenth-century date. Figure 196 indicated a little of the evidence. The consistency of dimension of strips and ploughlands and the integrated droveways suggest a co-operative or corporate manorial effort for the whole development. The master and the men are at work together here.

Similar outfield patterns exist in Greencombe, west of Lettaford (a hamlet with more than one longhouse still) in North Bovey parish, and across the road (B3212) west of Challacombe Cross, at Blackslade, east of Widecombe, on Aish Ridge above South Brent, at Hentor in the upper Plym valley and between Higher Godsworthy and Webland below Cox Tor (Fig. 222). Clearly arable use of what we now know as moorland was intense for its time at a number of 300 m OD sites right around the southern half of the Dartmoor moorland fringe between the twelfth and the seventeenth centuries. For detailed analysis of some of these early mediaeval outfields shows them to have been used again in the sixteenth and seventeenth centuries, with ploughing lines differently oriented from the original axes. Such fields, visited with the plough perhaps only briefly in any one mediaeval generation and perhaps for a year or two at most, were used again generations later when food-crop demand motivated it. Rye is seen to have been a staple cereal throughout, though its use seems to have died out by the end of the seventeenth century.

Seventeenth to nineteenth centuries

The seventeenth century saw two reports that refer to the continuing evolution of Dartmoor land use. The coming of age of the Prince of Wales who was to become Charles I seems to have triggered an examination of the management of the Duchy estate in 1621. We learn *inter alia* from it that many newtakes seem to have been created beyond the mediaeval generation change rule, and of acreages in excess of that same rule. It is also recorded that they were often ploughed until exhausted and then reverted to grazing, so suggesting an outfield replica, but unlike the standard outfield they were permanently walled. The report writer also refers to the appropriation by adjacent landowners of some of the Commons of Devon that he believed were rightly still Duchy lands. Walkhampton (a royal manor in 1086) was one such, along with land around Sheepstor that earlier must have been part of the manor of Meavy. The obvious effect of this was to reduce the Duchy's potential income from summer grazing. But astonishingly that was still at the same rate in 1621 as in 1345, 'one and a half pence' a head for cattle and 'seven and a half pence' for 20 sheep, described as a bargain then. Taken together with the inflation of the sixteenth century, it may account for the laxness of the Duchy local collectors, for it was hardly worth the effort. In 200 years the Duchy's income from Dartmoor had fallen to a quarter of its 1420 level and the pound had slumped to a third of its value in the same time.

The eldest son of Charles I probably never knew what his Dukedom had to offer on Dartmoor but, after the Civil War and Commonwealth ended, it was he who created the Royal Society whose Georgicall Committee commissioned a survey of agriculture 'in all shires'. In 1667 Samuel Colepresse (vicar of Plympton) responded and in a *Georgicall Account of Devon and Cornwall* confirms the continuation of the outfield practice. He refers to the outfields as brakes, other authors have 'breaks' and 'breaches' and it is interesting that bracken is etymologically connected with these dialect terms. The report also refers to 'Devonshiring' or 'denshiring' of such lands, the practice of paring the vegetated surface, heaping up the parings and after drying, burning them and spreading the ash back on the bared soil before ploughing; a critical part of the process when returning to a long-rested outfield.

So, the arable farmers' marks that are still to be seen in the moorland, and as widespread around its edge at their preferred altitude as those of their contemporary tinning colleagues, have their origin in the ebb and flow of cultivation and quasi-enclosure over at least 900 years. The periodic opportunity to indulge such cultivation has to be related to the considerable amount of moorland grazing available at the same time and, especially in the summer, to a farming economy slowly shifting otherwise to livestock dominance.

More than a century after Colepresse reported, Vancouver could write of 'the ancient moorlands' that they differed from his various forms of bog and heath 'only of their surface having been left under ridge and furrow and consequently bearing evident marks of a former cultivation'. Thus it would seem that the Dartmoor infield–outfield system at the historically fluctuating edge of the moorland had finally withered during the eighteenth century. After all, general agricultural technique had advanced considerably and the improvement of arable production in the lower country combined with increasing livestock emphasis all over the southwest caused a permanent change in local land use. It also finally confirmed the function of the future hill-farmer as a producer of store cattle and lambs for finishing elsewhere. Vancouver has been quoted already in connection with summer cattle numbers in May 'standing shoulder to shoulder' (!) on Widecombe Town Commons, thus underlining for us in this new context the continuation at the turn of the eighteenth century of the Saxon summer transhumance. He was reporting to the new Board of Agriculture and obviously felt obliged to produce recipes for the reclamation of the wetter areas, invoking paring and burning of the vegetated surface layer similar to Devonshiring but also identifying 'soil' types whose surface should 'on no account be broken'. While respecting the very valuable grazing pasture of the Commons of Devon, Vancouver may be part responsible nevertheless for triggering some of the unfulfilled ambition which resulted in the enclosure of the largest newtakes in the Forest which characterise its central belt now and which were mostly 'taken' in the early nineteenth century.

By the time he reported however, although the Ancient Tenements had been consolidated, or reduced, to 14 from 34, a new generation of farms had begun to appear within the Forest, extending moorwards from the 1780 outer boundary of the longest-established newtakes. About a dozen were created with Duchy consent in the 100 years from then on and they, such as Archerton and Stannon at Postbridge, Tor Royal and Beardown at Two Bridges, and the 'island' East Okement Farm at the north end of the Forest, still exist. Newtake creation, of much more extensive enclosures than the old Forest formula allowed, was a parallel process, in some cases intimately involved with the new farms and closely related to the construction of the turnpikes. The first of the latter connecting Moretonhampstead with Two Bridges and Tavistock was authorised in 1772 under Trusts in the two towns and was operative by 1780. The road to Ashburton from Two bridges was begun in 1772 and completed by 1800 or so. Donne's 1765 map of Devon, at one inch to the mile, has none of that new road.

FIG 224. Western Dartmoor newtakes (made under the Enclosure Acts) at Longbettor in Peter Tavy parish.

Other newtakes were enclosed in the same time span round the outer edge of the moorland, mainly under private Act of Parliament. Important enclosures occur north of Ashburton on Halsanger and Horridge Commons, at Holwell Down, Holwell Lawn and Hedge Down north of that, and at Blackaton and Challacombe Downs further west. In the far west others were enclosed at Merrivale under Great Mis Tor and in from Longbettor in the north of Peter Tavy parish (Fig. 224). Most of these nineteenth-century newtakes have retained their moorland vegetation and scattered rocks and more than one contain tors. However, many have had more than one liming in their lives so far, and some – Hedge Barton and Blackaton for instance – had their clitter cleared into heaps before ploughing as recently as the 1960s (Fig. 225).

Vancouver's report makes observations about the in-bye land and the stock at the end of the eighteenth century that many would recognise today. Of the fields between the Lyd and Tavistock, through Mary Tavy and Peter Tavy, it says they 'produce a very good pasturage, on account of which the ordinary operations of tillage are very much foreborne; the sward being once broken would require ages to produce an equally valuable herbage'. References to the 'rich feeding grounds' around Ashburton must ring bells in farmers' minds in the twenty-first century. The report dismisses Widecombe barley as an 'inferior sample' but lists the parishes to the north and east, especially those on the metamorphic aureole, as having better soil and 'by judicious cultivation produced excellent turnips, barley, clover, wheat, oats (and where too strong for permanent pasture) beans and pease'. Potatoes were clearly an important crop especially in northeastern

FIG 225. Hedge Barton Newtake, Houndtor, with heaps of cleared boulders in 1970.

Dartmoor, Moretonhampstead having a particular reputation for growing them. 'Lazy beds' (one had to bend less) were a medium for that growth, being 0.9–1.2 m wide and separated from the next bed by a ditch whose content had been used to raise the bed – the system is still observable in the Hebrides. The 1765 map already quoted has a 'potatoe market [sic]' at Two Bridges which suggests permanent trade routes (towards Plymouth?) predating the turnpikes.

Vancouver saw that packhorses were still used for most burdens in Dartmoor, even 'packing lime and dung' as well as the more easily 'packed' cereals, still on the stalk, and coppice wood. He also refers to 'butts', which were still in use in the twentieth century. They were low-bodied and might be wheeled or on sleds (or a combination of both) behind one horse and having barrow-like handles. They were used to carry stone among other things and to move bottom headland soil – surplus after downhill creep – from the bottom of a sloping ploughed field to the top, where a single universal coupling between butt and traces and semi-circular tops to front and tail boards, allowed the driver to tip over and empty the load sideways almost without stopping the horse.

North Devon cattle were seen to be commonest then though their value as draught animals, or oxen, was less than the 'South Hams' breed on steep slopes. The latter reference is almost certainly to the South Devon cows that are still kept by some Dartmoor farmers, and are considerably bigger than the 'Red Rubies' of the north. Their milk and butter yields pleased Vancouver, and the milk quality in the lower country is still rated with that of Channel Island breeds. South Devons are very similar to Limousins in colour and shading but longer and taller, and there is a theory that cross-Channel trade from prehistoric times, but boosted by the Conquest, may well account for a real connection between the breeds. Dartmoor Sheep are referred to as a breed, and modern breeders would assume that they were the whiteface Dartmoor seen in Figure 238 still kept by a number of them, but landowners even then are credited with already crossing them with Dorsets and the 'new Leicesters'. Vancouver could not complete his missive without telling the Board of Agriculture that, 'sheep stealing is carried on to an atrocious extent particularly in the vicinity of the forests of Exmoor and Dartmoor ... and it is no uncommon case for farmers to lose twenty sheep in the course of a season'. It still happens, numbers quoted are greater now, and doubtless modern transport makes it simpler and the get-away speedier.

By default this 1808 record is also telling us that neither the Scotch blackface sheep nor the hardy Scottish cattle, especially Galloways, had yet arrived. Both were to have a major influence on Dartmoor hill-farming, its working seasons and the creation and maintenance of the vegetation mosaic of the commons and newtakes of the Moor.

RABBITS

Before moving on into twentieth-century times it is necessary to deal briefly with another Dartmoor crop which has left its physical mark widespread across the middle-level moorland and happens to link the two great modifiers of scenic moorland detail whom we have just examined – the tinners and the farmers.

The rabbit, not native to these islands, was brought in from France soon after the Normans and the Saxons had settled down together. Their potential for meat and fur made them a valuable mediaeval adjunct to agriculture, and both products came to be staples for those who had specialised in other trades locally and even to more distant populations in Devon's towns. Rabbits on Dartmoor

FIG 226. Headland Warren: (above left) the current farm, the warrener's house until the 1940s; (left) a 'warren' or pillow mound at Ditsworthy Warren in the Plym valley. (DNPA)

were undoubtedly 'farmed' from at least the thirteenth century until the twentieth. Trowlesworthy Warren is referred to in 1272 and alongside it are Legis Tor, Hentor and Ditsworthy Warrens in the Plym valley, others are scattered around the Moor – at Skaigh near Belstone, Headland Warren due east of the Warren House Inn on the B3212, and Huntington Warren moorward from Buckfastleigh. A warren was a collection of artificial 'buries' built as long, low broad banks of boulders covered with earth and providing many tunnels within. They are often but not always contained in walled enclosures and invariably aligned up and down the slope. The four named above in the Plym valley all had a warren house within the site, as did Huntington Warren on the south moor. The Warren House on the B3212 may not always have been an inn, though Headland Warren that it abuts has a house of that name in the next valley head (Fig 226). The buries are now referred to by archaeologists as 'pillow mounds' and in some warrens are very dense; there are 50 within 200 hectares at Legis Tor Warren alone.

The whole process of 'warrening' was quite sophisticated. Vermin predation was dealt with by the construction of artificial tunnels and surface passages leading to box-like granite traps with slate doors that the stoat sprang shut. Rabbits were caught by netting, either over burrow entrances, or as long nets into which grazing rabbits were driven, usually in the dark by dogs and noisy warreners. Nests of young rabbits from near or distant farmland found during harvest were introduced, when mature enough, to warrens to ensure new blood and a healthy population. The detail is known to farmers in Widecombe parish now whose grandparents knew related warreners at work. The concentration of warrens in the Plym valley is certainly related to the market for rabbit flesh and fur in Plymouth itself, and to railheads well beyond it – rabbits were sent as far as Liverpool in 1900, when the skins alone could pay the rent. Ditsworthy Warren was the largest, the 1901 census shows the warrener was Mrs Ware ('Lady Ware' to most) who lived on site and she had at least three other 'staff'. It was worked until the middle of the twentieth century. The Headland Warren in Figure 226, the latest known to be active in the east, probably began and continued its life in close relationship with tin working in the Vitifer mining complex.

The pillow mounds, associated walls, vermin traps and ruinous houses are all still marking the 'moorland'. Like deserted villages, fallen field boundaries and tin streamworking surface detail, they provide new micro-habitats for plants and invertebrates and nesting sites for wheatears and, in the right site, redstarts. Men, in an even more specialised form of work, earnt a living while modifying what is now, because of their effort, a much more intricate moorland surface

FIG 227. The long view: Fur Tor (left) and Great Mis Tor (right) on the skyline from Dinger Tor – viewpoint accessible and view possible because of high moorland grazing and burning by commoner hill-farmers. Their Galloways are in the middle distance (and remember Figure 24).

than it appears from any distance. Although that distant prospect, from without and within, gives Dartmoor its splendid singularity, as soon as one sets off from the internal viewpoint something of that intricacy is revealed with every step. Both the landscape of the long view and its close-up surface detail are the outcomes of the work of men. Miners (of the tiny detail) have long gone from Dartmoor, warreners contributed to it until the 1940s. Farmers (of the long view), for the time being, remain.

CHAPTER 8

Farming Dartmoor and Sustaining Moorland: The Last Hundred Years

The main object of Dartmoor farming is to raise cattle, but not to fatten them. When they are of store age, that is from two to three years old, they are sold to graziers who have rich lands in the in-country, and are there fatted.
     William Crossing, 'The Farmer' in The Dartmoor Worker, 1903

A large number of cattle and sheep are pastured on the Forest, remaining there from May until September. William Coaker of Runnage, who rents the east quarter, receives probably not less than 2000 head of cattle each season. John Edmonds of South Brent rents the south quarter, succeeding his father, a fine type of old moorman ... 'Upright and down straight'.
     From 'The Moorman', op. cit.

The Dartmoor of today which draws attention and affection is that of open commons, close grazed turf at the foot of a tor or side of a stream, pony herds, stone wall lined fields, sheep or cattle tracks weaving through grassland. This is the Dartmoor landscape that farmers create maintain and change ... it is the farmers' presence which under-pins Dartmoor's economy, culture and vibrancy.
     Richard Povall and Nancy Sinclair, Focus on Farmers, 2007

THE SIGNIFICANCE OF THESE quotations lies partly in their dates, spanning the 100 years of this chapter. Crossing describes his own observations of a process or processes that are exactly the same as those rehearsed throughout Chapter 7 of this book and so 800 or more years old and still going strong when he wrote about them. His series of essays for the Western Morning News in 1903 in that sense underlined the well-tried suitability still of the farming that he saw for its Dartmoor context and for the maintenance of the moorland throughout that time. It had clearly persisted regardless of the economic and climatic fluctuations that Britain had witnessed from the twelfth century on. Moreover, he is writing less than a decade after the lowest point of the agricultural recession of the late nineteenth century and implying, by reference to longstanding practice and personalities then, that the farmers of this hill, at least, had survived that recession perhaps without noticing its devastation of the agricultural economy of England further east. Dartmoor's longstanding socio-economic resilience had persisted into modern times, even though canning and maritime refrigeration, the first innovations to affect the domestic meat supply chain for centuries, were already in place when Crossing wrote. That resilience was at least partly based on survival, when necessary, by a low-input/low-output agricultural routine but with enough mixed farming flexibility in the group of small fields at the homestead to grow more corn when mean summer temperatures rose a little – as in the fourteenth century, or minimal cereal cropping in the Little Ice Age. The same principle is evident in the detail too, and can even be produced if we move forward another hundred years. There is still a Coaker at Runnage, an Ancient Tenement since at least 1317 AD, and his father was also still the agister for the East Quarter before the Forest became common in 1983. There is a successor John Edmonds at Gribblesdown in South Brent in 2008 who agists part of the South Quarter by virtue of a grazing tenancy from the Duchy. The resilience of the systems and of the landscape in which they work and which they sustain, has wrought a different, but equally strong, resilience in the people of this remarkable southwestern hill.

At this end of the 100 years, Runnage and the present Coaker family feature as one of three Dartmoor hill-farms and their incumbents in *Focus on Farmers*, a book produced by a contemporary group called Aune Head Arts based in Princetown. (The other two Dartmoor farms in the book are Frenchbeer in Chagford parish and Greenwell, already listed in the preceding chapter. Both, like Runnage, are on longstanding sites, Greenwell is mentioned in 1181 AD, Frenchbeer in 1346, both in pipe rolls.) The book is in part a reaction to the foot-and-mouth disease outbreak of 2001 and its aftermath, which hit the central basin and the northern fringe and called upon farmers' resilience in a new way (Fig. 228). Artists of various disciplines, including writing, lived on the farms for at least six months and were exposed to all that modern hill-farming involves. The farmers, their wives and their children, bared their souls, and both of these exposures are documented in the book. Resilience, as a theme, is illustrated, but a new, and essential, flexibility also emerges as the twenty-first century begins. The remarkable revolution in communication throughout society in the 100 years in question has introduced aspirations to every family which the majority never imagined in all the preceding 1,000. Survival on a hill-farm in a depression because you could eat what you grew if your back was against the wall is probably

FIG 228. Moorland farmers about their business: (left) Phil Coaker at Runnage; (below left) Will Hutchings at Yardworthy. (Chris Chapman)

FIG 229. Yellowmead: just into the moorland edge there is still a collection of isolated farmsteads, many still occupied by those keeping stock against the economic odds.

no longer an option. But, as we shall see, the principle or at least its effect, may well be tested again quite soon. The farmer of a remote holding said in my hearing recently, 'Yes, I could turn off the power, heat and cook with my own wood, and eat from what I breed and grow, but the family wouldn't stay to share that way of life these days.'

INTRODUCTIONS AND THE QUESTION OF NUMBERS

Crossing, who is one of Dartmoor's literary heroes primarily through his *Guide to Dartmoor* of 1909 – following Wordsworth's *Guide to the Lakes* after almost 100 years – provides some other important information about the modern evolution of Dartmoor's farming in that other *Dartmoor Worker* essay, 'The Moorman'. Almost by chance he pinpoints the beginning of the most important changes in moorland grazing since mediaeval times when he records that Scotch blackface sheep were introduced to the Moor, appropriately by Mr Lamb of Prince Hall, in 1880 (Fig. 230). By the time Crossing wrote, Mr Lamb's grandson had 1,000 head of the blackface sheep at Foxtor Farm and newtake and another 100 were on Walkhampton Common. Whether this indicates the rate of their spread in the new southern habitat is not clear, but if there were more by 1900, Crossing would

FIG 230. Scotch blackface ewes and a lamb on the raised bog at Challacombe.

FIG 231. A Galloway calf on Walkhampton Common – as Crossing said, 'as rough and shaggy as young bears'.

have known if anyone did. Near the same time, Scottish black cattle were also brought in, and from Crossing's description they were Galloways. 'Beside our red Devons they look quite fierce and their calves are as rough and shaggy as young bears' (Fig. 231). The dramatic significance of both these introductions is that they rang the death knell of the centuries' old summer grazing routine on the commons and the Forest. Both the blackface and the Galloway could be out-wintered on the moor and lamb and calve out there, so two age-old parts of the system fell by the wayside. Letting grazing-with-care up here to farmers from the South Hams and mid-Devon from May to September would become untenable quite soon as available grazing was reduced by winter consumption; and the old legal principle of levancy and couchancy – not being able to graze on the common more than you could winter on your own in-bye land was blown. Grazing effects and its resulting patterns must have changed almost overnight. The old intense summer grazing had begun well after a long winter's rest for the moorland vegetation and its spring re-growth, as demonstrated in that early nineteenth-century observation by Vancouver about knee-high grass on Widecombe Town Commons in May. Once all-year-round grazing began, the numbers of commoners' sheep and cattle plus the in-country visitor herds of 1,000 summers would never be sustained again. The landlord's 'surplus' ('after the commoners are satisfied' is the legal advice) had for centuries been quantified largely by his own decision, confirmed by his own court, which was peopled only by his own tenants. It, too, was obviously challenged by the new year-long grazing. His easiest income: from letting that surplus in the summer to in-country lowland stockmen, disappeared, and in many cases his personal interest in the management of his common disappeared with it. Slowly this led to the breakdown of the disciplines required to manage the commons properly and by 1950 only two manor courts were still held in the whole National Park and they rarely dealt with disciplinary matters. Soon after that enough commoners agreed that something had to be done if valued commoning was to survive, and that involved the reinstatement of discipline on all the commons. That led to the formation of the Dartmoor Commoners' Association in 1954 as a federation of local associations, its evidence to the Royal Commission on Common Land which sat from 1955 to 1958, and eventually to the Dartmoor Commons Act of 1985 referred to in Chapter 1, of which more anon.

A classic illustration of the problems which had developed by the second half of the twentieth century, 50 years after Crossing wrote, is partly related to the beginning of political intervention in Dartmoor, and all other hills, from afar. The public, or at least governmental, decision to support farming from the early 1940s, onwards to sustain the food supply and keep it cheap, was effected in the hills through subsidies calculated per head of cattle and sheep kept. The incentive thus created led to a new and eventually vast increase in cattle and sheep kept on the common, some would say rivalling the numbers Vancouver had seen – but then they were only there in the summer. By the 1960s out-wintered stock, especially cattle, reached numbers that demanded the transporting of 'feed' out to them for lack of natural 'keep' (not, it should be noted, a historic right of common, which was to take in what was growing through the mouths of one's stock). That meant the development of tractor tracks, cattle waiting close by all day for the next delivery and consequent poaching and damage to the vegetation which ironically was the 'asset' held in common (Fig. 232). Some commons' edges had become simply the site of outdoor 'sheds' or yards, and the less energetic used the same feeding area day in day out. Commoners themselves began to differ about damage to the grazing, and some local associations nearly fell apart because of it. Devon County Council, as the then NPA, became involved in 1971 because of the perceived effect on the 'natural beauty' of the National Parks and Access to the Countryside Act of 1949 and even on that access. By 1990 attitudes would have changed enough for the new Commoners' Council (see below) to make, without much debate, a regulation prohibiting any commoner from damaging or (significantly) allowing damage of

FIG 232. The effect of supplementary feeding of stock in winter. The picture was taken in the mid-1970s and the erosion of the roadside edge of the common is clear (see also Figure 179). By 1990, the practice had effectively ceased as the Commoners' Council and management agreements both matured.

the natural beauty of the commons. This effectively ended the taking of hay or silage on to the common or causing damage by the use of vehicular transport. Tractors had been the real culprits but smaller four-wheel drive vehicles such as Landrovers were already commonplace as bale carriers. The commoners' transport system continued to evolve however and within a decade quad-bikes had replaced many of the ponies which moorland farmers had until then habitually used to look at stock, and to drive it home and 'out over' again. Quad bikes represent the latest important innovation in moorland management with their virtues of lightness and 'go-anywhere' capability, thus reducing the need to make, and the incidental making of, new tracks (Fig. 233).

The general question of numbers of stock on the moor led almost inevitably to accusations of over-grazing from the 1960s onwards, and any observer could take one to a hard-bitten site. They were nearly always just inside cattle grids at the moorland edge and alongside roads. They thus involved short-cropped turf, ideal ironically, for picnicking and games for the burgeoning numbers of

FIG 233. Contemporary shepherding by dog-and-quad-bike on Brent Moor. (T. Eliot-Reep)

FIG 234. Hemsworthy Gate below Rippon Tor, now a cattle grid whose gate is clearly visible. Short-cropped grass is close to the grid and round the signpost, but also extends up the slope on the common side of the newtake wall. Winter grazing is being conserved on the newtake side.

weekend and summer visitors (Fig. 234). But only a slightly more diligent search would reveal within a few hundred yards under-grazed vegetation, often rank and making for uncomfortable walking. Sheep and ponies are attracted to roadsides and stay close to them for long periods and for a variety of reasons, including visitors' ill-advised offers of tit-bits (to ponies), the warmth of the road surface on summer nights (to sheep) and the salt-lick innocently provided by the highway authority in winter (to both). This all concentrates numbers near roads and car parking sites and partly explains the close-cropped vegetation seen by all passers-by, but the concentration was also a symptom of a shortage of time for traditional stockmanship or lack of experience of it. This latter because the headage payment tempted new and inappropriate stock, dairy cattle breeds for instance, on to the common according to rights registered but long unused. The perception for some observers was that many could not or did not spare the time to drive animals to lears further into the moor and away from entrances to the common and from the roads that cross them, even fewer could actually spend time learing stock having got them to the appropriate site.

Lears and stockmanship

'Lear' and its derivatives need explanation. It has the same root as 'lair', and learing is the Dartmoor equivalent of 'hefting' in the north. Well cared-for flocks of sheep have their own lear, graze in it and certainly return to it wherever grazing has taken them during the day, and lamb there so the next generation 'know their lear' from the start. Good shepherds, too, will speak of their own lears and recognise that those of other commoners adjoin theirs. They help each other, as being a commoner demands, by driving the straying ewe – or cow – back to, or at least towards, its rightful place. Part of the good management of a common is its division into enough lears which function well because they fit together in a mosaic without spare space. In effect the animals themselves maintain the lear pattern once it is firmly established. It is said that (in the old days!) a simple whistle would trigger the rapid return of ewes to their lears whether a dog appeared or not. Two other things flow from the principle. One is the clear virtue of selling established breeding flocks with the farm that holds the common rights, when it changes hands, because they 'know their lear'. The other is the converse which is the effort involved in establishing a lear for sheep newly acquired from elsewhere. Sons and daughters, within our 100 years, given a new set of ewes to start a flock of their own, would be made to go out with the dog and sleep with them on the common to ensure their more rapid adherence to their lear.

Headage versus hectarage

The over-grazing argument was taken up by conservation ecologists, elsewhere as well as on Dartmoor, and steadily a head of steam was built up in a campaign to end headage payments and instead to subsidise, or compensate, hill-farmers according to the area of in-bye they occupied, and of the common grazings they used. A significant change, and a step towards that perceived Valhalla, was tested in the late 1980s via 'management agreements' and a shift from the 50-year-old social and production support in the hills began. The UK persuaded the EEC of the virtue of the experiment and by the mid-1990s Dartmoor farmers were being offered 'contracts' under various agri-environment schemes which paid for fixed stocking levels and annual grazing routines and compensated for stock withdrawn. Ironically, on the commons, rights unused for decades became a passport to compensation for not grazing by those who had not indulged it in any case, because grazing availability was the criterion, rather than actual use of it. It is still a matter of huge contention. Dartmoor became an Environmentally Sensitive Area (ESA) in 1993 under which such formulae were applied and its detail and effects are dealt with in the next chapter. However the ideal management system (involving stock units per hectare and annual grazing times) was still a theoretical one and the translation of it from a quasi-academic beginning to an agricultural practicality was to elude the innocent agents of government for some time yet. Fitting the simple matter of a seasonal and headage grazing limitation into the farmer's business context – into a whole farm year, into the rest of the farm's land, plant and buildings, and into the normal cycle of a suckler herd – seemed too difficult. Initially perhaps, out of innocence on both sides, the complete equation may not even have been considered. Most cattle withdrawn by the active grazier had nowhere else to go but market. Replacing them when initial grazing calculations were shown to be less than accurate was not a simple matter, for the disposal had had to lead to other economic initiatives if the books were to be balanced. Before these difficulties could be properly addressed, more changes were to be made in environmental and support systems at government and European level. But addressed they were, and the 'Dartmoor Vision' process, described in Chapter 5, which had been set in train by the NPA in 2003 was playing a substantial role in that by 2006.

The effect of all this on the individual farmer's income and expenditure account was to underline, and even to increase, the real significance and value of the public support which had been available since 1948 in one form or another in that account. But it also began the overt acceptance by the farmer himself that he had another role to play besides producing marketable stores for others to finish.

He no longer had to think of it as free 'park-keeping', now it was the management of a public asset or set of them for which there was a going rate. For all its initial blemishes the ESA process had the makings of achieving the best balance in the farmer's perception of his new and his age-old roles. We will look at it all from the environmental viewpoint and in up-to-date detail very soon but it is necessary first to assess the farming situation that had developed within the National Park by the end of the 100 years in question.

THE FARMS AND THEIR BUSINESS

At the beginning of this century there are 1,300 holdings in the National Park but under a third of them are full-time farms, though that third does include nearly all the moorland ones. Just over half of those 425 farms are owner-occupied and the rest are tenanted. Some of the large terrain principles of the Bronze Age which evolved in socio-economic terms through the Dark and Middle Ages and into the eighteenth century are still there at the end of the last 100 years. The Duchy's tenanted land, to make sense under my theoretical claim, would be interpreted as comprising more than one large terrain now. The Ancient Tenements probably count as four of them from north to south, centred on Postbridge, Dartmeet and Hexworthy, with another up the West Dart to Prince Hall. A fifth terrain lies south and east of Princetown, a sixth from Two Bridges northeast to Powder Mills, and finally an extensive one centred on Chagford Common. Outside the Duchy's central core, at least five private single estates exist from north to south on the western fringe and almost abut each other. In the middle east, the Hambledon estate of the 1900s stretching from Drewsteignton south to Becka Falls, and the Whitley holdings from Houndtor to Ashburton, have both been broken up, the latter only in the last two decades of our 100 years. The Spitchwick/Holne Park estate still holds on.

The freehold farms average 63 ha in area and the tenancies 50 ha; but the range shows that only 10 per cent of all the farms are over 300 ha and two-thirds of the rest are under 100 ha. Nearly one in three of all the farmers now have some lower land outside the Park farmed in conjunction with that of their Dartmoor holding and it may form nearly a quarter of the land inside the boundary of the 'business'. Many of the tenants in the Park actually own their in-country land, which gives them the added benefit of somewhere to go when their time in the tenancy ends and hopefully their children take over.

All the farmers are livestock producers and a little under two-thirds of them still regard stores as their primary end product, but nearly 40 per cent finish some animals somewhere, and in 2002 most thought that the proportion of fattened animals in their total output would increase, according to the answers to a questionnaire circulated on behalf of the NPA by the University of Exeter. They also expected the total numbers of sheep and cattle kept would be reduced, which does not bode well for the grazing regime needed to sustain the ideal moorland vegetation pattern. In fact cattle numbers (in the whole Park) had declined from 60,000 in 1972 to 53,000 in 2000, while sheep headage had risen from 151,000 to 240,000 over the same period. Cows and calves had peaked in 1985 and sheep in 1990, the latter just after the Common Agricultural Policy (CAP) sheepmeat regime was put in place, but before agri-environment-scheme grazing formulae started to bite.

Just less than half the total number of full-time farms actually used the commons, though many more still have common rights attached to their hearths or to some fields. The stock numbers estimated as grazing the commons in the 1950s were only 2,000 cows and 13,000 ewes, by the mid-1960s they had risen to 5,000 and 40,000 respectively, and in 1996 20,000 cattle and 130,000 sheep were registered with the Commoners' Council, reflecting the overall increases in the whole Park.

Since then, the livestock industry in general has suffered dramatic change, its Dartmoor component included – the cattle population 'crash' here was reported in Chapter 5. The overall change started with the attempt to curb beef mountains in Europe (associated with those dramatic increases in stock in the 1970s and 1980s just mentioned), then came the BSE scare that cut off UK exports to Europe. The foot-and-mouth Disease (FMD) epidemic of 2001, which saw outbreaks in the central basin of Dartmoor and on the northern edge (and especially the invidious contiguous culling policy that was deployed around it), seemed like a final blow. However, Bovine TB, though currently a dairyman's problem, touches the hills in the end as all those other things have done. The hill-farmer produces stock to be finished by lowland men, so everything that affects them has a knock-on effect that ends up in his kitchen. Alongside all this the reform of the Common Agricultural Policy, which finally disconnected support for farming from food production, has had massive effects upon farmers' cash flow already, and in time, as currently planned, will reduce the actual amount of that support. That direct support is, in 2008, via a Hill Farm Allowance (HFA) – soon to disappear – and a Single (Farm) Payment (SP) which is paid per hectare farmed and has two rates above and below a 'moorland line' and a far greater one for all land outside the Severely Disadvantaged Area (SDA). Much hill grazing is inevitably above the moorland line, where the rate is nearly a sixth of that outside the SDA, with the added complication of shared rates for common land depending on the number of unit rights to graze registered on a particular common and the area of that common.

FIG 235. The arable component of the traditional homebase of the hill-farm was still evident throughout the eastern valleys until the 1970s. Hay Tor is in the background.

Given all that, it is perhaps understandable that the number of graziers has diminished and that the next generation in farm households wonders whether it is worth staying to do the job that was satisfying in grandfather's day – or so he says. It also explains why under-grazing has overtaken over-grazing as the major management problem affecting the future of the Dartmoor moorland as a source of livelihoods, as a unique upland ecosystem, as a remarkably rich archaeological landscape and as the biggest public open space south of the Pennines in England.

Arable farming and dairying are now of little significance in the overall Dartmoor picture, though the former dominates patches of the fringe farmland, south of Buckfastleigh for instance. Small dairy farms had been widely scattered through the eastern half of the Park and down the narrow western fringe right up to the 1970s and their decaying milk-churn collection stands still punctuate hedge-banks near farm gates from Widecombe eastwards.

The farming population

Farmers and their spouses provide two-thirds of the whole workforce on Dartmoor farms, and a small proportion confesses to relying on unpaid help from other members of the family whose day job is elsewhere. Over half of the full-time farmers claimed to have at least one successor, which, given that the average age of all Dartmoor farmers is now nearing 60, is very important. The obverse side of that coin – the half that don't have family successors – is a cause for concern in the context of retaining skills associated with the care of moorland stock, its deployment on the commons and the maintenance of the low-level vegetation mosaic. The same proportion of that farming family total – fathers, mothers, sons and daughters – have other agricultural work off their own farm. That can range from being a farm secretary to contracting out manual labour and driven machinery, but also includes technical things like scanning pregnant ewes and travelling long distances to provide such a service, and thus only possible if there is cover at home. 'Diversification', long extolled as the saving for farmers whose main business is no longer producing a good enough income, is widespread. Some is close to farming itself, commonly processing produce and selling direct to the public at the farm gate or in a farm shop or

FIG 236. Campsite backed by bunkhouse barns (here at Runnage Farm) doubles the workload but runs easily alongside the livestock farm routine. Income is supplemented as a new set of skills emerge in the farm household. (Christine Coaker)

farmers' market, part-time contracting already mentioned, or using land and buildings for holiday accommodation of one kind or another (Fig. 236). These things can naturally combine to their mutual benefit because a full camp site provides a ready market for lamb chops, say – one purchase leading to barbecue smells, can have a snowball trading effect that persists beyond that evening. All of this increases the total household income, but a large number of farmers still claim that off-farm income is crucial to their whole-year results.

Current and future public support

Those results still involve receipt of the just-still-alive HFA, successor to the longstanding Hill Livestock Compensatory Allowance, itself having origins in the Hill Cow subsidy of the 1940s. Three-quarters of our farms receive HFA, and more than two-thirds of them were contracted under ESA schemes in 2002. The HFA is due to end in 2010 and its promised replacement is an Upland Entry Level scheme under Environmental Stewardship (the current umbrella for all agri-environment schemes now). It is interesting that a core support payment of long standing (and recognising the hardship in the hills) is 'to be replaced' by an agri-environmental one for which a farmer needs to earn points. ESA schemes will not be renewed after their present contracted term ends and in 2012 the SP (see above), introduced as a consolidation of previous core support systems in 2005, will be wholly based on area farmed in England, shrinking the while, and more of that below. One tenant farmer claims that in 2012 his SP will be less than the agricultural wage. So the confidence in a fair payment for the provision of public goods as part of the income and expenditure account that ESA establishment boosted in the 1990s and in the recognition by society that those goods in the hills are managed under severe difficulty compared with lowland, and especially arable farming, is already waning, as of course is the value of the public investment made since then. Indeed the potential waste of that investment for lack of its maintenance in the next decade or so is an underlying theme of the next chapter.

SHEEP, CATTLE AND PONIES

We have already seen something of the importance of the combination of the three major domestic grazers in sustaining the vegetation mosaic of the open moorland and the newtakes. For this record, cattle tear coarser grasses, especially purple moor grass in the spring, ponies bite heather and gorse but crop better grasses lower, and sheep almost mow the turf. Sheep also turn to heather and gorse in winter snows and new heather and gorse shoots for vital minerals in early summer. All play a significant and complementary role.

FIG 237. Texel-fathered crosses in Gawler newtake at Postbridge.

Scotch blackface ewes still dominate the sheep scene on the moorland proper but many are now put to rams intended to improve the quality of lambs. The 'tupping' is in October/November in in-bye fields and newtakes in the fortnight when the moor is cleared of sheep by Commoners' Council regulation. 'Entire' male animals except stallions are excluded from the common by the same regulations. Dartmoor farmers will go to ram and bull sales as far away as Scotland and France almost as part of an annual routine. Many of the new rams are Texels of Dutch origin, but Germans are used and sometimes lighter French rams on first tupping of a hogget – or yearling ewe. The resulting 'mules' or cross-bred lambs are now commonplace and attempts to brand them, when finished, as 'Dartmoor mules' are being made (Fig. 237). Lambs are marketed from June onwards until the following March, so a variety of finished sizes are available to discerning butchers. Whiteface Dartmoor sheep, and a few Grey-faced ones, are still kept by those keen to keep older breeds going (Fig. 238). There are still some Welsh Mountain ewes in the northwest, and Exmoor Horns on Widecombe Town Commons and Haytor.

Galloways and their belted siblings (black or dun with a white band round the middle) are the commonest cattle across the whole high moor, but as with the sheep many cross-bred cows and calves also occur on lower slopes in an attempt to increase the size of carcass (Fig. 239). Welsh blacks, blue greys, Luings

FARMING DARTMOOR AND SUSTAINING MOORLAND · 315

FIG 238. Whiteface Dartmoor ewes – 'prapper sheep' to a devotee. Soussons Plantation is in the background.

FIG 239. A reminder of the South Devons and belted Galloways, but remember the Highland cattle in Figure 24 (see also Figs. 147, 227 and 231).

FIG 240. October, Merrivale Pound, the West Quarter: drift of mainly Dartmoor hill ponies.

and some Highland cattle are still kept by their different devotees and there are a number of herds of South Devon cows lingering from the old transhumance days, many now wintered in sheds but out on the moor from spring to autumn. The Galloways and some Highlands, as might be expected, are the cows which penetrate furthest into the high plateaux in the summer and retreat to the mid-level slopes in the winter, while the other breeds and crosses are most likely to be seen from roads all year round.

Ponies are of two main types. The Dartmoor hill pony (Fig. 240), usually 'coloured' or carrying patches of different hues, is probably now the commonest, while the Dartmoor breed is always of a single colour usually bay, but greys are accepted. The latter are more often in newtakes and the in-bye than out on the common, and of course are bred in other locations in England now. There are pockets of Shetland ponies on Okehampton Hamlets Common and around Haytor. During our 100 years Shetlands were introduced first, in an attempt to reduce the Dartmoor indigenous ponies' leg length to 'improve' them for the coal-mining market, and the Duke of Cornwall who was to become briefly Edward VIII, tried to redress the resulting 'stunted' mares by releasing Arab stallions on to the Forest in the 1920s. So the feral pony total herd is by now of

FARMING DARTMOOR AND SUSTAINING MOORLAND · 317

FIG 241. The Dartmoor Pony Show at Princetown in September, entry confined to the Dartmoor breed. The President, an ex-NPA Chief Officer, in attendance.

FIG 242. Chagford Pony Sales – a singular hill pony in the ring, September 2007.

mixed descent, and hence the enclosed or at least the protective grazing of the Dartmoor breed itself.

The moorland herd is difficult to count but it seems to have numbered some 1,200 in 2008 of which 200 were stallions, and 800 or so foals went through the autumn markets.

The Dartmoor Commoners' Association's evidence to the Royal Commission in 1956 had included what became known as the 'Nine Point Plan' to improve the husbandry of all the animals on the common. It consisted of i) the culling of old ewes; ii) the dipping of all hill sheep in the autumn; iii) the culling of old cows and any unthrifty cattle; iv) the weaning of calves at the proper time; v) the provision of fodder as conditions demanded; vi) the voluntary attestation of hill cattle; vii) making sure ponies bred on the moor were hardy; viii) proper feeding and watering of ponies in severe weather; and ix) limitation of stallion numbers. It clearly dealt with all three species, and part of it was triggered by the national publicity given to unhappy animals in hard winters, but it did mean that national attention was now drawn to the Dartmoor commoners' corporate recognition of the need to put their own, shared house in order.

MORE ABOUT NUMBERS

The Royal Commission published its findings in 1958 and a research team was charged soon after with surveying the state of some commons in anticipation of legislation which it was hoped and expected would introduce management systems for common land. Among many others nationally, it surveyed the stock on Peter Tavy, Whitchurch and Walkhampton Commons on western Dartmoor and looked at one or two other commons such as Okehampton Hamlets and Holne. It visited the surveyed commons in March, June and October and found the grazing poor, sufficient and moderate at those three respective times. In June, on Peter Tavy and Whitchurch taken together it found 1,701 sheep of which Scotch Blackfaces were over 75 per cent, far less than half the 90 cows had calves and the 1,223 ewes had 478 lambs between them; 35 mares had 19 foals. It calculated that the average grazing density was some 3.5 livestock units per acre (0.4 ha) – a livestock unit then was one bovine or pony, or five sheep. In March, there were 'many old ewes' and nine dead ones were found. Friesians and Shorthorns were found among the expected hill-cattle breeds and hay was being fed near the road where severe poaching was seen.

Today, on Peter Tavy Common alone, 45 commoners are recorded in the Dartmoor Commoners' Council register with rights to graze 9,104 sheep,

FIG 243. Looking up toward Peter Tavy Great Common from below Cox Tor; Roos Tor is on the right, Wedlake fields on the left.

1,527 cattle and 237 ponies – or 3,035 livestock units (a livestock unit now equals six sheep). But only 16 commoners actually turn out stock and they put only 624 livestock units on the common. The commoners have an ESA contract; their common carries parts of two separate SSSIs, and is partly within a military live firing range, involving clearance of stock on to that part of the common outside the range sometimes four times a week. Under the ESA scheme all cattle have to be withdrawn from the common from December until May, some from October to May. Sheep numbers have also been reduced, and the effect of both is that lears cannot be maintained. The reductions, combined with milder recent winters, means that considerable areas of rank and unpalatable grasses have developed.

There is thus a very confused picture of the common grazing situation over the last 50 years. The cattle and sheep numbers out on Peter Tavy Common now are still far greater than they were when those surveyors counted in the 1960s and reported over-grazed space, even though they are much reduced from the situation in the mid-1980s. But contemporary commoners see the effects of under-grazing all around them, and in their view there has been a massive deterioration of the quality of the vegetation since they took over from their fathers. It is worth noting that it was their grandfathers who attended the first meetings of the Dartmoor Commoners' Association in 1953 and who were worried about the state of affairs on the commons then.

To a neutral observer it is clear that something had to be done about the headage on the commons at the end of the 1980s, but it looks as though the combined effect of disease mitigation, changes in support payments and official well-meaning but innocent regulation of numbers and seasonal timing has moved too far in the opposite direction. The optimal balance between a farm's satisfactory economy, the common grazing's place in that and the incentivisation of the maintenance of moorland vegetation in the interests of biodiversity, archaeology, the scene and access to it, clean water, and carbon storage in the peat is still to be worked out. The pursuit of the Dartmoor Vision should ultimately yield the formula that solves the equation if all parties remain committed to it. Then the potentially powerful alliance of farmers and agencies, represented by that shared and published Vision, has to sell the visionary equation to government and to the EEC, if the only labour force that can realise it is to remain available. Dartmoor has always been farmed, it never needed to keep its farmers contentedly at work more than it does now.

CHAPTER 9

The Contemporary Conservation Scene: Its History and Its Future

A National Park may be defined, in application to Great Britain, as an extensive area of beautiful and relatively wild country in which for the nation's benefit ... the characteristic natural beauty is strictly preserved, access and facilities for public open-air enjoyment are amply provided, wild life and buildings and places of architectural and historic interest are suitably protected while established farming use is effectively maintained.

John Dower, May 1945

It must then be an essential purpose of National Park policy to harmonise man's material needs with the protection of natural beauty.

Arthur Hobhouse, July 1947

As Duke of Cornwall I have had wonderful opportunities to get to know the Moor at all seasons and in all weathers ... and to understand the high level of skill and care that is required from those who manage such a precious and finely balanced environment – to the benefit of all of us.

HRH the Prince of Wales, 2001

DARTMOOR, AS WE HAVE just seen, has been an Environmentally Sensitive Area for agricultural management purposes since 1993 but a national park since 1951. The National Park contains 48 Sites of Special Scientific Interest (SSSI) covering about 26,150 ha; some have been there since 1952. It also includes three national nature reserves that are nearly as old (Fig. 244), and also carries more than one 'candidate' Special Area for Conservation status (SAC). SACs are a European Union designation under the 'Natura 2000' system. In Dartmoor they are those three big SSSIs and the Bovey Valley Natural Nature Reserves (NNRs). The National Park is itself some 99 per

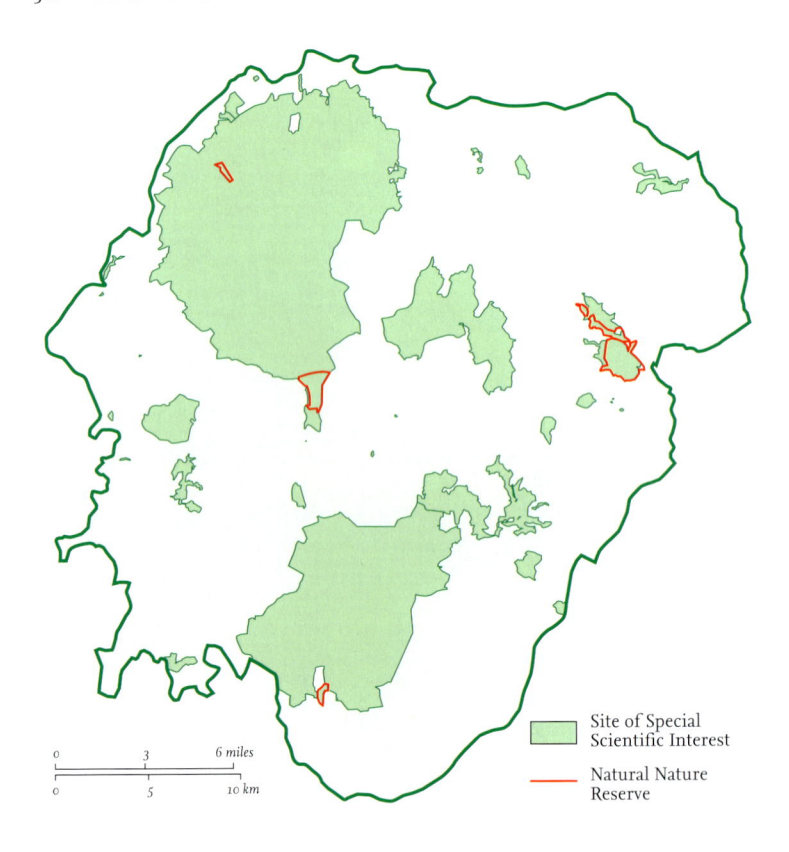

FIG 244. Designated nature conservation sites in the National Park. (DNPA)

cent of the Dartmoor Natural Area born out of the Joint Character Area family delineated for the whole of England's landscape by the Countryside Agency and English Nature in 2005. That Area includes the whole Park and then the low hills just east of the north–south reach of the Teign and a strip from Trusham Quarry to Bovey Tracey to include the foot slopes of the far-east block – the only extensions on the east side of the Park. The china clay deposits of Lee Moor with Crownhill Down and the slopes southwards from there to Hemerdon Ball are included in the southwest. West Down, at the northern end of Roborough Down and the fields beyond it, Fernworthy Down north of Lydford and a triangle east of Bridestowe stretching up to Sourton are the only parts of the Natural Area outside the western boundary of the National Park (Fig. 245). This accumulation of designations and the space they take up tells its own story in quasi-political terms

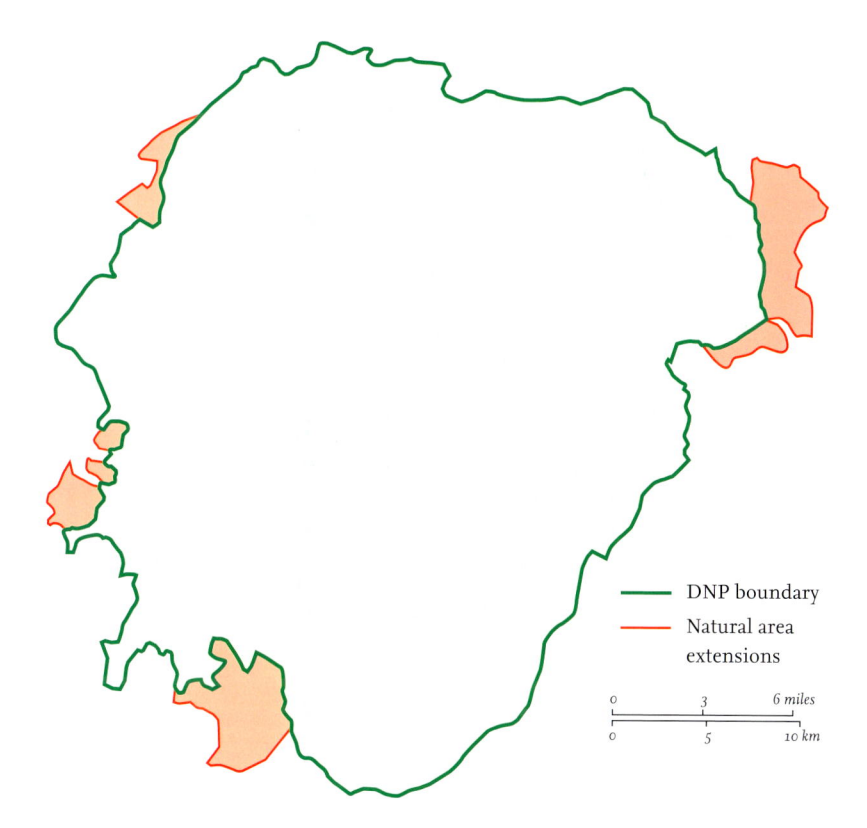

FIG 245. Extensions beyond the National Park that complete the Dartmoor Natural Area. (DNPA)

both for Dartmoor's landscape and natural history, and for the protective broth which increasing numbers of cooks have stirred in the last 50 or more years.

When the first New Naturalist volume about it was published in 1953, Dartmoor was simply a national park – with one slightly younger national nature reserve, Yarner Wood, declared in 1952 and low down just inside its eastern boundary, a wood not a moor. The National Park had been designated in the first group of nominated landscapes after the 1949 Act invented the designation, alongside the Lake District, the Peak District and Snowdonia in 1951. Still, in 2006, the man in the urban street, asked to name British national parks, remembers (or guesses!) 'Dartmoor' at least third and usually second in his list and can often only name three in any case. It was listed as a candidate from the moment the public discussion about British national parks began (Wordsworth having invented the idea when he said in the *Guide to the Lakes*, that that district should be a 'kind of national property'). Dr (later Viscount) Addison reported in 1931, recommending the creation of British national parks to a government sadly swamped by a depression and a financial crisis. Lord Justice Scott reporting on post-war land use in rural areas in 1942, recommended the establishment of national parks and in the parliamentary debate of his report reference was made to creating them 'in the first year of peace'. John Dower was then asked to study the question of establishing them and produced what is still regarded as the seminal work on the subject in May 1945, before that first year of peace had begun. He ends with the sentence: 'There can be few national purposes which at so modest a cost offer so large a prospect of health-giving happiness for the people.' He also said that further work was necessary and the government, only two months later so urgently was the prospect regarded, asked Sir Arthur Hobhouse to do that work, and he reported his results in July 1947. Dower (who was a member of Hobhouse's Committee) had argued that his central 'National Parks Authority' should also control a system of national nature reserves, but the Hobhouse Committee thought otherwise and set up a Wildlife Conservation Special Committee under, the then, Dr Julian Huxley to examine a nature conservation system for the country as a whole separate from the national parks. It reported in the same year, recommending a national 'Biological Service' which should acquire and manage 'national nature reserves' even in national parks, but that the proposed National Parks Commission should be empowered to create other nature reserves within the parks which it considered would be necessary to conserve local breeding populations of wild animals.

Government accepted this strange separation of landscape and nature conservation and in the legislative foundation year of 1949 created a Nature Conservancy (i.e. 'Biological Service') by Royal Charter under a committee of the Privy Council, and a National Parks Commission, under the National Parks and Access to the Countryside Act. That Act, a veritable conservation compendium, contained the means with which to define and set up national parks in England and Wales *and* the tools which it was thought the Nature Conservancy and local authorities would need to protect and manage wildlife, habitat and geological sites throughout Great Britain. In that regard, it invented 'areas (not then 'sites') of special scientific interest' and local, but oddly not 'national', nature reserves. It also dealt with 'areas of outstanding natural beauty' (AONB), long-distance footpaths and surveys for definitive maps of rights of way, access agreements and access orders. Strangely it offered no positive connections between any of these things, though some negative ones: an SSSI was one 'not being a nature reserve' and an AONB one 'not being a national park'. But it was a protection and access omnibus that offered various lines on, and degrees of 'shading' for, the 'white land' of the contemporary planning jargon. White land was to all intents and purposes 'undeveloped countryside' born out of the twin Acts of 1947 (Agriculture and Town and Country Planning) which had produced permanent and comprehensive public support and protection for agriculture on the one hand and an equally comprehensive regulatory system for the control of all the remaining use of land on the other.

From Scott, Dower and Hobhouse there was a clear message that (in Dowers' words) 'established farming use should be effectively maintained' in national parks, and thus an explicit acknowledgement that farming contributed much of the beauty of the landscape of England and Wales. Whether the word 'established' implies either that farming better not change methodologically, or better not extend its then surface limits in national parks is open to conjecture. Clearly the tools of the Town and Country Planning Act of 1947 were meant to regulate change in spatial and design terms for the whole of the rest of the domestic economy. So in the innocence of the early post-war years a dilemma was created for national park overseers whoever they were to be. Farmers were to be trusted with the heritage and the rest were not. Those overseers had a potentially powerful tool called development control (popularly generalised as 'planning') to deal with the mistrusted majority and at that time no real means of 'doing a deal' with the few (the farmers) who could influence, benignly or otherwise, the great spread of the rural landscape. No one, not even the apparently far-sighted founding fathers of the landscape and wildlife conservation system, foresaw the potential of the combination of that 'odd couple': public subsidy and hydraulic power, for modifying field, hedge and moor, even less the likely demand for housing, and the revolution in recreation mounted by the explosion of private motorised mobility and a weekly televisual invitation to examine things natural.

NATIONAL PARK EVOLUTION

Nevertheless the national park system was inserted remarkably rapidly into the landscape of England and Wales. The National Parks Commission began work with energy and as early as 1951 had designated its first four parks, though not without some battles lost. The Peak District and the Lake District, without much local fuss, were given free-standing Joint and Special Planning Boards. Such boards were invented in the Town and Country Planning Act of 1947 and recommended for application to national parks by Hobhouse, writing when that Act was still only a bill before parliament. However the burghers of northwest

Wales, and of the three counties (the same number in the Lakes and even four in the Peak) overlapping the area designated, rose up and resisted the idea of such a board, saying that they could well care for Snowdonia without such elaboration. The Commission withdrew and oversight of the park was given to a joint, but only advisory, committee of the three county councils, leaving actual planning, development control and management decisions with each of them in its own space. That clearly risked inconsistency of decision, lack of uniform policy and thus of unity across the new national park.

No further attempt was made to create an independent body to plan and manage a national park in the 1950s and the Dartmoor National Park, designated at the end of the year of the Snowdonia debacle, was thus set to be 'administered' by a special committee of Devon County Council, though at least it was within one authority's area. The committee inevitably had a majority of councillors of that one authority and the occupational hazard of being over-ruled by the County Council, most likely on substantial matters of policy. The officers reporting to that committee, planning, legal and financial, were effectively part time and hence easily distracted from the national park purpose. Whatever its status, each of the four national park boards or committees of 1951, and eventually each of the first ten, had a third of its members appointed by the Minister of Town and Country Planning of the day to represent the national interest. He or she actually appointed them to the boards, but the County Councils could accept, or not, his or her nominations.

All this is to create the background for the evolution of the system of public management of Dartmoor as a national park over the last 50 years. That evolution had three main phases. The first, ruled as already described, lasted for 23 years, until 1974; the second, with new structures, obligations, a budget and staff of its own, though still 'of the County Council', another 23 until 1997; and the third, under a fully independent authority, is still with us.

Within each of those phases were milestones, or at least landmarks. In the first they were almost all about land-use battles: three reservoir proposals, china clay and afforestation extensions and a 200 m-high television transmitting mast. The third potential reservoir, at Swincombe, was beaten off, the extension of plantations never materialised, but reservoirs in the Avon and West Okement valleys were built and the transmitter, high above Princetown, was agreed to by the casting vote of the chairman. Road improvement and the military presence were, to the close observers of the performance of the national park committee of the day, continual irritants. All of the developments listed, it must be noted, were designed to have outcomes, and provide for people, well beyond the boundaries of the National Park, and a countywide parent committee or its parent council were likely to place more weight on that fact than those attempting to protect a less material national interest. Even they, the latter, needed to take into consideration the fact that the 30,000 people who lived within the Park were bound to be beneficiaries of all or some of those outcomes, as the chairman who swung the vote on the BBC TV mast made clear.

Meanwhile, the need for a daily presence on the ground did become clear, if at least recreational management for the national park purpose was to mean anything. One full-time warden was appointed in 1961 and two more later in that decade, and they led a large number of voluntary wardens, especially at weekends. Their powers were to 'help and advise the public' and to enforce any bye-laws that might exist. At the same time one mobile information centre was acquired and placed seasonally in that roadside pit with the 'buried' tor in it (Chapter 2) at Two Bridges (where the scissor roads crossed). A short footpath led up the West Dart valley to Wistman's Wood from outside the information centre, a situation that slightly perturbed the Nature Conservancy. By 1970, too, the County Planning Officer had been persuaded to dedicate the services of more than one of his officers to national park business, but all this in a time when expenditure on that business, whether wages, the making of a car park or the erection of a public lavatory, had to be agreed in Whitehall item by item.

Reformation and renaissance

But a revolution in this limited arrangement was on the way and the second phase about to begin. Government, no less, had recognised at last that public taste and mobility had changed and recreational use of the whole countryside had exploded in the 20 years since those high-minded days of 1949. In 1968 the National Parks Commission was wound up and replaced by a Countryside Commission. It had its predecessor's responsibilities for national parks and indeed all of the 1949 Act powers, but a wider remit both to advise government and to implement an innovative experimental power for landscape and recreational management purposes throughout rural England and Wales. (A Scottish Countryside Commission had been established in 1967.) Within three years the Government asked the Commission to 'take a fresh look' at national parks and long-term policies for them and a committee under Lord Sandford was appointed to do just that. However, before it could report, a bill to reorganise local government came before Parliament, and the Director of the Countryside Commission (Reg Hookway, who also sat on the Sandford Committee) saw and seized an opportunity to improve the national park management situation beyond all recognition. His achievement was the first and fundamental change in the evolution of Dartmoor's governance since 1951.

The Local Government Act of 1972 established a single National Park Committee for each park that was to be a 'senior' committee of the county council with the largest area of the park within its boundary, but having seats for other counties which overlapped the park. It would be the planning authority for the whole park and would appoint its own chief officer – the National Park Officer (NPO) named in the Act; both the appointment and the naming gave the arrangement an unprecedented strength in local government terms. The Act also required the national park committee to publish within three years of 1974 a National Park Plan setting out its policies, implementation intentions and expenditure. It was to be a management plan, not a 'planning' plan. In the debate on the relevant part of the 1972 Act ministers promised that central government would meet directly 'the lion's share' of the expenditure of a national park committee. It turned out to be 75 per cent of the accepted bid for funds year-on-year, which also strengthened the committee's hand in budgetary arguments within the county council. The national park case often ending with the line: 'and you only have to find 25 per cent of the cost of this modest proposal, Mr Chairman!'

Imagine the change in Dartmoor's prospects for real conservation management of its then 945 sq km landscape – suddenly there was a single-minded authority (the NPA) with its own officers and a budget. The new NPA set about its task with vigour, it met for the first time a year before vesting day – and advertised for and appointed its National Park Officer by October 1973, the first in the land. He was able to appoint many new colleagues before 1 April 1974, and so on that day the NPA hit the ground running.

Lord Sandford's report was published in that same April, though the Government's response to it took until January 1976 to emerge. It, Circular 4/76, deserves its place in the printed record of the history of landscape conservation. It broadly accepted the Committee's recommendations, most importantly what has become known in the trade as the 'Sandford principle'. It stated that where an irreconcilable conflict is revealed between the two statutory purposes for which a national park then existed ('preservation' of its natural beauty and the promotion of enjoyment of it) then the conservation purpose must prevail. The Committee had asked for it to be made clear in statute that public enjoyment of the parks must 'leave their natural beauty unimpaired for the enjoyment of this and future generations', and I quote it only because of the resonance it has with the definition of general 'sustainability' that became internationally agreed some 20 years later. The government forbore to put in hand legislation to that effect immediately, but in the Environment Act of 1995, which began the third phase of our history, it did turn the Sandford principle into a statutory duty not only for NPAs but for all public bodies whose work found them, however temporarily, within national parks. Similarly, in 1976, it agreed to regard the promotion by the NPA of the social and economic well being of its area as 'an object of policy', but not a third statutory purpose. With hindsight that was a blessing in disguise, for while most NPAs including Dartmoor pursued the object of policy with some energy as Hobhouse had determined, none then had to wrestle with the effect on the Sandford principle of having more than two purposes. (For the record, three purposes were accorded to the Broads Authority in 1988, and four to the Scottish NPAs in 2003. It still remains to be revealed whether in practice on the ground such complications really can be made to work and the landscape conservation record of the original ten NPAs repeated in higher mountains and on coastal flats given their added socio-economic responsibilities.)

By 1977 the first Dartmoor National Park Plan was published on time. Its Foreword ended with this:

The communities of people in the hills, however physically dispersed, are close knit. They and their individual members are vital to the national park, they manage the surface and make it a living healthy organism. Their well-being is a prerequisite of the care they take of, and the part they play in the Park. The circulation system of their organism – the 560 miles of road and 460 miles of path – is also a critical network for the visitor and must be kept equally healthy, by the right pruning, maintenance and sensible growth.

The total resource which is Dartmoor goes well beyond the national park purpose. Indeed recreation is the latest, least tangible and most volatile function for the hills. Farmers, foresters, engineers, quarrymen and soldiers also use it for society's benefit and to some recreational users each of them provides an additional fascination. The farmers carry on an essential service and are also asked to carry a huge responsibility to society for the management of the scene. The new concept which is the national park plan could be used to co-ordinate the activities of all users, in order to ensure the continuing optimum yield from this Dartmoor resource for all those who can benefit from it.

The Sandford Committee had asked for the involvement of landowners in the planning and management of the national park and for a power for the NPA to make management agreements with them. It was to take a few more years before the powers were forthcoming, but the writing was on the wall and explains some of the sentences just quoted.

The new NPA decided early that it needed to practice landscape and recreation management itself if it was to influence others to indulge in such things for the public benefit. To do that it needed to occupy land, enough to allow the right scale of practice and experiment, but not so much as to overstretch its labour force or its budget. The half of the park covered by farmland and buildings would be sustained by its occupiers, who might or might not be susceptible to advice or persuasion – but there were tools to help the process. Moorland and woodland offered most scope for active public enjoyment and were the landscape characteristics that made the Park different from its context. They also sheltered a unique biodiversity, though no one spoke in those terms then. *They* were where the NPA needed to produce tried-and-tested management action to demonstrate what was needed if national park principles were to be fulfilled.

NPA LAND

The neglect of much broad-leaved woodland in the park was, as in much of late twentieth-century England, very clear. Many estates had committed themselves to developing and maintaining conifer plantations under a dedication scheme that gave them tax advantage and grant aid as the woods developed and this had often involved the replacement of native woods (Chapter 4). The NPA recognised the need to demonstrate what could and should be done if the existing woodland

FIG 246. Wray Cleave Wood from Wheelbarrow Lane on the opposite side of the valley. More than one valley-side tor protrudes through its canopy and Pepperdon Mine house is at the far right. In the foreground is one of a set of curiously separate hills which occur along both sides of the Wray – part of the Sticklepath Fault zone.

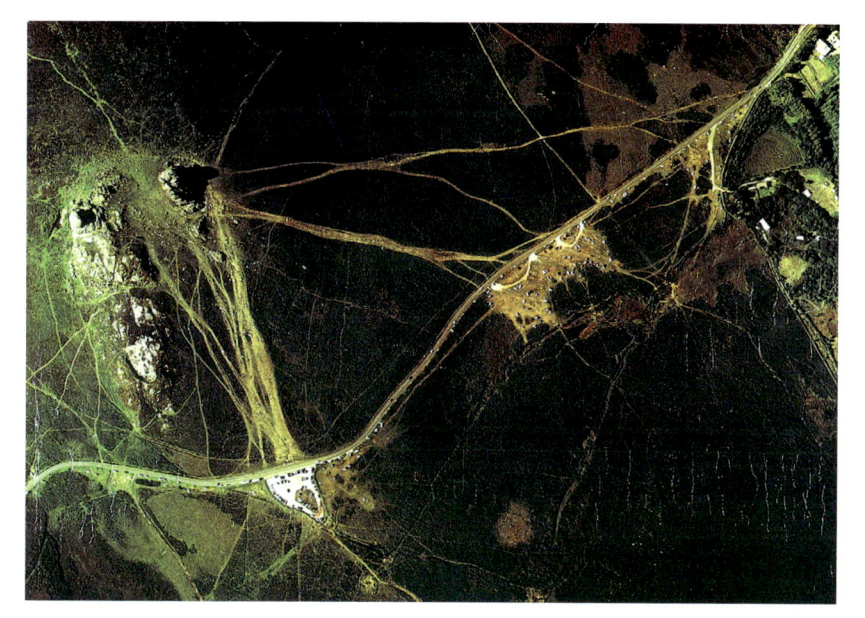

FIG 247. A vertical aerial image of Haytor Down taken in the early 1970s. The Widecombe road runs across from top right – the car parks, cars on verges and wide pathways to Haytor Rocks tell their own story. (DNPA after Brunsden)

resource was to be improved and sustained for all its potential values. It also accepted that conifer planting was an acceptable exercise within any one estate at the right scale if income from it could be applied to the costs of management of the broad-leaves. Its predecessor National Park Committee had been persuaded, only just before April 1974, to buy 74 acres (30 ha) of woodland in the Wray valley, Wray Cleave (Fig. 246), because a) the valley was described as a 'major scenic wooded valley' in the County Development Plan and b) the sale could risk further conversion to conifers already evident in the same valley. Eventually more plots on both sides of the River Wray – Sanduck, Huntingpark and Caseley Woods – were added to form a sort of eastern woodland collection.

As far as moorland was concerned, soon after the NPA took office Haytor Down came on the market. It straddled the B3387 from Bovey Tracey to Widecombe (Fig. 247). Here was the first open space, the first natural stopping place on the third most significant entrance road to the National Park in traffic terms (only those from Plymouth and past Ashburton carried more cars in the 1970s). Here also was Hay Tor, easily reached from the road on foot, easily climbed – the Victorians had cut steps in it so that their ladies could ascend to

FIG 248. Dartmoor is not blessed with a welter of rock-climbing sites, but Hay Tor offers a number of potential pitches, often used by learners under supervision and military trainees – climbing congestion is commonplace. (DNPA)

take in the view … to seaward! This massive pile had a multiple attraction, its own intrigue for the sightseer, its educational demonstration of all the Dartmoor granite characteristics, and short climbs that challenged amateurs, soldiers and trainee professionals (Fig. 248). Haytor quarries and their granite tramway only added to these public virtues of the space. Most of these attributes have appeared in earlier pictures. Few bid at the auction and the NPA became the owner and thus a necessary new relative of the Haytor and Ilsington Commoners' Association with the redoubtable Herbert Whitley in the chair (see Chapter 1).

In the same year a complementary move was made when the owner of Holne Common decided to move away and offered the moorland part of the common to the NPA. It, too, sat across a road, but this time a minor one chiefly notorious

THE CONTEMPORARY CONSERVATION SCENE · 333

FIG 249. Some of Holne Moor's public benefits: (left) Combestone Tor from its inevitable car park; (below left) the view northwest from Combestone across the Ancient Tenement landscape from Bellever at the far right across to Sherberton, with a Dunnabridge Copse beyond – the skyline is the edge of the north plateau; (bottom left) the west edge of Holne Moor from a Huccaby field – Combestone Tor is on the extreme left of the skyline that runs up to Ryder's Hill.

for being on the return half of a coach-drivers' loop from Torquay to Dartmeet, where tea could be had. It thus functioned as the obligatory Torbay holiday-makers' Dartmoor visit on a day too wet for the beach. Buckfast Abbey lay beyond Holne on the way back in case the moorland experience had itself been too dampening of the spirit. For some it was their first, maybe their only sampling of Dartmoor.

Holne Moor also had a tor, Combestone, even nearer the road than Hay Tor and level with it (Fig. 249). As a viewpoint it commands the central basin all the way to Princetown on the western rim, and overlooking in the foreground the landscape of six of the Forest's Ancient Tenements. It thus also has its educational potential as an instructive viewing platform and as a rock outcrop. From it to the south runs a relatively short transect through the Dartmoor soil pattern set out in Chapter 3, from brown earth to the blanket bog on the plateau top, with their appropriate plant cover; to the north the same line runs rapidly downslope through woodland and clitter to the River Dart. It is altogether the pivotal point in a splendid Dartmoor profile. Since the acquisition of Holne Moor and partly because of it, as we have already seen, the common has become a veritable archaeological laboratory from Combestone eastward right across to Fore Stoke and spanning at least 2,000 years, from the Bronze Age to the end of the mediaeval period.

In the next year the same owner offered White Wood to the Authority who snapped it up. It was the remaining part of Holne common, which he had retained in 1975 to protect his fishing in the River Dart. Here was a rare chance to test the management of a commonable wood, almost unique now in Dartmoor terms. The wood is home to strong populations of wood warblers, redstarts and the pied flycatchers who have circumnavigated Dartmoor since the Yarner Wood entrapment already described in Chapter 5. Its own historical attributes, vegetation and easy access route, for people and foresters, were hinted at in Chapter 4, and the qualities of Bench Tor, overlooking it, in Chapter 2. Altogether it was a very appropriate purchase and the icing on this last slice of the cake was that with the wood came the Lordship of the Manor of Holne. The Manor Court was and is still functioning, one of only two alive in Dartmoor. The National Park Officer became steward of the Manor, and thus more embroiled with the homage – the collective noun for the commoners assembled now, originally for all the tenants of the manor – than on Haytor. The present record of the Court proceedings is kept in a book begun in 1790 when Sir Bourchier Wrey of Holne Park was lord of the manor and when changes in the 'lives of the manor' were registered at each session, their successors accepted or rejected and their dwellings or farmsteads assigned. Now the business is only about the common, but it, its management and that of its watercourses gives the NPO and, through him or her, the NPA a valuable insight into the detail of this 1,000-year-old labour. Two successive NPOs have proved good enough stewards to have had permanent marks erected on the Moor by the commoners on their departure, one a new bound-stone on the col between the Mardle and the Holy Brook, the other a new clapper bridge over the Aller Brook.

The NPA and the commoners

These two essays into moorland ownership and thus management proved invaluable to the young NPA, but because they both ventured into commoners' territory that value was more than doubled; critically because a working relationship with the whole community of commoners in the National Park also began early. Almost as soon as the new NPA had taken office the chairman of the Dartmoor Commoners' Association (DCA), the same Herbert Whitley who led the Haytor and Ilsington Association, came to the chairman of the NPA and said, in as many words, 'You have the means to promote private legislation (through the County Council) and we need it.' He explained that with the general demise of active lords of the manor as overseeing, benevolently or otherwise, their tenants as the sole graziers of their commons, discipline had largely disappeared and only a legally binding statute could correct the situation. The DCA, whose origins have already been described, had seen a national Commons Registration Act passed in 1965 with the promise of a second stage of legislation that would deal with the management of commons. (That second stage did not happen until 2006, so the Dartmoor commoners' frustration of 1974 was justified.)

Thus began a partnership between the NPA and those commoners – the real managers of Dartmoor moorland – that still exists in 2009. It took 11 years, a defeat in the House of Commons in 1979 and many long and crowded meetings to achieve a Dartmoor Commons Act, known even nationally as the '1985 Act', but still locally as 'the Bill' because for 11 long years it was just that. The NPA had responded positively and immediately to the DCA's proposals in 1974, saying that what it needed were seats on whatever management body was sought and a public right of access to the commons in perpetuity which would be its responsibility. Devon County Council, to its everlasting credit, bore the financial brunt of the whole legal expeditions to Parliament, so the NPA's annual budget was never unduly strained.

The 'Act of '85' created a Commoners' Council to protect the interests of commoners, the status of the commons and to regulate their use. It was to be elected as to 20 of its members by the commoners who registered as electors and paid dues according to their quantifiable rights to graze and whether they used

FIG 250. Holne commoners clearing the leat to the Stoke farms. An old hay knife stuck in the ground on the left makes a good tool for shearing the leat sides. The homage foreman supervises and a then national park ranger, the late Mrs Dot Hills, is helping further down the leat, at the extreme left.

them or not. A duty was imposed on the Council to keep a 'live' register of actual graziers, and non-grazing right-holders who wished to vote for it. The elections were to be held in the historic quarters, each for five seats, one of which must be occupied by a 'small' grazier (with less than ten livestock units attached to his/her right). The NPA should appoint two members and two more to represent the private common landowners, and the Duchy of Cornwall would appoint one. The Council had to co-opt a vet and could co-opt up to two more individuals. The National Park Officer became honorary adviser to the Council. The NPA was empowered to make bye-laws to control public excesses should they arise out of a right to walk and ride on the commons, or liberties taken beyond those rights. The Council could make regulations to control the commoners' exercise of grazing and burning, about animal welfare and to prevent abuse of the commons by those not entitled to graze. Both parties were to consult each other over the implementation of both powers and before any other actions relating to open moorland and its vegetation.

The Act was, for its time, as comprehensive as its promoters could make it, its few deficiencies were only revealed as those who had to implement it faced the changes that were to be imposed by national and international regulation, and in public support for agriculture as the twentieth century proceeded into the twenty-first. Its electoral machinery more closely resembled eighteenth-century hustings than modern polling stations. Its statement, for the 'avoidance of doubt', that the custom on Dartmoor was that the adjoining landowner should fence his land 'against the common' was not strong enough, while its prohibition of the severance of rights of common from the in-bye land to which they were attached (accidentally empowered by the 1965 Act) was ahead of its time. For a number of legal and financial matters the Council was given the powers of a local authority. Suffice it to say that Part III of the national Commons Act of 2006 is modelled on the Dartmoor Act.

There were some 1,500 Dartmoor commoners listed on the 1965 Act register, with rights on 104 Common Land (CL) Units belonging to 93 owners. One effect of the Dartmoor Bill's passage was to speed up the Commons Commissioners' hearing of disputes about land and rights that arose from the registration process. By 1985 they had declared 15 CL units void – for lack of commoners or non-grazing history – amalgamated some and reduced others in size. The 1985 Act records 32 commoners' local associations in a Schedule and one, that for the Forest of Dartmoor, has been added to the list since its creation, though not for election purposes.

The 'Forest' was not a common prior to the 1965 Act but registered as such in 1967 and the Commons Commissioner sorted out, as far as he was able, who had rights upon it in a hearing in 1983. The Commoners' Council decided in 1996 that those rights could not logically be regarded as historic and thus must be separate from any others held by the same commoner on other older commons. MAFF then accepted that decision for the purposes of paying grant under the ESA system for the better management of the commons. The separation of the Forest from other commons in this way is now disputed by MAFF's partial successor, the Rural Payments Agency of the Department of Environment, Food and Rural Affairs (DEFRA) which has recently decided that the Forest rights in most cases duplicate rights held on the 'home' commons of the grazier. It therefore discounts them in any calculation related to rights and common land area for the purposes of support payments. The situation has excited the European Union, which has difficulty understanding British common land in any case. In 2008 the matter was still in dispute, among others, between the commoners and the government.

Land management by agreement

DEFRA's interest, apart from its responsibility for common land in law, arises out of payments to farmers for agri-environmental purposes which have existed for some 25 years or more in one form or another.

During the 1960s one of the effects of farming's newer technical and financial power began to show, especially on Exmoor but on Dartmoor too. It involved the conversion of moorland by ploughing into 'agricultural land' – rough grazing being defined as other than farmland for some reason. In the Countryside Act of 1968 the Minister had taken powers to apply an order to any 'moor and heath' prohibiting its conversion by ploughing, but attempts to get such orders made came to little or nothing. In the same legislation the Nature Conservancy was empowered to agree, with the owner and occupier of any SSSI, the details of its management and to pay for that or carry it out, and to compensate for any restrictions that were part of the deal. However, progress was slow and while the most important tool so far devised for conserving habitat and landscape in the face of economic ambition began its gestation, the moorland ploughing process still proceeded. A campaign to protect moorland resulted in an inquiry into the problem on Exmoor. As a result, in 1978, Lord Porchester advised the government that the Exmoor NPA needed power, and a budget, to pay would-be converters of moorland compensation for profit forgone, based on an annual assessment of that profit by Exeter University's Agricultural Economics department. The management agreement was born.

Pressure mounted for its application in all national parks from the Countryside Commission, and in 1979 the Ministry of Agriculture removed the need for farmers to get prior approval for grant-aided works 'except in national parks' where the farmer had to show that the NPA had no objection to the work in question. Thus almost by default a necessary dialogue between all farmers and NPAs was triggered for the first time. It was bound to include discussion of at least income forgone and the public value of the status quo, or even its improvement for the public purpose. Only two years later the Wildlife and Countryside Act gave to NPAs and the Nature Conservancy Council (revitalised and renamed by its own Act of 1973) powers to make management agreements with owners and occupiers of land. These management agreements became the building blocks of all the agri-environment schemes that have followed and spread from England and Wales to the whole of Europe.

In Dartmoor, management agreements became the order of the day in the NPA/farmer partnership. The first was made in the year of the enabling legislation and in ten years from then there were 56 covering 5,262 ha of land.

FIG 251. Management agreement land: (top) Babeny, the farmstead is left of centre with parallel hedge-banks to its right – the driftway to Riddon Ridge beyond it can be seen snaking away behind the farm. It is an Ancient Tenement and site of the first management agreement made by the NPA, and here with a tenant farmer; (above) Emsworthy, with Hay Tor beyond – the farmstead abandoned in the 1920s can be seen in the trees under the cloud shadow. At the head of the Becka Brook the land allowed access on foot from Haytor Down to Widecombe Town Commons, avoiding the road. A single sum bought a 21-year agreement with the owner-occupier.

They ranged from less than 0.5 ha at Spinsters Rock in Drewsteignton parish, which also ensured public access to the monument, to the 526 ha of Tor Royal Newtake, just south of Princetown, and the 1,662 ha of the Meavy catchment above Burrator. Some were for five years, with potential annual extensions after that – some were in perpetuity. More than half of them provided for public access. Tenant farmers were to be paid annually when money was involved and their landlord was entitled to a percentage, but owner-occupiers could be paid a single sum for, say, a 21-year agreement. Accepting the argument that the NPA could not predict a threat that might trigger management agreement negotiations when budgeting ahead of the year in question, a national sinking fund was set up by the Countryside Commission on which an NPA could draw for payments in the first year of an agreement. If, therefore, an agreement was struck with an owner within that year, the whole of the cost of the 21 years could be drawn from the sinking fund. Dartmoor used more than half the fund in each of its early years.

The Duchy of Cornwall and the NPA

By the 1980s too, another partnership had emerged, this time with the biggest landowner – the Duchy of Cornwall – and it also involved management agreements. The Duchy owned more than 28,000 ha including an enclosed block of the central basin and the heart of each of the high moorland plateaux. A new Secretary and Keeper of the Records, John Higgs, arrived at the head of the Duchy's professional arm. He was a land-use academic from Oxford, just returned from the Food and Agriculture Organisation in Rome, and took the management of the Dartmoor Estate to a new level within the Duchy. It was, he claimed, never going to be a major contributor to the Duchy's coffers so why not use it to demonstrate the environmental contribution that could be made by hill-farmers through the work of its tenants with the conservation agencies. His master concurred. John Higgs met the National Park Officer on his first visit to Dartmoor and a personal partnership also began. The NPA grasped this new opportunity and did much of the work that resulted in the 'Future Management of the Dartmoor Estate', a report to the Prince of Wales in 1983 that ran to more than 50 pages. Out of 19 'proper' farms on the estate, ten had management agreements by the end of the 1980s, though not without some protracted negotiation, sucking of teeth and working out tricky formulae for calculating actual costs. To avoid a new fence across a large moorland newtake in shared tenancy, which was proposed to keep two herds apart at critical times in the cattle-keeping calendar, the calculation involved time for a stockman to police the herds, keep for his horse and for his dog for the whole of the critical period. The cost of maintenance of all

FIG 252. Huccaby Farm, in the centre, like Babeny a Duchy tenancy, just passed to the son of the tenant with whom the NPA made an agreement in the 1980s which allowed him to return to work alongside his parents.

the walls on an Ancient Tenement, continuing to make labour-intensive hay in far-too-small fields rather than take walls out, and grazing the newtake to a new seasonal timetable, added up to the wage for a man for a year. That allowed a son, 'working away', to return to the farm and prepare himself for the tenancy succession in the time-honoured way of slowly acquiring his parents' stock and machinery. He is the farmer now. Thus arose the human and conservation satisfactions in the 1980s for landlord, tenant and for the new farmed landscape broker – the NPA (Fig. 252).

At another Ancient Tenement, where a proposal was received to divide the farm, ignoring the current field pattern, into a set of silage-making rotation blocks, a reorganisation of the proposed plan allowed existing walls to remain. The NPA's survey of the fields revealed a hitherto unknown colony of greater butterfly orchids. The NPA alerted the Nature Conservancy Council, which, eventually, declared it an SSSI and took the four small meadows involved into a separate management agreement. The two bureaucracies were in great contrast as far as performance speed was concerned, but the story serves to introduce the second major player in the nature conservation game in Dartmoor in the second half of the twentieth century.

Nature conservation and the NPA

We have already seen that the functions of national parks and the statutory nature conservation system were born together in the same legislation in 1949, also that the Nature Conservancy had acquired three nature reserves within the national park in the 1950s. All three were woodland, Dendles Wood straddling the River Yealm two miles upstream from Cornwood, Yarner Wood clothing a broad blunt spur with a narrow valley on either side joining at the toe of the spur and forming Reddaford Water, a tributary of the Bovey, and the Bovey Valley Woodlands in the bottom of that valley. Yarner, the first to be acquired, is much the best known and the site of much research work almost from the beginning of its life as a National Nature Reserve, and well before the research arm of the Nature Conservancy was split off as the Institute of Terrestrial Ecology. Clearings were created to encourage various butterfly species, notably the purple hairstreak; and experimental work on woodland management for nature conservation purposes began in earnest. Pied flycatchers, however, provided Yarner with its greatest claim to fame, and their story has already been told. Research there continues and, as recently as 2006, work by Dr David Stradling of the University of Exeter showed that ants in Yarner use the earth's magnetic field to navigate. Suffice it so say here that Yarner Wood remains the premier Dartmoor base for Natural England, the contemporary successor of the Nature Conservancy of the 1950s whose officers established so much there.

The Nature Conservancy Council – of Great Britain – had been split between the three mainland countries in 1990 and thus English Nature had become the national nature conservation actor in Dartmoor from 1991 until 2006 when Natural England hit the streets incorporating English Nature, the bulk of the Countryside Agency (which had succeeded the Commission) and the Rural Development Service of DEFRA.

While nature reserves, dubbed 'National' long before that was a legitimate title, became early showcases and the home of pioneering field research, the designation of Sites of Special Scientific Interest also proceeded apace. By the mid-1960s there were 25, the biggest of which were two great expanses of moorland, one a rough triangle in the northwest with a base from Blackdown to Cut Hill and an apex near Okehampton Camp, and the other a broad swathe diagonally across the southern plateau, southwest to northeast from Shell Top to Holne Moor. Gidleigh Common, Blackslade Mire, Tor Royal Bog and High House Moor adjoining Dendles Wood were the other moorland SSSIs. Nine others were woods including the 200 ha of Holne Chase and Piles Copse, the only one of the three high-level oakwoods which did not have 'Forest Nature

FIG 253. The entrance to Joint Mitnor Cave at Buckfastleigh (see also Figure 155).

Reserve' status (then in the gift of the Forestry Commission). The newtake in which Wistman's Wood sits was declared an SSSI to buffer the wood and accommodate its (then suspected) natural expansion, which, as we now know, has actually continued throughout the last 100 years. This suite of sites of secondary protection also included five designated at least in part for their geological importance. Meldon Quarry and its tiny neighbour Meldon Aplite Quarry, the big one working, the little one long abandoned, and Haytor and Smallacombe Iron Mines are all in the metamorphic aureole. Lydford Gorge and Buckfastleigh Caves are beyond it. The former was declared as much for its damp, shaded habitat for lower plants as for its impressive geomorphology – by far the most spectacular gorge in the National Park, and outside the granite/aureole complex. Buckfastleigh Caves too had a combination of reasons for designation. Their complexity as a subterranean limestone system in a landscape floored by predominantly acidic rocks might have been reason itself. That they hold interglacial deposits containing a rich mammalian fossil fauna making, *inter alia*, a major contribution to the interpretation of the history of the middle reaches of the Dart valley has to be even more important. It was detailed in Chapter 2. The presence of winter populations of greater horseshoe bats, with their 'lesser' cousins also around, is the icing on the SSSI cake and another subject of detailed research (Fig. 253).

Almost inevitably the nature conservation designatory system has been applied ever more intensively as the last 50 years have proceeded. New knowledge of risk and rarity, more careful searching and the growth of public interest in things natural have all played a part in that expansion. The system itself has been refined, more powers to support it have been developed and the overview of the protection of wildlife and habitat has become European and even more widely international. The UK, along with many other governments, signed the International Biodiversity Convention demanded by the Earth Summit of 1992, out of which Biodiversity Action Plans for both species and habitats were born. The European Union created new designations, notably the SACs (coupled with existing Special Protection Areas – for birds) under the banner of 'Natura 2000' in the mid-1990s. The government published the UK Biodiversity Action Plan in 1994 and demanded a new appraisal of the biological and surface geological resource at local level as building blocks for the national contribution to the international action demanded by the Earth Summit. In 1997 the NPA and English Nature had published, in response to the UK Action Plan, their shared appraisal of Dartmoor's natural history, 'The Nature of Dartmoor – a biodiversity profile'. By 2001 the NPA produced its biodiversity action plan, 'Action for Wildlife', alongside a second edition of the profile

The original five geological SSSIs had meanwhile grown to 21, now including the sites of important pollen and charcoal profiles in the peat at Blacklane and

FIG 254. The corner of Whitchurch Down protected for its Irish lady's tresses in the 1970s.

FIG 255. Dunsford Wood alongside the Teign. Innocent despoilers were finally persuaded by a campaign by nature reserve managers and local lady volunteer wardens to leave daffodils to their pollination, bee-feeding and for others to enjoy. The Devon Wildlife Trust still occupies the reserve but now as a tenant of the National Trust.

Black Ridge which were described in Chapter 3. The exposure of the actual contact margin of the granite in Burrator Quarry and the migmatite boulders and outcrops on Leusdon Common south of Widecombe are also designated. Extensive periglacial features around and northwestward of Merrivale, including Cox Tor, now constitute the most significant geomorphological site in the National Park that is specially protected. Woodland sites have increased to 17 in number and cover 2,378 ha. The two moorland plateaux are now totally of SSSI status, called North and South Dartmoor respectively, and East Dartmoor covers 2,000 or more hectares centred on Bush Down straddling the B3212, which all agree is the most significant stand of ling in the National Park. Blackslade Mire and Tor Royal Bog still stand alone, and with Okehampton Park flushes complete the 'wet moorland' suite. Five hectares of Whitchurch Down east of Tavistock protect a small stand of Irish lady's tresses (Fig. 254), and Lydford Railway Pools, at 1.3 ha the smallest protected wildlife site in the park, support the fairy shrimp. There is little of the River Dart and its headwaters that is not within an SSSI, and the Bovey, the Lyd, the Okements, Tavy, Teign and Walkham all have reaches within SSSIs.

Some of these nationally protected sites are actually owned or occupied by bodies dedicated to conservation of nature or landscape. The Devon Wildlife Trust has occupied Dunsford Wood and the 'Dart Valley Woods' since the early

1960s, and in the former conducted a successful campaign to stop the quasi-commercial picking of wild daffodils before that decade was out. The Trust brokered a deal between the then Society for the Protection of Nature Reserves and the Devon Speleological Society which involved itself taking a lease of the Buckfastleigh Caves from the former and sub-letting part of the quarry floor and the caves to the latter. It also has two tiny woodland reserves, at Mill Bottom almost in Lustleigh village and Lady's Wood southwest of South Brent. They were the first reserves it ever acquired and both carry a significant dormouse population. The Dartmoor Preservation Association owns High House Moor adjoining Dendles Wood, now within the South Dartmoor SSSI, and carries out a long-term bracken control experiment there.

THE NATIONAL TRUST AND THE NATIONAL PARK

The National Trust owns the major part of Shaugh Prior Commons, a block which comprises the southeast side of the valley of the moorland River Plym above Cadover, all the way up to the watershed from Shell Top through Broad Rock to Plym Head. This extensive moorland landscape includes Great Trowlesworthy Tor, with that distinctively pink felspar in its granite blocks, Trowlesworthy Warren, Willings Walls Warren and Hentor Warren, companions to the warrens described in Chapter 7. The Trust owns other significant properties in the National Park. The best known is the Castle Drogo estate in Drewsteignton parish, despite its reference back to a Domesday tenant, the castle was built by Julius Drewe at the beginning of the last century, and is regarded as one of Edward Lutyens's unfinished masterpieces (see Fig. 57). Standing on a spur-end overlooking the Teign valley opposite Chagford, the castle is at one end of an estate that runs down both sides of the Teign valley to beyond Fingle Bridge. The south side of the valley is almost completely wooded, but the north side is open, bracken and scrub-covered, but very steep. The Huntsman's Path takes the walker out from Drogo along the lip of the valley side and the Fisherman's Path brings him back along the river's edge after a descent to Fingle Bridge. Whiddon Deer Park, exactly opposite the castle, has already been named and also comprises much open space and its higher slopes boast small fragments of the 210 m Calabrian shoreline carved at the beginning of the Pleistocene (Fig. 256).

The Parke estate abutting the boundary of the National Park outside Bovey Tracey is both the Dartmoor office of the National Trust and the headquarters of the National Park Authority. The house is a small (by NT standards) four-square early-nineteenth-century building with the Egyptian embellishments – entrance columns with no bases and parapet rising in steps to the centre of the front, all

FIG 256. Whiddon Deer Park, part of the Castle Drogo estate of the National Trust and well known by lichenologists (see also Figures 69, 114, 123 and 276).

tomb-like – made fashionable by Napoleon's (and Nelson's) eastern Mediterranean campaign and also visible at other big Trust houses in Devon such as Arlington Court and Saltram. Adjoining and behind it is a wing of older buildings which form two sides of a courtyard and themselves link with an even older farmstead. The NPA and the National Trust occupy all of this as offices and stores and a spacious room, large enough for the authority's formal meetings with the public present, has been built in what was the yard of the farmstead. The parkland of scattered big trees in a neutral and patchily damp grassland is the valuable part of the site in our terms – with moonwort *Botrychium lunaria* and adder's tongue *Ranunculus ophioglossifolius* among the grasses (Fig. 114). It comprises a substantial parcel of the floodplain of the River Bovey and a gently sloping spur into the side of which the buildings just described have been inserted. Upstream of the house the valley floor is flanked by woodland on steeper slopes. The former railway line from Newton Abbot to Moretonhampstead flanks the estate throughout its length offering easy walking and cycling from a lay-by on the A382. The Trust also owns Dunsford and Cod Woods near Steps Bridge, Holne Woods downstream of White Wood below Holne Moor and Hembury Woods above Buckfast. All three are SSSIs or parts of the same. At Sticklepath, included in the Park at the 1991 review of the boundary, is a workable – and thus for visitors working – iron foundry and knap mill. The Finch Foundry uses the available power of the River Taw as it leaves Belstone Cleave. The Trust acquired it in the 1980s soon after it ceased trading.

So, in one way the National Park Authority has a number of important and strong allies in its effort to conserve quality in the landscape and all that underpins that. Some are more powerful than others, and that power lies in legislative duty but also in both membership and funds. While Natural England designates land and occupies some to fulfil its own functions, it also makes enforceable contracts with many an owner and occupier and even commoners, to try to achieve a wider spread of 'favourable conditions for conservation' – to use its own language. English Heritage does much the same and via the Dartmoor Vision has done a deal about grazing levels with the other agencies and the commoners specifically geared to the visibility of ancient monuments. The Environment Agency, in monitoring river and stream quality, promoting and protecting fish stocks and overseeing pollution risk on farms as well as in streams, plays another significant part in the maintenance of a healthy Dartmoor. Like Natural England it has a set of interesting antecedents the Devon River Board spawned the Devon River Authority to be absorbed by the National Rivers Authority – with the best logo a conservation body ever had – which then got lost in the great monolith we now live with. When every river had a water bailiff they were all honorary wardens of the National Park, as Rangers of the NPA were honorary bailiffs. The former were not expected to pick up litter, the latter had no power of arrest so did not nab poachers, but the increase in pairs of eyes watching each others' areas of responsibility was to everyone's advantage. The other side of this 'allies' coin is of course the number of cooks actually in the kitchen and whether the broth is stirred too much for the peace of mind of observers and land managers who produced the ingredients in the first place.

OTHER POTENTIAL CONSERVATORS

There are even more – cooks, that is. The County Council has five smallholdings in the National Park still and the Royal Agricultural Society of England owns a small farm at Stowford near Ivybridge. The South West Lakes Trust, a creature of South West Water, owns the catchment of the Meavy, the Ministry of Defence (MOD, and see below) owns Willsworthy Common (Fig. 257), whose commoners were bought out in the first decade of the twentieth century by its predecessor, the War Office. Both licence grazing now, and both have public consciences that a wise National Park Authority can prick if it so chooses. The MOD leases its Okehampton and Merrivale ranges from the

THE CONTEMPORARY CONSERVATION SCENE · 349

FIG 257. Willsworthy ranges with Hare Tor beyond; the only MOD freehold, the commoners were bought out by the War Office in the 1900s – grazing is now by licence. The NPA's long-time chief planner, Keith Bungay, is approaching from the northeast.

FIG 258. Members and officers of the NPA inspecting a new shell-hole in 1981 about which complaints had been made about the scene and the hazard. The licence to fire shells technically required the prompt filling in of craters, not a happy pause in battle practice. Artillery firing ceased in 1996.

Duchy of Cornwall, and has licenses on South West Lakes Trust and Maristow Estate land to the south, both for 'dry' training, i.e. without live ammunition (Fig. 258). Substantial areas of common land are owned by South West Water on Holne Moor and Brent Moor, and by an electricity company on Blackdown at Mary Tavy, where a small but active hydroelectric power generation plant still exists. They also offer persuading opportunities to conservation authorities, as do the plantations in the Teign valley and around the Trenchford Reservoir complex. The Forestry Commission still occupies the three highest plantations described in Chapter 4 and has long shared a memorandum of agreement with the NPA.

The MOD's relationship with the NPA and with Dartmoor is perhaps the most enigmatic of all, in the 'public body' and the Sandford principle (of the 1995 Act) stakes. Its presence on Dartmoor is of long standing, the Napoleonic Wars saw army camps in the south, and in 1875 the Mayor of Okehampton invited the War Office to indulge an annual artillery camp where it still is, though in buildings now. (The first permanent buildings were erected there in 1892.) So, it is important to remember, Dartmoor was designated a national park in 1951 in the knowledge that soldiers fired shot and shell within it regularly. The shells ceased falling, on or off target, in 1996, but live firing with mortars and small arms is still indulged and so public access continues to be impaired by that. More significantly, for our purposes, a major public inquiry into the military presence was held in 1975 with some useful results. Lady Sharpe, who conducted the Inquiry, concluded that military activity in the Dartmoor National Park was 'discordant, incongruous and inconsistent'. She reported to the Secretaries of State for Environment and for Defence who remarkably agreed with her phrase; but seeing no early opportunity for the ending of the relationship, which is perhaps why they agreed so readily, she proposed that formal relations between NPA and MOD should be established which would involve regular and joint consideration of the mitigation of the military effect on landscape and public access to it. Despite intractable problems such as elderly unexploded ammunition surfacing from the peat, the net effect in the last decade at least has been the deployment of a military budget for nature conservation purposes on the high moor. Substantial surveys of vegetation and particularly of breeding birds have been carried out at no expense to the NPA; and professional minds have been bent on high-altitude land management as a result which extend into grazing detail, re-wetting of blanket bog and fire control. Everything in the plateau garden with military gardeners is not necessarily rosy but it would take another book to go into that in adequate detail.

THE VOLUNTEERS – *PACE* THE NATIONAL TRUST

At the voluntary end of the spectrum the picture can get somewhat confused. The Devon Wildlife Trust and the Dartmoor Preservation Association have already been listed as occupying designated nature conservation sites, but the former for instance occupies that land which is actually owned by the National Trust at Dunsford Wood, and White Wood within its Dart Valley Woods reserve is owned by the NPA itself. Some might say conservation energy is being duplicated, but busy and cash-strapped landlords may be relieved to know that a management job is being done on their behalf, if it is. The Dartmoor Preservation Association owns High House Waste upslope from Dendles Wood, but also what might be called 'preservation monuments'. A strip straddling the valley of the Swincombe, which might have been the site of a dam had the Association and others not defeated the proposal, ranks with another tiny plot on the ridge between Sharpitor and Peek Hill which once was occupied by a wartime radar station whose remnants the Association successfully fought to have removed.

On an altogether bigger scale the Woodland Trust was founded in the early 1980s by Kenneth Watkins, a millionaire woodland devotee, at Harford near the southern end of Dartmoor. It is now a nationally significant organisation with a headquarters in Lincolnshire, but it owns parcels of land known as Pullabrook, Hisley and Houndtor Woods in the Bovey valley adjoining the national nature reserve of that name. It also has scattered woodland blocks at Higher Knowle Wood near Lustleigh, above East Wrey Barton and Hawkmoor in the Sticklepath Fault zone on the line of the Wray valley, at Westcott above the little valley running down to the Teign from Doccombe and at Blackaton Bridge near Gidleigh Mill. Some of these were acquired as conifer plantations with the express aim of converting them back to broad-leaved woods. All are publicly accessible and thus add to the National Park walking portfolio, helping to meet the aspiration in the first National Park Plan that it should be as easy to walk alone in the woods as on the moorland. That Plan also recognised the 'concealment capacity' of woodland, not only in terms of coloured anoraks but of parked cars, information displays and public lavatories, so the occupation of it by public-spirited bodies can only be a good thing for the National Park version of landscape management.

The simplest expression of the potentially major alliance – or set of alliances – just rehearsed is, that of the 94,500 ha of the National Park, 41,500 ha are owned by the bodies referred to so far in this chapter. By dint of complicated calculation and adding in the remainder of the total area of commons, whose commoners are NPA partners by virtue of the Act of 1985 and which land's status is nationally protected in any case, much more than half the Park is in safe hands. The ultimate protection in a property-owning democracy is ownership. The public service companies and authorities listed so far are under a statutory duty to have regard for the National Park purposes in their own management decision making (the Environment Act of 1995), hence their inclusion under that safety cliché.

THE FUTURE OF RURAL CONSERVATION DELIVERY

However, while the land-holding part of the equation, even with the occasional 'duplication of effort concern', is a fairly concrete basis for an alliance in the interests of conserving landscape for the public benefit, the regulatory and supportive administration part is more tenuous. The NPA is the sole planning authority and ostensibly controls potential change in the use of any plot of land in the Park from one category to another. This is universally regarded as applying mainly to the erection of buildings (for any purpose) and the creation of their curtilages (so that field to garden is a 'change of use'). It also involves considerations of appropriate design and thus should be a means for the maintenance of local character in villages and farmsteads, very significant in a national park landscape where the planning authority is effectively acting in the nation's interest. That is why the importance of the 'development frameworks' (as opposed to the National Park Management Plan) which the NPA as planning authority makes to guide the aspirations of any would-be 'developer', from large corporation to humble individual, cannot be understated. But in overall park-wide landscape terms it is the administrative influence and the scientific interpretation feeding it, wielded by Natural England, English Heritage, the Environment Agency, at arms-length: DEFRA, and from even further away the European Union, that cannot in this day and age be gainsaid.

A man who lives in a listed building with a national trail passing his front doorstep, inside a national nature reserve, itself within an SSSI and the whole well inside a national park within an ESA can be forgiven for feeling he's a bit over-supervised. The farmer next door feels he's under the cosh, and their landlord is the National Trust! OK, it's not in Dartmoor, but the actual situation still exists and in 1970 I was the 'man' (Fig. 259). It is merely another illustration, but this time in the detail, of the early reference in this chapter to the conservation broth and the number of cooks who want a ladle in it. In fact it all

THE CONTEMPORARY CONSERVATION SCENE · 353

FIG 259. The Old Farm at Waterhouses, Malham Tarn, with the Pennine Way passing the front door; the house is in a nature reserve, itself in an SSSI, in a national park and is owned by the National Trust with the Field Studies Council as tenant – how protected can you get?

began in 1947 when Hobhouse *et al.* decided that landscape and nature conservation couldn't be handled by one body and yet there should be national agencies to oversee both. The contrast in the briefs for those agencies stems from the fact that the natural scientists had got their act together by 1949 and knew exactly what they wanted or thought they needed, but the romantics and ramblers had delved very little into what makes landscapes work. In their defence, perhaps no one had. John Dower's retrospectively valuable recognition of the need for farming to continue did not then represent a wide understanding of the subtlety of optimal grazing and burning management which sustains the mosaic of ground cover outside the moorland wall, and which we now know to be critical, at least in Dartmoor.

In both cases the relationship between national strategic policy-making and action on the ground and how both should be organised, was not thought through and the seeds of a conservation competition were sown. The evolution of both processes has been registered as the development of the contemporary Dartmoor quasi-political scene has unfolded in the last few pages. Both of course also found themselves rubbing shoulders with the historic and archaeological conservation system, because one had to deal with bats and birds in buildings and the other had all the functions of a planning authority about those buildings. All three operators, late in the day, had to take a mutual interest in grazing; and the happy coincidence of the virtues of short-cropped grassland for bird feeding, easier walking and the visibility of elderly and now low-level stone structures brought them together on Dartmoor in 2005 in that attempt to create, with farmers on board, the shared 'Vision' for Dartmoor's vegetation in 2030 to which I have often referred.

That 'Vision' process brought together in a strategic judgement, hopefully not too briefly, those three organisations with nearly 50 years' separate existence. Others joined in, much younger, like the Rural Development Service and the Environment Agency, and the really old, like the Ministry of Defence lately apprised of its wildlife conservation responsibility and spatial potential for it, through its agent joined at the hip – Defence Estates – on a training estate of which Dartmoor bears a fair-sized chunk. The separate existence of the three strictly conservation agencies was probably always inevitable, possibly necessary at the Whitehall level and workable as long as a single minister had oversight of all three. On the ground lie the questions. On Dartmoor things were peaceable enough throughout the first 20-odd years of the life of the National Park from 1951. The committee had little power and no full-time staff, the Nature Conservancy had a remote regional officer based at Furzebrook near Wareham in Dorset, eventually a warden living in the reserve at Yarner Wood, and even later a Chief Warden for South Devon and Dartmoor. But, as we have seen, the 1970s saw a remarkable set of changes in responsibility and powers, a relatively rapid growth in staff and funds and an increased expectation of action by all communities of interest from government downwards. This applied to newly created national park authorities, the youthful Countryside Commission and the newly independent and newly titled Nature Conservancy Council. As the 1980s wore on, more and more farmers were enticed into management by agreement by the NPA, and the Countryside Commission invented a 'Countryside Stewardship' experiment targeted at particular landscape features – hedgerows, valley floors and the like. Soon the Ministry of Agriculture joined in with Environmentally Sensitive Areas (ESA) in which farmers could volunteer land on which a specific management formula would be pursued – all for cash of course. UK ministers persuaded the European Union, in the early 1990s, that all this was a good thing for the whole continental membership, and thus corporate international funds were deployed by local MAFF ESA project officers and a third force of ecologists joined the fray.

Ecological expertise with agricultural innocence

The potential for a fray must be obvious. Add to the competitive risk the fact that ecology is not an exact science at the best of times. Opinions, theories and the imposition of thinking from one hill – in this case – to another, ignoring simple geographical variations, bedevils the art. The calculation of optimal sheep-grazing numbers per unit area of heather 560 km to the north and in the Pennine rain shadow is unlikely to work on a Dartmoor hill-farm exposed to the southwest wind and all that it carries – enjoying a much longer growing season and higher summer temperatures. But such a grazing formula became a mantra that must be obeyed. A timetable for haymaking is inserted into another formula to foster the biodiversity of the hill-farm home meadows. The necessary time for cutting the grass which will be made into hay varies from year to year on a real farm, and not just with the weather of that season but with the variable demands on the available labour from day to day. Sheep graze the northern hills almost alone but we have already seen that cattle and ponies play a vital role in Dartmoor, complementing the work of sheep to a greater degree than even old MAFF hands had realised. If a farmer is asked to, and paid to, reduce the numbers of cattle on his common, say, it is unlikely that he will keep the balance removed, at all. Where can they go? Poaching the home pastures? Feeding expensively in a shed? Or to market, and release some cash? The last is the likeliest. When the formula is shown to be lacking, there are no cattle to be swiftly redeployed to eat off the now-rank vegetation. Over-grazing symptoms have turned into an actual under-grazed state. But when the ESA 'contract' ends (and the maximum length is ten years) the hill-farmer has fewer beasts than made his livestock enterprise viable as a simple stock-producing operation, and in any case he has looked elsewhere in the meantime to seek profit because that is his normal motivation, and nowadays necessity.

In truth, the imposition of the ESA de-motivated the NPA as management agreement maker for financial reasons if no other, and while English Nature (EN, the successor to the NCC) tried to use the grazing formulae in its search for achievement of SSSI 'favourable condition' (a DEFRA target for 2010), it hasn't worked yet. By 2007 the RDS (Rural Development Service, of DEFRA) and EN had become the greater part of Natural England. European writing was on the wall for ESAs, and its successor combination: Single (farm) Payment (with its perverse Moorland Line) and Environmental Stewardship (with its entry-level and higher-level schemes) was proving inadequate for common land and rejected by farmers as unviable for moorland in single ownership, such as newtakes. The Upland Entry Level Scheme may help in 2010, but in effect it merely replaces the Hill Farm Allowance that ends then.

WHAT NOW?

Natural England and its parent DEFRA now not only have to resolve this motivational conundrum if upland moorland is to survive on Dartmoor but almost certainly review the organisational set-up. For NE has also become the parent body of National Park Authorities via its third constituent, the Countryside Agency, successor of the Countryside Commission, itself successor of the National Parks Commission. Ironically we have just achieved a single operator for landscape protection, nature conservation and recreation promotion at national level in England (which Scotland and Wales have had since 1991) but we still have a sad competition and worrying confusion on the ground. Because Natural England includes the old RDS, it administers whatever agri-environmental financial farm support DEFRA can produce. This is new and unlike the situation in Wales and Scotland; it thus remains to be seen whether the whole complex is capable of easy management and the comprehensive success all involved would want it to have.

Logic suggests that Natural England might recognise the virtue of having a set of conservation agents on the ground for areas already statutorily protected. One body, in Dartmoor's case that charged with the care of the National Park for more than 50 years now, and on which it thus has an inherited grip, could be that agent and deliver all the advice, regulation and financial support available to farmers, who alone have what is needed to maintain the Park's publicly valued attributes. They would then know with which single authority they were dealing, and that its officers were accessibly based and on the spot. A working relationship between officer and farmer would be developed anew, which the original National Park Plan claimed was necessary for the smooth delivery of public goods by private operators. Of course, in matters of irreconcilable disagreement, there would have to be an appeal system involving the parent body, who still calls the necessary financial tune. The NPA could be required to account for its stewardship annually, be monitored by NE as necessary – *but* work on the ground would be continuous and constructive. The broth would have one cook, or at least one sous chef.

The broth of course, cooks apart, has an age-old recipe and we have examined most of its constituents. It remains to consider them and their freshness, new alternatives, and how the heat of the kitchen may vary not too long hence.

CHAPTER 10

Dartmoor From Now On

The tor and its surroundings epitomise what makes Dartmoor a national asset. But this is not the whole story. From the blanket bog and valley mires through the high moor to woodland and enclosed fields, Dartmoor National Park remains a unique and varied landscape, with habitats of international importance, an extraordinary range of wildlife and wide expanses of wildness. It is a cultural landscape where extensive remains testify to generations of human activity. At the same time it is a place where people live, work and play ... This vision for Dartmoor National Park is therefore one of balance in which stability and change benefit local people and visitors alike and the special qualities are conserved and enhanced for future generations ... Our aspirations demand a common philosophical and cultural ethos towards Dartmoor and as ever, innovation, partnerships and new approaches to old problems will be of great significance.
Adapted from the 'Introduction' to the Management Plan
for the National Park, 2007

For most purposes, land use and social context is much more important for species survival than the amplitude of climatic change.
Ian Simmons, The Moorlands of England and Wales, 2003

MOST PREDICTIONS ABOUT THE future of any particular landscape are usually wide of the (eventual) mark, and the further ahead they fly, the wider they well may be. So in some ways in its *Management Plan 2007–2012* the NPA's 'vision' of balance sounds like a safe bet, and may well be calculated, very reasonably, to ensure the widest possible support. It echoes fairly precisely Eric Hemery's introduction to *High Dartmoor*, written in spring of 1972. He actually writes that he believes there is an 'indisputable need to maintain a balanced order in all things – industry, technology, preservation, conservation, access'. Perhaps that is another safe bet, perhaps bravely independent, given the polarisation of views about activity around the moorland at that time. The chairman of the National Park Authority in the quotation above justifiably calls for a shared philosophy between all his potential partners and for new approaches, even innovation, in facing the future for the landscape his Authority is charged to cherish and sustain. He is clearly speaking to those who deal in land uses and social activity, though his plan also faces up to the one big popular environmental question – climate change – spending nearly a third of its 'Passing Dartmoor on to Future Generations' section on the subject. Which is why, to me, the quotation from the last chapter of *The Moorlands of England and Wales*, to which I have already referred, is so important. No look at the future for Dartmoor can ignore the changing climate discussion, and most longstanding Dartmoor men think they detect changes in weather patterns already, as Chapter 6 hinted. To that we must return. But there is little doubt that land-management change, even cessation of moorland management, threatened just now as never before in at least two centuries, must cause most disquiet if any attempt to maintain what we may call 'a Dartmoor balance' is to succeed. The threat is palpable as I write in 2008, as may already be clear from what has gone before in this book. That threat also involves more players than any other, and they range from a goodly number of remote European politicians and public servants to a tiny handful of hill-farming apprentices as close to the ground as you can get.

We have, in passing, already examined some of the ingredients that will have to be in the balancing recipe, and we need to rehearse them again and complete the list, if we are to predict anything. We can at least look at the options for producing a better broth than is currently being cooked, soon perhaps in too hot a kitchen, and to hope – as Ian Simmons says 'more is not possible' – that the decision-makers in Brussels and in Godsworthy farmhouse kitchen come up with the joint best answer themselves.

GRAZING – THE MANAGEMENT OF THE PUBLIC ASSET

Whatever the weather does, and whether that adds up to a permanently changed annual climatic regime or not, it is already clear that more animals are needed to graze, if anything like the recent vegetation mosaic and its publicly beneficial attributes are to persist. If, in this context, the Dartmoor Vision of 2006, agreed by the Commoners' Council and all the relevant agencies, is to be fulfilled. On the south-facing slope below Birch Tor, in the 1960s, I used to line up 25 students to struggle abreast, high-stepping downslope, through part of the best heather stand on the Moor. They were told to sing out when they came across a rowan seedling. The chorus soon began, and two points were quickly made, the potential for a moorland take-over by trees or scrub was very clear; and that no seedling or sapling protruded above the heather, and all had bitten leaders, told

FIG 260. Under-grazing: (top) Trendlebeare Down, birch, willow and pine – strangely reminiscent of the pre-Mesolithic pioneers – spreading above the heathers; (above) conifer saplings spreading out from Bellever Plantation in to the adjacent newtake, Laughter Tor is beyond them.

what kept the take-over at bay. There in 2008, and even more obviously on the contiguous ridge north of Soussons Down, just west of Haytor, and on the north slope of Chinkwell, to name but a few, those rowans are emergent, and already standing a metre or more proud of the heather crowns. That commentary, on the lifting of grazing pressure beyond the right intensity for heather moor management on a common, is only more emphatically underlined by the scatter of spruce saplings visible across the newtakes west and southwest of Bellever. There is thus a potential scissor movement waiting to overtake the mid-level moorland, the native shrubs are standing-to universally and the plantation seed source is poised to join in. So on the commons and, perhaps more surprising, in the privately occupied moorland enclosures, not enough managed grazing is now taking place. However, the elderly hawthorns scattered in the drier bracken cover of gentler foot-slopes all around the Moor suggest that such things may have happened before, without so eliminating edible plants as to deny control of woody seedlings when grazing returned to a useful level.

A greater number of grazing animals deliberately deployed on the moorland demands:

a) an improving market for the annual crop of calves, lambs and foals which gives the stockmen a valid return on their labour and their own investment in their terms;
b) a regime of public support that pays a proper rate for environmental maintenance and enhancement and the provision of access to it – Adam Smith's corporate purchase of 'public goods';
c) a population of hill-farmers happy at their work because of a) and b), with sons and daughters wanting to carry on that work and its demanding routine;
d) a healthy working relationship between the farmers and those who carry the professional (and political) responsibility to the nation for the creation and management of the regime at b); and
e) an understanding of, and thus a respect for, the work of the hill man and his animals by everybody, from politicians to those walking and riding, and especially those of them with dogs.

The balanced state of affairs, which the bulk of that scenario implies, actually existed in the late 1990s as the ESA agreements spread, even if the regime still needed refinement for a Dartmoor application. Indeed from the early 1980s, onwards the developing balance was probably perceptible in the minds of the farmers and of the NPA. So, logic says that it could be achieved again; but there are underlying human considerations which everyone involved has to understand. The most significant is the industrial psychology of the hill-farmer on his hill and within his wider profession. For a 1,000 years he has produced store cattle and lambs to finish off the hill, all sold from home or at a market close to it. The measure of his performance – not least to himself – was by comparison with last year and with his peers at the market. In the mid-1970s when the NPA started its real work, farmers were blunt about having no intention of becoming 'park-keepers'. By 1979 they were having to consult the NPA prior to indulging any grant-aided matter as we have seen, and the farmhouse back doors opened wider as management agreements came on offer. By the mid-1990s a majority of farmers were contemplating entering their in-bye land into the Environmentally Sensitive Area Scheme and local Commoners' Associations were sitting down to agree formulae for supportable commons management, the distribution of funds corporately earned, and forming Trusts to hold the annual income from the new public contract. Many Associations, with their Trusts, decided to use some of that income to carry out corporate works in the same 1,000-year-old 'working in common' tradition, as well as dividing out the graziers' individual income. Such work ranged from setting up a wildfire response team and equipping it with protective clothing and all that goes with moorland fire control, to installing cattle grids in minor roads at the boundaries of commons, and paying for research into combating tick-borne diseases. Thus the return from selling public goods was applied so that the individual felt fairly paid for his or her work, and the corporate management of the commons was also improved. The environmental psychology was catching up with that related to production. In a sense the late 1990s saw the basis for a new heyday for environmental hill-farming which was very much of its time, and a new balance had been struck. The European taxpayer had joined the national taxpayer (who had been supporting production in the hills since 1948) and both now shared some of the conservation and production costs of running a successful Dartmoor National Park with internationally recognised assets. The managers of the land and its cover were as content as they might ever be, even though there would not necessarily be any overt admission of that to the outside world.

A succession of disconnected events has since distorted the perceivable balance of 1999, say, and reference has already been made to some of them. But they have implications for the future of the Dartmoor moorland that must be teased out here. Some ESA contracts may still have a few years to run, but the Scheme itself has been closed, ending after a short life that promised so much. Reform of the CAP was proceeding as Foot and Mouth Disease hit Dartmoor in early 2001. The outbreak was widespread in England and Wales but Cumbria, Devon and North

Yorkshire were the hardest-hit counties. One knee-jerk reaction of the politico-bureaucratic hierarchy to that rural nuisance was to cancel the Ministry of Agriculture Fisheries and Food (which had admittedly acted lamentably in the face of the crisis) and substitute for it a Department of Environment, Food and Rural Affairs (DEFRA). Where had 'agriculture' gone? Farmers who had had a cabinet-level champion for more than a century considered themselves deprived of political support, to put it rather more politely than they did.

One faintly flickering light on the Dartmoor skyline was a 'Task Force for the Hills' that had been set up wisely by the ill-fated MAFF late in 2000. It was led by the chief executive of English Nature, who had, himself, been a national park chief officer, and it included a Dartmoor farmer's wife, Rosemary Mudge. Its leader, David Arnold-Forster, was sadly fatally ill as his report was published in March 2001, and action on it about hill-farmer support never emerged, perhaps because Lord Haskins was asked, in the aftermath of FMD, to look at the whole of the rural land administrative situation. After discovering that there were more than 70 funding streams available to a single farm and some 19 or more bodies involved in managing them, he proposed a thorough shake-up of at least the main public sector bodies involved. Sadly, implementation of that 'shake-up' was left to others, and significantly he, a new life peer, left the Labour benches soon afterwards.

Natural England, as we have seen, was born out of that shake-up, though it took until 2006 for the birth to happen. Farmers lost their last direct servicing agents within DEFRA when the Rural Development Service was transferred out and into this new all-purpose rural agency. National parks, too, lost their free-standing landscape and access specialist go-between with government when the Countryside Agency was also absorbed. English Nature, as was predictable given the experience in Scotland and Wales 15 years earlier, formed the dominant core of the new organisation.

Haskins's logic about funding streams is unassailable, and the merging of nature and landscape conservation functions also has a longstanding logic and even an 18-year-old precedent (in Wales and Scotland) attached to it. But adding in the actual operation of land management schemes and their funding on the ground, in a space the size of England, already seems to have been a step too far. Once there is a single national organisation responsible for nearly everything to do with the rural environment bar water and pollution, then spending priorities between its components emerge as a major influence on outputs. Internal competition in any organisation does not always lead to good external performance. The longstanding separation of policy-making from the delivery of it is seen to have had advantages now lost. Ironically, the calculation and paying out of the funding streams, now bundled together as core support for all farmers and called the Single Payment, was given to a new Rural Payments Agency, detached from the land and any consideration of the reasoning behind entitlement, need and the achievement of the good agricultural and environmental condition (of land), or GAEC, demanded by the SP rules. Dislocation, within the public environmental service, support for the food supply chain, and its administration, seemed to be the order of the day despite all of Lord Haskins's effort.

Dartmoor is not alone in needing a simplified situation that is specifically designed for the hills and their carers if the future of such places is to be secured, and it was necessary to describe the present turmoil to clarify that need. One of proposals of 'The Task Force for the Hills', out of 15 labelled 'longer term', said it all:

> *the long term aim for Less Favoured Area support should be an integrated tiered payment scheme reflecting environmental and social benefits, actual costs of landscape, wildlife and access maintenance, and the economic difficulties of traditional hill farming.*

DEFRA and its creatures will claim that that's what now exists, but it doesn't quite, and the social and economic components are lost somewhere. So the devising of a proper formula for Dartmoor is still needed, and if Europe continues to insist on a Single Payment underpinning it, so be it. Simplicity and flexibility must become watchwords again, for present attempts to approach the Task Force's proposal become more and more complex and attempt to fit lowland and northern square pegs into upland and southwestern round holes. Whatever emerges has to be better tailored to all the upland and capable of adaptation to regional differences if not to specific hills. The Moorland Line should be cancelled and the SP per hectare over the whole hill should be at least as good as those in the immediate lowlands, and logic would say they should be better than those for metropolitan England, for all the reasons cited by the Task Force and made obvious here. The arable inland landscape of the Golden Triangle – Isle of Wight/Scarborough/North Foreland – with its minimal if any environmental public benefit, needs only a token payment per unit area, and the bulk of its current £200 plus per hectare could be used to fund a proper share per upland hectare where public assets burgeon.

The delivery of this support for the real managers of Dartmoor and the purchase of the public goods involved – natural beauty, access to it, heritage care, biodiversity contributions, clean water, carbon storage and soon food security, demands the consideration only a local agent can effectively give. The argument was made at the end of the last chapter. It is called, in European terms, 'subsidiarity'. There sits, as close to the farmer as you can get, a potential agent:

the all-purpose NPA. Dartmoor commoners were talking in 2008 of a need to work even more closely with the NPA as their survival formula is debated. In July of that year their Council and the NPA set up a permanent Joint Meeting essentially to keep all mutual interests under review and especially to monitor the life of the Dartmoor Vision.

The market and future output

As for the market for livestock, the hill-farmer is at the very beginning of a supply chain whose other end is bedevilled by a demand for the cheapest possible meat. The Dartmoor farmer's traditional role finishes nothing, so his chance to add value to his twenty-first-century product is very low if he stays only on the hill. Even if he brings some of his output inside, for one or more reasons the cost of feed and bedding, most from further east, is growing apace – and that means weekly in 2008. His eastern and lowland arable colleagues suddenly have markets of which they never dreamt. Demand from the far east for grain for human consumption as living standards there rise exponentially, combined with new uses at home: grain for fuels such as ethanol, and straw for fuel and insulation, mean that the two pre-requisites for wintering cattle at home in Dartmoor, for fattening or as part of a wise personal routine, are fast getting out of reach.

FIG 261. Tree stems waiting to be sawn up on the Swincombe valley floor below Sherberton – the sale of planks enhances the farm income and the work can be fitted well into a hill-farm routine.

An obvious recourse is, by hook or by crook, to finish stock within the business boundary, and that means acquiring the occupation of other land whether as tenant or owner, even of whole farms, off the moor or at least in the eastern valleys. Many of Dartmoor's highest-level farmers already indulged in some occupation of fringe lower land before the present crisis struck. Some now have three or four separate farms and at some farm-gates retail sales may be developable – finishing and adding value certainly is, even if the trade is still wholesale. A tiny proportion have found an additional specialisation within the farming enterprise. Pig and turkey rearing are carried on at home in buildings, and forestry and other tree and timber work including sawmilling and the sale of planks, poles and firewood come within that bracket (Fig. 261). Some, too, have diversified in the time-honoured reaction to years of MAFF socio-economic advice, and the on- and off-site options were listed in Chapter 8. The extreme in Dartmoor is probably the case of the Duchy tenant who, with his landlord's encouragement, has created a conference centre and even enhanced his own market for meat by selling to attendees at meetings and seminars (Fig. 262). Dartmoor Farmers Ltd is a new, wider meat marketer.

All that is fine and some of it has gone on somewhere for a century or more. Always, some farmers have shared their skills and grouped together to achieve

FIG 262. Brimpts Farm gate – the sign demonstrates the ultimate in farmstead building adaptation.

savings or efficiency. The essence of being a commoner is about sharing some common-wide jobs and swaling and the drift are the most obvious examples. Farmer's wives have taken in visitors since travel and the visitation of the Moor started in the nineteenth century. There is one major drawback associated with all diversification now and in the immediate future, and it is the scale and the intensity of what is required. The more other activities must be pursued, and however close they are to the original main enterprise, the less time and concentration is available for the proper work of a moor man.

I have written elsewhere very recently:

The greatest fear must be that they, the high moorland farmers and commoners, by dint of even professional distractions, take their eye off the moorland ball, and the game their fathers taught them to play begins to be lost in the face of a greater game, survival.

This is a real risk with even those who have simply added acreage to their holding or added other holdings to their home hill farm, for those other fields make their own maintenance demands and stock must, properly, be seen daily wherever it happens for the moment to be. The generation just contemplating for the first time taking on their parental business, its base and all its hectares, must be looking at the spectrum on offer. They will quickly calculate what is worth doing, what fits in a twenty-first-century portfolio of aspirations, even what is most and what is least arduous, set against the likely return. It is said of their parents and all their predecessors come to that 'hill-farmers are ever resilient'. They have stayed in high Dartmoor since the Mesolithic, and Mesolithic genes, we now know, are still carried by them. They can survive if necessary on their own produce as was hinted in Chapter 8, but will their wives and children put up with it, and stay? Some have already demonstrated their reluctance to do that, and some young families are no longer all in the farmhouse they entered with joy and enthusiasm not very long ago. All this predicates a major change in the way Dartmoor hill-farmers look at their businesses and thus the way they look at the moor, especially that beyond their own boundary walls.

In the medium term, Dartmoor hill-farmers as a whole may resign themselves to becoming openly – where some already indulge quietly – a kind of hybrid corps of livestock breeders, rearers *and* finishers. They might conduct their own private transhumance in the face of its loss as a traditional corporate process between clear-cut upland and lowland cultures. For some, this routine would be possible entirely within the National Park, for they already have

FIG 263. The Forder valley northwest from Moretonhampstead, also seen in Chapter 2, is typical of the eastern valleys of the National Park where fields capable of holding cattle for fattening may be rented or bought by a hill farmer now intent on finishing a product.

appropriate land in those valleys from Widecombe eastwards or even at the edge of the farmland fringe. Such a change must cause a re-examination of labour needs, and thus the output would have to justify the new wages bill as a valid part of the total outgoings. The 'new' labour demand could only exacerbate the thesis just propounded, about at least a partial withdrawal from attention to the detail of the moorland end of the system. Dartmoor's extreme southwesterly location can only be seen to facilitate such a development, for in the right year already, lambs can almost be finished on the edge of the hill given good summer temperatures and a long enough growing season. Hill cattle progeny would have to be shifted downslope, they need longer than their eastern and lowland counterparts to get to a good butchering state and shortening that could only be achieved on lower grass or under a roof – quicker to change breeds. If a twenty-first-century Dartmoor NPA is to keep its moorland in 'good environmental condition' it needs to cherish its farmer allies more than ever. Its own duty to society demands that all other of society's agents support it in that. Hence the long argument here, the natural history of Dartmoor can only falter if the hill-farmer turns his back on it.

THE GREAT BOWL OF THE SKY

Nothing can diminish the alarm that the present plight of the Dartmoor hill-farmer, and even only the tentative withdrawal of his cattle and sheep from the moorland and especially the common, arouses in everyone concerned. Whether that concern is about the overgrowth of the vegetation, its pending impenetrability and its height against the view, the loss of habitats uniquely developed as the history of Dartmoor unfolded, or the visual loss of the evidence of the last 5,000 years of that same human history. But other changes loom, especially from the sky, and their quality and timetable is still a series of big questions. In this new century it can be safely claimed that weather patterns seem different now from those that we, who are here, think we remember ten, even perhaps 20, years ago. Rainfall totals remain much the same, but they come in more concentrated bursts rather than steadily spread through the year, and 'bursts' is an appropriate description on many occasions nowadays. More violent weather is experienced more often than ever before, though notably the two most significant recent windstorms were nearly 20 years ago, in 1987 and 1990. Nothing of their intensity has been experienced since though their effects still show, not least just west of the prison at Princetown (Fig. 264). The ice and snow of the late winters of the last quarter of the twentieth century, even then never the long-lying stuff of its first three-quarters and certainly less than in the post-Little-Ice-Age winters from 1850 on, has not recurred for more than a decade (Fig. 265). Then, in-winter periods could be characterised by shepherds searching field-corner drifts by prodding for buried ewes, by cut-off villages and farmers selling milk from the backs of tractors in their squares, by National Park rangers delivering meals-on-wheels and manning the perimeter cattle grids at weekends to turn back inadequately clothed snowy-sightseers. Such periods, of very variable length, happened in nearly every winter. They and their challenges were expected and the annual test of resilience was relished, for it often, though not always, separated Dartmoor and its people from the softer landscapes and their softer inhabitants around it.

No longer can men say with Chapter 6: 'Dartmoor, the place with three months' winter and nine months' wet weather' – for the jocular distinction between just two seasons in a year has ceased to apply. Nevertheless, the suggested Mediterranean-type hotter and drier summers have not yet appeared at a scale or a length to rival those of 1959 or 1976, though shorter periods of drought-like conditions, as in the high summer of 1995, have punctuated what used to be winters and distinct summers. So the jury seems to still be out on at

DARTMOOR FROM NOW ON · 369

FIG 264. West of Princetown: (top) the state of the woods on 26 January 1990; (above) the replanting mainly substituting broad-leaves for the blown-down conifers.

FIG 265. Snowed-up eastern Dartmoor village in 1985 (and remember Figure 192).

least the pace of a climatic regime-change of any permanent character. A ten-year moratorium on it has recently been suggested as the earth's axis wobbles, as it often does, and the effects of that temporarily cancel recently observed trends. Most apparent symptoms observable so far on Dartmoor are winter ones and the higher hills of the southwestern peninsula, in any case, may see the least effective medium-term change, and that at a slower rate than anywhere else in England.

Models from the UK Climate Impacts Programme use regional models by the Hadley Centre of the Meteorological Office, conveniently for Dartmoor, now in Exeter. Different models produce different patterns involving different magnitudes, so they are bound to cause the uncertainty based on amateur observation to persist. But these models, as maps attempting to display predicted change by isobar-like lines of equal temperature change differences, demonstrate a kind of southwest to northeast grain with northern high Dartmoor as the southwest end of a 'ridge' defined by those contours and following that grain. On the other hand the equivalent mean annual precipitation-change map shows Dartmoor largely outside an island of greatest change which – 'banana like' – wraps round its western and northern flanks. In support, the summer and winter

FIG 266. Fair-weather cumulus in the rain shadow of the northern plateau. Cosdon is at the centre of the skyline.

precipitation change maps show Dartmoor's regime changing least, and the areas immediately to leeward of it changing most, by drying, in summer. The longstanding rain shadow bites again!

The implications for plants and animals, given that predicted trends from the present mixture of observations persist, must be a likely northeastward drift given the axis of that temperature change map 'grain'. The nice illustration of the possible detail of that on the small scale would involve moorland butterflies. High brown and pearl-bordered fritillaries, finding that their hitherto favoured habitat – a bracken-covered south-facing foot-slope with violets in the under-storey – becomes too warm, might well move round the hill to the east side first (morning sun is cooler than that of the afternoon) and even end up on the north-facing slope if warming continues. On the larger scale, birds common right up to the Channel shore of France, say red-backed shrike or honey buzzard, may quickly cross the said Channel and spread round the Dartmoor fringe, where they were, not so long ago, in any case. Among their prey, the warming by then should have caused both common lizard and wasp to have burgeoned in population terms.

Clearly even native birds are likely to be equally mobile respondents to climatic change. Dartford warblers, as we have seen, are moving in on Dartmoor's

FIG 267. 'Blue grey' cattle in a mire in late summer – there may have to be more and more carefully leared around mires like this to improve the waders' chances.

'upper end' of the lowland heath spectrum, perhaps the only slightly warmer summers have already boosted the insect population of gorse and bramble thickets which they have always favoured (Fig. 267). The other side of that coin maybe the otherwise unexplained loss of moorland bird numbers, especially nesting waders in the mires, but also skylark, meadow pipit and wheatear on the dry moor. While losses in lowland birds over the last 50 years have always been ascribed to changes in agricultural techniques and in seasonal arable and silage-making patterns, no such dramatic changes have characterised hill-farming. However it is observable that ring ousel and wheatear need access to sizeable areas of short-cropped turf on which to feed. Its total has diminished as sheep grazing levels have so recently fallen along with the deposition of animal droppings – feeding and breeding medium for many invertebrates. A double whammy has hit those two totemic Dartmoor dry moorland birds. The same lessening of grazing, this time by cattle, seems to have produced another dual-edged problem for wading birds in valley mires. Even slightly taller vegetation reduces the available area of mire surface for probing beaks, however long, and open pools grow over from their outer edges inwards. These changes may be easily ascribed to changes in grazing density, but is there already a cumulative weather change under the

FIG 268. The 'bracken and bushes' suite on a south-facing slope in Dartmoor's western fringe. It is happily spreading uphill; will it want a cooler site in time?

great open sky where moorland birds have thrived for centuries, too subtle for us yet to observe, let alone measure? Does it affect populations of their insect food, even their nesting success in, say, timing or shading terms? Comparisons with northern moors could tell us something of this if rigorous enough, though completion of meaningful work on that score might be overtaken by the movement of southwestern climate change pole-wards. It might thus be little help with any adaptation aids we are able to offer the birds on Dartmoor by land management means with its attendant difficulties just rehearsed.

Our 'offers' would have to be in not only restoring the vegetation pattern to something more akin to that of the 1980s, but actually boosting those parts of the mosaic, in area at least, which host the food supply. They are essentially the short-cropped grass and open valley mire just mentioned. We would have to ensure at the same time, the proximity to such sites of cover for concealment, shelter and nesting. If we become convinced that northward and eastward traffic is part of the scenario then working with others to be sure of appropriate vegetation staging posts in Exmoor, the Quantocks, Mendip and the Welsh Border, may become significant. All the species concerned already have populations well settled further north, and some pause here seasonally *en transit*, so routes are well established. We may wish, of course, to delay total loss of Dartmoor representatives for as long as possible, but replacements to the southwest of us do not exist and climate change affects the winter habitats of our summer visitors as well as those we offer them, so there is much well beyond our reach about which we can do little or nothing.

The obvious corollary of present upland animal species moving northward in the context of milder winters and warmer summers is of lowland species moving upslope. Here there is more of a dilemma for future managers and ecological, even National Park, policy-makers. The generality of Devonian lowland inland birds, mammals and insects seek cover, and while the 'Vision' for Dartmoor incorporates some scrub development, it's a minor component with minority support. The Vision is after all 'of a farmed moorland landscape' and that implies holding on to the wide open scene for as long as is feasible. One can foresee an eco-political debate about biodiversity and rarity that ranges woodland against moorland and deer fanciers (stalkers?) against pony keepers, if historic all-rounder hill-farmers actually quit the field. As for the other plants, while bracken clearly has a low temperature limit on the global scale – and it *is* a round-the-world plant – not so much seems to be known about the subtlety of its high-temperature boundary. We might find it migrating round the hill as well if summers get too hot for it. Heather does well, even better than ours, on the North York Moors under less than half our present rainfall, greater sunshine hours and higher temperatures.

THE USERS OF THE PUBLIC ASSET

There is no sign yet of any real diminution of public recreational use of the moorland, in fact walking and riding may even be increasing. Orienteering and the hunt the 'letter box' game begun by the Victorians are really variations on the walking theme, as are the burgeoning challenge and charity industries, though the mass presence and processional progress which both the latter invoke can be a real trial for lambing shepherds, and attempted learing. Indeed organised events on foot, horseshoes or wheels may be very good for lots of urban folk in many ways, but they can be the bane of a hill-farmer's life. A more sophisticated society would have a serious debate about what a wild landscape can take if its management on the one hand, and the real enjoyment of its uniqueness on the other, are to be properly achieved. Mountain biking is perhaps the epitome of the dilemma. To some extent it emulates other forms of riding, mountain bikers even use bridleways, but suddenly belting round a remote tor they can seem as incongruous as Lady Sharpe thought military activity was.

DARTMOOR FROM NOW ON · 375

FIG 269. Pony trekking which uses the same routes regularly creates bare tracks which are easily eroded in heavy rain, but riding is marginally kinder to wildlife and lying-up lambs than walkers in the mass.

FIG 270. The epitome of organised mass walking – the start of the 'Ten Tors' event. Some 55 tors are actually visited by the most senior contestants in 24 hours. (DNPA)

FIG 271. The crow – patently the most successful species of its size, springtime predator of nests and their content and so far the likeliest survivor of almost any change. (C. Tyler)

Otherwise, while accurate total visitation of the National Park is as incalculable as ever, the impression is not of any great change in density. It is individual recreational habit that seems to be evolving. More folk walk and more walk much further into the remoter moorland, than did in the third quarter of the last century. There has always been a strong school of thought about disturbance of lambing and breeding birds by people and especially by people-and-dogs. That no tor, however remote, now carries a raven's nest is often quoted (even earlier in this book) as an effect of the promotion of long-distance challenges inevitably using tors as navigational markers and targets, but it is ground-nesting birds that are, on the face of it, most at risk. Disturbance can affect nesting, nests and parental loyalty to them. It can also prevent territorial establishment in the early spring. But neither predation nor parasitism can be ignored in this discussion. Northern moorland gamekeepers are amazed by the number of carrion crows that Dartmoor appears to carry, and their easiest meals away from road-kill in the summer consist of eggs and nestlings (Fig. 271).

FIG 272. Cuckoo – needs perches if it is to observe its host's location and timetable well enough. (C Tyler)

Ravens and magpies join them in the depredation as a change from their more habitual carrion and, in the spring, the lambing after-births. Disturbance by people and predation have one direct relationship. Some studies on Dartmoor have shown that the crow family are inhibited close to car parks and popular tors near roads. The nesting success of small ground-nesting birds is greater in the same places – pipits and skylarks especially seemed to have weighed the crows against people and found the latter friendlier. Parasitism may be affected in the same way. Cuckoo numbers have been maintained in the face of other changes, but pipits in the well-peopled areas may be safer from compulsory hosting than those in more remote locations. Cuckoos, of course, need perches, both to track their potential host's homeward journey and for their own courting purposes (Fig. 272). If the scattered rowan and thorn saplings continue to rear their heads above the heather, for a time the cuckoo opportunities may increase and their population spread. Sheep and cattle also veer away from places popular with humans; though ponies regard them as sources of tit-bits and hang around there (hence the bye-law prohibiting feeding of ponies, for it attracts them to roadsides and makes traffic accidents more likely). But the absence of the other two grazers means that future shrub survival may be more successful where people congregate. Here is another dilemma: is the moorland which attracts people in the first place, even if only because its 'different from home', at risk of scrubbing-up locally at least in part because people affect its management?

On all counts Ian Simmons's quote would appear to be borne out on contemporary Dartmoor: 'Land use and social context is much more important for species survival than the amplitude of climate change.' The managing farmers' survival as a species is more immediately critical to the survival of the mosaic of stands of moorland plants. It alone provides the shelter and the feeding sites in closest proximity vital for the sustaining of the present animal biodiversity of the upland heath, the mires and the blanket bog. The visitors, who enjoy the huge benefit that the wide open moorland and its mosaic convey, as we have seen, play contradictory roles: interfering innocently with both wildlife and animal husbandry on the one hand, justifying public support for hill-farming by their use of all the public goods on offer on the other, and even more innocently aiding and abetting predator protection for small birds. This adds up to a significantly more weighty argument for society to ponder. The urgent re-appraisal of the way the upland farmed environment is administered, with its proper conservation and enhancement the prime target – versus the same time spent worrying about the effects upon it of climate change, mitigation of it or adaptation to it. After all, we can correct the former – we had it nearly right less than a decade ago, we really have little understanding of the latter, even less what might be done about it.

That said, the two things are not wholly disconnected. Ninety per cent of Devonians get their drinking water from moorland, and South West Water spends less on cleaning water than any other water undertaking in England. Dartmoor's peatlands, especially the blanket bog, retain their iron oxides better than any bogs in the North Country or in Wales for reasons still inadequately understood, but like them they also store carbon more effectively and efficiently than trees and herbs, even than other soils. Sustaining bog and mire needs the attention that only hill-farmers and their stock can give. Dealing with wildfires requires hill-farmers' navigational and pyrotechnical knowledge and their manpower as well as any professional aid that is on hand. The re-wetting of over-dry peat will only be achievable using that same long-established experience. Both are critical to the containment and better the improvement of the blanket bog to the point where peat accumulates again. We may desperately need grazing at the right intensity and in the right places for the public enjoyment benefit to be sustained, but we need the moorland nous of the grazier for the protection of these other, more material, public assets almost as much. The ecosystem services approach, which government has just begun to preach, demands that our rather important share of the world's moorland and blanket bog is conserved for its own sake. Public support for that, based on enjoyable use of it, and the skill of those who live with these complex ecosystems day by day ought to be a powerful combination for the achievement of that conservation. National Park as a designation could come to have a new meaning as our need to live with the natural system, rather than off it, becomes better understood.

ENJOYABLE DARTMOOR NOW AND TOMORROW

Having rehearsed the problems that loom and what may be needed to confront those capable of further reaction, some more urgently than others, it is important to register that much of what has inspired so many observers of Dartmoor for so long is still there to be enjoyed as the twenty-first century starts to gather momentum. The vast expanse; the morning light on low slopes; mist pouring down steeper ones; a foreground mosaic of wind-combed grasses and shaking heather, sheep-pruned gorse and rusty deer grass, rush-clump 'fountains' and red-brown autumn bracken – all still evoke the same wonder. They form together the vast backdrop for a collage of a myriad small pictures, some in slabs of paint of every rocky grey hue there is; some well-worked dark deep-green in sloping woods, some lighter aquatints of many-domed pale-green mossy clitter, and some delicate etchings that alone can catch the fine lines of the life of the streamside. Each has its devotees, but none will forget the moorland context just left to enter and absorb any one of them, and to each we must attend if we are to understand that whole. They are our counterpoint to the vast Moor. This great work, the function of structure, process and time in the original physical but also in the natural and human history senses is mounted and framed by an intimate patchwork of fields and farms, lanes and villages right round it, and fingering up its wider valleys for all the world like an intricate old moulding of greening gilt relief and verdigris.

Ironically it is the small pictures that will survive longest, in the face of the challenges just described, if they do indeed persist. Grazing withdrawal and lack of daily attention will affect the backdrop and its foreground first, but farming withdrawal may only be to the farmland of the moorland edge and into the valleys and thus into that frame-and-mount, whose fields and villages will be protected as they already are. But then only the kind of building stone, the fieldwalls and perhaps field size would separate the Dartmoor pattern from

FIG 273. Pioneer trees – as White Wood spreads outwards.

that stretching out into all of Devon. The woods will recycle themselves in due time, even though that will involve a bramble-and-thicket phase if entirely self-induced, but the process is likely to be assisted in the immediate future by a growing interest in their sensitive management. If left all alone, they are likely to stretch upwards and outwards to the detriment of the edges of the great backdrop. We should note that the three high-level oakwoods could spread outwards as soon as any of the lower ones if grazing retreated from them; after all Wistman's Wood did so throughout the first half of the last century.

Climatic oscillation might affect everything living in the very long term, whether grazing of the moor is sustained or not, but drier summers would favour heather for some time to come – think of those splendid heather stands in the North York Moors. However, the heather's actual survival to reap that benefit will depend upon rather more than pony grazing continuing.
Of course the rocks of the moorland backdrop and of the small pictures will not change, tors and clitter will still be there, and so will the 5,000-years' worth of rock-built artefacts. Whether they will all be visible is a different matter. It is already clear that many a prehistoric monument is being rapidly swamped by

FIG 274. Challacombe stone row in 2008 – compare with Figure 71.

gorse and grasses (Fig. 274), a sad reflection on the grazing density over-reduction under eco-driven ESA formulae. Special victims are the lesser-known artefacts with the least human visitation. The longest rows and widest circles of lowest stones, and the remnant isolated tin-mill mortar block or burial cist are most vulnerable. The stone row southwest of Headland Warren and the circle on Mardon Down demonstrate what might be afoot, given the worst case.

On the other hand, in that case, summit tors will doubtless survive as landmarks one from another for a century or two, though they will eventually only protrude above a sea of scrubby woodland and their visibility from below on what was well-grazed moor and heath may be compromised long before that; Blackingstone Rock above its conifer curtain demonstrates the point, even if better in the winter (Fig. 275). Their clitter skirts will probably scrub over and assume the mantle of a Wistman's precedent at least in the east. Another landscape irony is that the present 'hidden tors' on the convexities of oak-covered valley sides, like Wray Cleave or White Wood on the Double Dart, will remain the same, offering the same surprises to families on winding woodland walks and challenges to their younger members. Thoroughly wooded clitter, too,

FIG 275. Blackingstone Rock – a northeastern tor which, except at its own foot, is seen only across the tree tops. This could be the fate of many a summit tor if moorland gives way to scrub for lack of maintenance by hill-farmers.

will still be there and for a long time retain its mossy blanket as it does in Figure 119, as the even temperature and relative humidity of the deep woods provides a shield against open air drying. Streamsides, especially those at the foot of a wood, will probably remain as entrancing, and though the annual mean discharge may diminish and show in summer most, the spates of winter will be encouraged by the predicted increase in that season's rainfall and its periodic storminess.

Dartmoor as major water resource could persist as long as the blanket bog stays, is made wet enough again, its erosion minimised, and if its sphagnum species survive the summer drying. But there isn't much blanket bog south of us now. All that demands that people who know about bog are up there, and up there often enough, to monitor change, fight fire and tend the grazing. Valley mires pose a more complex question and their sustenance depends on the upstream catchment and the management of the outflow. If the former contains blanket peat, so much the better; but the latter will require a 'keeper' after the manner of the leat-watching water-man of old if we are to take our mires seriously.

So, Dartmoor's early twenty-first-century contribution to biodiversity, already a complex of variable fortunes, may be in for a roller-coaster ride. If the woods can retain their enormous insect populations then the tits, pied flycatcher, wood warbler and redstart may stay and thrive, as should all three woodpeckers as long as management respects the need for a volume of dead wood, both standing and fallen. At the woodland edge chiff chaff and willow warbler, blackcap and robin; hedgerow dunnock, whitethroat and yellowhammer, and streamside alder siskin and marsh tit populations should all stay at their posts. Their predators, especially the sparrowhawk, ought then to remain happy too. Deer populations are already burgeoning and managers better beware potential for browsing and fraying increase. The badger population, already high and unhealthy for lack of predation, may go into a cyclical state with the kind of crashes that the smallest mammals already experience, but for different reasons.

The greatest and most awful risk for Dartmoor is that the moorland that has given it its name for more than 1,000 years, given the whole of this great work of natural art its uniqueness, and given to us a special sense of place, succumbs faster to climatic variability than it should *because* its management has become impossible. Momentarily the biodiversity of the space that was moor, in numerical and species terms may well increase, but its own kind, its moorland kind, may be lost. Moorland ecosystems were never rich in genera, let alone species – hermit-like they are ascetic, but the very sparsity of species is one of their great and subtle attractions. The skylark punctuates that great bowl of the sky, tormentil dots the turf and a stags horn club moss tuning fork spikes a sea of dark ling.

The sparsest of all the species or at least of one of its varieties, is the truly native people. The people whose families have been within the Dartmoor boundary, or wandering back and forth across it for generations. They are those whose surnames appear in mediaeval tin coinage rolls, seventeenth-century muster rolls and the presentments of Lydford courts. Names like Coaker, Dicker, Edmonds, Endacott, French, Hodge, Jordan, Nosworthy and Perryman are among them.

Their number includes those who now have no moorland rights or, having registered them between 1965 and 1970 rather than lose them, have not used them since. They are the wholly in-bye farmers of this National Park, able to finish their own stock themselves and perhaps only at market contributing to moorland management by buying moor-bred stores from their near neighbours up the hill. But still they are part of the complex family that, without thinking about it, cherishes Dartmoor for the rest of us. Those who remain in the Moor,

FIG 276. Arnold Cole of Greenwell (1181 AD) and a quarterman of the West Quarter of the Dartmoor commons, standing on Broad Rock on the boundary between the Forest and the National Trust's Shaugh Moor near the head of the Erme. The still-active commoners need society's support and confidence for the future if Dartmoor is to retain its moorland heart.

on its surface daily and actively managing it, have been joined, within the last century, even the last few decades, by new recruits, some from close by, some from other moors. The need now is to retain all of them, their longer-standing colleagues and their skills. For their sparsity affects that of all the other moorland species, and their departure, or even only their backs turned on the high tops, will herald the disappearance of most of those *we* know as the collection that makes Dartmoor the place it still, just, is.

References and Further Reading

CHAPTER 1

Early writing still available: Rowe, 1848; Crossing, 1901 *et seq.* (but new editions 1960s onwards by David and Charles, Devon Books and others); Hawkings, 1987; HMSO (Acts of Parliament and Circulars), 1949, 1972, 1976, 1995, 2006; Hemery, 1983; Hamilton-Leggett, 1992; Harvey & St Leger Gordon, 1953; DNPA, 2005; Beeson & Greeves, 1993.

CHAPTER 2

Gill (ed.), 1970; Brenchley & Rawson (eds), 2006; Dearman, 1964; Dineley, 1986; JNCC, 1993; Edwards & Scrivener, 1999; Sutcliffe, 1986; Durrance & Laming, 1982; Brunsden, 1963, 1968; Waters, 1954, 1957, 1964, 1965.

CHAPTER 3

Simmons, 1964, 2003; Amesbury *et al.*, 2008; Blackford *et al.*, 2006; Fyfe *et al.*, 2008; Fleming, 1978, 2008; Beckett, 1981; Gerrard, 1997; Griffith, 1998; Butler, 1991–7; Clayden, 1964; Mackney, 1983.

CHAPTER 4

Vancouver, 1807; Harvey & St Leger Gordon, 1953; DNPA, 2001, 2008; Ward *et al.*, 1972; JNCC, 2004; Denman *et al.*, 1967; Simmons, 1965; Baldock & Walters, 2008; Streeter, 2009; Rackham, 2004; Preston *et al.*, 2002; Gilbert, 2000; Benfield, 2001; Proctor *et al.*, 1980; DNPA, 1997, 2001.

CHAPTER 5

Harvey & St Leger Gordon, 1974; DNPA, 1997, 2001; Baldock & Walters, 2008; Smaldon, 2005; Sitters (ed.), 1988; Stanbury *et al.*, 2006; Chinery, 1993; Bristow *et al.*, 1984; Baines, 2000.

CHAPTER 6

Harvey & St Leger Gordon, 1953; Crowden, 2008; Simmons, 2003; Environment Agency (data sets), annual; Hawkings, 1987; Hemery, 1991; Smaldon, 2005; Chinery, 1993; Croft, 1986; Baldock & Walters, 2008; Devon County Council, 2005.

CHAPTER 7

Linehan, 1962; Thorn (ed. Morris), 1985; Greeves, 1981, 1986, 2003; Newman, 1998; Gill (ed.), 1970; Thurlow, 1997; Gerrard, 1997; Crossing, 1986; Woods, 1988; Gill (ed.), 1987; Colepresse, 1667; Stoyle, 1994; Vancouver, 1807.

CHAPTER 8

Crossing, 1903 (1966); Aune Head Arts, 2007; HMSO, 1985; Turner et al., 2002; Martin, 1965; Yarwood, 2006; Denman et al., 1967.

CHAPTER 9

Dower, 1945; Hobhouse, 1947; HMSO, 1949, 1968, 1972, 1974, 1977, 1995, 2006; DNPA, 1977, 1997, 2001; Duchy of Cornwall, 1983; Edwards & Scrivener, 1999; DCC, 2002; Defence Estates, 2007; Smout (ed.), 2000.

CHAPTER 10

DNPA, 1987, 2005, 2007; Simmons, 2003; Hemery, 1991; DCC, 2002, 2005; HMSO, 2006; RSPB, 2007; Harvey & St Leger Gordon, 1953; Greeves, 2005.

LEGISLATION

National Parks and Access to the Countryside Act (1949)
Countryside Act (1968)
Local Government Act (1972)
Nature Conservancy Council Act (1973)
Wildlife and Countryside Act (1981)
Dartmoor Commons Act (1985)
Environment Act (1990)
Environment Act (1995)
Countryside and Rights of Way Act (2000)
Commons Act (2006)
Natural Environment and Rural Communities Act (2006)

CIRCULARS AND WHITE PAPERS

4/76 – 'Report of the National Parks Review Committee'
Cmd 6837 – 'Statement on the Non-statutory Inquiry by Baroness Sharp (v.i)
12/96 – 'Environment Act (1995) Part III. National Parks

REPORTS

National Parks in England and Wales (1945), John Dower.
National Parks Committee (1947), Sir Arthur Hobhouse.
Conservation of Nature in England and Wales (1947), Dr J. S. Huxley.
National Parks Review Committee (1974), Lord Sandford.
Dartmoor (1977) – of a public Inquiry into the use of it for Military Training, Lady Sharp.
Fit for the Future (National Parks Review Panel), Prof. Ron Edwards.

FIG 277. Haytor sunset.

Select Bibliography

Abbreviations: DAS – Devon Archaeological Society; DNPA – Dartmoor National Park Authority; DCC – Devon County Council; FSC – Field Studies Council; JNCC – Joint Nature Conservation Committee; NERC – Natural Environment Research Council; RSE – Royal Society of Edinburgh; Trans. DA – Transactions of the Devonshire Association; Trans. IBG – Transactions of the Institute of British Geographers

Amesbury, M. J., Charman, D. J., Fyfe, R. M., Langdon, P. G. & West, S. (2008). Bronze Age settlement decline in S.W. England, testing the climate change hypothesis. *Journal of Archaeological Science* **35**.

Aune Head Arts (2007). *Focus on Farmers: Art and Hill Farming.* Halsgrove, Wellington.

Baines, D. (2000). *Breeding Wading Birds in the Dartmoor National Park.* DNPA.

Baldock, N. & Walters, J. (2008). *The Wildlife of Dartmoor.* John Walters.

Beckett, S. C. (1981). *Pollen analysis of the peat deposits* In: Shaugh Moor Project 4th Report. *Proceedings of the Prehistoric Society* **48**.

Beeson, M. & Greeves, T. A. P. (1993). *The Image of Dartmoor.* Trans. DA.

Benfield, B. (2001). *The Lichen Flora of Devon.* Barbara Benfield, Cullompton.

Berridge, P. J. (1984). *A Flint Collection from Hedgemoor Farm Bridford.* DAS **42**.

Blackford, J. J., Innes, J. B., Hatton, J. J. & Caseldine, C. J. (2006). Mid-Holocene environmental change at Black Ridge Brook, Dartmoor, S.W. England: a new appraisal based on fungal spore analysis. *Review of Palaeobotany and Palynology* **141**:1–2, 189–201.

Brenchley, P. J. & Rawson, P. F. (Eds) (2006). *The Geology of England and Wales.* Geological Society of London, London/Bath.

Bristow, C. R., Mitchell, S. H. & Bolton, D. E. (1984). *Devon Butterflies.* Devon Books, Exeter.

Brunsden, D. (1963). *Denudation*

SELECT BIBLIOGRAPHY · 389

Chronology of the River Dart. Trans. IBG.
Brunsden, D. (1968). *Dartmoor: British Landscapes Through Maps.* Geographical Association, Sheffield.
Butler, J. (1991–7). *Dartmoor. Atlas of Antiquities.* Vols 1–5. Devon Books/Halsgrove, Exeter.
Chinery, M. (1993). *Insects of Britain and Northern Europe: The Complete Insect Guide.* HarperCollins, London.
Clayden, B. (1964). *Soils of the Middle Teign Valley District of Devon.* Rothamsted Experimental Station/Agricultural Research Council, Harpenden.
Clayden, B. & Manley, D. J. R. (1964) *The Soils of the Dartmoor Granite.* In: *Dartmoor Essays* (Ed. Simmons, I. G.). The Devonshire Association, Exeter.
Croft, P. S. (1986). Freshwater invertebrates. *Field Studies* **6**, 531–79. FSC.
Crossing, W. ([1901] reprinted 1967). *A Hundred Years on Dartmoor.* Devon Books, Exeter.
Crossing, W. (1902). *The Ancient Stone Crosses of Dartmoor* (facsimile 1987).
Crossing, W. (1909). *Guide to Dartmoor: a topographical description of the Forest and Commons* (reprinted as *Crossing's Guide*, latest 1990). David and Charles, Newton Abbot.
Crossing, W. (1966). *Crossing's Dartmoor Worker.* David and Charles, Newton Abbot.
Crowden, J. (2008). *The Bad Winter.* Flagon Press, Chard.
DCC (2005). *A Warm Response – Our Climate Change Challenge.* DCC, Exeter.
Defence Estates (2007). *Environmental Appraisal – Dartmoor Training Estate.*
Dearman, W. (1964) Dartmoor: its geological setting. In: *Dartmoor Essays* (Ed. Simmons, I. G.). The Devonshire Association, Exeter.
Denman, D. R., Roberts, R. A. & Smith, H. J. F. (1967). *Commons and Village Greens.* Leonard Hill, London.
Dineley, D. (1986). Cornubian quarter-century advances in the geology of S.W. England. *Proceedings of the Ussher Society* **6**.
DNPA (1977). *Dartmoor (First) National Park Plan* (et seq. 1983, 1991, 2001, 2007).
DNPA (1987). *Dartmoor Seasons.* Devon Books, Exeter.
DNPA (2001). *Action for Wildlife. The Dartmoor Biodiversity Action Plan.*
DNPA & English Nature (2001). *The Nature of Dartmoor – a biodiversity profile.*
Dower, J. (1945). *National Parks in England and Wales.* HMSO, London.
Duchy of Cornwall (1983). *Future Management of the Dartmoor Estate.*
Durrance, E. M. & Laming, D. J. C. (Eds) (1972). *The Geology of Devon.* University of Exeter.
Edwards, R. A. & Scrivener, R. C. (1999). *The Geology of the Country Round Exeter.* NERC.
Fleming, A. (2008). *The Dartmoor*

Reaves: Investigating Prehistoric Land Divisions. Oxbow Books, Oxford.
Fyfe, R. M., Bruck, J., Johnston, R., Lewis, H., Roland, T. P. & Wickstead, H. (2008). Historical context and chronology of Bronze Age land enclosure in Dartmoor UK. *Journal of Archaeological Science* **35**, 2250–61.
Gerrard S. (1997). *Dartmoor: Landscapes Through Time.* B. T. Batsford/English Heritage, London.
Gilbert, O. (2000). *Lichens* (New Naturalist **86**). HarperCollins, London.
Gill, C. (Ed.) (1970). *Dartmoor: A New Study.* David and Charles, Newton Abbot.
Gill, C. (Ed.) (1987). *The Duchy of Cornwall: 650th Anniversary.* David and Charles, Newton Abbot.
Greeves, T. A. P. (1981). 'The Devon Tin Industry 1450–1750' (PhD thesis). University of Exeter.
Greeves, T. A. P. (1986). *Tin Mines and Miners of Dartmoor.* Devon Books, Exeter.
Greeves, T. A. P. (2003). *Devon's Earliest Tin Coinage Roll 1302-3.* Trans. DA **135**.
Greeves, T. A. P. (2005). *Dartmoor: Images of England.* NPI Media Group, Stroud.
Griffith, F. (1998). *Devon's Past: An Aerial View.* DCC, Exeter.
Griffiths, D. M. (Ed.) (1996). *The Archaeology of Dartmoor: perspectives from the 1990s.* DAS **52**.
Hamilton-Leggett, P. (1992). *The Dartmoor Bibliography.* Devon Books, Exeter.
Harvey, L. & St Leger-Gordon, D. (1953, 1974). *Dartmoor* (New Naturalist), HarperCollins, London.
Hawkings, D. (1987). *Water from the Moor.* Devon Books, Exeter.
Hemery, E. (1983). *High Dartmoor.* Robert Hale, London.
Hemery, E. (1986). *Walking the Dartmoor Waterways.* Peninsula Press, Newton Abbot.
Hobhouse, A. (1947). *Report of the National Parks Committee.* HMSO, London.
JNCC (2004). *An Illustrated Guide to British Upland Vegetation.* JNCC, London.
Linehan, C. D. (1962). *A Forgotten Manor in Widecombe-in-the-Moor.* Trans. DA.
Mackney, D. (1983). *Soils of S.W. England.* Lawes Agricultural Trust, Harpenden.
Martin, E. W. (1965). *The Shearers and the Shorn.* Routledge and Kegan Paul, London.
Newman, P. (1998). *The Dartmoor Tin Industry: A Field Guide.* Chercombe Press, Newton Abbot.
Pennington, R. R. (1973). *Stannary Law,* David and Charles, Newton Abbot.
Preston, C. D., Pearman, D. A. & Dines, T. D. (2002). *New Atlas of the British and Irish Flora.* Oxford University Press, Oxford.
Proctor, M. C. F., Spooner, G. M. & Spooner, M. F. (1980). Changes in Wistman's Wood, Dartmoor. Trans. DA, **112**.

Rackham, O. (2004). *Woodlands* (New Naturalist). HarperCollins, London.

Rowe, S. (1848 [reprinted 2007]). *A Perambulation of the Forest of Dartmoor and its Venville Precincts.* Kessinger Publishing, Whitefish, MT.

RSPB (2007). *Climate Change: Wildlife and Adaptation.* RSPB.

Sale, R. & Chapman, C. (2000). *Dartmoor: The Official National Park Guide.* Pevensey Press, Cambridge.

Simmons, I. G. (1963). *The Blanket Bog of Dartmoor.* Trans. DA **95**.

Simmons, I. G. (Ed.) (1964). *Dartmoor Essays.* The Devonshire Association, Exeter.

Simmons, I. G. (1964). *An Ecological History of Dartmoor.* In: *Dartmoor Essays.*

Simmons, I. G. (1965). The Dartmoor oak copses. *Field Studies* **2**, 225–35.

Sitters, H. P. (1988). *Tetrad Atlas of the Breeding Birds of Devon.* Devon Bird Watching and Preservation Society, Okehampton.

Smaldon, R. (2005). *The Birds of Dartmoor.* Isabelline Books, Falmouth.

Smout, T. (2001). *Nature, Landscape and People since the Second World War.* RSE, Edinburgh.

Stace, C. A. (1997). *New Flora of the British Isles.* Cambridge.

Stanbrook, E. (1994). *Dartmoor Forest Farms.* Devon Books, Exeter.

Stanbury, A., Salter, A., Slader, P. & Tayton, J. (2006). *Breeding Bird Survey of Dartmoor Training Area.* RSPB/Defence Estates.

Stoyle, M. (1994). *Loyalty and Locality.* University of Exeter.

Streeter, D. (2009). *Collins Flower Guide.* HarperCollins, London.

Sutcliffe, A. J. (1986). *On the Track of Ice Age Mammals.* British Museum (Natural History), London.

Thorn, C. & F, (1985) *Domesday Book: Devon.* Phillimore & Co. Ltd, Stroud.

Turner, M., Barr, D., Fogerty, M., Hart, K. & Winter, M. (2002). *The State of Farming on Dartmoor 2002.* DNPA.

Ward, S. D., Jones, A. D. & Manton, M. (1972). *The Vegetation of Dartmoor,* FSC.

Waters, R. S. (1954). Aits and breaks of slope in Dartmoor streams. *Geography* **38**.

Waters, R. S. (1957). Differential weathering and erosion on Oldlands. *Geographical Journal* **123**.

Waters, R. S. (1964). *Denudation Chronology of Parts of S.W. England.* FSC.

Waters, R. S. (1965). *The geomorphological significance of periglacial frost action in S.W. England.* In: *Essays in Geography for Austin Miller* (Ed. Whittow, J. B.). University of Reading.

Woods, S. (1988). *Dartmoor Stone.* Devon Books, Exeter.

Vancouver, C. (1808). *Agriculture of Devon.* Board of Agriculture.

Yarwood, R. (2006). *Devon Livestock Breeds: a geographical perspective.* Trans. DA **138**.

Index

Page numbers in **bold** indicate the subject is the main topic of the section in question; those in *italic* denote illustrations/captions.

adder (*Vipera berus*) *180*, 180–1, 208, 210
adder's tongue (*Ranunculus ophioglossifolius*) 347
Agricultural Development Advisory service (ADAS) 108, 190
agriculture 185–7, 254–5, **276–320**
 crops 6, 26, 97–8, 243–4, 291, 294–5
 early modern developments 292–5
 early settlements 14, 90–1, 92–3, 96–9, 246–7
 economic viability 300–2, 312–13
 governmental support/subsidy 304, 308, 310, 313
 impact of climate change 243–4, 358, 368, 371
 impact on landscape 104–5, 281, 325
 problems 305–7, 308–9, 311, 319–20, 355, 368
 workforce 312–13
Agriculture, Fisheries and Food, Ministry of (MAFF) 108, 136, 189, 337, 338, 362
alder (*Alnus glutinosa*) 87, 148, 199, 202, 214
 decline/use as fuel 103
alder fly 208
amoeba 85, 97, 218
amphibians 180–1
'Ancient Tenements' 106, 134–5, 253, 261, **278–81**, *280*, 309, 333, *339*
Anglo-Saxons 1, 5, 8–9, 99, 135, **249–54**, 281–2
 building 139–41
 impact on landscape 105
 place names 99, 135, 162, 249–51
 villages 251–2
Antitrichia curtipendula (moss variety) 161–2
ants 206–8, 342
aphids 204, 208
arable land 311, *311*, 363
 subsidy 363
Arctic white heather (*Cassiope tetragona*) *83*, 83
Arctic willow (*Salix arctica*) *82*, 82

Areas of Outstanding Natural Beauty (AONBs) 324–5
arsenic mining 266
ash (tree) 89, 146
Ashburton 26, 35, 51, 144, 252, 263–4, 293, 309
Avon, River 5, 48, 177, 213, 266
 waterworks 225, 226, 227–8, 255, 267, 275, 326

Babeny 14, 75, 135, 279, 280, 281, 339
badgers 185, 197–8, 216, 383
ball clay 40, 42, 43
bank vole (*Clethrionomys glareolus*) 173, 210
banks 139, *139*–41, *140*, 210
barn owl (*Tyto alba*) 194, 195
bats *see* Buckfastleigh; greater horseshoe bat
beak sedge (*Carex rostrata*) 118
beard lichens (*Usnea spp.*) 148, 161
Beardown 7, 20, 106, 143, 144, 240, 293
Becka Brook/Falls 75, 76, 309, 339
Beckamoor Combe 255, *258*, 259, 275
Beckett, Stephen 91–3
bedstraw *see* heath bedstraw; marsh bedstraw; upright bedstraw
bee hawk moth (*Hemaris tityus*) 170, *171*, 195
beech 193, 146, 199
beetles 128, 172, 199, 201
 as food 175
 woodland 205–6
Bellever 135, 178, 184, 333
 Forest 20, *20*, 106, 143, 199, 200, 203, 359
 Tor 63, 69–70, *71*
Belstone 63, 251–2, 278, 348
Bench Tor 16, 45, 62, 65, 75, 151, 157, 208, 213
benched hillsides 68–9
bent grasses (*for Latin names see individual species*) 121–2, 129
betony (*Betonica officinalis*) 138
bilberry (*Vaccinium myrtillis*) 121, 123–4, 129, 153, 155, 170, 171, 208, 211

biodiversity 146, 151–2, 206, 236, 330, 383
birch 84, 87, 103, 359
 see also dwarf birch
Birch Tor 177, 183, 184, 261, 358–60
birds **173–84**
 aquatic 228–9, 237–9
 carrion 192, 376–7
 in disused mine workings 262
 farmland 196–7
 ground-nesting 128–9, 180–1, *182*, *183*, 210–11, 377
 impact of climate change 371–3
 impact of human presence 376–7
 insectivorous 201–2, 208
 plantation residents **202–5**
 predatory 173, 192, 196–7, 203–4, 376–7, 383
 as prey 184, 185, 192, 196–7, 204, 210
 research/conservation 344, 350
 wading 181–3, 372–3
birdsfoot trefoil (*Lotus peduculatus*) 132
Black Death (C14) 99, 243, 277, 278–9, 289
black grouse (*Tetrao tetrix*) 184
Black Tor Beare 141, 160–4, *163*, 210, 216
Black-a-Brook 48–50, 51, 70, 91–2, 222–3, 225, 235–6, 237, 275
Blackaton 5, 243, 287, 288, 294, 351
blackbird (*Turdus merula*) 215, 239, 262
blackcap (*Sylvia atricapilla*) 202, 383
blackcock *see* black grouse
Blackdown 7, 101, 342, 350
blackfly (*Simulium spp.*) 234, 235
Blacklane Mire 87, 88, 89, 344–5
Blackslade 16, 130, 182, 291, 342
blanket bog 78, 88, 107, **115–20**, *116*, *118*, 123, 130, 131, 243
 as habitat 181
 management 119–20
 pools/streams 118, *118*, 221–4
 risk of damage to 191
 surveys 108–9
 survival 382

INDEX · 393

blue ground beetle (*Carabus intricatus*) 205–6, 206, 209
blue-tailed damselfly (*Ischneura pumilio*) 223–4, 270
bluebell (*Hyacinthoides non-scripta*) 127, 127–8, 138, 153, 154, 155, 211
Bodmin Moor 7, 81, 84, 87, 121
bog asphodel (*Narthecium ossifragum*) 117, 117
bog bean (*Menianthes trifoliata*) 131, 132
bog impernel (*Anagallis tenella*) 132
bog pimpernel (*Anagallis tenella*) 132
bog pondweed (*Potamogeton polygonifolius*) 233, 233
Bovey, River 5, 19, 50, 75, 230, 251
 acidity 230
 conservation measures/areas 345, 347, 351
 fauna 214, 239
 geology 41–2
Bovey Tracey 40, 147, 252, 283, 322
bracken (*Pteridium aquilinum*) 89, 111, **125–8**, 126, 187, 243, 360, 373
 control 126–7
 as habitat 173, 177, 181, 371
 problems posed by 127–8
 woodland 155–6, 163–4
brambles 205, 237
brambling (*Fringilla montifringilla*) 196
Brent Hill 8, 9, 68, 69, 248
Brentor 2, 7, 9, 248
Bridestowe 252, 265, 278, 322
bristle bent (*Agrostis curtisii*) 121, 121–2, 129
broad-leaved woodland 146, 369
 conservation measures 330–1, 342–3, 345–6
 ecology 205
 fauna **205–16**
 see also oaks
Broad Rock 158, 346, 384
Bronze Age 1, 14–15, 18–19, 92–7, 246–8, 252, 255, 269, 309
 settlements 94, 96, 247, 247–8, 252, 281–2; distribution 93, 95
'brown earths' 13–14, 15, 95, 100, 102, 164
brown hairstreak butterfly (*Thecla betulae*) 208, 209
brown hare (*Lepus capensis*) 184
brown trout (*Salmo trutta*) 236–7
Buckfastleigh 4, 35, 35, 57, 124, 141, 145, 177, 203, 252
 bat caves 195, 195–6, 273, 343
Buckland 16, 42, 62, 124, 144, 188–9, 208
buckler fern (*Dryopteris dilatata*) 155
burning (of moorland vegetation) 114–15, 119, 243, 298, 366
Burrator reservoir/woods 20, 66, 143–4, 225, 226–7, 227, 259, 275, 280, 340, 345
 fauna 199–200, 203, 228–9
Bush Down 111, 112, 114, 124, 243, 345

buttercup
 bulbous (*Ranunculus bulbosus*) 136
 meadow (*Ranunculus arvensis*) 136
butterflies/moths 127–8, 156, **168–71**, 194, 195, 199, 208–9
 food 169–70
 impact of climate change 371
butterwort (*Pinguicula grandiflora*) 132, 132–3
buzzard (*Buteo buteo*) 173, 174, 192, 197, 203, 215

caddisflies (*Rhycophilidae/Hydropsyche spp.*) 199, 208, 234, 235–6
Cadover Bridge 91–2, 178, 230, 346
 as centre of mining industry 266, 268, 269, 270
campion (*Silene dioica*) 82, 138, 138
Canthocampus (copepod genus) 228
carbon dating 81, 84, 85–6, 87, 98
Carboniferous period, geological formations 36, 37–8, 41, 273, 274
carnation sedge (*Carex panicea*) 129
caseless caddis (*Rhycophilidae goeridae*) 234
Castle Drogo 53, 346
cat's ears (*Hypochoeris spp.*) 138
cattle 27, 295, 298, 372
 breeds 187, 295, 303, 303, 314–16, 315, 318
 diseases 127, 310
 grazing 114–15, 119–20, 126, 134–5, 186, 187–90, 277, 302–9, 305; habits/preferences 313
 impact of human presence 377–8
 numbers 187–90, 278, 304, 310–11, 318–19
celandine (*Ranunculus ficaria*) 138, 138, 139
cereals, cultivation 97–8, 291, 294
Cetti's warbler (*Cettia cetti*) 166
Chagford 5, 14, 196, 248, 283, 285
 Common 119, 124, 125, 309
 as stannary town 24, 263–4
Challacombe 16, 130, 131, 243, 288, 290, 294
 stone row 94, 381
charcoal 89, 103, 150–1, 152
Cherry Brook 50, 130, 178
cherts 34, 37, 41
chiff chaff (*Phylloscopus collybita*) 210–11, 383
china clay
 formation 39–41, 43
 mining 25, 40, 100–1, 237, **266–70**
 pits, working/abandoned 223, 231, 267–9, 268
 waste tips 268, 269
 workmens' villages 267
cirl bunting (*Emberiza cirus*) 196
climate 65–6, **217–21**
 changes 218, 241–2, 300, 358, **368–74**, 380–1, 383; national patterns/predictions 370–1
 modern 4, 216, **240–4**

pre-human 53–4, 59–62
 Stone/Bronze/Iron Age 84, 87–8, 97, 218
 see also Ice Age
'clitter' 62, 62, 65, 65–6, 69, 79
 declining visibility 381–2
cocksfoot (*Dactylis glomeratus*) 136
collared dove (*Streptopelia decaocto*) 197
Combestone Tor 14, 240, 333, 334
common bent (*Agrostis tenuis*) 121, 129, 136
common blue damselfy (*Enallagan cyathigerum*) 195
common land 22–3, 26, 100, 151, 277–8, 282
 boundary markers 193, 193
 erosion 304–5, 305
 management 28, **335–7**, 383–4
 organization 23, 24
 see also grazing, public rights
common lizard (*Lacerta vivipara*) 181, 210, 371
common polypody (*Polypodium vulgare*) 155
common redstart (*Phoenicurus phoenicurus*) 211–12, 212, 216, 262, 334, 383
common sandpiper (*Actitis hypoleucos*) 214
Commons Registration Act (1965) 22–3, 188, 335, 337
conifer plantations 19–20, 106–7, **143–6**, 145, 246, 330–1, 350, 359
 fauna **199–205**
 species 145–6
 conservation **21–9**, 146, 151–2, 225
 common interests 26–9, 105
 designated areas 322 (*see also types of area e.g. SSSI*)
 governmental prioritisation 328–9, 344
 groups 21–2, 24, 28–9, 155, 189, 206, 308, 351–2
 legal measures/obligations 26–8
 need for 216, 244, 308–9, 358
 NPA role in 328–9, **342–6**
 overlapping/competing authorities 352–4, 353
 projects/action plans 28–9, 206, 216, 236, 269, 270, 344, 352–6
 see also biodiversity; natural beauty
coot (*Fulica atra*) 229
copper mining 249, 265–6
coppicing 151–3, 152, 153, 216
cormorant (*Phalacrocorax carbo*) 228, 240
cornditches 193, 193, 289
Cornwall, Duchy of 1, 22–3, 99, 109, 348–50
 agricultural management 277–8, 280–1, 291–2, 309–10
 authorisation of newtakes 134, 253
 conifer plantations 19–20, 143
 conservation activities 26, 182
 oak woods 162–3

role in National Park management 336, 340–1
rural/urban development 253
tenants/tenancies 70, 178, 276, 280–1, 309–10, 340–1, 365
Cosdon (Cawsand Beacon) 6, 6–7, 27, 31, 137, 219, 220, 285, 371
tinworks 257, 259
cotton grass (*Eriphorum angustifolium*) 116, 117, 129, 169–70
'country rock' 36–8
Countryside Agency 28–9, 322, 342, 356
Countryside Commission 327, 338, 340, 354, 356
cow parsley (*Anthriscus sylvestris*) 138
cow wheat (*Melampyrum pratense*) 155, 211
Cowsic, River 4, 50, 70, 119, 144, 221, 225, 275
Cox Tor 7–8, 66, 68, 68, 69, 265, 291, 345
Cranmere Pool 10, 11, 181, 184, 219, 222
creeping thistle (*Cirsium arvense*) 136
crested dogstail (*Cynosurus cristatus*) 136
cross-leaved heath (*Erica tetralix*) 89, 117
crossbill (*Loxia curvirostra*) 202–3
Crossing, William 299–300, 302–3, 304
crow (*Corvus corone cornis*) 192, 197, 204, 376
 interaction with humanity 376–7
crowberry (*Empetrum nigrum*) 82, 84, 123
cuckoo (*Cuculus canorus*) 168–9, 169, 262, 377, 377
Culm, river/geology 34–5, 39, 191
curlew (*Numenius arquata*) 181–2, 182
Cut Hill 12, 31, 101, 181, 218, 219, 342
Cyclops (copepod genus) 228

daffodils 154, 155
 protection 345, 345–6
damselflies 118, 195, 199, 200, 223–4, 233, 270
dandelion (*Taraxacum officinale*) 138
Daphnia (pond-dwelling invertebrates) 228
Dart, River/valley 2, 4, 4–5, 5, 7, 47, 48, 74, 219
 agriculture 98
 conservation 345–6
 fauna 213, 237, 239, 240, 343
 geology/mineralogy 235, 256
 gorges 75
 headstreams 4, 48–50, 51–2, 237
 naming 4–5, 141, 249
 vegetation 141, 146, 153, 156, 157
 waterworks 225, 276
Dartford warbler (*Sylvia undata*) 370–1
Dartmeet 4, 14, 75, 159, 180, 237, 309

Dartmoor
 changing landscape 379–83
 future, plans/needs 28–9, 109–15, 216, 236, 244, 356, **357–85,** 373–4
 geographical extent 2
 geology 2–3, 11, 30–78, 34
 high points 2, 6, 7–9, 47–8, 160–4, 218–19, 220
 naming 141, 249–51
 native families 383–4
 Natural Area, defined 321–3, 323
 ownership 1, 22, 253, 277, 278, 329–30
 unique character 379, 383
 views 6, 6–9, 27, 331–2, 334
 visual/sensual appeal 379 (*see also under* tourism)
Dartmoor Biodiversity Action Plan (DBAP) 236, 270
Dartmoor Commoners' Association 22, 126, 189, 243, 304, 318, 320, 335, 361, 364
Dartmoor Commoners' Council xii, 22, 26, 29, 304–5, 337
 creation/functions 335–6
Dartmoor Commons Act (1985) xi–xii, 22, 26, 304, **335–7**
Dartmoor Preservation Association 3, 21–2, 346, 351
Dartmoor Prison 23, 229
 farm 25–6, 143–4, 182
 quarry 273
deer 191, 197–8, 205, 383
 culling 205
deer grass (*Trichophorum caespitosum*) 117
Defence, Ministry of 109, 348–50, 349, 350, 354
Defence Estates 29, 354
DEFRA *see* Environment, Food and Rural Affairs, Department of
Devensian (glacial) phase 57, 81
devil's bit scabious (*Succisa pratensis*) 133, 136
 insects feeding on 170, 171
Devon County Council 27, 304, 326
 smallholdings 348
Devon Wildlife Trust 345–6, 351
Devonian period, geological formations 34–6, 37–8, 102
dew ponds 223, 223, 224, 243
Dicranium scoparium (moss variety) 153
dipper (*Cinclus spp.*) 237–9, 238, 240
dog's mercury (*Mercurialis perennis*) 155
Domesday Book x, 14, 105, 134, 251–2, 253, 254–5, 281, **283–5,** 346
dor beetle (*Geotrupes stercorarius*) 128
dormouse (*Muscardinus avellanarius*) 210, 210
Double Dart 4, 4, 5, 19, 48, 52–3, 75
 fauna 208, 214
 vegetation 147, 149
dragonflies 199, 200, 200–1, 201, 236
drainage 17–18, 48–53

Drewsteignton 35, 224, 251, 274, 309, 340, 346
driftways 136–7
dry stone walls 77, 77, 135, 139–41, 140
dunlin (*Calidris alpina*) 181–2
dunnock (*Prunella modularis*) 196, 383
Dunsford Woods 154, 155, 345, 345–6, 347, 351
dwarf birch (*Betula nana*) 84
dwarf shrubs 121, 123–4, 173, 190–1

early human habitations 1, 4–5, 14–15, 18–19, 80, 83, 86, 88, 246–7
earthworms 197, 205, 214, 215
East Dart 4, 11, 42, 50, 75, 200, 221, 230
ecosystem(s),
 functioning/complexity 167, 179, 185–7, 216, 243–4, 378–9, 383
Elatobium abietinum (aphid species) 204
elm(s) 87, 92
emperor moth (*Saturnia pavonia*) 168, 168–9, 172
enchanter's nightshade (*Circaea lutetiana*) 155
enclosure(s) 12, 21, 23, 99–100, **134–41,** 279–80, 293
English Heritage 28, 29, 109, 348, 352
English Nature 28–9, 109, 342, 344
English oak (*Quercus robur*) 146, 162, 164
Environment, Food and Rural Affairs, Department of (DEFRA) 109, 136, 337–8, 342, 352, 355, 362–3
Environment Agency 28, 29, 109, 232, 348, 354
Environmentally Sensitive Area(s) (ESAs) 352, 355, 360–1
 Dartmoor designated as 108–9, 136, 190, 216, 308–9, 313, 321
Eocene Age, geological formations 43, 51–2
Erme, River/valley 5, 48, 77, 101, 130, 229, 266
European Economic Community (EEC) 308, 320, 363
 Common Agricultural Policy (CAP) 310, 361
European gorse (*Ulex europaeus*) 124,
European Union (EU) 337, 352, 354
 conservation measures 321, 344, 355
Exmoor 191, 338, 373

fallow deer (*Dama dama*) 191, 198, 205, 216
farmers
 changing ways/outlook 366–7
 conservation responsibilities 26–7
 expansion/diversification 312, 365, 365–7
 long-resident families 319–20, 383–4
 problems facing 365–7, 368
 psychology/motivations 361
 relationship with authorities 338–41, 361–4

farmland
  boundary with moorland 99–100, 105
  distribution 105–6, *106*
  ecological management 330, 338–40, 339
  management agreements 338–40, 354, 361
feldspar 31, 32, 39
ferns 149, 155–6, *156*
Fernworthy reservoir/woods 20, 94, 106, 143, 225, 226, 227, 243, 275, 322
fauna 184, 199–200, 203, 228–9
field grasshoppers (*Chorthippus spp.*) 128
field vole (*Microtus agrestis*) 172–3, *173*, 204
fieldfare (*Turdus pilaris*) 179
fields
  delimitation 193
  grazing 193–5
  patterns *98*, 137, 287, 288, 290, 291
finches 174, 196, 214
fire(s)
  dealing with 361, 378
  early use/incidence 89–90
  impact on landscape/economy 116, 186, 190–1, *191*, 243
fish 236–7
  growth 236
  impact of water acidity on 232, 236
  as prey 228, 236, 239–40
'flats' 51, *51*, 53, 55–6, *56*
flatworms (*Planaria/Polycelis spp.*) 234
flax-leaved St John's wort (*Hypericum linariifolium*) 155
Fleming, Andrew 94–6, 281–2, 289–90
floating sweet grass (*Glyceria fluitans*) 224
foliose lichen (*Hypotrachyna [=Palmelia] laevigata*) 161
Fontinalis (moss variety) 233
Foot and Mouth Disease 310, 361–2
foot travel
  dangers 11–12
  rights of access 22, 28
  route markers 1, 2, 11
Forest of Dartmoor 22–3, 253, 276
  establishment of farms within 134–5
  legal status 337
  parish boundary 250, 384
forestry 19–20, 25, 199–205, 365
Forestry Commission 20, 143, 199, 343, 350
fossil remains, mammalian 35, 57–8, 343
fox moth (*Macrothylacia rubi*) 169
Fox Tor 119, 130, 184
Foxtor Mire 11, 75, 101, 130, *130*, 182, 225
foxes 173, 184, *185*, *185*, 192, 197, 216
foxglove (*Digitalis purpurea*) 138–9, *139*
freshwater limpet (*Ancylastrum fluviatilis*) 236

freshwater pearl mussel (*Margaritifera margaritifera*) 236
froghoppers (*Aphrophoridae spp.*) 235, 236
fruticose lichen (*Sphaerophorus globosus*) 161
Fur Tor 62, 65, 69–70, *70*, 88, 157, 298
furze (*Ulex spp.*) 122, 123, 129, 131–2
Fuscidea cyathoides (lichen species) 157

Galloway cattle 187, 295, 303, *303*, 314
gatekeeper butterfly *see* hedge brown butterfly
Gidleigh 251, 280, 285
  Common 86, 93, 119, 182, 342
  Mill 351
goat willow (*Salix caprea*) 148
goldcrest (*Regulus regulus*) 202, 204, 213
golden plover (*Pluvialis apricaria*) 181, 181–3
golden ringed dragonfly (*Cordulegaster boltonii*) 201, *201*
golden saxifrage (*Chrysosplenium oppositifolium/C. alternifolium*) 156
golden scale male fern (*Dryopteris affinis*) 155
goosander (*Mergus merganser*) 228, 228–9, 240
gorges
  conservation 343
  distribution 74
  formation 73–7, *74*
gorse (*Ulex spp.*) 111, *112*, 124, *124*, 372
  grazing 187
  as habitat 177, 181
  proliferation 380–1
goshawk (*Accipiter gentilis*) 203–4, 215
granite 2–3, 30–46, 47, 269
  age 31, 33, 34
  'blue' 31–2, 33
  boulders 77–8, 141, 153, *158*, 180
  chemical instability/decay 39, 54, 61, 64, 71–2, 77
  faulting 41–3, 54
  formation/emplacement 31–3, 38–9
  'giant' 31–2, *32*, 33
  impact of climatic changes 54, 61–2, 70, 71–2
  jointing 44, 44–6, 64
  kaolinisation 39–41, 43, 46, 100–1
  quarrying 44, *270*, 270–3
  relationship with younger formations 34, *34*, 37–8
  scientific investigation 345
  weathering 54, 63, 64, 65–6, 71–2
  see also clitter; growan
Graphidion (lichen genus) 157
grass moth (*Crambus pratella/Caleptris pinella*) 169–70
grass(es)
  first appearance 53–4
  as food/habitat 172–3
  proliferation 380–1
  types 117–18, 121–2, 136

grasshopper warbler (*Locustella laevia*) 202
grasshoppers 128, 172, 196, 206
grassland 109–11, **120–4**
  categories 128–9, 194–5
  diminution 190–1
gravel 79, 80
  plant life 82, *82*
  taking for domestic use 70–1, 276
grayling butterfly (*Hipparchia semele*) 170
grayling (*Thymallus thymallus*) 236
grazing 134–5, **183–95**, 216, **302–13**, 318–20, **358–67**
  all-year 303–4
  changing patterns 303–4
  fees 277–8, 291
  importance to moorland ecosystem 185–7
  licensed 348, 349
  as means of vegetation control 114–15, 119–20, 126
  problems 305–7, 308–9, 311, 319–20, 355
  public rights 1, 23, 304, 335–6, 383
  reduction 308–9, 372–3, 380–1
  regulation 188–9, 277
  requirements for proper functioning 360–1, 378–9
great green grasshoppers (*Tettigonidae spp.*) 206, *207*
great hairy woodrush (*Lusula sylvatica*) 153, 211
Great Links Tor 7, *8*, 172, 257
Great Mis Tor 63, *63*, 219, 298
great spotted woodpecker (*Dendrocupus major*) 196, 204, 215
Great Staple Tor 7–8, 62, 63, 64, *66*, 66, 68
greater butterfly orchid (*Platanthera clorantha*) 136, 137
greater horseshoe bat (*Rhinolophus ferrumequinum*) 195, 195–6, 273, 343
green hairstreak butterfly (*Callophrys rubi*) 170, *171*, 208
green oak tortrix (*Tirtrix viridiana*) 208
green woodpecker (*Picus viridis*) 196, 215
grey squirrel (*Sciurus carolinensis*) 204, 216
grey wagtail (*Motacilla cinerea*) 202, 216, 237–9, 238, 240
grey willow (*Salix cinerea*) 148
Grimspound x, 232, 261, *261*
  Bronze Age settlements 94, 247
growan (rotted granite) 61, 70, 178, 235

hair lichen (*Bryoria smithii*) 162
Halshanger
  Common 11, 16, *16*, 294
  Newtake 130–1, 181, 294
Hameldown 101, 126, 220, 257, 283, 309
hard fern (*Blechnum spicant*) 155, *156*
harestail (*Eriphorum vaginatum*) 117

Harford 42, 141, 251, 273
Reservoir 223
harts-tongue (*Phyllitis scolopendrum*) 155
hawkbits (*Leontodon spp.*) 138
hawk's beards (*Crepis spp.*) 138
Hawks Tor (Cornwall) 81, 84
hawkweeds (*Hieracium spp.*) 138
hawthorn (*Crataegus monogyna*) 240, 241, 360
Hay Tor 7, 8–9, 9, 16, 27, 63, 64, 280, 311, 339, 385
 fauna 177, 316
 iron mine 343
 NPA purchase 331–2
 quarry/pools 224, 270, 270–1, 271, 272
 tinworks 257–8
 vegetation 124, 158
hazel 87–8, 89–90, 103, 146, 152
 manufacturing use 152–3
Headland Warren 124, 183, 261, 261, 296, 297, 381
heath bedstraw (*Galium saxatile*) 129
heath grass (*Sieglingia decumbrens*) 129
heath rush (*Juncus squarrosus*) 117, 173
heather 89, 89, 109–13, 114, 117, 123, 123–4, 125, 131–2, 374
 as food/habitat 172, 184, 187
 proliferation 190, 380
heather beetle (*Lochmaea suturalis*) 168, 172, 243
hedge brown (gatekeeper) butterfly (*Pyronia tithonus*) 170
hedgehog (*Erinaceus europaeus*) 197, 210
hedgerows 140, 141, 159
hemp agrimony (*Eupatorium cannabinum*) 138–9, 139
hen harrier (*Circus cyaneus*) 173
heron (*Ardea cinerea*) 228, 236–7, 240
Hexworthy 135, 309
 Series (soils) 101, 102
hieroglyphic ladybird (*Coccinella hieroglyphica*) 172
high brown fritillary (*Argynnis adippe*) 127–8, 167, 208–9, 371
High Willhays 2, 6, 31, 47–8, 157, 218–19, 220
Hill Farming Allowance 185, 310, 313
Hill Livestock Compensatory Allowance 313
hogweed (*Heraclium spondylium*) 138
Holne Chase 4, 4, 53, 147, 148, 248, 284, 342
Holne Common 151, 318, 336
 NPA acquisition 332–5
Holne Moor xi, 3, 14, 18, 225, 280, 284, 332–4, 333, 342, 350
 enclosure 99–100
 fauna 177, 178
 settlements 93, 94–5, 95, 252, 289–90
 soil 14–15, 101
 vegetation 124, 124
Holne Park 147, 284, 309, 334

Holocene period 73–8
honey buzzard (*Pernis apivorus*) 371
Hookeria lucens (moss variety) 156
hornet robber fly (*Asilus crabroniformis*) 128
horsetails (*Equisetum spp.*) 149
Hound Tor 16, 219, 294, 309
 medieval village 14, 99, 243, 286–9, 287
humans, interaction with landscape 216, 244, **245–320**, 308–9, **374–9**, 383–4
hunter-gatherer societies 83, 86, 135, 246

Ice Age(s) 2–4, 31, 56–7, 58, 73
 close/aftermath 73–8, 79, 81, 221
in-bye land *see* farmland
insects **168–72**, 199–202
 aquatic 234–6
 as prey 174, 176–7, 178, 195–6, 199, 200–2, 206, 210–11, 213–14, 215–16, 236, 383
 woodland **205–9**
Ipswichian (interglacial) phase 57–8
Irish lady's tresses (*Spiranthes romanzoffiana*) 133, 344, 345
iron, working/trade 151, 347–8
Iron Age 97–9, 246–7
 community structure 247–8
 field layout 98
 hill forts 98, 248, 282
Isothecium myosuroides (moss variety) 153
ivy-leaved bellflower (*Wahlenbergia hederacea*) 133
ivy-leaved toadflax (*Cymbalaria muralis*) 141
jackdaw (*Corvus monedula*) 192, 196–7
jays (*Garrulus/Podoces spp.*) 204
juniper (*Juniperus communis*) 84, 87

kale 191, 194
kaolinisation *see* granite
Kennick reservoir/plantation 203, 225, 227
kestrel (*Falco tinninunculus*) 173
knapweed (*Centaurea nigra*) 136

lady fern (*Athyrium felix femina*) 155
lapwing (*Vanellus vanellus*) 128–9, 181–2, 195
larch 145–6
large black slug (*Arion ater*) 172
large mammals **185–92**, 198, 216
Laughter Tor 63, 81, 199, 359
lead mining 265–6
lears/learing 307, 372
leats 17–18, 18, 200, 221–2, 229–30, 247, 256
 fauna 233, 236–7
 impact of climate change 243
Lecanora (lichen genus) 157
Lee Moor 7, 31, 91–2, 98, 108–9, 178, 223

china clay works 39–40, 266, 267, 322
leeches (*Helobdella stagnalis*) 235
Leigh Tor 38, 38, 53, 69, 248
lesser redpoll (*Carduelis flammea*) 202–3, 203
lesser spearwort (*Ranunculus flammula*) 132
lesser spotted woodpecker (*Dendrocupus minor*) 196, 213–14
lesser water boatmen (*Corixidae*) 235
lichens 148, 157–9, 158, 159
 see also names of species
limestone 35, 37, 57, 69, 139–41, 273
 quarrying 273–5
ling (*Calluna vulgaris*) 89, 111–13, 112, 202, 243
linnet (*Carduelis cannabina*) 174
little grebe (*Tachybaptus ruficollis*) 229
liverworts 153
livestock **313–18**
 changes to industry 310–11
 dangers to 11
 grazing **185–91, 302–9**
 market 364–5
 out-wintering/supplementary feeding 304–5
Lobarion (lichen genus) 157
long-tailed field mouse (*Apodemus sylvaticus*) 173, 173, 204, 210
longhorn beetle 199
longhouses 288–9, 290
lungwort *see* tree lungwort
Lustleigh
 Cleave 62, 75, 156, 248, 265
 village 346
Lyd, River 5, 48, 146, 345
Lydford 223–4, 251, 278, 283
 Gorge 343
 High Down 122, 122
 Railway Pools 345
lynchets 288, 288

MAFF *see* Agriculture, Fisheries and Food, Ministry of
magpie (*Pica pica*) 192, 197, 204, 377
male fern (*Dryopteris felix mas*) 155
mallard (*Anas platyrhynchus*) 229
management agreements 338–40, 354, 361
Manaton 251–2, 283, 284
map lichen (*Rhizocarpon geographicum*) 157
marram grass *see* arctic white heather
marsh bedstraw (*Galium palustre*) 132
marsh fritillary (*Eurodryus aurinia*) 170, 170, 171, 195
marsh lousewort *see* red rattle
marsh marigold (*Caltha palustris*) 148
marsh orchid *see* orchid
marsh orchid (*Dactylorhiza praetermissa*) 133, 133, 170

INDEX · 397

marsh pennywort (*Hydrocoytle vulgaris*) 132
marsh tit (*Poecile palustris*) 214, 383
marsh violet (*Viola palustris*) 132
Mary Tavy 38–9, 46, 231, 274, 280, 283, 294
  mining 251, 265, 265–6
matt grass (*Nardus stricta*) 129
mayflies (*Baetis spp.*) 199, 234, 235–6
meadow brown butterfly (*Maniola jurtina*) 170
meadow grasshopper (*Chorthippus parallelus*) 172
meadow pipit (*Anthus pratensis*) 168–9, 169, 174, 262, 372, 377
meadowsweet (*Filipendula ulmaria*) 138
Meavy, River 5, 48, 66, 144, 146, 259, 340
  fauna 237, 239
Meldon
  Quarry/chert 37, 37, 273, 343
  reservoir/viaduct 224, 225, 226, 227–8
meltwater, impact on topography 73–8, 221
Merripit Hill 71, 173, 184, 188, 223, 242, 275
Merrivale 134, 316, 345
  Quarry 179, 223, 270, 270–2, 272
Mesolithic era 83, 86, 89–91, 96–7, 103, 104–5, 135, 246, 366
metamorphic rocks 34–8
  'aureole' 38–9, 68–9, 273
  ground cover 153–5
  quarrying 273–6
mica dams 268, 269
Middle Ages 99–100, 134–5, 254–5, 285–91, 309
  agricultural practice 289–91
  architecture 288–9
  distribution of settlements 286
  remains 286–9
  military, use of moor 24–5, 25, 246, 348–50
  damage caused by 349, 350
milkwort (*Polygala serpyllifolia*) 117
minerals
  (attempted) extraction 25–6, 254–76 (*see also* china clay; copper; tin)
  deposits 36
mines, disused, as animal habitat 179, 185
mink (*Mustela lutreola*) 239–40
mires 11, 16, 114, 130–4, 372, 372–3
  vegetation 131–3, 233
mistle thrush (*Turdus viscivorus*) 178–9, 204
mites (*Hydracarinae*) 228, 234
Mnium hornum (moss variety) 155
mole (*Talpa europaeus*) 94–5, 197–8
molluscs 236
moonwort (*Botrychium lunaria*) 347
Moorgate Series 13
moorhen (*Gallinula chlorophus*) 229

moorland 108–34
  agriculture 299–320, 301, 338
  boundary with agricultural land 99–100, 105
  colouring 123–4, 128, 131–2, 379
  conservation potential/measures 330
  distribution 106, 110
  grazing 185–91, 298, 302–9
  impact of climate change 371–4, 383
  (problems of) classification 108–15, 123, 124, 128–9
  recreational use 26, 374–9
  surveys 108–15
Moretonhampstead 26, 184, 193, 208, 251, 283
  agriculture 294–5
  Court of the Stannaries 263
  Series (soils) 13, 101, 102
mosses 117–18, 129, 133, 153, 153, 155, 156, 156, 233, 259, 259–60
  see also names of species
mottled grasshopper (*Myrmeliotettix maculatus*) 172
mountain avens (*Dryas integrifolia*) 82
mud snail (*Lymnaea glabra*) 195
Muddilake 11, 119, 120, 130, 134, 182
muntjac deer (*Muntiacus spp.*) 198
myxomatosis 183–4

National Park Authority/ies (NPA(s)) xi, 22, 109, 216, 274–5, 310, 324, 327–46
  adminstrative policies 328–30
  conservation obligations 26–7, 28–9, 328–9, 356
  creation 324, 327–8
  land management 335–46
  land purchases 329–30, 331–5
  legal/financial powers 328, 336, 352
  Management Plan 2007–12 357–8
  membership 27–8
  relations with Duchy 340–1
  relations with farming community 338–41, 361, 363–4, 367
  relations with other authorities 348, 350, 352–4, 356
  staff 327, 328, 348, 349
National Park Officer, position of 328, 334–5, 336, 340
National Park(s) 1, 105, 383
  administration 26–9, 325–30; 1972 reorganisation 327–8
  boundaries 25, 47, 321–2, 322, 323
  creation 321, 323–5
  defined 321
  government policy towards 327–9
  Management Plan 28
  planning authority/procedure 352
  Planning Board(s) 325–6
National Parks and Access to the Countryside Act (1949) 304, 324, 327
National Parks Commission 324, 327, 356

National Trust 346–8, 351
  properties 147, 345, 347, 353, 384
natural beauty, legal obligations towards 26–7, 304–5, 324–5, 328–9
Natural England 28–9, 342, 348, 352, 355–6, 362
Nature Conservancy (Council) 108, 212, 324, 327, 338, 341, 342, 354
nature reserves 60, 61, 212–13, 321–3, 342–3, 353
Neolithic era 91–3, 96–7, 246
New Bridge 4, 75, 208, 209, 235
newtakes 12, 134–5, 189, 253, 293, 293, 294, 306
  fauna 191, 199
nightjar (*Caprimulgus europaeus*) 178, 179, 202
non-biting midges (*Chironomidae*) 234, 235–6
Norman invasion/occupation 281–2
  see also Domesday Book
nuthatch (*Sitta europea*) 196
oak eggar (*Lasiocampa quercus*) 169
oaks/oak woods 5, 14, 19, 141, 145, 146, 148, 148, 150–6, 153, 342–3
  expansion 380, 381–2
  height 161
  high-level 160, 160–4, 161
  pests 208
  pollen records 87, 89
  species 162, 164
  use of materials 150–1
  variations 150–6
Okehampton 68, 210, 248, 252
  army camp 25, 175, 342
  Deer Park 98, 127, 147, 159, 286, 345
  Hamlets 278, 316, 318
  quarries 37, 37, 273
Okement (West/East), River 5, 48, 219–21, 345
  acidity 232
  fauna 179, 209, 213
  geology 42
  mineral resources/extraction 103, 258, 259
  vegetation 146, 160, 163
  waterworks 225, 227, 229, 326
Oligocene period, geological formations 42
Oligochaete (worm genus) 235
openworks (tin workings) 260–3
Ophioparma (lichen genus) 157
orchards 149–50, 150
orchids *see* greater butterfly orchid; marsh orchid; purple orchid
otter (*Lutra lutra*) 239
over-grazing 278, 305–7, 308–9, 311, 355
ovine encephalomyelitis *see* louping ill
ox-eye daisy (*Chrysanthemum leucanthemum*) 138

pale butterwort (*Pinguicula lusitanica*) 132, 132–3, 167
parasitic wasp (*Asecodes mento*) 172

parasitism 376–7
patch-forming plants 81–2, 82
patterned ground 66–8, 67
pearl-bordered fritillary (*Boloria euphrosyne*) 208–9, 209, 371
peat 11–12, 15, 89, 91, 107, 243, 257
  chemical composition 378
  distribution 100, 100–1
  formation 80–1, 84, 221
  preservation of plant/animal remains 80, 84
  scientific investigation 344–5
  types 101, 102
  use as fuel 115–17
peregrine falcon (*Falco peregrinus*) 192, 196–7
periglacial zone/climate 59–62, 67, 71–2, 275–6
permafrost 73, 79
Permina period, geological formations 36–7
Peter Tavy 231, 248, 251, 274, 283, 293, 294
  Great Common 86, 278, 318–19, 319
pheasant (*Phasisnus colchicus*) 196–7
pied flycatcher (*Ficedeula hypoleuca*) 211–13, 212, 216, 334, 342, 383
pill sedge (*Carex pilulifera*) 129
pine weevil (*Hylobius abietis*) 204
place names 4–5, 8–9, 69, 141, 183, 283
  Saxon 99, 135, 162, 249–51
Plagiothecium undulatum (moss variety) 153
plant life
  aquatic 234
  re-emergence following Ice Age 81–4
plateaux 10, 47–8, 89, 116, 219
  conservation 345
  geomorphology 31
Pleistocene Epoch, climate/topography 55–8, 72, 73, 78
Plym, River/valley 5, 48, 146, 223, 346
  acidity 230–1
  fauna 183–4, 237, 239, 297
  Iron Age dwellings 248
  mine workings 266, 268
Plymouth 297
  City Council 143–4, 225
  hinterland 141, 159
  railway links 273
Plympton, as stannary town 263–4
pollen analysis 85, 85–6, 87–8, 92, 97–8, 103
pond skaters (*Gerridae*) 234, 235
pondweed (*Potamogeton spp.*) 132, 233
ponies 187–90, 189, 192, 222, 242, 307, 316, 316–18, 377–8
  numbers 187–9, 318–19
pools 118, 222, 222–4, 223, 224
  in abandoned mines/quarries 223–4, 270
Postbridge 75, 91, 106, 135, 143, 178, 239, 240, 241, 274, 309
potatoes, cultivation 294–5
primrose (*Primula vulgaris*) 138

Prince Hall 135, 143, 178, 275, 302, 309
Princetown 7, 14, 23, 105, 229, 241, 262, 309, 334
  development 253, 278
  railway link to Plymouth 271, 272
  Series (soils) 101, 102
  storm damage 368, 369
  see also Dartmoor Prison
purple hairstreak butterfly (*Neozephyrus quercus*) 156, 208, 342
purple moor grass (*Molinia caerulea*) 117, 118–20, 119, 120, 128, 134, 194–5
  as food/habitat 173, 187, 313
purple orchid (*Orchis mascula*) 138
purple saxifrage (*Saxifraga oppositifolia*) 81, 81–2

quarries/quarrying 37, 71, 71–2, 72, **270–6**
  abandoned, pools in 223–4, 270
  as animal habitat 179
  roadside pits 275–6
  small enterprises 274–5
quartz 38, 38, 39, 42, 46, 53, 69

rabbit (*Oryctolagus cuniculus*) 183–4, 194, **296–8**
  farming 296–7
  human consumption 184, 296
  as prey 167, 185, 198, 204, 215
ragged robin (*Lychnis flos-cuculi*) 133
railways 271, 272, 273, 347
  abandoned lines 223–4, 266
rainbow trout (*Oncorhynchus mykiss*) 228
rainfall 4, 217, 218–21, 219, 241, 243–4, 368
raised bogs 130–1, 131
raven (*Corvus corax*) 192, 192, 376–7
reaves (stone banks) 93–5, 94, 96, 252
  abandonment 97
red-backed shrike (*Lanius collurio*) 166, 371
red deer (*Cervus elaphus*) 191, 205
red fescue (*Festuca rubra*) 129, 136
red grouse (*Lagopus lagopus*) 183, 183, 184
red rattle/marsh lousewort (*Pedicularis palustris*) 132
Redlake 22, 39–40, 52, 130
  china clay pit 100–1, 102, 223, 266, 267
redstart *see* common redstart
redwing (*Turdus iliacus*) 179
reed bunting (*Emberiza schoeniclus*) 149, 195, 262
reptiles 180–1
reservoirs **225–9**, 274–5
  construction 25, 225, 246, 326–7
  fauna 228–9
  impact of climate change 243–4
  negative impact 225, 226–7
  positioning 227–8
  refusal of permission for 225, 326, 351
  supply areas 226, 326–7, 378–9

rhos pastures 134, 136, 194–5
Rhytidiadeplhus undulatum (moss variety) 153
Riddon Ridge 23, 101, 135, 280, 339
ring ousel (*Turdus torquatus*) 179–80, 262, 372
Rippon Tor 8, 16, 63, 121, 124, 130–1, 306
rivers 4–5, 48–53, 49, 200–2, **229–40**
  chemical composition 229–32, 236
  waterworks 225–7, 229
roads/road traffic 331, 376–7
roadsides, grazing 305, 305–7, 306
robin (*Erithacus rubecula*) 196, 201–2, 213, 262, 383
Roborough Down 56, 109, 124, 322
rock tripes (*Lasallia pustulata*) 157
roe deer (*Capreolus capreolus*) 191, 198, 198, 205, 216
Roman occupation 99, 218, 249
rowan (*Sorbus spp.*) 89, 146, 199, 358–60, 377
Royal Commission on Common Land 126, 304, 318, 337
royal fern (*Osmunda regalis*) 149
Rural Development Service 354, 355, 362
Rural Payments Agency 362–3
rushes 116, 133, 134, 173, 194–5
Ryder's Hill 3, 10, 14, 31, 123–4, 219, 333

Saddle Tor 15, 16, 63, 272
sallow (conifer) 199, 200, 202
salmon (*Salmo salar*) 237
sand martin (*Riparia riparia*) 178, 202
sandstone 34, 36, 38
saxifrage *see* golden saxifrage; purple saxifrage
schist 139–41
Scotch Blackface sheep 187, 216, 295, 302, 314
  introduction 302–3
  leaping ability 193
  numbers 318
sea level, changes in 55, 55–7, 73, 87
sedges (*Carex spp.*) 118, 129, 148
  as animal food 173
self heal (*Prunella vulgaris*) 136
sessile oak (*Quercus petrea*) 146, 162, 164
shale 34, 37
Shapley Common 111, 193, 283
Sharp Tor 16, 44, 45, 59, 62
Sharpitor 8, 63, 222, 351
Shaugh Moor 31, 92–3, 266, 269, 269, 384
sheep 187–90, 192, 193–4, 216, 277, 295, 307, 372
  breeds 187, 193, 295, 302–3, 315;
  crosses 314
  grazing habits/preferences 313, 355
  impact of human presence 376, 377–8
  learing 307
  numbers 187–90, 304, 310–11, 318–19

INDEX · 399

sheep's bit (*Jasione montana*) 136
sheep's fescue (*Festuca ovina*) 121, 129
Sheepstor 8, 9, 63, 144, 291
Shell Top 266, 342, 346
shore weed (*Littorella uniflora*) 227, 227
short-eared owl (*Asio flammeus*) 173, 195
short-tailed vole *see* field vole
shrews (*Sorex spp.*) 197, 210
shrimps (*Gammaridae*) 234
sika deer (*Cervus nippon*) 198
silver-washed fritillary (*Argynnis paphia*) 208, 209
Simmons, Ian x, 79, 86, 87, 88, 90, 91–2, 96, 97–8, 103, 163–4, 217, 357, 358, 378
Single Payment (farming subsidy) 310, 313, 355, 362–3
  propsed adjustment 363
siskin (*Carduelis spinus*) 196, 196, 383
Sites of Special Scientific Interest (SSSIs) 130, 224, 225, 273, 321–2, 322, 341, **342–6**, 347–8, 353
  creation 324–5
  management obligations 338, 355
Sitka spruce 145–6
skylark (*Alauda arvensis*) 173–4, 175, 262, 372, 377, 383
slate 34, 36, 39, 102, 153–5
slugs 172, 201
small heath butterfly (*Coenonympha pamphilus*) 170
small mammals **172–3**
  human consumption 184
  as prey 181, 185, 195, 204–5, 210, 215
small red damselfly (*Ceriagrion tenellum*) 223–4
snails 195, 201
snakes 180–1
snipe (*Gallinago gallinago*) 181–3, 195
snow 241, 242, 368, 370, 382
Snowdonia 67, 81, 323, 325–6
Society for the Protection of Nature Reserves 346
Soil Survey (1983) 109
soils
  distribution 100, 100–3
  types 101, 102, 107
  see also 'brown earth'; peat; silt
Sourton Tors 7, 68, 69, 134, 273
Soussons Down 261, 261, 360
Soussons Plantation 20, 21, 106, 143, 315
  fauna 200, 203
South Brent 196, 210, 251, 291, 300, 346
South Hams 3, 3, 5, 7
  geology 36, 56–7
  naming 249
South Tawton 35, 37–8, 224, 251, 274, 278, 283, 285
  Domesday record 284–5
South West Lakes Trust 348–50
South Zeal 38, 265

southern damselfly (*Coenagrion mercuriale*) 195, 233, 234
Spaders Newtake 130, 182
Spanish slug (*Arion lusitanicus*) 172
sparrowhawk (*Accipiter nisus*) 196, 203, 215, 383
spear thistle (*Cirsium vulgare*) 136
Special Areas for Conservation (SACs) 321, 344
speckled wood butterfly (*Pararge aegeria*) 208
sphagnum 116, 117–18, 133, 156, 191, 382
spotted flycatcher (*Muscicapa striata*) 202, 213
wildlife damage 205
St John's wort (*Hypericum spp.*) 132, 155
stag beetle 199
stagshorn club moss (*Lycopodium clavatum*) 259, 259–60
stannary towns/Courts 24, 263–4
starling (*Sturnus vulgaris*) 174–5, 175, 208
starwort (*Callitriche stagnalis*) 233
Sticklepath Fault 41, 41, 42, 43, 330, 351
stitchwort (*Stellaria holostea*) 138, 138
stock dove (*Columba oenas*) 197
stone, domestic use 70–1, 77, 274–5, 276
Stone Age *see* Mesolithic; Neolithic; Palaeolithic
stone circles/rows 94
stonechat (*Saxicola torquata*) 176–7, 178
stoneflies (*Plecoptera*) 199, 208, 234, 236
streamworks (tin workings) **256–60**, 258
  appearance 258–9
  distribution 257, 257–8, 259
  subsidiarity 363–4
sundew
  narrow-leaved (*Drosera intermedia*) 132–3
  round-leaved (*Drosera rotundifolia*) 117, 118, 132–3
swaling *see* burning
swallow (*Hirunda rustica*) 178, 202
sweet vernal grass (*Anthoxanthum odorata*) 129, 136
Sweltor 272
swift (*Apus apus*) 178
Swincombe, River 4, 51, 75, 76, 130, 182, 351
  fauna 235–6, 237
  waterworks 225, 326
sycamore 146
tanning industry 150–1
tansy (*Chrysanthemum vulgare*) 138
Tavistock 26, 252, 274, 283
  as stannary town 24, 263–4
Tavy, River 5, 19, 48, 146, 221, 231, 345
  acidity 230–1, 236
Tavy Cleave 63, 65, 179

Taw, River/valley 5, 11, 48, 219–21
  fauna 179, 209, 228
  mineral resources 103
  waterworks 226, 347–8
Taw Head 91–2, 219–21
Taw Marsh 11, 25, 130
tawny owl (*Strix aluco*) 204, 204–5, 215
Teign, River/valley 2, 5, 15–16, 50, 74, 219, 251
  acidity 230–1
  conservation 345–6, 350
  fauna 182, 191, 206, 209, 213, 236, 237, 240
  forestry 19, 20, 145
  headstreams 5, 52, 230
  mineral resources/extraction 235, 266, 271, 273
  natural vegetation 146, 151, 155
  settlements 248, 251, 251
television transmission mast, erection of 326–7
'Ten Tors' walk 375
Tertiary Era 53–62
thrift (*Armeria spp.*) 82
Throwleigh 251, 280, 285
Throwleigh Common 182
thrushes (*Turdus spp.*) 178–80
Thuidium tamariscinum (moss variety) 155
tilting, geological 42, 53, 78
tin mining 249, **254–64**, 255
  archaeological finds 255
  buildings 256
  impact on landscape/plant life 102–3, 200
  implements 258–9
  legal right of 264
  market/economy 263–4
  methods 256, 262
  mine remains 260–2; as habitat 262
  scale/productivity 262–3
  waste heaps 258, 259, 259–60
  see also openworks; streamworks
tits (*Parus spp.*) 196, 201–2, 204, 213, 262, 383
topography (of Dartmoor) 2–29
  divisions 13, 13–20
  evolution 2–4, 11, 47–78
  human impact on 90–1, 96–7, 102–3, 104–5, 115–17, 167
Tor Royal 293
  Bog 97, 101, 342, 345
  newtake 340
  plantation 143
tormentil (*Potentilla erecta*) 117, 129
Torquay Urban District Council 144–5, 225
tors 10–11, 61, 62–72, 79
  (attempts at) classification 64
  composition 31, 69
  etymology 69
  locations 62–3, 69–70, 74, 157
  structure/shape 64, 71
  survival in changing landscape 380, 381–2

tourism 26
  nature of Dartmoor's appeal 16–17, 107, 331–2, 379
tramways, serving quarries 271, 271–2
tree clearances
  Bronze Age 92–3, 96–7
  Dark Age 105
  medieval 103, 105
  Neolithic 91–2
tree lungwort (*Lobaria pulmonaria*) 148
tree pipit (*Anthus trivialis*) 216
treecreeper (*Certha familiaris*) 196, 197
Trenchford reservoir/plantation 203, 225, 227, 275, 350
turnpike roads 26, 134, 271
  creation 293–4
  verges 137, 275–6
tussock sedge (*Carex paniculata*) 148
Two Bridges 71–2, 72, 119, 160, 185, 293, 295, 309

under-grazing 307, 311, 358–60, 359, 372, 380–1
upright bedstraw (*Galium mollugo*) 138
Usnion (lichen genus) 157

valley bogs 131–4
  as habitat 181–2
  risk of damage to 191
valleys
  fauna 208
  formation 41–2
Vancouver, Charles 104–5, 107, 115, 136, 188–9, 292–5, 303, 304

Venford Reservoir 65, 225, 225, 226, 227, 240, 275
Vigur's eyebright (*Euphrasia vigursii*) 121–2, 122, 128
villages 14
  abandonment 243
  medieval 286, 287
  mining 267
violets (*Viola spp.*) 127–8, 128, 132, 371
'Vision for Dartmoor' 28–9, 29, 109–13, 111, 115, 123, 124, 133–4, 308, 320, 348, 354, 374
visitors (to moor) 26, 374
  impact on wildlife 376–9
  see also tourism
Vitifer 179, 182, 200, 223, 261, 262
Vixen Tor 62, 156, 258
voles 172–3
  as prey 181
voluntary work 351–2

Walkham, River 5, 19, 48, 63, 146, 156, 345
wall pennywort (*Umbilicus rupestris*) 141
Walla Brook(s) 4, 11, 50, 106, 135
Walna 135, 200, 261, 280

Ward, Stephen 108, 109, 111, 113, 114, 115, 117, 119, 120, 123, 129, 134
wardens, appointment/functions 327, 354
Warren House 200, 223
  Inn 261, 280, 297
wasps 172, 371
waste-of-the manor 105
  creation of farms in 135–6
water boatman (*Notonecta glauca*) 235
water crowfoot (*Ranunculus aquatilis*) 132, 235
water dropwort (*Oenanthe crocata*) 235
water milfoil (*Myrriophyllum alterniflorum*) 235
water starwort (*Callitriche spp.*) 235
water treatment works 25, 226–7
wavy hair grass (*Deschampsia flexuosa*) 121
wax caps (*Hygrocybe spp.*) 128
Webburn (West/East) 4, 11, 16–17, 19, 19, 50, 106, 232, 261
  fauna 177, 237, 240
  vegetation 130, 144, 145, 149, 200
West Dart 4, 48, 51, 51, 75, 221, 225, 229, 230, 276, 309
  fauna 178, 237, 240
Western Beacon 3, 6, 8, 13, 37, 47–8, 62, 273
western furze (*Ulex gallii*) 113, 188, 243
'western heath,' (problems of) definition 109–11, 113, 124
Wheal Betsy 265, 265
Wheal Friendship 265–6
wheatear (*Oenanthe oenanthe*) 176, 176–7, 262, 372
Whiddon Deer Park 147, 158, 159, 346, 347
whinchat (*Saxicola rubetra*) 127, 156, 176–7, 177, 262
whirligig beetles (*Gyrinus spp.*) 234
Whitchurch Down 93, 111, 112, 251, 255, 280, 318, 344, 345
white admiral (*Limentis cammila*) 208
White Wood 151, 153, 157, 212, 213, 216, 284, 347, 351, 381
  NPA acquisition 334–5
whitethroat (*Sylvia communis*) 383
Widecombe 12, 15, 15–16, 98, 134, 140, 226, 242, 283, 286, 294, 297
  Common 177, 188–9, 278, 303, 339
wild boar (*Sus scrofa*) 192
wild garlic (*Allium ursinum*) 155
wildlife
  duty of care 216
  habitats 165–6
  limited variety 383
  methodology of analysis 165–7
  rarity 166–7
  see also biodiversity; conservation; ecosystems; types of animals/plants
willow (*Salix spp.*) 148, 149, 214, 359

willow tit 214
  see also tits
willow warbler (*Phylloscopus trochilus*) 202, 210–11, 262, 383
willowherb (*Chamaenarion angustifolium*) 138
wind
  damage 240, 241, 369
  prevailing 65–6
winter moth (*Operophtera brumata*) 208
Wistman's Wood x, 75, 141, 142, 160, 160–4, 210, 327, 343
  etymology 162
  expansion 163, 380, 381
wood ants (*Formica rufa*) 206–8, 207
wood cricket (*Nemobius syvestris*) 206
wood mouse *see* long-tailed field mouse
wood pigeon (*Columba palumbus*) 192, 196–7, 204, 215
wood warbler (*Phylloscopus sibilatrix*) 210–11, 211, 216, 334, 383
woodcock (*Scolopax rusticola*) 195, 214–15
woodland **141–64**
  beginnings 83–4, 87
  conservation potential/measures 330, 345
  distribution 105, 106
  expansion 380–2
  fauna **198–216**
  ground cover 153–5
  wet 148–9, 149
  see also broad-leaved woodland; conifer plantations
woodlark (*Lullula arboris*) 196
woodpeckers 196, 183
woodruff (*Galium odoratum*) 155, 211
woodrush *see* great hairy woodrush
worms, aquatic 228, 235
worms, terrestrial *see* earthworms
Wotter 38, 91–2, 266
Wray, River 5, 19, 50
  geology 41–2, 330
  mineral resources/extraction 251, 272
  vegetation 146, 331
wren (*Troglodytes troglodytes*) 196, 199, 213, 262

Xanthorion (lichen genus) 157

Yar Tor 16, 63
Yarner Wood 207, 221, 228–9
  National Nature Reserve 60, 61, 212–13, 323, 334, 354
Yealm, River 5, 48, 146, 213, 229
yellow marsh St John's wort (*Hypericum spp.*) 132
yellow rattle (*Rhianthus minor*) 136
yellowhammer (*Emeriza citronella*) 196, 383
Yes Tor 6, 6–7, 13, 47–8, 63, 68, 219, 220
Yorkshire fog (*Holcus lanatus*) 136

The New Naturalist Library

1. *Butterflies* — E. B. Ford
2. *British Game* — B. Vesey-Fitzgerald
3. *London's Natural History* — R. S. R. Fitter
4. *Britain's Structure and Scenery* — L. Dudley Stamp
5. *Wild Flowers* — J. Gilmour & M. Walters
6. *The Highlands & Islands* — F. Fraser Darling & J. M. Boyd
7. *Mushrooms & Toadstools* — J. Ramsbottom
8. *Insect Natural History* — A. D. Imms
9. *A Country Parish* — A. W. Boyd
10. *British Plant Life* — W. B. Turrill
11. *Mountains & Moorlands* — W. H. Pearsall
12. *The Sea Shore* — C. M. Yonge
13. *Snowdonia* — F. J. North, B. Campbell & R. Scott
14. *The Art of Botanical Illustration* — W. Blunt
15. *Life in Lakes & Rivers* — T. T. Macan & E. B. Worthington
16. *Wild Flowers of Chalk & Limestone* — J. E. Lousley
17. *Birds & Men* — E. M. Nicholson
18. *A Natural History of Man in Britain* — H. J. Fleure & M. Davies
19. *Wild Orchids of Britain* — V. S. Summerhayes
20. *The British Amphibians & Reptiles* — M. Smith
21. *British Mammals* — L. Harrison Matthews
22. *Climate and the British Scene* — G. Manley
23. *An Angler's Entomology* — J. R. Harris
24. *Flowers of the Coast* — I. Hepburn
25. *The Sea Coast* — J. A. Steers
26. *The Weald* — S. W. Wooldridge & F. Goldring
27. *Dartmoor* — L. A. Harvey & D. St. Leger Gordon
28. *Sea Birds* — J. Fisher & R. M. Lockley
29. *The World of the Honeybee* — C. G. Butler
30. *Moths* — E. B. Ford
31. *Man and the Land* — L. Dudley Stamp
32. *Trees, Woods and Man* — H. L. Edlin
33. *Mountain Flowers* — J. Raven & M. Walters
34. *The Open Sea: I. The World of Plankton* — A. Hardy
35. *The World of the Soil* — E. J. Russell
36. *Insect Migration* — C. B. Williams
37. *The Open Sea: II. Fish & Fisheries* — A. Hardy
38. *The World of Spiders* — W. S. Bristowe
39. *The Folklore of Birds* — E. A. Armstrong
40. *Bumblebees* — J. B. Free & C. G. Butler
41. *Dragonflies* — P. S. Corbet, C. Longfield & N. W. Moore
42. *Fossils* — H. H. Swinnerton
43. *Weeds & Aliens* — E. Salisbury
44. *The Peak District* — K. C. Edwards
45. *The Common Lands of England & Wales* — L. Dudley Stamp & W. G. Hoskins
46. *The Broads* — E. A. Ellis
47. *The Snowdonia National Park* — W. M. Condry
48. *Grass and Grasslands* — I. Moore
49. *Nature Conservation in Britain* — L. Dudley Stamp
50. *Pesticides and Pollution* — K. Mellanby
51. *Man & Birds* — R. K. Murton
52. *Woodland Birds* — E. Simms
53. *The Lake District* — W. H. Pearsall & W. Pennington
54. *The Pollination of Flowers* — M. Proctor & P. Yeo
55. *Finches* — I. Newton
56. *Pedigree: Words from Nature* — S. Potter & L. Sargent
57. *British Seals* — H. R. Hewer
58. *Hedges* — E. Pollard, M. D. Hooper & N. W. Moore
59. *Ants* — M. V. Brian
60. *British Birds of Prey* — L. Brown
61. *Inheritance and Natural History* — R. J. Berry
62. *British Tits* — C. Perrins
63. *British Thrushes* — E. Simms
64. *The Natural History of Shetland* — R. J. Berry & J. L. Johnston

65. *Waders* — W. G. Hale
66. *The Natural History of Wales* — W. M. Condry
67. *Farming and Wildlife* — K. Mellanby
68. *Mammals in the British Isles* — L. Harrison Matthews
69. *Reptiles and Amphibians in Britain* — D. Frazer
70. *The Natural History of Orkney* — R. J. Berry
71. *British Warblers* — E. Simms
72. *Heathlands* — N. R. Webb
73. *The New Forest* — C. R. Tubbs
74. *Ferns* — C. N. Page
75. *Freshwater Fish* — P. S. Maitland & R. N. Campbell
76. *The Hebrides* — J. M. Boyd & I. L. Boyd
77. *The Soil* — B. Davis, N. Walker, D. Ball & A. Fitter
78. *British Larks, Pipits & Wagtails* — E. Simms
79. *Caves & Cave Life* — P. Chapman
80. *Wild & Garden Plants* — M. Walters
81. *Ladybirds* — M. E. N. Majerus
82. *The New Naturalists* — P. Marren
83. *The Natural History of Pollination* — M. Proctor, P. Yeo & A. Lack
84. *Ireland: A Natural History* — D. Cabot
85. *Plant Disease* — D. Ingram & N. Robertson
86. *Lichens* — Oliver Gilbert
87. *Amphibians and Reptiles* — T. Beebee & R. Griffiths
88. *Loch Lomondside* — J. Mitchell
89. *The Broads* — B. Moss
90. *Moths* — M. Majerus
91. *Nature Conservation* — P. Marren
92. *Lakeland* — D. Ratcliffe
93. *British Bats* — John Altringham
94. *Seashore* — Peter Hayward
95. *Northumberland* — Angus Lunn
96. *Fungi* — Brian Spooner & Peter Roberts
97. *Mosses & Liverworts* — Nick Hodgetts & Ron Porley
98. *Bumblebees* — Ted Benton
99. *Gower* — Jonathan Mullard
100. *Woodlands* — Oliver Rackham
101. *Galloway and the Borders* — Derek Ratcliffe
102. *Garden Natural History* — Stefan Buczacki
103. *The Isles of Scilly* — Rosemary Parslow
104. *A History of Ornithology* — Peter Bircham
105. *Wye Valley* — George Peterken
106. *Dragonflies* — Philip Corbet & Stephen Brooks
107. *Grouse* — Adam Watson & Robert Moss
108. *Southern England* — Peter Friend
109. *Islands* — R. J. Berry
110. *Wildfowl* — David Cabot

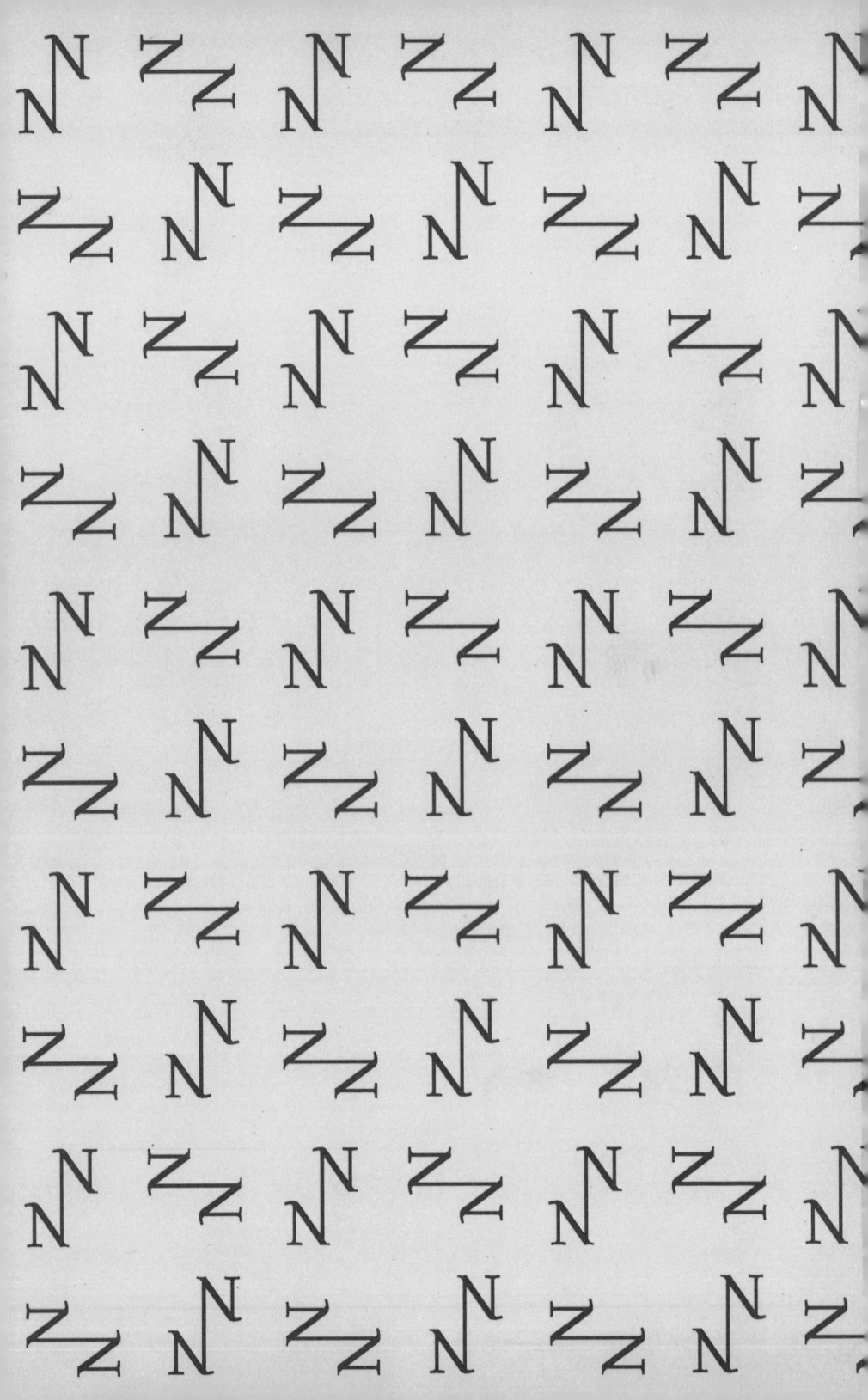